WORLDMAKING IN THE LONG GREAT WAR

WORLDMAKING IN THE LONG GREAT WAR

HOW LOCAL AND COLONIAL STRUGGLES SHAPED THE MODERN MIDDLE EAST

JONATHAN WYRTZEN

Columbia University Press
New York

Columbia University Press
Publishers Since 1893
New York   Chichester, West Sussex
cup.columbia.edu

Copyright © 2022 Jonathan Wyrtzen
All rights reserved

Library of Congress Cataloging-in-Publication Data
Names: Wyrtzen, Jonathan, 1973– author.
Title: Worldmaking in the long Great War: how local and colonial struggles shaped the modern Middle East / Jonathan Wyrtzen.
Description: New York: Columbia University Press, [2022] | Includes bibliographical references and index.
Identifiers: LCCN 2021053905 | ISBN 9780231186285 (hardback) | ISBN 9780231186292 (trade paperback) | ISBN 9780231546577 (ebook)
Subjects: LCSH: World War, 1914–1918—Middle East. | Geopolitics—Middle East. | Middle East—Politics and government—1914–1945. | Middle East—Foreign relations—20th century.
Classification: LCC DS63.W97 2022 | DDC 956—dc23/eng/20220210
LC record available at https://lccn.loc.gov/2021053905

Cover images: First World War map of the Middle East. Everett Collection, Inc. / Alamy; Ibn Saud's Ikhwan Army on the March near Habl, 1911 (W. Shakespeare, Royal Geographical Society)
Cover design: Milenda Nan Ok Lee

CONTENTS

Preface vii
Acknowledgments xvii

INTRODUCTION   1

I. UNMAKING THE GREATER OTTOMAN ORDER

1. GEOSTRATEGIC QUESTIONS, COLONIAL SCRAMBLES, AND THE ROAD TO THE GREAT WAR   31

2. THE MANY FRONTS OF THE OTTOMANS' GREAT WAR, 1914–1918   53

II. REIMAGINING THE POST-OTTOMAN MIDDLE EAST

3. THE MIDDLE EAST'S SO-CALLED WILSONIAN MOMENT, 1918–1920   91

4. EMERGING POLITIES IN THE EARLY 1920S   123

III. REMAKING THE MODERN MIDDLE EAST

5. KURDISH UPRISINGS, THE RIF WAR, AND THE GREAT SYRIAN REVOLT, 1924–1927   169

6. ENDGAME STRUGGLES IN KURDISTAN, CYRENAICA, AND ARABIA, 1927–1934   216

CONCLUSION   249

Notes   259
Bibliography   287
Index   301

PREFACE

This book retells the origin story of the modern Middle East: how an extended period of conflict that I term the Long Great War (1911–1934)[1] unmade a centuries-old Ottoman regional system and opened up a tumultuous window of time during which the Middle East's political order was fundamentally reimagined and remade. The revisionist twist concerns *how* this took place. The usual account of this period is top-down, focused on how the British and French imposed artificial new political boundaries on the region after World War I, which are then blamed for ensuing unrest. In its place, I offer a new version, arguing that the modern Middle East was actually shaped by power struggles on the ground that were fueled by competing local and international visions for the post-Ottoman future.

The following chapters trace this process over a two-decade period of transition and upheaval in the Middle East as the Long Great War progressed through three distinct phases. In the first (1911–1918), the last vestiges of the greater Ottoman political order were unmade in an interempire global conflict. This opened up a second moment in which a wide range of post-Ottoman polities became imaginable for both local and colonial actors. In the last phase of the Long Great War (from the mid-1920s through the mid-1930s), these visions clashed violently. It was these struggles that narrowed down the types of political structures, generated locally or by colonial powers, that survived in the region; transformed how political communities could be imagined; and ultimately produced the new polities and redefined boundaries that constituted the region's new map.

Focusing less on peace settlement pen strokes and more on the realities of state formation and violent conflict—recognizing that it was war that made borders in the region from Morocco to Iran, rather than the reverse—forces a rethinking of the modern Middle East's origins. My hope is that it also helps us reimagine the region's present and future. The greater Middle East has been passing through a similar critical transitional period in the early twenty-first century, during which political orders have again been undone in revolution and civil war, new polities have been imagined, and political boundaries have become both more fluid and more rigid.

Over my years of research for this book, I have repeatedly been struck by the complicated entwinement of the Middle East's century-old Great War past and its present-day violent processes of state and boundary formation. One of these times was physical, when my face was pushed down in the hard dirt, about a hundred yards from the Syrian border, by a Jordanian soldier in early January 2017.

I was in northern Jordan to do field site visits in the southern reaches of the Jabal al-Druze and the Hawran volcanic plain that extend across the border from Syria. In the aftermath of World War I, these areas were initially under Faisal's Damascus-based Arab Kingdom, which briefly governed an inland territory stretching from Aleppo down to Amman before being crushed by France in the summer of 1920. This region was then split between French and British zones of control roughly laid out in a secret 1916 wartime agreement divvying up the Ottoman Empire, known by the names of its negotiators, Mark Sykes and Georges Picot. Five years later, however, the Hawran was the launching point and epicenter of the Great Syrian Revolt, a countrywide uprising in 1925 that threatened the French Mandate granted by the League of Nations over Syria and Lebanon. Druze communities traversed more or less freely across the porous frontier, using northern Transjordan, nominally under British control, as a refuge during the fighting and again fleeing there when the conflict ended in 1927. To guard against another uprising, French forces occupied many of the villages in this area until a bilateral commission finally settled and surveyed the international boundary in 1931 and 1932.²

That Saturday morning in early 2017, my brother-in-law and I had driven up the international highway heading north from Amman toward Damascus, passing through the towns of Zarqa and Mafraq to the Jaber-Nassib checkpoint. This was once the busiest crossing into Syria, but it had been closed as a result of the civil war that escalated after the Assad regime cracked down on protests just over the border in the city of Daraa in March 2011.³ From Jaber, our plan was to cut southeast down to the village of Umm al-Jimal to see the ancient black basalt ruins. This Nabatean city had thrived through Roman, Byzantine, and Ummayad periods before being destroyed by an earthquake in 749 CE. In 1925, with the outbreak of the Syrian revolt, the British stationed armored-car units at the Umm al-Jimal ruins and further east at Azraq to try to control movement across the ostensible international border.⁴ Along the route, we would have views to the north toward al-Suwayda and Salkhad, key Druze strongholds during the Great Syrian Revolt, now inaccessible because of the ongoing conflict in Syria.

On our way, we decided to cut north slightly from the village of Elemtaih to get to a well-paved road that, on Google maps, paralleled the border and would take us to Umm al-Jimal. Soon after making this turn, though, I started hearing the pinging sounds of (what I later realized were) warning shots. A minute later, two 4x4 Toyotas with mounted guns and a squad of Jordanian soldiers on foot, with machine guns drawn, raced at us, pulled us out of the car, and pinned us on the ground. Turning my head slightly, I watched as they immobilized the car, systematically shooting out the tires and windows. Thankfully, the patrol's sergeant got his men to stand down once he realized we were not a threat and loaded us into the pickups. In the back of the truck, the gunner kept looking at us, smiling and laughing, pointing to his right and saying "Suria, Daesh"⁵—Syria, ISIS—and to his left "al-Urdun"—Jordan—as we sped on the well-paved road feet away from the Syrian border to the nearest army post. The rest of the day we were treated with the utmost courtesy (and countless cups of tea and coffee) while we tried to explain to higher-ranking officers why we had gone so foolishly close to the border, hearing the refrain, "You should thank God, you should be dead," over and over.

Unwittingly, we had entered a no-go zone established along the entire Syrian frontier by the Jordanian military, who had a shoot-to-kill protocol for anyone approaching the border from either side. This had been established after ISIS launched several attacks in the summer of 2016 against Jordanian border posts, including a suicide attack in which a bomb-filled truck was driven into a post at al-Rukban, killing seven Jordanian soldiers. Afterward, the Jordanian military installed a U.S.-funded, Raytheon-built, hundred-million-dollar security system, including ground radar, communications infrastructure, and quick-response vehicles along the length of the Syrian and Iraqi borders. We had just had a traumatic, much-too-close encounter with one of the most highly securitized territorial boundaries in the world. Echoing the aftermath of the Great Syrian Revolt, when the threat of Druze mobility forced the British and French to demarcate and police the frontier, the twenty-first-century Syro-Jordanian border had been drastically hardened because of the Syrian civil war and the specific cross-border threat of the self-proclaimed Islamic State.

The past and present negotiation of the region's emerging states, political identities, and boundaries became viscerally real to me during another research trip, this time in May 2016 to northern Iraq, on the opposite edge of the archipelago of territory amassed by ISIS since 2014. In the northwest Duhok governorate, I was at the Rabban Hermizd monastery (founded by Christian monks in the 640s), standing on the first ridgeline of the Kurdish highlands that rise from the Nineveh Plains, twenty-five miles north of Mosul. A hundred years ago, in the last weeks of World War I, the British raced up to these plains from Baghdad to stake a claim to the Mosul province, despite the fact that the Anglo-French Sykes-Picot land-share agreement designated it part of a French zone after the war. Throughout the rest of the 1920s, the Mosul Question—the nexus of competing British, French, and Turkish claims to the former Ottoman province—remained an ongoing tension until a series of League of Nations commissions finally apportioned Mosul province to British-mandate Iraq in 1926, though it took six more years to finally negotiate and demarcate its boundaries with the Turkish Republic and French-mandate Syria. None of these settlements, however, accommodated the Kurdish political aspirations that had been stoked by the Great War, an omission with long-term repercussions.

By 2016, a new iteration of the Mosul Question had crystallized in the aftermath of U.S. invasions of Iraq in 1991 and 2003, namely, the emergence since the early 1990s of a functionally autonomous Kurdish Regional Government (KRG) in Iraq's northern provinces and the spectacular rise of a self-proclaimed Islamic State, which occupied the city of Mosul in 2014. In contrast to Jordan, territorial boundaries in this area were in extreme flux. In the summer of 2014, on the plain right below where I stood, ISIS forces had reached within less than a mile from a Christian Assyrian village, Alqosh, before Kurdish Peshmerga forces stemmed the tide. In the wake of their dramatic push from Syria into Iraq—taking Mosul, Tikrit, and much of the west and north of the country—the Islamic State released a video on June 29, 2014, proudly titled "The End of Sykes-Picot." Clips showed a bulldozer plowing through a berm on the Iraq-Syria border and a border checkpoint being blown up to dramatically illustrate the erasure of the "artificial" boundaries imposed on the region by Britain and France a century before.[6] The same day, at the al-Nuri mosque in Mosul, the Islamic State's leader, Abu Bakr al-Baghdadi, declared the creation of an Islamic caliphate, a postnational polity intended to encompass Muslim lands.

Standing there two years later, the boundary between the KRG and the Islamic State was about six miles south of Alqosh. The Kurdish Peshmerga—with significant North American, European, and Middle Eastern material and advisory support[7]—were pushing that boundary back down toward Mosul from the north while the Iraqi army prepared a campaign to retake the city from the south. Aid agencies had already constructed additional refugee camps near Dohuk to try to deal with the flood expected to flee the fighting in the city. In October 2016, the Peshmerga and Iraqi army launched the Battle of Mosul. Victory was declared in July 2017 by the Iraqi prime minister.

The contemporary Mosul Question, however, remains far from resolved. The claims of the KRG and the Iraqi state clash in the Nineveh and Kirkuk northern governorates, as do the economic, political, and strategic interests of regional powerhouses Turkey and Iran. These concerns remain deeply interconnected with complex neighboring conflicts. In Syria, emergent polities like the Islamic State and Kurdish-dominated Rojava have vied with the Assad regime and a myriad other militia forces, and Turkey has taken an increasingly aggressive interventionist posture across the border. The Turkish military also continues to wage a counterinsurgency in the southeast against the Kurdistan Workers' Party (PKK), a Kurdish group that uses cross-border support bases in Rojava and Iraqi Kurdistan. While hiking in the Gara Mountains just south of the Turkish border in Iraqi Kurdistan, we saw PKK shelters, craters made by Turkish airstrikes, and, far below, PKK groups driving Toyota pickups on tracks in the valleys. In this complicated political topography, the guide coordinating our trip had had to notify the Kurdish Peshmerga, the Turkish air force, and the PKK to give them a heads-up that our group was hiking in the area.

Today's Mosul Question is one manifestation of a deeper question hanging over the region: How are political orders reconfigured in historical moments of profound change? In 2003, the U.S. invasion of Iraq functionally demolished state control over a strategic space right in the center of the Middle East. Seizing this opening, multiple local political-military networks and external nonstate and state actors—al-Qaeda, the proto-Islamic State grouping created by Abu Musab al-Zarqawi, al-Sadr's and other Iraqi Shi'i militias, the Kurdish factions, Iran, Turkey, Syria, Saudi Arabia and the Gulf States, and the occupying U.S. military—joined the fray to reshape Iraq. With the 2011 Arab Uprisings, the region's interstate system was further destabilized as bottom-up pressures threatened incumbent regimes, with some successfully reconsolidating, reforming, and co-opting resistance or waging a counterrevolution (Egypt, Morocco, and Jordan) while others were overthrown or functionally destabilized (Libya, Syria, and Yemen). Since then, the region's most intense conflicts have raged at these friction points where, in the absence of a functioning state even loosely approximating a monopoly of force, a wide array of local, regional, and international forces clash for control on the ground. Hundreds of thousands have been killed and millions displaced over the past two decades within and across what constitute the world's most fluid and most hardened political boundaries.

My experiences in Jordan and Iraq have driven home how the past is inextricably tied to the Middle East's present, how the early twentieth century is connected to the early twenty-first century. This book focuses on the critical earlier window during which the Ottoman political order was unmade and reshaped into the modern political map, but, like any historical analysis, it is deeply influenced by the present moment. This is perhaps even more true in this instance, as the century-old post–World War I settlement is continually invoked to explain the current crisis by present-day politicians and analysts. Particularly in the case of the Middle East, though, history is unfortunately often paradoxically invoked in ways that dehistoricize the actual processes that shaped the present. Though the contemporary Middle East has striking parallels to and resonances with the past century (as the old adage goes—history doesn't repeat itself, but it does often rhyme), figuring out the historical rhyming schemes through which the past and present are connected is complicated and requires a careful study of that past on its own terms.

This book represents my best attempt to do that. The earliest seeds for this project were planted long ago when I took my first undergraduate class about the Middle East—Clement Henry's Arab-Israeli Conflict course at the University of Texas–Austin—and first learned the standard narrative about the impact of World War I and the postwar settlement on the region. Over subsequent decades of study, research, and teaching about the Middle East, this period continued to be of great interest to me, but it was working on the Rif War (1921–1926) for a chapter in my first book on Morocco that eventually led me back to the Great War.

This process happened in two stages. First, while studying how the erstwhile Rif Republic achieved astounding success before being snuffed out by a vast Franco-Spanish joint military force, I realized that what was happening in Morocco in the 1920s was deeply connected to similar political projects launched at the same time across the region. Some of these ultimately ended in failure (the Sanusi state in eastern Libya, the Idrissid Asir emirate in southern Arabia, Kurdish polities in the Zagros, the Arab Kingdom in Syria), and others were spectacularly successful (the Kingdom of Saudi Arabia and the Turkish Republic). As I started to work on a comparative study of these concurrent cases, the twenty-first-century present began to resonate with that past as virtually every one of the sites at which there was significant conflict a century ago began to reemerge in the wake of the 2011 uprisings as primary friction points: Syria, southeast Turkey, northern Iraq, the Arabian Peninsula, eastern Libya, and, most recently, the Rif region of northern Morocco (from which I was banned by the Moroccan government from doing research for this project during a Fulbright year in 2017 and 2018). The memories of these earlier episodes have been palpable, whether it is Kurds constructing a narrative of national resistance, Benghazi rebels invoking Omar al-Mokthar (the hero of Sanusi anti-Italian resistance in the 1920s) in their fight against Qaddafi, ISIS defying "Sykes-Picot," Houthis mobilizing against a Saudi threat in Yemen, or Moroccan *hirak* protesters in al-Hoceima waving the Rif Republic's flag.

Noticing the connectedness of conflict and fluidity across the region from northwest Africa to the Iranian Plateau (well after the Paris Peace Conference supposedly wrapped up World War I) in the region's early-twentieth-century past and in my twenty-first-century present led me to a second stage: questioning the basic narrative that I had been taught and that I had taught about the making of the modern Middle East. This project's main focus became to critically reevaluate and retell the Great War genesis story, particularly with respect to its widely diagnosed original sin, "Sykes-Picot." Beyond the specific 1916 secret Anglo-French (and Russian, until the 1917 revolution) agreement to divide up the Ottoman Empire after the war, this phrase invokes a deeper explanatory paradigm: that the root of the region's problems traces back to artificial political boundaries the British and French imposed on the Middle East after World War I.

The Sykes-Picot shorthand is widely accepted across the spectrum at a popular level, from ISIS propaganda to the *Daily Show* segment in which John Oliver plays a gin-soaked British colonial official, Sir Archibald Mapsalot III, drawing and redrawing "arbitrary lines betwixt Middle Eastern tribal allegiances" on a white board.[8] This is also the basic causal story, though more nuanced and complex, informing most of the policy-oriented and academic interpretations of this period of history. The way I myself have taught the making of the modern Middle East largely centers on a catechism of dates including (a) the 1915 Husayn-McMahon correspondence, in which the British promised the Arabs a state; (b) the 1916 Sykes-Picot Agreement, in which the British and French divided up colonial spheres of control; (c) the 1917 Balfour Declaration, in which the British promised the Jews a homeland/state in Palestine; and the (d) 1920 Treaty of Sèvres, in which the League of Nations gave mandates to the British and French closely resembling (b) with the promises of (c) included in the Palestine mandate. After this litany, the 1923 Treaty of Lausanne recognizing the gains made by Mustafa Kemal Atatürk in creating modern Turkey is tacked on as an addendum, and the story of the Arab Middle East (with North Africa and the Arabian Peninsula out of the frame) carries on within the mandate system's arbitrarily defined boundaries.

In both its more blatant and implicit forms, the Sykes-Picot standard narrative privileges a linear causal arrow in which the European colonial powers unilaterally imposed boundaries on the post-Ottoman Middle East map in the postwar settlement negotiated in Paris in 1919 and 1920. As other scholars have argued, however, the Sykes-Picot "myth" actually obscures the obvious fact that the 1916 map of British, French, Russian, and international zones of direct and indirect control never translated *directly* into a concrete reality in Iraq or Syria and definitely not in Anatolia or Palestine.[9]

At a deeper level, the myth perpetuates a misconception that the whole of the modern Middle East was "made" by agreements and treaties drawn up by western Great Powers and that artificial borders they imposed have hence been the root cause of conflict in the region. This story, though intuitive, rests on at least three fundamental errors. First, the Sykes-Picot standard narrative glosses over the difference between treaty terms and realities on the ground: it tells us nothing about why there was a decade-long gap between the 1918 armistice and the actual, physical demarcation of the region's post-Ottoman territorial map in the early 1930s, skipping over the puzzling large-scale military conflict from the Rif to the Zagros that persisted after the matter was supposedly settled. Second, it implicitly assumes there were "natural" political boundaries that could and should have been set, a presumption that begs the question of what they might be. And, third, it reifies the mandate fates of a particular part of the region (Syria, Lebanon, Palestine, and Iraq) as representative of the whole.

Erasing the record of local political agency in these cases, this narrative does not even get the mandate story right, much less account for what happened in the vast majority of the region that did not come under the mandate system (Anatolia, Arabia, Iran, and Northern Africa). In sum, the red herring of misdrawn borders diverts attention from the more important question: What kind of worlds—identities, politics, and political systems—emerged, evolved, and survived through this period of intense colonial intervention, local mobilization, and ongoing warfare from 1911 through the mid-1930s? And, secondarily, how did those processes shape the region's political boundaries?

In telling an alternative narrative of the making of the modern Middle East, this book aims directly at those gaps. Opening up a wider field of view temporally and geographically, this revised account looks at how regional and local political orders were undone and reimagined through the Long Great War from Morocco's Atlantic Coast to the Iranian Plateau. It focuses carefully on the local and colonial political projects envisioned and mobilized during this period and how they clashed head-on, examining how winning and losing polities and governance structures were narrowed down in the late 1920s and early 1930s.

The modern Middle East was not made by international actors unilaterally imposing their will after World War I; it was shaped by warfare between colonial powers and local movements as they tried to do so. The borders eventually negotiated and demarcated among the surviving political units were neither arbitrary nor natural; they were, as in the rest of the world, produced through historical processes. By tracing how complex interactions among local, regional, and international actors forged the modern Middle East in the early twentieth century, I hope to also provide context for how we can reimagine the present moment, as political orders are, in many parts of the region, being unmade and remade through violent conflict in the early twenty-first century.

ACKNOWLEDGMENTS

It feels like I have been working on this book about as long as the period it describes. Through this long journey a host of people have shaped me, shaped the project, and come alongside in critique and encouragement. Books are truly collaborative endeavors that rest on the labor of so many people, and I am humbled by the generosity that has been showered on me by so many in the process.

At the head of the list is my partner in life, Leslie Gross-Wyrtzen. She has humored my endless processing, encouraged me when self-doubting, challenged me intellectually, broadened my perspective, been more than game to do a lot of traveling together as a family for different stages of research, and sacrificed much time to make this possible, many times at the expense of her own work. As with the first book, this project simply never could have happened without so much help from you. Thank you for walking with me on the path this book has taken. Similarly, I want to thank all three of my daughters: for bearing with my sketchy drives over Rif peaks in the July heat and all of the other travels over the past seven years. Leila, for your creative visual ideas; Nora, for your help with the title; both of you for bearing with my semi-crazed rants about the periodization of World War I during your AP history classes; and finally, to Alia, especially for being my travel buddy to the *qasr* and wetland preserve at Azraq and sharing tea by the camel well near al-Haditha on the Saudi border.

I thank my dad, Dave, for again being the first person to read completely through the manuscript and for your invaluable input; and to both him and my mom, Mary, who passed on a love for history and lifelong encouragement. Jimmy and Rachel, thank you for your generosity and hospitality in Amman, and Jimmy, for your courage and humor during that adventure together. To Joel, Josh, and Jenae, and to the rest of my family, thank you for your love.

I also want to thank the key teachers who have shaped my understanding of the Middle East through undergraduate and graduate training: Roger Louis, Esther Raizen, Clement Henry, the late Ehud Sprinzak, Abraham Marcus, the late Bob and Elizabeth Fernea, John Voll, Aviel Roshwald, Osama Abi-Mershed, Amira Sonbol, Judith Tucker, John McNeill, and Elizabeth Thompson. All of you deeply influenced how I thought about this book.

Yale has provided an incredibly supportive environment in which to carry out this project. I was able to present parts of it in several forums, including the Comparative Research Workshop, the Political Violence and Its Legacies Workshop, the Council on Middle East Studies, and International Security Studies. I received incredibly helpful input on the book over the past several years from Julia Adams, Phil Gorski, Emily Erikson, Alka Menon, Isaac Nakhimovsky, Marcia Inhorn, Alan Mikhail, Frank Griffel, Paul Kennedy, Libby Wood, Chrystal Feimster, Louisa Lombard, Rohit De, Liz Nugent, Nick Lotito, Jean-Baptiste Gallopin, Anne Taylor, Gulay Turkmen-Dervisoglu, Mehmet Kurt, Ulla Kasten, Bayan Abubakr, Ayse Cicek Unal, Ramon Garibaldo Valdez, all the undergrad students in my WWI and the Making of the Modern Middle East seminar, and especially Rene Almeling and Daniel Karell (whom I thank for close last-minute reads!). I also deeply thank my research assistants—Lina Volin, Ronay Bakan, and Julia Hontaruk-Levko—who did invaluable work on Italian, Turkish, Kurdish, and French archival materials.

This project was incubated at an NEH World War I workshop hosted at Georgetown by Elizabeth Thompson and Mustafa Aksakal, to whom I owe deep gratitude, along with the other amazing participants that summer from whom I learned so much (and continue to learn as your books keep coming out!). I have also benefited from interactions and conversations about this project with Beth Baron, James Gelvin, Kevan Harris, Eugene Rogan, Terry Burke, George Lawson, Toby Dodge, William

Gallois, Peter Wien, Ariel Ahram, Daniel Neep, Fred Wehrey, Ellen Lust, Jonathan Krause, Stathis Kalyvas, Charles Kurzman, Hussein Omar, Aaron Jakes, Marwa Elshakry, Nada Khalifa, and Anupama Rao. Over the years, I had the privilege to present this work and receive feedback in invited talks at Northwestern's MENA Program, UCLA's Middle East Historiography Group, CUNY's Middle East Historiography Group, Boston University's Sociology Department, LSE's Middle East Centre, the University of Arkansas–Little Rock, Al Akhawayn University, the Understanding Insurgencies workshop at Oxford, and Columbia's Global 1919 workshop. In 2016, I had the opportunity to join Al Sharq Reise on an invaluable study trip in Kurdistan, and I thank Christoph Dinkelaker, Amina Nolte, and especially Schluwa Sama for making that possible.

During a wonderful Fulbright year in Morocco (2017–18) working on this project, I had the privilege of being hosted at Al Akhawayn University in Ifrane, our true second hometown, and I thank Nizar Messari, Katja Zvan-Elliott, Derek Elliott, Karen Smith, Kevin Smith, Driss Ouaouicha, Matt Lehnert, Jack Kalpakian, Doris Gray, Driss Maghraoui, Eric Ross, Khalid Mouna, and Paul Love for your generous input into the book, interactions, and friendship.

At an earlier stage, Martin Thomas and Fatma Müge Göçek both did close readings of multiple chapters and provided invaluable help in moving the book forward. Near the end, Ethan Bueno de Mesquita, at the University of Chicago's Harris School and Pearson Institute, convened a group to workshop the entire manuscript, and I am utterly indebted to them for the time, energy, and deep thought you invested, which helped so much in the final shaping of the book. Thank you to Ethan, Paul Staniland, Julian Go, Orit Bashkin, Holly Shissler, Roger Myerson, Carl Shook, Darryl Li, Steve Pincus, and Jim Robinson.

Thank you to the editorial team at Columbia University Press—Caelyn Cobb, Eric Schwartz, and Monique Briones—for making this book happen, to Milenda Lee for the beautiful cover and interior design, to the copyediting team, and to the two anonymous reviewers for their productive critiques and encouragements. And to Yo-Yo Ma for recording Bach's Cello Suites, which I have listened to hundreds, maybe thousands, of times while writing this book. And finally, this project would not have been possible without financial support from Yale's MacMillan Center Faculty Research Grants, the National Endowment for the Humanities, and the

Fulbright Scholar Program. The author and press also want to thank the Frederick W. Hilles Publication Fund of Yale University for assistance in the publication of this book.

Jonathan Wyrtzen
New Haven

WORLDMAKING IN THE LONG GREAT WAR

INTRODUCTION

A wide new world seemed imaginable in the Middle East[1] in the spring of 1920. In late October 1918, the Armistice of Mudros had officially ended hostilities between the Ottoman Empire and the Allied armies of Britain and France in the eastern theater of World War I.

After more than a century of creeping European encroachment, the global conflict had unmade the last bulwarks of Ottoman sovereignty and the vestiges of the wider regional system they had anchored. What would replace the centuries-old Ottoman order, however, remained an open question.

The war's onset had made it thinkable for a large cast of local and European players to completely reenvision the region's map. In the liminal period just after the armistice, a wide array of political futures for the Middle East were imagined and began to be put in motion, at the international level and on the ground. The tensions among these emerging local and colonial political projects to replace the Ottomans were soon evident, however, portending a violent collision course.

At the local level, new political entities proliferated in the spaces opened up by the war. In the eastern Mediterranean, the Syrian National Congress convening in Damascus proclaimed the independence of the Arab Kingdom of Syria in early March 1920 and declared Faisal, the hero of the Arab Revolt, king of a polity aspiring to encompass Syria, Palestine, and Lebanon. In the former Ottoman North African provinces, a group of rural and urban notables announced the formation of the Tripolitanian Republic (al-Jumhuriyya al-Tarabulusiyya) in the fall of 1918 and attempted to get its independence recognized the next spring at the Paris Peace Conference. To their east, the Italians had already diplomatically recognized the functional independence of a Sanusi state in the interior of Cyrenaica in three successive treaties between 1916 and 1919.

New polities were also taking shape in the Arabian Peninsula and other margins of the Ottoman system. The Kingdom of the Hejaz had been created during the war under Sharif Husayn; the Najd-based Abdulaziz Ibn Saud was expanding an area of control in the interior by attacking the al-Rashidis in Ha'il; and the Imam Yahya in Yemen was warring with the Idrissid Amir of Asir in the south. The newly created Armenian republic in the Caucasus had designs on the former eastern Ottoman Anatolian provinces, and in Mesopotamia, the future of the Basra, Baghdad, and Mosul provinces occupied by the British during the war was still to be determined. The fall of the Ottomans had also reshaped expectations for the Kurds, Assyrians, and other highland groups of the northern Zagros Mountains who had long lived on the marches between rival empires of the Anatolian and Iranian Plateaus, most recently between the Ottomans and Qajars.

In that area, the heady blend of new notions of local ethnic and religious collective identity and political expectations, stoked by the principle of self-determination, that became conceivable at this historical moment is captured well in the person of Shaykh Mahmud Barzanji. The British appointed this Sufi Kurdish leader as divisional governor in Sulaimaniya, the eastern sanjak in the Mosul province, just after they came north into the area in December 1918. That winter Shaykh Mahmud consolidated his position; then in late May 1919, he imprisoned the British personnel in Sulaimaniya, evicted troops garrisoned in the district, and tried to rally the local tribes with a call for a jihad to defend a free, united Kurdistan.

Two British brigades promptly sent over from Baghdad defeated his five-hundred-man force at the pass leading from Kirkuk through the Bazian Mountains toward Sulaimaniya and eventually captured the injured leader. In a meeting at the hospital while Shaykh Mahmud was recovering, the British civil commissioner, Sir Arnold Wilson, recalls the shaykh haranguing him about the illegitimacy of the British actions against him or against an independent Kurdish polity given the wartime pledges of the American president and the British themselves: "I had seen him in hospital when, with a magnificent gesture, he denied the competence of any Military Court to try him, and recited to me President Wilson's twelfth point, and the Anglo-French Declaration of 8th November 1918, a translation of which in Kurdish, written on the fly leaves of a Qur'an, was strapped like a talisman to his arm."[2] Wilson had promised the "nationalities" under Turkish rule "autonomous development" after the war in the twelfth point of his January 1918 "Fourteen Points" speech to Congress. The Anglo-French declaration that Shaykh Mahmud had translated into Kurdish and was quoting back to the British commissioner had been issued the week after the Armistice of Mudros. It aimed to reassure the local populations about Anglo-French intentions, declaring that the lofty war objectives of the British and French had been to emancipate the peoples "so long oppressed by the Turkish" and to establish "national governments and administrations deriving their authority from the initiative and free choice of the indigenous populations" in Syria and Mesopotamia.[3]

At the same moment that these new local political entities were emerging that spring, at the international level the colonial powers were nailing down their own visions for the post-Ottoman Middle East. In late April 1920, the prime ministers of Britain, France, and Italy and the ambassador from Japan (the four principal Allied powers still active in the Paris Peace Conference)[4] met for a week at the Villa Devachan in San Remo, Italy. Their task was to reconcile their colonial ambitions with the competing pledges for self-governance they had made in the region over the past five years, like the one referenced by Shaykh Mahmud. These included British assurances to Sharif Husayn of Mecca in 1915–1916 about a postwar Arab Kingdom and to the Zionist movement in the 1917 Balfour Declaration about creating a postwar Jewish "national home" in Palestine. The French, for their part, had created an Armenian Legion in 1916 with the explicit purpose of liberating "Little Armenia," or Cilicia (the Adana vilayet in southeast Anatolia), and creating an Armenian state there. They also actively supported Maronite desires to greatly expand the size of the Mount Lebanon *mutasarifiyya*. Britain and France had issued the joint declaration, reassuring the peoples in Syria and Mesopotamia that they supported freely chosen national governments and administrations. Justifiable local concerns about colonial designs on the region stemmed from the recent publication of a series of secret accords about post-Ottoman spoils, including the infamous 1916 Sykes-Picot Agreement in which the British, French, Russians, and Italians divvied up respective postwar zones of control in Anatolia and the Arab-majority Ottoman provinces.[5]

At the Paris Peace Conference, an international legal mechanism, the mandate system, was devised to marry these seemingly opposed imperial and local aspirations for what would replace the Ottoman Empire: the newly formed League of Nations would provisionally recognize the existence of independent nations of peoples formerly under Ottoman rule and then put them under the tutelage and administrative control of a European power. At San Remo in April 1920, the European stakeholders finalized the allocation of these mandates: Britain got Palestine (with the Balfour pledge about a Jewish national home built into the mandate charge) and Mesopotamia; France got Cilicia (Adana), Syria, and Lebanon; and the Italians registered their interests in southern Anatolia. The treaty terms were circulated to the Ottoman government in May, and in early August 1920, the fifth and final treaty of the Paris Peace Conference was signed in a suburb six miles southwest of the city.

On paper, the 1920 Treaty of Sèvres described a dramatically reimagined post-Ottoman political space, with multiple delineated zones of European tutelary control. For the rump Turkish state left in Anatolia, the treaty involved major immediate and impending territorial amputations. Greece took western Thrace and a substantial coastal enclave inland from Smyrna, on the Aegean coast, where it had landed troops in May 1919. Istanbul and the Bosphorus region were put under the authority of the British-dominated Straits Commission. In the east, the treaty provided for creating a Kurdish state in the next six months in southeastern Anatolia, with a clause stating it could eventually absorb Kurdish areas from the Mosul province.[6] The newly created Armenian Republic would absorb three former northeastern Ottoman provinces.[7] The treaty also laid out a southern boundary with Syria and partly with Mesopotamia, with a Boundary Commission appointed to determine the remaining borders of the Mosul province.

However, the map that European planners drew up in Paris in August 1920 bore little resemblance to facts on the ground. As diverging local and colonial ideas about the shape of the post-Ottoman Middle East clashed, the gap between treaty terms and reality continued to grow. One of the

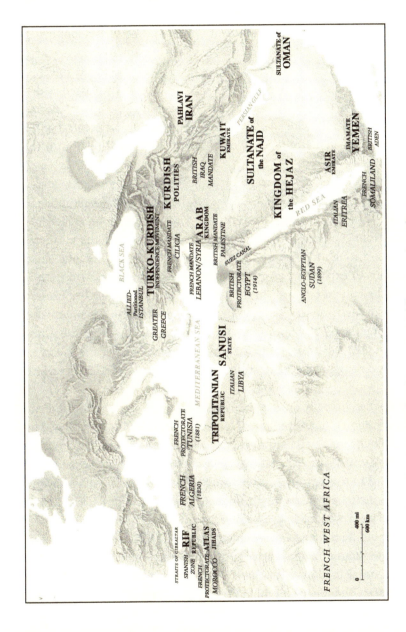

FIGURE 0.1 Emerging political topography of the greater Middle East in the early 1920s.

Source: Author adaptation from public domain.

most intense pushbacks against Sèvres occurred in the Anatolian core. Months before the San Remo conference, the nucleus of a Turkish governing structure rivaling the impotent Ottoman state in Istanbul began to form in late 1919 under the leadership of the charismatic military hero of the Gallipoli defense, Mustafa Kemal. In January 1920, at the final Ottoman parliamentary session, this group successfully passed a distilled vision for the post-Ottoman Turkey they imagined, the National Pact (Misak-ı Millî), which laid out specific territorial and political goals, including the defense of a core homeland of the Turkish nation in the whole of Anatolia.

Kemal and other officers had already begun deploying reconsolidated former Ottoman army divisions to act on these territorial aspirations in the field. Over the next two years, Turkish forces expelled the French and Italians from southern Anatolia and secured control over the northeast provinces through treaties with Soviet Russia, shutting down Armenian aspirations to expand westward. By the fall of 1922, Kemal's troops had launched a counteroffensive in the west that pushed the Greeks back to the Aegean coast and were threatening British positions in the Straits zone and Istanbul. Forced by the Turks back to the negotiating table, the Allied powers signed the Treaty of Lausanne in 1923, abrogating the Treaty of Sèvres and recognizing the postwar realities the newly declared Turkish Republic had forged in Anatolia.

In other areas of the former empire, the distances among the European powers' vision of the post-Ottoman Middle East, the future envisioned by its inhabitants, and facts on the ground also continued to widen. In Mesopotamia, the British faced a massive uprising starting in June 1920, as Shi'i, Sunni, and Kurdish groups in the former vilayets of Baghdad, Basra, and Mosul violently protested the mandate formalized at San Remo. Relying on brutal air power, the British military eventually put this revolt down by October, but their hold over the emerging Iraqi polity remained tenuous. That same summer, French forces pushed inland into Syria to quash the nascent Arab Kingdom, defeating Faisal's forces at the Maysalun Pass on July 24, 1920. Though in control in Damascus, the French faced significant military resistance led by Ibrahim Hananu in the Aleppo region and by Shaikh Saleh al-Ali in the Alawite highlands of Latakia that took more than a year to quell. The veneer of stability finally achieved in the French mandate would be blown apart in the summer of 1925 with the launching from the Jabal Druze of the Great Syrian Revolt, a two-year conflict that would inflame virtually the whole country.

In the Arabian Peninsula, the Hashemite Kingdom of the Hejaz and the Emirate of Kuwait, both British clients, were threatened by their expansionary Najd-based Saudi rival, another British client. At the peninsula's southern tip, the Imamate in Yemen also stood poised to expand, worrying officials in the British crown colony at Aden. In Northern Africa, Egypt exploded into months of revolt after the British arrested and deported Saad Zaghlul and other members of a delegation (*wafd*) attempting to argue for full Egyptian independence at the Paris Peace Conference in March 1919. In the former Ottoman provinces of Tripolitania and Cyrenaica, the Italians vied for control with the nascent Tripolitanian Republic and the more established Sanusi network, and further west, the French and Spanish faced intense tribal resistance to reinitiated military operations into the interior areas of Protectorate Morocco.[8] Spain's campaign to subdue the Rif Mountains provoked the creation of the Rif Republic, a local polity that soon took over most of Spain's designated northern zone.

The point of this survey of the state of play in the early 1920s from the Caucasus and Zagros Mountains in the east to the Rif and Atlas Mountains in the west is to highlight a glaring puzzle: how, years after World War I had supposedly ended and the postwar peace had been settled in Paris, was virtually the entire map of the Middle East still fluid and in tumult? The obvious but overlooked fact is that the maps and treaty terms that European empire builders in London, Paris, and San Remo drew up of how they wanted to partition former Ottoman territories did not translate directly into reality. They had to keep redrawing these maps because new polities were also being reimagined in places like Damascus, the Rif Mountains, and the deserts of Arabia. Local movements from Morocco to Iran vigorously fought throughout the 1920s and into the 1930s to create and defend their own visions of political autonomy. Some of these reimagined units survived in the long term (the Turkish Republic, the Pahlavi Iranian State, and the Kingdom of Saudi Arabia) while others did not (the Kingdom of the Hejaz, the Arab Kingdom, the Rif Republic, the Kingdom of Kurdistan, the Ararat Republic, or the Sanusi state). Regardless of the outcomes, it was these clashes between emerging local and colonial political post-Ottoman projects—not Great Power agreements and treaties—that actually reshaped the modern Middle East. Even for those that did not survive, the memory of these polities and struggles persists in ways that still affect the region a century later.

This book is about how the greater Ottoman political order that had shaped the region for centuries was unmade and how the new political worlds of the modern Middle East were remade during what I call the Long Great War. Running against the standard narrative of European colonial powers more or less unilaterally imposing artificial borders in the postwar settlement, this revisionist account of the formative moment in the Middle East's modern history presents a much more complicated story. First, it shows how the cataclysm of the war, by undoing the status quo, opened up the possibility for both European *and* local actors to reimagine post-Ottoman futures and mobilize toward them. Then, instead of either a top-down account of international intervention and imposition or a bottom-up story of local agency and resistance, *Worldmaking in the Long Great War* traces how it was at the intersection of both, where competing local and colonial projects came into violent conflict on the ground, that the political order of the modern Middle East was forged through the 1920s and early 1930s.

THE LONG GREAT WAR IN THE MIDDLE EAST

World War I marked a particularly transformative juncture in the history of the Middle East, and questions about its impact in the region are perhaps more salient now than ever before. One reason is the war's centenary, which has brought a resurgence of scholarly and popular interest as anniversary after anniversary of major events in the European theater and elsewhere are marked. The other reason is that, in the aftermath of the destabilizing American interventions in Afghanistan and Iraq and the 2011 uprisings that swept the region and opened up a period of revolutionary upheaval and civil war, the Middle East is again at a similar seismic historical juncture. The interstate political system established in the previous century has been shaken, political boundaries are fluid, and emergent political projects in places like Libya, Syria, Iraq, and Yemen are in violent conflict and competition with more established national, regional, and supranational actors. Many of these war zones were sites of intense contention a century ago and, for those with stakes in these struggles, World War I and its controversial settlement in the Middle East constitute an ongoing present-day concern.

This study joins a surge of scholarship revisiting the Great War, with specific respect to the Middle East, by engaging one of the central questions relevant to the region as a whole: How did World War I transform the political topography—in terms of power, identity, and territorial boundaries—of the Middle East? In joining this long-running discussion, I propose three related interventions needed to reassess and rethink the Great War's impact on the region. These include (1) reperiodizing World War I from the vantage of the Middle East, (2) expanding the geographical scope through which we view the war to encompass the whole region, and (3) rethinking the conventional explanation of how new polities emerged and political boundaries were redrawn after the war.

RE-PERIODIZING THE GREAT WAR

The first issue relates to when the war started and ended in the Middle East. The conventional 1914–1918 World War I bracket is limited by two entwined biases that distort our overall understanding of the conflict and warp it in specific ways with respect to the Middle East. The first is a bias toward a judicial definition of wartime that is bookended by the dates of formal declarations, armistices, and treaties carried out by recognized state actors. Using this shorthand occludes complicated realities of continuing violence and political fluidity that extend beyond those dates. The second bias is a myopic privileging of the beginning and ending of hostilities in a single theater of the war to periodize the whole of the conflict. In this case, fixating on the Western Front diverts attention from what was happening in the conflict's other interconnected maritime and overland theaters, minimizing the true interregional scope of *World* War I.

In June 1914, a Bosnian Serbian nationalist assassinated the Hapsburg heir, Archduke Franz Ferdinand, activating a series of continental alliances that brought Europe to war by the beginning of August. But, for the Ottoman Empire and the wider Middle East, this event marked not the beginning but rather a phase shift in a period of multilateral warfare that had already started three years earlier with two related crises in Northern

Africa. The first was the inland occupation of Morocco in June 1911 by France and Spain, which provoked the Agadir Crisis and almost brought France and Germany to war. The second was Italy's decision, in the midst of the Morocco-related diplomatic turmoil, to unilaterally declare war on the Ottoman Empire in late September 1911 and invade Ottoman Tripolitania and Cyrenaica. The Italo-Ottoman War escalated, spreading the next year to the Red Sea, the Eastern Mediterranean, and the Dardanelles, before eventually metastasizing into a war between the Balkan League and the Ottoman Empire that set up the conditions for the 1914 July Crisis. In sum, the Great War in Europe grew directly out of armed conflicts that started back in 1911 and escalated to span the greater Ottoman region in the southern Mediterranean and Balkans.

With respect to the end date of the Great War, using the formal armistices signed by the Allied and Central powers in the fall of 1918 to neatly mark it in the Middle East is even more problematic. This judicial periodization completely obscures the fact that high levels of military conflict continued unabated in much of the region well into the next decade. From the vantage of the Middle East, a Europe-focused Great War chronology, which relies on clean starting and stopping points in 1914 and 1918 and which treats the peace settlement as an event that occurred in Paris in 1919 and 1920, misdirects attention from significant wartime processes extending before and beyond these dates.

Recent scholarship has already begun to move in the direction of re-periodizing the Great War to range from Italy's 1911 invasion of Libya to the 1923 Treaty of Lausanne, acknowledging that, as Gerwarth underscores, the war "failed to end" in 1918 in many places, among them Eastern Europe, the Balkans, and Anatolia.[9] Looking beyond the Western Front, it is obvious the war was prolonged several more years during this "violent peace-time" in a zone that stretched from Central Europe to the Caspian Sea.[10] For the greater Middle Eastern theater, an even longer window is needed to account for region-wide conflicts that continued more than a decade past the formal cessation of interstate hostilities in either 1918 or 1923.

This book uses a Long Great War framework that explicitly brackets an epochal transition of extended wartime in the wider Middle East, roughly from 1911 to 1934, as its own historical period. This move combines two transitional decades typically split up among multiple other periods, correcting a fragmented dating schema in which Middle East history switches abruptly from wartime to peacetime, and from Ottoman to Turkish or from Ottoman to Mandate periods. Leaving room to account for the violent fluidity and complexity that blur these temporal boundaries, the following chapters show how the Middle East proceeded through three sometimes overlapping phases of transformative wartime from 1911 through 1934. The first was the final unmaking of the greater Ottoman order. Through most of the nineteenth century, the Ottoman Empire, like the Alawites in Morocco and Qajars in Iran, was pressured by expanding neighboring European empires because of its proximity and geostrategic position commanding Eurasian and African links.[11] The hostilities that began in 1911 in Morocco and in Tripolitania and Cyrenaica signaled the start of the final chapter of this struggle, with the Ottoman Empire operating almost permanently on a wartime footing through its defeat in October 1918; the Alawites surviving as titular sovereigns in a Franco-Spanish protectorate created in 1912; and the Qajars suffering Russian, British, and Ottoman occupation, despite their official neutrality, that functionally eliminated their last pretensions to territorial sovereignty.

During the second phase of this wartime period, roughly from 1918 through 1923, local and colonial actors reimagined a wide array of post-Ottoman worlds and began to put these in motion, with several of these projects falling quickly by the wayside. One of this study's major innovations is to include a third phase in the Long Great War, from the mid-1920s to mid-1930s. During this period, the remaining political visions for the post-Ottoman order—colonialist, nationalist, regionalist, and local—vied for supremacy in violent clashes that determined the region's new political topography. By 1934—a year French conquest operations in Morocco concluded, the Italians merged Tripolitania and Cyrenaica to create Libya, and the Saudi-Yemeni War ended in a peace treaty—this critical period of polity and boundary formation had more or less wound down, though conflicts continued within these units.[12]

De-Europeanizing the Great War by Ottomanizing it underscores how the greater Middle East was central to the causes, course of, and outcomes of World War I as a whole. For Middle East history, thinking in terms of a Long Great War offers an essential framework for identifying, analyzing, and interpreting the complicated processes through which the region's political order was unmade, reimagined, and remade in a period that extends beyond that conventional dating. Recent work by scholars including Zürcher, Philliou, Schayegh, and Provence emphasizes that 1918 was not an absolute rupture separating late Ottoman versus the Turkish Republic or colonial mandate periods, as evidenced in the complex trajectories of "the last Ottoman generation" through the "Ottoman twilight" in the 1920s and 1930s.[13] Not locking too quickly into separate Turkish or mandate containers is not just important for the Eastern Mediterranean. It also keeps our eyes open to what was happening beyond the post-Ottoman core, helping us see broader patterns in the war's impact on the whole of the Middle East.

EXPANDING THE GEOGRAPHICAL SCOPE OF THE WAR

Toward this end, the book's interlinked second intervention is to expand the geographical scope through which we view the Great War and its effects on the region. To the extent that the Ottoman Empire is even considered in the wider historiography of World War I, the spatial focus is typically on the Eastern Mediterranean—on Gallipoli, the Arab Revolt, or perhaps Britain's campaign in Mesopotamia. This is also true for analyses of the postwar settlement and the partitioning of the Ottomans lands. Most attention is focused on the promises made, kept, or broken by the British and French in the creation of mandates for Syria, Lebanon, Palestine, and Iraq in a single subregion—the Arab East, or al-Mashriq in Arabic. This bias can lead to a generalization of a part of the Middle East to represent the whole in ways that ignore or disregard the variation of experiences and outcomes elsewhere in the region.

From the start, re-periodizing the Long Great War to begin with France and Spain's inland military occupation in Morocco and Italy's invasion of Ottoman Libya in 1911 forces open the geographical lens to include Northern Africa, or in Arabic, al-Maghrib.[14] Though too often bifurcated into separate historiographical bins, Northern Africa and the Middle East continued to be deeply interconnected through the Long Great War. This is also true for other areas of the wider post-Ottoman Middle East—Anatolia, the Iranian Plateau, the Arabian Peninsula, and the Balkans—that continued to be both connected to and express variation beyond the Mashriq experience through these decades.

In this book, the Long Great War plays out across a wide-angle frame resembling the regional system approach outlined by Fernand Braudel for the Mediterranean world but with the center of gravity shifted eastward.[15] This greater Middle East geography includes the interconnected landmasses—littorals, plains, hinterlands, mountain chains, and deserts—and waterways—seas, rivers, and canals—that join Eurasia and Africa. Laterally, this unit stretches from the Atlantic Coast of Northern Africa to the Iranian Plateau (including the Balkans) and spans the Mediterranean, the Black Sea, the Red Sea, and the Persian Gulf. On the edges of this primary frame, the book also keeps neighboring regions in view including the northern shores of the Mediterranean and Black Seas, the Caucasus, Afghanistan and the Indian subcontinent, the Arabian Sea and the Gulf of Aden, the Horn of Africa, the Sudan, and the Sahara.

Using this region-wide scope illuminates the overlapping zones of control, interest, and interaction among the various empires involved in this interconnected system. While several scholars have begun to emphasize that the Great War was fought among empires, not nation-states, many empire-oriented approaches are structured around single cases (the Ottoman, the Russian, the German, etc.) or perhaps two-case comparisons typically focused, in regards to the Middle East, on the British and French Empires.[16] This is one of the first accounts to explicitly address interactions within and among the multiple empires involved in the region during this period. Though the Ottoman Empire is at the center of this cartographic projection, it is situated in relationship to neighboring Islamic empires to the west and east—the Alawites in Morocco and the Qajars in Iran—and to a host of neighboring or more distant European empires—French, British, German, Austro-Hungarian, Italian, Spanish, and Russian/Soviet empires—whose interests intersected in this system.

This wider geographical lens, by not locking down on a single empire, mandate, or other unit, also shows how various local politico-military movements traversed established or emerging international borders. Colonial and local struggles in one subregion of the greater Middle East system had direct and indirect consequences on others throughout the Long Great War. Kurdish movements, for example, emerged at the nexus of the emerging boundaries of Turkey, Iran, Mandate Iraq, and Mandate Syria and Lebanon; the Sanusi were active across what became the international borders of Libya, Egypt, and Chad; the Syrian revolt spilled over into Transjordan and Turkey; and the Rif War affected not just Spanish Morocco but also the French zone and Algeria. Several, like the movements in the Rif and Syria, had global dimensions, being linked directly to each other and to solidarity organizations as far afield as Buenos Aires, New York, and Edinburgh.

One final important way this study expands the geography of the Great War is in shifting the focus outside of urban centers like Paris, London, Cairo, Istanbul, Tehran, Baghdad, Damascus, or Fes to include the countryside, centering rural history in this account of the region's unmaking and remaking. Between 1911 and 1918, the multiple fighting fronts of the Great War were located primarily in rural regions. In the second half of the Long Great War, the hinterlands of the greater Middle East were then the true epicenters from which powerful and novel conceptions of political order and politico-military institutions were mobilized. Though rarely the object of global, transnational historical analysis, rural populations—their internal dynamics, relations with various urban centers, and transnational connections—were incredibly influential through this period of the Middle East's history.

REVISING THE SYKES-PICOT STANDARD NARRATIVE

These shifts to a longer and wider view of the Great War are integral to the book's third and most important intervention: revising the dominant explanation for how the modern Middle East was remade by World War I. I refer to this as the "Sykes-Picot standard narrative." The specific reference is to a 1916 secret agreement in which the British and French drew a lateral line from the Mediterranean to the Zagros Mountains on the map, designating desired spheres of direct and indirect control after the war in the post-Ottoman Middle East. More expansively, Sykes-Picot serves as shorthand for the conventional genesis story told for the modern Middle East.

In brief, the basic plot centers on a sequence of overlapping, often downright contradictory, secret agreements made by the British regarding what would happen after the war if they won. The first promise was to the "Arabs"—specifically to Sharif Husayn of Mecca in a series of letters exchanged with the British high commissioner, Henry McMahon, in Cairo between July 1915 and March 1916—that the British would support the creation of one or more Arab states (with some caveats about the coastal regions of Syria and the Basra and Baghdad provinces) as a quid pro quo for them revolting against the Ottomans. The second was to the French, in the aforementioned infamous 1916 Sykes-Picot Agreement, which promised them Greater Syria, southeast Anatolia, and Mosul province, while the British took everything to the south (with an exceptional international zone designated in Palestine). The third promise was to the Zionist movement, in the 1917 Balfour Declaration, which pledged British support for the creation of a Jewish national home in Palestine.

The central tension in the story is the British betrayal of the Arabs after the war. Instead of honoring their pledges to support Arab self-determination, the British divvied up the post-Ottoman Arab provinces among themselves and the French in the postwar settlement negotiated in Paris, partitioning and imposing de jure colonial rule in the Syria, Lebanon, Iraq, and Palestine mandates. In Palestine, the British added insult to injury, honoring the Balfour promise and functionally privileging Jewish nationalism over Palestinian nationalism in the mandate administration.

This plot is compelling because it has clear-cut main actors, a legible progression of events, and a straightforward causal arc. The British, the central protagonist, and the French, playing a supporting role, concluded secret deals during the war while simultaneously making contradictory promises to local actors to get support. They then imposed a "peace to end all peace"[17] after the war, drawing self-serving artificial political boundaries that have been the source of conflict ever since. The story's intuitive appeal comes from the tragic moral valence of its answer to the question "What went wrong?" Quite simply, the British and French committed the original sin in the modern Middle East's genesis story by imposing the wrong borders and thwarting self-determination in the region.[18] Agency, causation, and blame are neatly assigned to the two European colonial powers.

The Sykes-Picot standard narrative (only slightly caricatured in this nutshell retelling) deeply influences popular and specialist perceptions of the Middle East's history. In David Fromkin's diplomatic history of this period, the definitive strong version of this paradigm is breezily and baldly stated:

Middle Eastern personalities, circumstances, and political cultures do not figure a great deal in the narrative that follows. . . . This is a book about the decision-making process, and in the 1914–22 period, Europeans and Americans were the only ones seated around the table when the decisions were made. It was an era in which Middle Eastern countries and frontiers were fabricated in Europe. Iraq and what we now call Jordan, for example, were British inventions, lines drawn on an empty map by British politicians after the First World War; while the boundaries of Saudi Arabia, Kuwait, and Iraq were established by a British civil servant in 1922, and the frontiers between Moslems and Christians were drawn by France in Syria-Lebanon and by Russia on the borders of Armenia and Soviet Azerbaijan.[19]

Much more nuanced studies do focus extensively on local rather than colonial actors, emphasizing the roles of various elite and non-elite groups including urban notables, nationalist movements, the middle class, workers, rural resistance movements, refugees, peasants, women's groups, or Islamists during and after the war. But here still, the standard narrative's presuppositions usually persist: the presumed starting point is that the British or French imposed the postwar unit—be it Palestine, Transjordan, Iraq, Lebanon, or Syria; the research and argument mainly addresses what happened within the unit.

Though intuitively persuasive, this widely held genesis story of the modern Middle East, in hard or soft forms, is deeply flawed. At its core, it leans heavily on the judicial fallacy already discussed: wartime agreements and postwar treaties are presumed to actually do work, converting more or less directly into realities on the ground. Narrating a progression of discrete events in this way, however, glosses over major gaps between aspirations and reality, concealing the complex and contingent processes actually happening over time.

A host of misconceptions flow directly and indirectly from this error. One is that studies of the war, of the peace settlement, or even local social, political, or resistance histories can accept settled political containers with fixed territorial boundaries as their starting point, rather than problematize them as outcomes. Tracing nation or state formation in a single case (like "Morocco," "Libya," "Syria," "Iraq," or even "Turkey") reifies an object that is actually emerging and obscures the fluidity and frictions that persisted well into the 1920s.[20] A too-ready acceptance that new post-Ottoman states and boundaries were imposed, rather than being formed over time, also leaves unchallenged a deeply problematic presumption that these are thereby artificial. First, this ignores overwhelming evidence that much of the map was fluid and contested for at least a decade beyond the peace settlement. More importantly, the whole notion that political spaces and their boundaries are ever artificial *or* natural in the Middle East or anywhere else is fundamentally mistaken. Political space, including territorial space, is always *produced* by political actors—in this case by both local and colonial actors struggling over the region's future.[21] None of the modern polities or borders in the greater Middle East were unilaterally imposed; all were negotiated over time; and virtually all were actually defined and demarcated, not with the stroke of a pen, but after extended periods of warfare.

A closely related flaw of the standard narrative is that it presumes the colonial and local actors involved in the story had fixed preferences. On the colonial side, the dominant impression is that the British and French articulated how they were going to divvy up Ottoman spoils in 1916 and then proceeded to do so after the war. In reality, the Sykes-Picot map only roughly resembles what anyone got in the end. The French and British (not to mention the Russian and Italian parties to the agreement who ended up with little to nothing of what they were promised) both had to recalculate and readjust for moves made by each other and by local actors. The process part of the story where the actual Sykes-Picot deal was deeply altered—with several parts totally abandoned—is completely underemphasized in the standard telling.

The same is true of assumptions made about populations and political entrepreneurs within the region itself. The betrayal trope deeply embedded in the standard narrative, though by no means completely false, overemphasizes fixed ethnonational identities and political preferences. The presupposition that natural or obvious ethnonational units actually exist as primordial givens in the Middle East or elsewhere is fundamentally flawed (as is the explicit or implicit corollary presumption that borders could have been "correctly" imposed around them).[22] This paradigm blinds us from seeing how dynamically communities in the region—just like the colonial powers—were able to adapt, recalculate, and reorder their political preferences as the opportunity context shifted through the Long Great War. What was betrayed was the pledge to allow these evolving preferences, negotiated among local stakeholders, to shape state institutions of self-governance. Instead, the British and French repeatedly intervened violently, crushing most of these emerging polities, including nascent liberal-democratic constitutional frameworks, and replacing them with authoritarian colonial state structures (emphasizing security, patrimonial politics, and divide-and-rule ethnoreligious classifications) that have left deep institutional legacies in the region.[23]

Finally, the Sykes-Picot standard narrative is seriously flawed because of its selection bias: the story is derived from a limited sample, the one part of the Middle East—Greater Syria and Mesopotamia—where the mandate system was eventually instituted. This *Mashriq* myopia leaves a host of questions unanswered even within the Arab East itself, much less for all of the other areas of the Middle East region that either immediately overthrew (Turkey) or never had mandate forms of colonial control (Iran, Arabia, Northern Africa). Overall, the standard narrative paradigm is blind to a host of processes and outcomes across the region that do not fit its storyline.

WAR AND WORLDMAKING

Countering these misconceptions requires a fundamental rethinking of the origin story of the modern Middle East. This first involves ground-clearing work, exposing the myths already described, and then it requires working out an alternative. Let me clarify that this book's intention is not to swap out the Sykes-Picot myth with another neat and tidy master model. Rather, the point is to set out a fresh region-wide canvas and begin to sketch out the initial outlines and patterns of a complicated picture. Much of that picture will need to be filled out and refined, and perhaps redrawn, by a broader community of scholars with more expertise than I have.

At its core, this book's counternarrative focuses on how war unmakes political orders *and* how it provides the conditions in which new political worlds can be made. It traces how three integral processes of this worldmaking—state formation, political identity formation, and territorial boundary formation—shaped the modern Middle East. In this account, interactions involving and entangling international and local actors drove these entwined, but distinct, processes. European colonial powers are neither all powerful nor absent but, rather, provincialized as one set among many contributing actors, including a cast of local leaders and movements, whose power also had potentials and limits.

Whereas Sykes-Picot is a creation myth in which mandate states and borders are simply spoken into existence by the godlike Great Powers, the Long Great War is an evolutionary origin story of punctuated equilibrium (to loosely extend the metaphor): after a long period of relative stability, the Middle East's political order experienced a short period of rapid change, initiated by the Great War, during which older forms were destroyed and new forms of states, identities, and boundaries rapidly emerged and evolved (with a historical natural selection process narrowing down the outcomes).

WAR MAKES (AND UNMAKES) STATES

This story emphasizes the intimate connections between war and state, identity, and boundary formation. To start with the first, though Charles Tilly's dictum, "War made the state, and the state made war," is one of the most succinct and well-known claims about modern state formation, the modern Middle East (and other colonized regions) is typically exceptionalized.[24] The dominant understanding is that, rather than war, the postwar *peace* settlement generated the (colonial) states in the region. Against that misconception, this study traces how state formation in the Middle East (colonial and local) was driven by war. In contrast to much of the state formation literature, which has focused on the early modern European context of war and state-making, this book turns to a much different type and scale of war and wartime: the interempire, hemispheric conflict of World War I.

For the Middle East and much of the rest of the world, it was this category of large-scale, interregional war among empires that radically unmade previous orders and deeply impacted subsequent trajectories of state formation. The Seven Years' War (1756–1763), the Napoleonic Wars (1803–1815), and the Russo-Turkish War (1877–1878) are earlier examples of this class of conflict that transformed empire states, at times driving the fragmentation and others the consolidation of state power. This is even more true of the two twentieth-century world wars. Both of these global interempire clashes and their aftermaths drove intense cycles of empire and state unmaking and making as the belligerents expanded or collapsed, catalyzing processes of colonization, decolonization, and nation-state formation that have shaped most of the world's present-day political topography. As Adom Getachew has recently argued with respect to mid-century anticolonial Black Atlantic thinkers and politicians after the World War II, these world historical moments also opened up the possibility for a "worldmaking after empire" that went beyond the nation-state.[25]

This study emphasizes the Great War as one of the most significant of these violent global historical junctures, especially for worldmaking in the Middle East. The war destroyed the centuries-old land-based imperial configurations—the Hapsburgs, Romanovs, and Ottomans—and the more recent Hohenzollerns, putting much of Central and Eastern Europe, Asia, and the greater Middle East in flux. The winning Allied empire-states (Britain, France, Italy, and the United States) were also transformed by the empire-wide mobilization of resources and population in total war and as they scrambled to absorb new imperial holdings in Africa, the Middle East, and Asia. Within the greater Middle East itself, this war completely unmade most of the prior state structures and then served as the crucible in which new colonial (mandate, protectorate, direct, and indirect) and local state-like structures (including proto nation-states and other forms) were forged and competed.

WAR REMAKES IMAGINED POLITICAL COMMUNITIES

Another key thread traced in the Long Great War narrative is how political identity—rather than being fixed and immutable—was dynamically reconfigured by communities in the greater Middle East as political orders were unmade and remade. Building off Benedict Anderson's influential theorization of the social construction of collective identity, the following chapters focus on a central question: How does war impact how political communities are imagined or reimagined?[26] As much as and perhaps often more so than longer-term social processes like the print capitalism and mass literacy discussed by Anderson, the tumult of war is a key factor shaping collective political identity, rupturing the status quo and transforming the conditions in which it is conceived.

This book shows how a range of scales of identification operating historically in the Middle East—local, regional, global—was affected by the war. Through this tumultuous period, multiple identities were in motion, with the nation emerging as one among many, often ambivalent and simultaneous, notions of political identification. These rapidly transitioned between becoming thinkable and unthinkable. Just before the war, for instance, the reinstitution of the 1876 Ottoman Constitution during the 1908 Young Turk revolution, as Campos and Der Matossian have shown, prompted individuals and groups across the empire of all different religious, linguistic, and regional stripes to celebrate and revel in a new sense of political identity as Ottoman citizens. Within months, though, the counterrevolution and outbreak of anti-Armenian intercommunal violence in the Adana massacres made these notions less tenable.[27] Similarly, the Turko-Kurdish Muslim post-Ottoman polity widely imagined in the early War for Independence became unimaginable following the intense crackdowns on Kurds by the Turkish Republic in the 1920s. This is similarly true for other political communities—from a reinvigorated caliphate, to a unified Greater Syria, to the Rif Republic—that seemed viable but then were shattered during the war. In the other direction, the idea of a Kingdom of Saudi Arabia, not thinkable ten to fifteen years earlier, had become an established reality by the mid-1930s.

As a world-historical event shattering imperial configurations that had shaped notions of identity for centuries, the Great War transformed conditions in which collective political identity was understood in the Middle East. This is not to say that the slate was wiped completely clean—a host of affinities and solidarities remained in place in terms of class, religion, language, and geography—but how these would be configured was very much put in play. Much of the book focuses on how people themselves rethought political community during this window of time in which it was possible to truly reimagine the future. How people reenvisioned new political worlds—in terms of empire, caliphate, mandate, emirate, kingdom, republic, religious network, tribe—was clearly not according to fixed or unchanging ethnonational identities and preferences (that were then necessarily either thwarted or consummated in the postwar settlement).

Historicizing these collective identification processes shows how political identities were relationally configured and reconfigured, over time, by moves others made and by changes in the broader international milieu.

WAR MAKES BORDERS

Lastly, the related but distinct thread the book traces is how the political boundaries of the modern Middle East, too, were remade through war, not secret agreements or the peace settlement. Borders drawn on maps did not directly create reality; borders were produced over time in tandem with state formation processes, primarily through clashes between rival contenders seeking to establish state-like authority in the post-Ottoman greater Middle East. While territorial space is at the core of definitions of the state, spatial boundary-making processes often are not explicitly theorized or addressed sufficiently in studies of state formation. The following chapters do so, tracking the litany of agreements worked out and reworked from the 1910s to the 1930s but carefully differentiating between aspirations and achievements with respect to stages of boundary formation—delineation, demarcation, and administration. The analysis emphasizes the process of local and colonial struggle through which the international borders eventually settled in the Middle East were generated. It also underscores that, rather than being uniform or static, various borders and borderlands in the region are diverse and dynamic. Produced through processes of contention, competition, and negotiation catalyzed by state-making, these boundaries remained integral to state-making and identity-making processes in terms of selective enforcement and uneven administration afterward. Against popular perceptions about the Middle East: borders rarely made war; war made borders.

WORLDMAKING IN THE GREATER MIDDLE EAST SYSTEM

The following chapters trace the entwined threads of state, identity, and territorial boundary formation, not within an individual country, region, or empire, but across the breadth of the greater Middle East—from the Atlantic coast of northwestern Africa to the Iranian Plateau. Examining how the Long Great War undid the greater Ottoman iteration of this interconnected system and reconfigured it highlights interactions at multiple scales.[28] These include the interregional context in which the greater Middle East system itself is embedded—its deep connections to parts of Europe, Asia, and Africa—as well as its subregions and the translocal interactions across them. Looking at the whole, it is also important to recognize the heterogeneity expressed within the Middle East system as it entered the Great War.

Before the war, a spectrum of state control was wielded in the region, with the Ottoman, Qajar, and Alawite empires projecting power more efficiently in certain areas and much less so in others. The latter were typically located in physical topographies—mountains, plateaus, and deserts—that have historically provided refuge from intensive levels of state control, or, in the case of Syria, contain pockets of these topographies. Some, like the Caucasus and Zagros represent "shatter zones," or peripheries at the meeting point of competing empire-states that provided refuge to a wide array of diverse ethnic and religious groupings.[29] Certain of these represent terrains within an ostensibly state-dominated territory (under Ottoman or Moroccan sovereignty, for example) where groups could sustain a high degree of self-governance and autonomy (the Jabal Druze, Mount Lebanon, and Jabal al-Nusayriyya in Syria; Jabal Akhdar in Cyrenaica; or the Rif in Morocco). Other nonstate spaces like the interior of the Arabian Peninsula were historically at the far margins of any form of state control.

The Great War was a tumultuous shock that transformed the Middle East's ecology of interpenetrating zones of state and nonstate governance, with all of these spaces profoundly transformed by new forms and intensities of state-building activity. In 1911, certain areas of the region had already long been colonized by European powers, namely Algeria, starting from 1830, and Tunisia, from 1881, by the French, and Egypt, from 1882, by the British. Having already experienced decades of colonial conquest and state formation, these passed through the war as relatively settled political units: undoubtedly, the war did catalyze serious contention in these areas, especially in Egypt in 1919, but this was focused on control within, rather than definition of, that unit.

The rest of the greater Middle East was different. The initial phase of interempire war (1911–1918) destroyed the last remnants of Alawite, Ottoman, and Qajar sovereignty, unsettling the political topography and opening up the possibility of redefinition. The last parts of this book focus primarily on these regions put in deep flux by the Great War, which include Anatolia, Greater Syria, Mesopotamia, the Arabian Peninsula, the former Ottoman Tripolitania and Cyrenaica, and the Alawite territories in Northwest Africa (with the Balkans and the Iranian Plateau kept in view). These unsettled political spaces on the map were themselves also unevenly patterned. For one, the multiple fronts of the 1911–1918 conflict in the Middle East theater played out differently in various subregions, with some deeply impacted by brutal battles, disease, famine, genocide and others less so. In addition, Ottoman and Allied (primarily British) armies were positioned at different points of the map at the moment of the Armistice of Mudros, priming, to an extent, the different contexts in which conflict would resume as local and colonial political projects were imagined and mobilized in the second phase of the war (1918–1923) and then competed in a last phase of less symmetrical warfare (1924–1934).

During this latter phase in the 1920s and 1930s, emerging state actors—including the colonial powers and their clients, such as the Hashemites in Iraq and Transjordan and to an extent Ibn Saud, as well as the revived Turkish Republic and Iranian state being consolidated by Reza Shah—were able to unleash military technologies created or perfected during World War I like machine guns, mobile artillery, and air power against populations in these terrains that had previously been largely beyond the state's direct reach.[30] The groups based in these areas—though by no means hermetically sealed off from economic, cultural, and political interactions with a respective state center—historically enjoyed high degrees of local political autonomy and the ability to negotiate the terms of their relationship with the state. The increased asymmetry of state power began to shift the balance of this equation. Some of the nonstate actors in remote areas simply tried to defend their autonomy, as individual tribes or loose confederations, against the encroachment of new British, French, Italian, Spanish, Turkish, and Iranian states. A number of others—including the Saudi, Rif, and Sanusi movements, however, began to systematically consolidate their own statelike military and administrative structures in these rural, nonstate areas to establish, defend, and extend their own new forms of state space.

This book highlights how the most sustained and violent conflicts of the latter phase of the Long Great War (1924–1934) played out in these liminal terrains where new types of emerging colonial and local political orders came into contact. The emerging European colonial states, as well as the nascent Turkish and Iranian states, referred to these clashes as "revolts" or "rebellions," while the local groups mobilizing them tended to frame their struggles for autonomy using the concept of "jihad," or struggle, which served as a multivalent idiom that could mobilize a wide constituency. The last chapters of the book are structured around these cases of major military conflict that played out in Greater Syria; the highlands of eastern Anatolia; the northern Zagros Mountains where eastern Turkey, northern Iraq, and northwest Iran meet; the Arabian Peninsula, including the deserts bordering Mandate Iraq and Transjordan to the north and the Sawarat Mountains running south from the Hejaz toward Asir and Yemen; the Jabal Akhdar upland interior of Cyrenaica in eastern Libya; and the Rif and Atlas Mountains in Morocco.

At the intersection of the international and the local, the warfare of the Great Syrian Revolt, the Rif War, Kurdish revolts against the Turkish and Iraqi states, the external and internal conflicts generated by the expansion of the Saudi state, and the Italo-Sanusi War deeply influenced the entwined processes of state, identity, and boundary formation and produced a range of outcomes across the greater Middle East system by the mid-1930s. War transformed the rival emerging polities and the long-term survival of these colonial and local projects was overdetermined by a combination of factors including the extent of state administrative and military consolidation, the entity's geographic situation with respect to the number of its rivals, availability of external support, and geostrategic importance and imperial cost-benefit calculations about the extent of intervention. In all the cases, these last phases of the war reshaped how political community was reimagined, with solidarities mobilized in these struggles around polities like the Rif State, the envisioned Syrian nation, or various Kurdish entities, though many of these did not survive. Finally, these final struggles—most of which took place in the fluid gaps of the post-Ottoman map—drove delineation and demarcation boundary-making processes on the ground that generated the borders of the modern Middle East.

This book represents one of the first attempts to stitch together a narrative at this scale of the transformative Long Great War period (1911–1934) across the greater Middle East system. As a multisited history, it draws on a targeted set of primary source material spanning Spanish, French, Italian, and British colonial archives; European and Arabic newspapers, journals, biographies, and pamphlets; and less traditional local sources including songs and poetry.[31] Because of its scope, it also integrates an extensive secondary literature, relying on and hopefully highlighting the invaluable work of past and present scholars who have way more expertise than me in much of this subject material and to whom I am indebted. These include older and more recent military, diplomatic, and social histories of World War I; works on the disparate postwar revolts and the colonial states and empires involved; and country-based case studies that I have tried to weave together into a comparative and synthetic analysis of this synchronic moment in which political worlds were being unmade and remade across the Middle East.

ORGANIZATION

The book's organization is broken into a three-part narrative arc. Part 1 examines how the onset of the Great War unmade the last vestiges of a centuries-old greater Middle East order. Chapter 1 provides background context on the Eastern Question and the position of the Ottoman, Alawite, and Qajar Empires with respect to European colonial expansion, including the "Great Game" in Asia and the "scramble for Africa," in the long nineteenth century. It then traces the road to Europe-wide war, starting with the international context and local implications of the Italian invasion of Ottoman Libya in 1911, the French and Spanish inland occupation of Morocco that same year, the Balkan Wars in 1912–1913, and the July Crisis in 1914. Chapter 2 examines the course of the war from 1914 to 1918 on multiple Ottoman fronts—the Caucasus, Mesopotamia, Northern Africa, the Dardanelles, the Hejaz/Syria, and the "home front"—looking at how the interempire conflict transformed the status quo and primed these key geographies as the terrains where struggles to shape the region's political future would take place in the 1920s.

Part 2 turns to how various local and colonial actors began to reimagine the postwar political order and to mobilize behind these visions from

1919 into the early 1920s. In tracing the early formation of rival political projects, these chapters explicitly address the relational process by which they interacted with each other. The colonial plans included the partitioning of Anatolia into spheres of European control, the formulation of a mandate system for the Arab-majority areas of Mesopotamia and Greater Syria, Italian aspirations for a Libyan "fourth shore," and French and Spanish plans in Protectorate Morocco. Local projects were simultaneously or reactively mobilized in opposition to these colonial schemas. In Syria, the Arab Kingdom projected by King Faisal and the Syrian National Congress was quickly snuffed out by the French, but armed movements in the Jabal al-Nusayriyya led by Shaykh Saleh al-Ali and around Aleppo by Ibrahim Hananu kept multiscalar visions for local and national autonomy alive. In the northern Zagros Mountains, Kurdish alternative political visions clashed with emerging Turkish, Iranian, and British-Mandate Iraqi state-building projects. State-like local structures were constructed in the Rif and in Cyrenaica to defend against Spanish and Italian colonial state expansion. In Arabia, state formation also gained traction in the early 1920s in the space opened up by the war, not against an invading colonial power, but in competition among multiple local power centers in the interior and on the coast.

The book's last chapters in part 3 analyze the sites at which the armed clashes between the opposing political projects set in motion during the war reached a climax and led to an end-game resolution in which the postwar polities and their political boundaries were settled. In the mid-1920s, these include the culmination of the Rif War in 1925–1927 during which, in response to Abd el-Krim's expansion south toward Fes, a combined Franco-Spanish force numbering over two hundred thousand was put in the field to crush the Rif Republic and guarantee the dominance of the Spanish and French protectorate states in Morocco for the next three decades; the Great Syrian Revolt between 1925–1927 that originated in the Jabal Druze in the southwest and eventually encompassed most of the country, including major urban areas, and whose defeat signaled the victory of the French mandate system over the dream of Greater Syria; and Kurdish revolts (Simqu Shikak in northwest Iran, Shaykh Said in southeastern Anatolia, and Barzanji in northern Mesopotamia) that challenged the state-building projects of Turkey, Iran, and Mandate Iraq.

They also include a second wave of clashes that climaxed in the late 1920s and early 1930s. The Ararat revolt against the Turkish state (1926–1930) signaled a final attempt to refashion the political boundaries of eastern Anatolia to create an independent Kurdish polity. During the Italo-Sanusi War in 1927–1931, the Italian military waged total war against the Sanusi guerilla forces led by Omar al-Mokhtar, building an almost two-hundred-mile fence on the border with Egypt and forcing over one hundred thousand Cyrenaican civilians into coastal concentration camps where over sixty thousand died, brutally crushing the Sanusi polity and unifying modern Libya. And, finally, I examine the internal struggle in the late 1920s between Ibn Saud and his Ikhwan forces over rival conceptions of political space—fluid boundaries of expansionary jihad versus a more fixed territorialized notion of state space—in which the proponent of the latter, Ibn Saud, won out. The resolution of these struggles in the north of the Arabian Peninsula in 1931–1932 and the end of the Saudi-Yemeni War in the south in 1934 signaled the close of this volatile period in which the new political contours of the modern Middle East were set.

The book's conclusion steps back to assess the different outcomes that emerged as a result of these political-military struggles between local and colonial actors across the new world of the broader Middle East. These include the successes of the state-building projects of Mustafa Kemal in reconstituting the Turkish Republic in Anatolia and Ibn Saud's creation of the Kingdom of Saudi Arabia as well as the apparent failures of projects like the Rif Republic, the Sanusi state, a Greater Syria entity, or a range of Kurdish polities. The conclusion also draws connections from the Long Great War to the present historical moment during which the political order of the region is—again in places like Libya, Syria, Iraq, Yemen, eastern Turkey, and even the Rif—being unmade and reimagined in new competing subnational, national, and supranational forms by international and local state and nonstate actors.

I

UNMAKING THE GREATER OTTOMAN ORDER

1

GEOSTRATEGIC QUESTIONS, COLONIAL SCRAMBLES, AND THE ROAD TO THE GREAT WAR

On the first day of November 1911, residents of the Tajura oasis in Tripolitania heard an engine noise. Looking up, they could just make out the semitranslucent, birdlike wings of an Etrich Taube monoplane several hundred feet up in the air, approaching them from Tripoli, eight miles down the Mediterranean coast to the west. As the plane flew overhead, they ducked for cover when pistol shots rang out. Moments later there was an explosion on the ground. The Italian pilot, Lieutenant Giulio Cavotti, had dropped a half-kilogram Danish Haasen hand grenade in what was the world's first-ever bombing attack made from an airplane. Circling back to the west, Cavotti dropped another grenade at Tajura and two more on the Ain Zara oasis on his way back to Tripoli.[1] Though no one on the ground was injured in Cavotti's attacks, the introduction of this new terrifying threat from the sky was a disturbing portent of the range of military technologies—air power, artillery, machine guns, motorized transport, wireless radio, and chemical weapons—that would be unleashed as the Great War engulfed the entire region.

Cavotti's air assault was launched in the early stages of an Italian invasion to wrest control of its presumptive "Fourth Shore" (*quarta sponda*), Libya, from the Ottoman Empire. The targeted Ottoman territories of Tripolitania, Cyrenaica, and Fezzan were situated between French-controlled Tunisia and British-occupied Egypt and represented the empire's last foothold in Northern Africa in the early twentieth century.

For over a century, the Ottomans and their neighboring Muslim empires, the Alawites and Qajars, had faced increasing European imperial encroachment in the Mediterranean and elsewhere that threatened to undo a centuries-old political order extending from northwest Africa to the Iranian Plateau.

The Ottoman Empire had anchored the center of this system since the early sixteenth century. In the 1300s, the House of Osman consolidated a power base in northwest Anatolia and the Balkans, eventually taking Constantinople in 1453. Fifty years later, the Ottoman sultan, Selim I, launched a massive phase of imperial expansion. To the east, the Ottomans pressed against the newly established Safavid Empire, defeating them in northwest Persia at the Battle of Chaldiran in 1514, annexing eastern Anatolia and northern Mesopotamia, and setting up the Zagros Mountains as an eastern borderland with rival Iran-based (Safavid then Qajar) empires. Turning southward, Selim I then incorporated Greater Syria, the Hejaz, and Egypt into the empire after defeating the Mamluks in 1516–1517. To the west, the Ottomans vied with the Hapsburgs for supremacy, pushing over land toward Vienna, which they first besieged in 1529, and vying with Spain in the Mediterranean.[2]

Northern Africa's coastline was of great strategic value in the struggle between the Spanish Hapsburgs and the Ottomans for control of the Mediterranean Sea. Both raced to establish strongholds from which to control sea lanes, and by the 1570s, Ottoman commanders, often privateer "admirals," had secured Algiers (1516), Tunis (first in 1534 and then taken again from Spain in 1574), and Tripoli (1551). The very Tajura oasis where the historic bombs had fallen in 1911 had served in 1531 as the base from which the famed Ottoman admiral Khayr al-Din (Hızır Hayrettin) Barbarossa, drove out the Knights of St. John from Tripoli.[3] Further west, the Ottomans and Spanish also vied throughout the sixteenth century for control of Morocco until the Saadian dynasty definitively consolidated the lasting autonomy of the al-Maghrib al-aqsa ("the Farthest West"), from Iberian and Ottoman foes, under Sultan Ahmad al-Mansur in the 1580s. Rising to power in the 1660s, the Alawites would maintain Morocco's independence up to the eve of World War I.

For the Ottomans, southern Mediterranean ports and their immediate environs served as important sea-facing military and commercial nodes, but less effort was invested in penetrating very far into the interior. Over time, local dynasties developed in several of these enclaves, as military commanders or governors amassed a high degree of autonomy while formally ruling under Ottoman suzerainty. In the nineteenth century, Northern Africa's function in the broader Ottoman political system shifted as it became the target of European colonial designs. In 1830, the French invaded the Regency of Algiers in 1830, executed the dey, and began steadily occupying the country southward from the coast. The Ottomans reacted swiftly to preserve their holdings elsewhere in North Africa. In 1835, they preemptively intervened in Tripoli, ousting the local Qaramanli dynasty and implementing a policy of more direct rule there and the eastern sanjak of Cyrenaica.

Within several decades, however, the Ottoman position in Northern Africa suffered further blows when the French and British established protectorates over Tunisia (1881) and Egypt (1882). Though functionally autonomous, both had still nominally been Ottoman vassal states, a diplomatic fiction the British maintained in Egypt until 1914, when they formally went to war with the Ottoman Empire.[4] These physical and symbolic losses in Northern Africa were compounded in the late nineteenth century by substantial setbacks elsewhere in the empire to Russian expansion, particularly in the 1877–1878 Russo-Turkish War, in which the Ottomans lost substantial territory in the Caucasus and the Balkans. Following directly in this progression of European colonial expansion at the Ottoman's expense, Italy's belligerent attack against Tripolitania and Cyrenaica in the fall of 1911 also signaled the start of a new phase: an endgame struggle in which the whole of the Ottoman Empire would have to fight for survival as it was drawn into the conflagration of the Great War.

This chapter traces how geostrategic tensions over Northern Africa and other key parts of the greater Ottoman system—stretching from the neighboring Alawite realm in Morocco to the Qajar Empire in Iran—paved the road to the Great War. I begin by charting the course of the "Eastern Question," the set of competing Great Power geostrategic interests that intersected at the Ottoman Empire. During the nineteenth century, a series of interacting processes related to the Eastern Question were set in motion, and they fundamentally destabilized the greater Ottoman system. The first of these was the pressure Russia applied from the north on the Ottomans and Qajars in the Caucasus, northwest Iran, and eastern Anatolia, and against the Ottomans in the Black Sea region and in the Balkans, where Russia supported local separatist movements seeking autonomy. Second, in the Persian Gulf and around the Arabian Peninsula, the Ottomans and Qajars faced intensifying British economic and diplomatic activity through the nineteenth century, including the solidification of "trucial" agreements with local rulers and the establishment of a crown colony coaling station at Aden. A third pressure on this system was exerted on the Ottomans and Alawites in Northern Africa and the Mediterranean during the "scramble for Africa." Here, the Ottomans contended with French and British expansion into Algeria, Tunisia, Egypt, and Cyprus, all while trying to consolidate and extend their own holdings in Tripoli and Cyrenaica. In the west, the Alawites likewise struggled to maintain Morocco's independence in the face of increasing European economic, then military, penetration.

The latter part of the chapter shows how intra-European tensions at the end of the colonial scramble climaxed in 1911 as German, French, British, and Italian claims in Northern Africa clashed. A British-brokered diplomatic solution to the Moroccan "Agadir" Crisis prevented France and Germany from going to war on the Western Front that summer. But, Italy's invasion of Tripoli in September 1911 engulfed the Ottoman Empire in a conflict that would expand from Northern Africa toward the Ottoman core, catalyze conflict in the Balkans, and set up the conditions in which the European powers went to war in 1914. The Italo-Ottoman War and Balkan Wars also served as key formative experiences for the Young Turk elites that rose to power through this turmoil, influencing why and how they led the empire into and through a war that would ultimately unmake the whole greater Ottoman order.

ASKING AND ANSWERING THE EASTERN QUESTION

Italy's invasion of Ottoman Libya in 1911 represented one of the final turns in a multiplayer chess match that had been in play for over a century. In this geostrategic competition among the European Great Powers, the game involved control and leverage over the Eurasian and African landmasses and connective waterways. Over the course of the nineteenth century, the Eastern Question referred to the variable resilience of the

Ottoman Empire, the physical, economic, strategic, and diplomatic linchpin at the nexus of powerful competing European interests and desires.[5]

Originating as a small emirate in northwest Anatolia close by Byzantine Constantinople, the Ottomans rose to power in the fifteenth to seventeenth centuries, consolidating a land-based empire astride the Black, Mediterranean, and Red Seas. For centuries, the Ottomans controlled primary overland and seaborne (after the completion of the Suez Canal in 1869)[6] trade routes linking Europe to the Indian Ocean, the Indian subcontinent, and East and Southeast Asia. At its territorial apex in the eighteenth century, the empire stretched west to east from Northern Africa (excluding the Sharifian Empire in the far west) to the Zagros Mountains bordering the Iranian Plateau, and north to south from Central Europe down to the Red Sea outlet to the Indian Ocean. Controlling most of the Eastern Hemisphere's nodal points, the Ottoman Empire was long a formidable geopolitical power. The Eastern Question became a question when it began to show signs of vulnerability—including the losses of the Crimean Khanate, southern Ukraine, and Bessarabia in defeats to the Russian Empire between 1768–1812—and expansionist European empires began to vie to exploit its weaknesses.

The Eastern Question's salience intensified as two trends came into conflict. One was a shared interest among the European powers to forestall another intra-European conflict in the aftermath of the Napoleonic Wars. Having blocked a French attempt to create a continent-wide empire, the Concert of Europe (Britain, Russia, Austria-Hungary, and Prussia) reapportioned France's annexed territories at the Congress of Vienna (1814–1815) to create a balance of power that ensured a long continental peace that lasted until 1914. The opposing factor that continually threatened that peace, however, was competitive expansion outside of Europe.

The Ottoman Empire, the so-called "sick man of Europe," was at the center of these tensions throughout the nineteenth century, as were, to a lesser degree, the Alawite and Qajar Empires. European expansion pressured the greater Ottoman system from four directions: (1) around the Black Sea and into the Balkans (by the Russian and Austro-Hungarian Empires); (2) in the Caucasus, Northwest Iran, and eastern Anatolia (by the Russian Empire); (3) in the Persian Gulf and Arabian Peninsula (by the British Empire); and (4) in Northern Africa and the Mediterranean (French and British Empires). Pressure on these fronts was interconnected

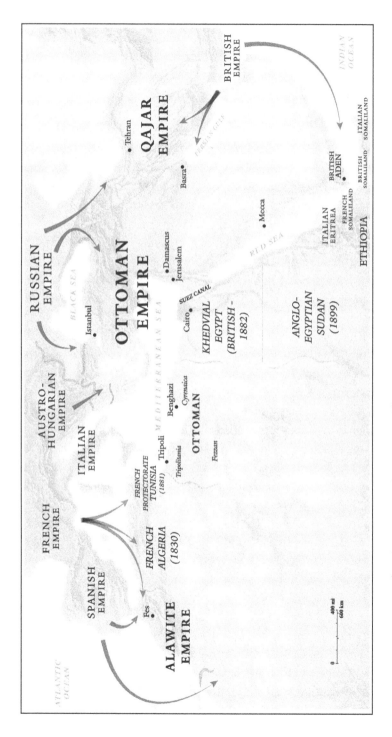

FIGURE 1.1 Expansionary colonial pressures on the greater Middle East in the long nineteenth century.

Source: Author adaptation from public domain.

in two perennially important ways. First, because of the intra-European balance of power and a zero-sum-game perception of empire, in which territorial gains by one was viewed as a loss by others, expansion to the detriment of the Ottomans, Alawites, or Qajars was never unilateral: each move by one player triggered countermoves by the others. Second, external pressures were usually closely linked to internal pressures within these three Muslim empires, particularly in the Ottoman Balkans.

The Greek Revolt (1821–1832) against Ottoman rule exemplifies how internal and external conflicts over Ottoman territory catalyzed multilateral interactions that spilled across the Balkans, the Caucasus, and the Mediterranean. In 1824, unable to defeat rebel Greek forces, the Ottoman sultan called on the functionally autonomous governor of Egypt, Mehmet Ali (himself originally from Albania), to send an expeditionary support force to Crete and Cyprus and then to the Peloponnese. The success of the battle-hardened Egyptian army, which had just conquered much of northern Sudan in 1820–1821, against the anti-Ottoman rebels drew in European pro-Greek intervention. After a combined French, British, and Russian naval force destroyed the Ottoman-Egyptian fleet at the Battle of Navarino in 1827, the Egyptian army was forced to withdraw, and the Ottomans eventually recognized Greek independence in 1832. The turmoil of the war, however, spilled over into other parts of the Ottoman Empire. In 1828–1829, Russia invaded Bulgaria and pushed into the Caucasus, forcing the Ottomans to recognize Serbian autonomy in the Balkans and Russian sovereignty over Armenia and Georgia in the 1829 Treaty of Edirne. In the summer of 1830, France occupied the Ottoman Beylik of Algiers and began expanding inland. Finally, in the eastern Mediterranean, Egypt's Mehmet Ali, though nominally an Ottoman vassal, seized the Syria and Adana provinces in the early 1830s and threatened the Ottoman capital, Istanbul itself. It took a British and Austrian naval blockade in Egypt, the shelling of Beirut in 1839, and the assurance of the hereditary title of khedive under Ottoman suzerainty, to force Ali and his son, Ibrahim Pasha, to withdraw back to Egypt and agree to downsize the Egyptian navy and army.[7]

During the second half of the nineteenth century, Russian southward expansion activated another intense round of interactions centered on the Eastern Question. By this point, British versus Russian imperial geostrategic competition, the "Great Game," was in full swing along a line extending from Istanbul through Iran to Afghanistan and India, and the

Ottoman and Qajar Empires were caught in the middle. For the British, the Ottoman and Qajar realms served as important buffers checking the Russians' ambitions to gain access to the Mediterranean and to the Indian Ocean. For the Russian Empire, "heir" of the Byzantines, the Ottoman capital, Constantinople, represented a religious, cultural, and strategic prize controlling the Black Sea's Bosphorus outlet, and the Ottoman-Qajar borderlands represented Russia's shortest path from the Caucasus to the Persian Gulf and seaborne access to the East. These tensions were palpable in the 1850s, when the British and French allied with the Ottomans in the Crimean War (1853–1856) to forestall Russian advances across the Danube in Central Europe and into the Kars province in eastern Anatolia.

Two decades later, they came fully into play when the shaky Ottoman bulwark was buffeted again during the Russo-Ottoman War of 1877–1878. Again, as with the Greek War, internal anti-Ottoman uprisings in Bulgaria, Herzegovina, and Bosnia in 1875 activated a web of interactions that escalated the conflict far beyond the Ottoman Balkans. First, the autonomous provinces of Serbia and Montenegro intervened on behalf of the rebels, and then Russia entered the fray when the Ottomans gained the upper hand, deploying troops to back the Serbs. In April 1877, the Russian Empire fully declared war on the Ottoman Empire, launching a western offensive in the Balkans and an eastern offensive into Anatolia. By January 1878, Russian forces were within sight of the gates of Istanbul, and Sultan Abdülhamid II agreed to an armistice. In March, the Ottomans signed the Treaty of San Stefano, declaring Romania, Serbia, and Montenegro independent of Ottoman rule and acknowledging an enlarged, autonomous Bulgaria, with access to both the Black and Aegean Seas, under Russian protection. The Ottomans also recognized the occupation and administration of the Austro-Hungarian Empire in the vilayets of Bosnia and Herzegovina, though these technically remained under Ottoman sovereignty.

Russia's extensive gains in the treaty greatly alarmed other European powers, leading the German imperial chancellor Otto von Bismarck to convene the Congress of Berlin that summer (June 13–July 13, 1878). The goal of the congress—which included Germany, Britain, France, Russia, Austria-Hungary, and the Ottomans—was to hash out a sustainable settlement for the Eastern Question. Its first step was to roll back Russian gains in the Balkans and contain the emerging Slavic states in the region. To this end, the Congress greatly reduced Bulgaria in size and made it an independent principality in the Ottoman Empire; Romania, Serbia, and Montenegro were allowed to remain independent but had to give back territory to the Ottomans; Austro-Hungary kept Bosnia and Herzegovina under their administration; and eastern Rumelia and Macedonia were returned to the Ottomans. It also recognized the formal and informal interests of other powers elsewhere in the Ottoman Empire. In eastern Anatolia, the Russian Empire took the three easternmost Ottoman provinces—Kars, Ardahan, and Batum. In the Mediterranean, the British took Cyprus, creating a protectorate that still formally recognized Ottoman suzerainty.

Though Russia's gains had been somewhat rolled back in the Berlin negotiations, the Ottomans still lost a devastating two-fifths of their territory and one-fifth of their population as a result of their defeat in the Russo-Ottoman War. The bulk of the European side of the Ottoman Empire had been effectively amputated, creating, for the first time, a Muslim-majority population in the remaining lands. This included over a million Muslims (and a large number of Jews) displaced from the Crimea, the Caucasus, and the Balkans during the previous decades of conflict and upward of two million who had to leave Russia and the Balkans after the 1877–1878 war.[8] These *muhajirs*, or refugees, had to be resettled across Anatolian and Arab-majority provinces, transforming intercommunal relations in numerous contexts.[9] The war's aftermath and settlement inflicted bitter wounds that would fester over the next three decades for multiple parties. For the Russian Empire and some Balkan states, the significant reversals imposed at the Berlin Congress set up grievances that would contribute directly to the outbreak of the Great War. For the Ottomans, too, especially for a generation of rising military officers growing up in the remaining Ottoman Balkan provinces, the experience of devastating territorial losses and population transfers sustained after the Russo-Ottoman war deeply shaped decision-making during the Great War.

In the 1880s, the Eastern Question's friction point shifted from the Balkans to Northern Africa, where it became entangled in the "scramble" on the continent. At the 1878 Congress of Berlin, the British and French had cynically agreed on a secret quid pro quo, with France supporting Britain's seizure of Cyprus in exchange for Britain recognizing France's prerogative in Tunisia. Three years later, the French Empire acted on these interests, using a cross-border raid into Algeria by the Khumayr tribe as a pretext to invade Tunisia in April 1881 and establish a protectorate that formally retained the Husaynid Bey in power.[10]

French expansion triggered several competitive moves elsewhere in Africa, including Britain's occupation of Egypt in 1882, which led to the convening of the Berlin Conference in 1885. This attempt to rationalize the "scramble for Africa" established the "principle of effective occupation"— colonial claims had to be substantiated by treaty, occupation, and some form of on-the-ground administration (a provision serving the interests of newcomer colonial powers, like Germany, wanting to expand in Africa). Though intended to diplomatically resolve colonial conflicts of interests, the principle of effective occupation set up powerful vectors of competitive inland expansion from coastal enclaves in Africa that eventually collided. The most serious of these was the 1898 Fashoda clash between French claims to a horizontal west-east African axis connecting Senegal to French Somaliland (Djibouti) and British aspirations to a north-south African axis connecting Cairo to the Cape. Still not reconciled to the British occupation of Egypt fifteen years earlier, the French sent a force out from the Congo under the command of Major Jean-Baptiste Marchand to traverse the interior of Africa and establish French claims on southern Sudan. The Marchand expedition ended up in a standoff at the Fashoda fort on the banks of the White Nile in late September 1898 with an Anglo-Egyptian contingent under the command of Sir Herbert Kitchener, which had just defeated the Mahdist army at the Battle of Omdurman earlier that month. The Fashoda incident came close to provoking an Anglo-French war before the French stood down, and both colonial powers negotiated an agreement recognizing separate spheres of influence west (French) and east (British) of the headwaters of the Nile and Congo Rivers.

THE MOROCCAN CRISES AND THE THREAT OF FRANCO-GERMAN WAR

Elsewhere in Africa, however, competing European imperial interests— French, British, Spanish, Italian, and German—continued to collide, particularly with regard to the still-independent Alawite entity in the northwest. The French, ensconced next door in Algeria since the 1830s, viewed the Sharifian kingdom in Morocco as the missing segment in an arc of hegemony extending from West Africa to Tunisia. For the British, in addition to their significant commercial interests in the country, Morocco's importance derived from its location on the southern shore of the Straits of Gibraltar, thereby controlling one of the three critical choke points of the sea lane to India (together with the Suez Canal and the Bab al-Mandab outlet of the Red Sea to the Indian Ocean). The Spanish retained centuries-old enclaves on the northern Moroccan coast and had expansionist aspirations following their ignominious defeat and territorial losses in the 1898 Spanish-American War, and Germany and Italy remained interested in grabbing whatever unclaimed territories were left toward the end of the "scramble for Africa."

The "Moroccan Question" thus emerged as a corollary to the Eastern Question in the late nineteenth century.[11] As with the Ottoman Empire and the Anglo-Russian competition in the Qajar Empire during this time, Morocco's geostrategic importance made the prospect of a single European power controlling it too severe a threat to the balance of power on the continent. As a result, Morocco was one of the few corners of Africa still not colonized by the early 1900s, though the Alawite state's effective sovereignty and ability to raise revenues had been severely compromised by this point by economic capitulations and onerous debt obligations to various European powers and the United States. In 1904, the two major colonial belligerents at odds over Morocco, the British and French, settled their differences in a secret accord, the Entente Cordiale, which included provisions recognizing the other's respective colonial interests in Egypt and Morocco, with a proviso that Spain's claims in northern Morocco be acknowledged. The latter move mollified British concerns that the French could shut down the Straits. Anglo-French diplomatic bargaining did not, however, settle the aspirations of the other newcomer colonial powers, particularly Germany and Italy, who respectively had designs on Morocco and Ottoman Tripolitania and Cyrenaica.

In the decade before the outbreak of World War I, Franco-German tensions over Morocco pushed Europe toward the brink of war on two occasions. The First Moroccan Crisis unfolded in the spring of 1905. On March 31, Kaiser Wilhelm II docked his yacht in Tangier, toured the city with great fanfare, and met with a group of emissaries from the Moroccan sultan Mawlay Abd al-Aziz. This was not the Kaiser's first excursion to a Muslim power in the Mediterranean in which Germany had strategic interests. In 1889 (a year after being crowned) and 1898, he had made high-profile visits to the Ottoman Empire to cultivate economic and military ties. In Tangier, the Kaiser vocally supported the Moroccan sultan's claims to sovereignty, particularly against French interests, emboldening Abd al-Aziz to reject proposed French economic and police reforms and call, with German support, for an international conference to resolve these issues.

The French strenuously rejected this proposal, and tensions began to escalate over the summer. With pressure from American president Theodore Roosevelt, the parties agreed to convene a conference to settle the Moroccan Question. Though preferring and expecting a diplomatic solution, both sides also initiated military preparations that fall: Germany took a few steps, calling up reservists and making some military purchases, but France issued more wide-ranging orders to ready the army on the border. (France's ally Britain kept naval concentrations near home ports, while Belgium fortified key bases on Germany's westward invasion path.)[12] The next year, between January 16 and April 7, 1906, thirteen nations with interests in Morocco deliberated in the Spanish port of Algeciras. In the negotiations, the Germans only had the backing of the Austro-Hungarian Empire, however, because Italy and France had previously come to a mutual agreement about their respective interests in Morocco and Libya. In the end, the terms of the Act of Algeciras ostensibly supported Moroccan autonomy by limiting European economic intervention, but the true outcome of the conference was to confirm tacit British, American, and Italian acceptance of France's and Spain's exclusive prerogatives in the sultanate.

A year later, the French used the murder of a French doctor, Emile Mauchamp, in Marrakesh (by a mob angry about the sultan's impotence in the face of European intervention) as a *causus belli* to move into Moroccan territory. In March 1907, they occupied the city of Oujda on the Algerian border, and then they shelled and occupied Anfa (Casablanca) on the Atlantic coast in June. French forces also began to press into Moroccan territory in the southeast, pushing into the Figuig and Tafilelt oases. In the north, the Spanish expanded control southward from one of its Mediterranean coastal enclaves, Melilla, engaging in battles with Rif tribes. With the country facing these threats, a civil war broke out in Morocco between rival claimants to the throne, with Mawlay Abd al-Aziz eventually supplanted by his brother, Mawlay Abd al-Hafidh. The new sultan had little means to stem France's increasing penetration in the country, and Middle Atlas tribes rose up in the spring of 1911 and besieged Hafidh in the inland capital, Fes, in early March. In April, the French ordered a relief column of fifteen thousand troops to be sent to Fes to support the sultan. That June, Spain landed forces on the northern Atlantic coastal port of Larache and began moving inland toward the Jbala region.

The French and Spanish colonial moves into the Moroccan interior caused the Second Moroccan Crisis in the summer of 1911 in which dangerously bellicose reactions threatened to escalate into a European war. In early July, Germany sent two gunboats, the *Panther* and the *Berlin*, to Agadir, ostensibly to protect German interests in Morocco's southern Souss region but also signaling a rejection of France's attempt to de facto occupy and colonize the country. Britain reacted strongly to the threat of Germany possibly gaining an Atlantic port, putting the navy on high alert, while France again heightened readiness on its German border. In negotiations early that fall in Paris, an agreement was reached by which Germany acknowledged a French protectorate in Morocco in exchange for the French transferring territory from the French Congo to German Kamerun.[13]

The two Moroccan crises demonstrated an increasing and dangerous willingness by the European powers to pair colonial competition in the greater Ottoman sphere with military saber-rattling on the continent. These interactions also clarified and solidified the emerging lines of alliance that would shape the Great War. The crises, of course, also profoundly transformed the Sharifian Empire, contributing to internal unrest, the outbreak of a civil war, and the inauguration a five-decade period of foreign intervention in Morocco. Just months after the Franco-German accord, the French emissary, Eugene Regnault, and the Moroccan sultan, Mawlay Abd al-Hafidh, met to sign the Treaty of Fes in March 1912. The internationally recognized treaty imposed a French protectorate over the Sharifian Empire in which the Third Republic took over the responsibility of diplomatic representation, the modernization of the state administration, and the military subjugation of "dissident" regions. That November, the French and Spanish agreed to a prearranged protocol acknowledging Spain's northern zone of control as well as its interests in the Saharan southern regions of the protectorate.

THE OTTOMAN AND ITALIAN SCRAMBLES FOR AFRICA

In the fall of 1911, as French and German negotiators finalized the Morocco for Kamerun swap to forestall a European war, the Italian decision that September to seize another part of Northern Africa—Ottoman Tripolitania, Fezzan, and Cyrenaica—ended up still catalyzing that conflict. Italy's project to "reclaim" Roman territories in North Africa had been decades in the making. Italy's national unification had been completed in 1871, the same year Prussia declared the creation of the Second Reich, and like the German Empire, the Italians were eager to catch up with other European colonial powers.[14] The prize Italy wanted initially was Tunisia, less than a hundred miles from Sicily and already home to a substantial Italian community numbering over eleven thousand in the 1870s. France's preemptive occupation and establishment of a protectorate in Tunisia in 1881 was a major blow to this ambition and to Italian prestige.

Looking further afield in Africa, Italy annexed the port of Massawa on the Red Sea in 1886, establishing the colony of Italian Eritrea. In 1888, it signed agreements with local leaders creating an Italian protectorate in Somaliland. The British supported these moves, preferring Italian expansion to the possibility that France, which had established French Somaliland (Djibouti) in 1883, would claim more strategic coastline opposite Britain's Aden at the Red Sea outlet of the route to India. Further Italian aspirations in the Horn of Africa were brutally cut short, however, with their devastating defeat by the Ethiopian army at the Battle of Adwa in 1896.

Over the next decade, pro-empire Italian groups like the Nationalist Association, founded in 1910 by Enrico Corradini, redirected expansionist enthusiasm toward the coast of Northern Africa, seeing the colonization of Ottoman Tripolitania and Cyrenaica as a means to avenge the humiliation of the defeat at Adwa, provide an internal migration outlet solving Italy's overpopulation problem, and revive Rome's mare nostrum.[15] Italian banks and business interests were already increasing activity in the coastal zones of Tripolitania and Cyrenaica in the early 1900s. In late summer 1911, having secured the tacit approval of the other European powers, the Italian prime minister, Giovanni Giolitti, ordered preparations for an amphibious assault on Ottoman coastal fortifications at Tripoli, Tobruk, Derna, Homs, and Benghazi. The Italian government ordered the Ottomans to cede Tripolitania on September 28, then declared war the next day.

On the other side of this conflict, the Ottomans themselves had not been passive bystanders during the three decades since the Congress of Berlin set out the framework intended to regulate the "scramble for Africa." In spite of, or perhaps because of, their losses to the French and British in Tunisia and Egypt in the early 1880s, the Ottoman Empire, as Ali Minawi has shown, fully joined the rush to make and buttress territorial claims on the continent in the late nineteenth century.[16] The Ottomans' base in Africa comprised three distinct geographical areas. In the west, the Tripolitania region encompassed the environs of Tripoli, the coastal plain, and the upland ranges including Jabal Nafusa; the Fezzan refers to the desert region directly south of Tripolitania; and Cyrenaica is the eastern region, including the coasts, the Jabal Akhdar mountainous plateau, and the Saharan reaches to the south.

Within these areas nominally under Ottoman control, the division between coast and hinterland marked an important spatial divide between areas under some degree of state administration and those exercising higher levels of local autonomy. Tripoli historically constituted a state center projecting power into its hinterland. To its south, the Fezzan preserved varying degrees of autonomy, and for a long period (1550–1813), the Fezzan-based Awlad Mohammed projected its own state-like influence farther south into the Chad basin.[17] In the east, in Cyrenaica, the Ottomans maintained small garrisons in coastal cities like Benghazi, al-Marj, Darna, and al-Qaiqab, but, from the 1870s, the upland areas of Jabal Akhdar (Green Mountain) were under the control of the Sanusi, a powerful movement of networked Sufi religious lodges founded in the 1850s by Muhammad bin Ali al-Sanusi, an Algerian scholar and religious reformer. Building off a strong base in Cyrenaica, the Sanusi movement extended nodes through the 1870s into critical oases southward across the Sahara and eastward into the Egyptian desert. By the late 1800s, the Sanusi had effectively built a robust governing institutional infrastructure that had executive and consultative councils, collected taxes, maintained a postal system, had military capabilities, administered a large-scale educational apparatus, and controlled important economic linkages across the Sahara and east to Egypt.[18]

In the late nineteenth century, the Ottoman Empire engaged in a series of strategies to try to consolidate its control on the coasts and extend its claims of "effective occupation" south into the Sahara and Sahel. After the French seized Tunisia in 1881, the Ottomans reorganized the administration in Africa and gave Cyrenaica, formerly part of the Tripoli province, a *mutassariflik* status as a separate governorate reporting directly to Istanbul.[19] The Ottomans also intentionally sought to coordinate more closely with the Sanusi, offering them tax exemptions, administrative recognition, and material aid. In exchange, the Ottomans wanted the Sanusis to use their network of lodges, fiscal and military apparatus, and solidarity enhancing religious ideology to project Ottoman influence southward across the Sahara into the Lake Chad region and mobilize local groups against French and British encroachment in the Sahara and Sahel regions.[20] In Egypt's Western Desert oases, as Matthew Ellis has shown, tensions about the overlapping spheres of sovereignty among the Sanusi, Ottomans, and Egyptian Khedivate (under a British "veiled protectorate" from 1882) began to activate the territorial importance of this boundary zone.[21]

With regard to the south, the Ottoman Empire addressed a note to the European powers in 1890, laying claim to large areas in the Sahara and Sahel, including Waday, Bornu, Borku, Kanem, Kewar, northern Congo, and Nigeria. A decade later, however, the post-Fashoda Anglo-French agreement of March 21, 1899, designated these areas west of Anglo-Egyptian Sudan as a French sphere. In the early 1900s, French military operations into the Chad Basin brought them into direct conflict with the Ottoman-Sanusi alliance. The Ottomans channeled limited amounts of supplies and munitions to their allies, but the French steadily pushed the Sanusis and their local allies back as they occupied Waday, Tibesti, and Borku between 1906 and 1914. Though not successful in holding the Ottomans' claims in the African interior, this previous history of Turkish coordination with local groups, the Sanusi in particular, would prove highly significant in the Italo-Ottoman War and in World War I. Though they had little capacity to field a large military force in their North African territories, the Ottomans could leverage local partisan groups as a potent military force.

THE ITALO-OTTOMAN WAR AND THE PRELUDE TO THE GREAT WAR

The Ottoman efforts to maintain an imperial stake in Africa during the 1890s and 1900s against French incursions in the Sahara and Sahel entered a much more intense phase when Italy declared war on the empire and directly invaded Tripolitania and Cyrenaica in the fall of 1911. In the first week of October, the Italians landed an expeditionary force of 34,000 troops—which included a large contingent of Somali and Eritrean colonial soldiers—believing it more than sufficient to overwhelm the 4,200 Ottoman soldiers on the ground and quickly pressure the Ottoman Empire into negotiations. Within the range of their vastly superior naval artillery, the Italian forces made rapid progress, occupying most of the coastal cities in Tripolitania and Cyrenaica in the first weeks of October. Their attempts to move inland, however, met stiff resistance from the Ottoman troops and local forces that had withdrawn outside the range of the Italian navy's guns. Within a month of the Italian invasion, this resistance began to be coordinated by several dozen Ottoman Young Turk officers affiliated with the Committee for Union and Progress (CUP) who covertly made their way via Egypt or Tunisia to Libya.[22] The war in Northern Africa would prove a profoundly formative experience for these officers, many of whom comprised the leadership cadre that rose to power over the next few years and led the Ottoman Empire through World War I.

The officer-dominated CUP had played a major role in the 1908 revolution that forced the Ottoman sultan, Abdülhamid II, to reinstate the 1876 constitution and hold parliamentary elections. In addition to domestic factors, their actions were partly driven by concerns that, having divided Iran and Afghanistan into separate zones of influences in the 1907 Anglo-Russian agreement, these two powers were pressuring the Ottoman sultan to partition Macedonia. In the midst of the tumult of the revolution, in October 1908, Bulgaria declared full independence and Austro-Hungary formally annexed Bosnia; until that point, both countries had still formally been under Ottoman sovereignty. In 1909, these Young Turk officers marched the Third Army from Salonika to Istanbul to quickly snuff out Abdülhamid's counterrevolution, replacing him with his younger brother, who took the title Sultan Mehmed V.

The Italian invasion of Ottoman North Africa two years later caused two reactions within the Ottoman leadership: on one side, the Grand Vizier and cabinet thought the cause hopeless and wanted to cut the empire's losses; on the other, the Young Turk officers, many raised in the Balkan provinces long beleaguered by separatist nationalism and imperial interference, believed this blatant assault on yet another zone of Ottoman territorial sovereignty had to be resisted. Despite an official decision not to send more troops, Major Ismail Enver, later one of the triumvirate that effectively ruled the Ottoman Empire during World War I, convinced the CUP leadership in Salonica of his plan's merits to help facilitate an irregular war against the Italians. He himself set out covertly for Alexandria on October 9, 1911, then proceeded west to Cyrenaica.

For Enver, the war in Libya was a proving ground in which he developed his own tactical and strategic thinking, view of Ottoman imperial space, and essential relational networks. The last included the nucleus of what would become the Teşkilât-ı Mahsusa, or Special Organization, an intelligence unit he would wield internally in the Ottoman Empire during World War I.[23] Upon arriving in Cyrenaica, Enver assembled around twenty thousand troops, including Ottoman and local Arab soldiers, at a base camp, Ayn al-Mansur, just inland from the Italian-controlled port of Derna. He also reached out to the Sanusi, liaising with their head, Sidi Ahmad al-Sharif. For the Sanusi and other local groups, Enver's marriage to Naciye Sultan, granddaughter to a former sultan and niece of the current sultan, enhanced his personal prestige and, for Enver, underlined the resonance of religious solidarity in the fight against an outside "Christian" invader. Enver strategically emphasized a shared Muslim identity while rallying resistance against the Italian occupying army.

That December, Ottoman-Arab forces made successive attacks on Benghazi and Derna in Cyrenaica but, despite inflicting heavy casualties, could not dislodge the Italian troops from their coastal strongholds. One success was the Battle of Tobruk, where an Ottoman force led by Adjutant Major Mustafa Kemal defeated an Italian detachment. Kemal, who would rise to distinction at Gallipoli five years later and go on to forge the Turkish Republic in the 1920s (gaining the honorific Atatürk, "father of the Turks"), was reassigned by Enver to his headquarters near Derna in March 1912 to help coordinate operations. Throughout the spring, both sides made counterattacks but shifted little in the basic balance of power:

the Ottoman and local Arab forces had the Italian troops trapped in seven coastal enclaves but were not strong enough to totally defeat them.[24]

Facing a stalemate on the ground in Northern Africa, Italy shifted the war to sea in early 1912, expanding operations against the Ottomans in the Red Sea and in the eastern Mediterranean. In January, two Italian destroyers and a cruiser engaged a flotilla of twelve Ottoman ships at the Kunfuda Bay on the Arabian Red Sea coast, sinking seven of the Ottoman vessels. The Italian navy blockaded Ottoman ports in the Hejaz and funneled resources to two anti-Ottoman separatist movements in the south of Arabia on the opposite coast from Italian Eritrea, the Idrissid Emirate of Asir and the Zaydi Imamate in the Yemeni highlands. In late February, two Italian cruisers attacked Ottoman ships off the coast of Beirut, destroying the entire Ottoman naval presence in the eastern Mediterranean.[25]

That summer Italy escalated the conflict, trying to end the war by moving through the Aegean Sea toward Istanbul. With the tacit approval of the British, the Italians occupied Rhodes (the Dodecanese Islands) and sent five torpedo boats north into the Dardanelles, the narrow straights controlling access through the Marmara Sea and Bosphorus Straits past Istanbul to the Black Sea. Italy's push against the Ottoman capital drew the Balkan Peninsula into the conflict and triggered the alarmed interest of the Austro-Hungarian and Russian Empires, particularly after Italy encouraged Montenegro to declare war on the Ottoman Empire on October 8, 1912. The Ottomans were now facing an escalating conflict near their core provinces, and within a week and a half, they signed a treaty with Italy ending the war in Northern Africa, agreeing to withdraw Ottoman military officers and troops from Tripolitania and Cyrenaica in exchange for Italian withdrawal from Rhodes. The defeat to the Italians and the loss of Tripoli (*Vilâyet-i Trâblus Gârp*) was lamented across the empire, even as far away as the Shiʻi suburbs of Baghdad, as related in the memoirs of Talib Mushtaq.[26] This outrage only increased when the conflict shifted to the Balkans.

BACK TO THE BALKANS

In the spring of 1912, sensing an opening provided by the turmoil of the Italo-Ottoman War, Serbia, Bulgaria, Greece, and Montenegro had formed the Balkan League with the goal of finally seizing Macedonia (comprised of the Ottoman provinces of Salonica, Manastir, and Kosovo). Open conflict did not break out, though, until Montenegro joined Italy in the war against the Ottoman Empire in October 1912. Serbia, Greece, and Bulgaria joined soon thereafter, bringing a combined force of 715,000 Balkan League troops against 320,000 Ottoman troops. Bulgaria attacked from the north, defeating the Ottomans in multiple engagements in Thrace and advancing through Ottoman defense lines at Kirkalareli and Lüleburgaz in late October and early November. On November 2, Bulgarian forces reached the Ottomans' last ring of defensive trenches at Çatalca, only twenty miles west of Istanbul. At the same time, Bulgarian units laid siege to Edirne (Adrianople), the principal city of Thrace and a significant base for Ottoman forces. In the Aegean Sea, the Greek navy occupied several islands and bottled up the Ottoman navy, freeing Greece to annex the island of Crete. Greek forces also pushed overland into Macedonia to occupy Salonica on November 8, 1912. Further west, the Greeks moved up into southern Albania, while Serb and Montenegrin forces occupied Albania from the north. All three countries successfully moved into Macedonia, joining forces to occupy Skopje by the end of October.

The Ottoman sultan and government, seeing their military collapse across the front in their European provinces, signed an armistice on December 3 and began peace negotiations in London with their Balkan opponents. Back in Istanbul, a group of CUP officers led by Enver, who himself had rushed back to Istanbul from Cyrenaica upon the outbreak of hostilities in the Balkans, carried out a coup d'état against the Liberal government on January 23, 1913, to shut down the peace negotiations. The Ottoman-Balkan armistice expired in early February, and the CUP-led Ottoman army resumed fighting. The war went very poorly, though, for them: the Bulgarians captured Edirne and the Greeks took Ioánnina that spring. The Ottoman government signed a peace treaty on May 30, ending the First Balkan War: Albanian independence was recognized, and the Ottomans lost Macedonia and most of Thrace, which were divided among the Balkan powers.

While hemorrhaging in the Balkans, the Ottoman Empire was also deeply threatened in eastern Anatolia in the summer of 1913. In June, the Russians, who had taken Kars, Ardahan, and Batumi at the conclusion of the 1877–1878 war, put forward a proposal to consolidate the Ottoman's six remaining eastern provinces (Van, Erzurum, Bitlis, Diyarbakir, Harput, and Sivas) into two semiautonomous units. Each would be administered by a foreign governor-general nominated by the Great Powers and have provincial councils with equal Muslim-Armenian representation. Coming just after the Balkan losses, the CUP leadership viewed the Russian proposal as an existential threat: in their view, it represented a de facto partitioning of Anatolia and signaled a broader Russian plan to create an independent Armenian polity and try to occupy Istanbul itself. To forestall another war, the government signed the proposal in February 1914, but the Russian threat to sever "Turkish Armenia" from the Ottoman core further reinforced deep insecurities about the empire's internal Eastern Question among the Ottoman military and civilian leadership, particularly among the top CUP figures. These strategic fears centered on eastern Anatolia would have tragic consequences over the next eighteen months and culminate in the genocide of Ottoman Armenians and Assyrians.

By the end of the summer of 1913, tensions arising among the victorious states over the division of Ottoman spoils after the First Balkan War led almost immediately to the outbreak of the Second Balkan War. Greece and Serbia formed an alliance within days after the end of the first war in June. At the end of that month, Bulgaria attacked Serbian forces along a front in Macedonia because Serbia had not handed over control of the city of Salonica. Throughout July and into August, the three Balkan states fought with each other over respective zones of control in Thrace and Macedonia. Seizing this opportunity, the Ottomans moved quickly to take back losses in Thrace, including the prize of the city of Edirne, which they reoccupied in July. Later that month, the conflict began to wind down as a series of treaties were signed among the various parties, though the final one between Serbia and the Ottoman Empire took until March 1914. For the Ottomans and the Balkan powers, there was a short period of calm in the spring of 1914, but the years of intense conflict had worsened significant rifts in the region, particularly hostility between Serbia and the Austro-Hungarian Empire and between Bulgaria, Serbia, and Greece. These fault lines would within months prove the epicenter for an earthquake after the assassination of the Austro-Hungarian imperial heir on June 28, 1914, in Sarajevo, the capital of the recently annexed former Ottoman province of Bosnia. By August 1914, all of Europe would be engulfed in the Great War.

In the multiplayer chess match that constituted the Great Game through the nineteenth century, the Ottoman, Alawite, and Qajar Empires had all been players and had supplied most of the game board. In 1911, a series of moves across the greater Ottoman region moved the game to its final stage, a two-decade Long Great War that would unmake and remake the political order from Morocco to Iran. In the west, the French and Spanish used political turmoil between the Moroccan sultan and tribes in April 1911 to justify an inland occupation and subdivide the Alawite sphere into respective protectorate zones. In the east, the British and Russians exploited the continuing upheaval of Iran's Constitutional Revolution to respectively intervene militarily against tribes in the south in October and begin occupying the northwest late that fall, with Russian troops capturing Tabriz in December. In the center, Italy's unilateral aggression in late September to seize Ottoman Tripolitania and Cyrenaica in Northern Africa cascaded into a conflict that drew in the Balkan states, the Russian Empire, and the Austro-Hungarian Empire. The successive Italo-Ottoman and Balkan Wars set up the powder keg that exploded into a full-blown European war in the summer of 1914 following the assassination of the Austrian Archduke Ferdinand and his wife, the Archduchess Sophie, by a Bosnian Serb nationalist protesting Austro-Hungary's 1908 annexation of Bosnia-Herzegovina. When they joined the European war in November 1914 on the side of Germany and Austro-Hungary, the Ottomans began playing the final, high-stakes round of the chess match, trying to save some part of the territorial board as the empire faced multiple fronts of attack.

2

THE MANY FRONTS OF THE OTTOMANS' GREAT WAR, 1914–1918

At three o'clock in the morning on Tuesday, August 4, 1914, the guard on duty at the port in Bône (now Annaba), a city on the northeast coast of Algeria, informed the harbor pilot that a warship with its lights darkened was coming in slowly from the east. At 4:08 a.m., the *Breslau*, a German battle cruiser, turned abeam the port's entrance and proceeded to open fire on the French ships anchored there then shell several prominent waterfront buildings including the rail station, the Palais Calvin, and the Palais Consulaire. An hour later, ninety miles down the Algerian coast to the west, another battle cruiser, this one falsely flying Russian colors, turned its starboard side toward the port area of Philippeville (now Skikda). A German flag was hoisted to replace the Russian, and the *Goeben* began shelling the city, hitting ships in the port, the train station, army barracks, and a gas plant.[1] The Balkans and Northern Africa had again become entangled in a widening conflict, this time one that was engulfing all of Europe.

Seven days earlier, on July 28, the Austro-Hungarian Empire had declared war on Serbia and invaded it, setting off a chain reaction that drew in the other European powers. Fearing Russia would mobilize to support Serbia against Austro-Hungary, Germany preemptively declared war on Russia on August 1. The next day the Germans swiftly moved west, invading Luxemburg and declaring war on France on August 3. The attack on French Algeria came within hours of this declaration, and the dozen

Algerian and French casualties in Bône and Phillippeville were among the first in a war that would claim 1.6 million French lives, largely in the trenches of the Western Front in the Belgian and French countryside.

Though those trenches dominate memories of the First World War, it is important to note that the conflict, from the very first shots fired, was global and that the greater Ottoman sphere from the southern Mediterranean to the Black Sea, Caucasus, and Persian Gulf were critical theaters. Germany started its war with France in Northern Africa, not on the Western Front, because German planners were well aware of the importance of France's manpower reserve in its African colonial possessions, which by 1918 would provide 450,000 troops (including Algerians, Tunisians, Moroccans, West Africans, Malagasies, and Somalis) to the war effort.[2] The German admiral Wilhelm Souchon preemptively ordered the *Breslau* and *Goeben* to the Algerian coast to disrupt the transport of French troops to Europe by bombing military infrastructure in the two ports.

Souchon's next orders would spread the unfolding conflict from Northern Africa through the Mediterranean to the Bosphorus Straits, eventually drawing the entire greater Ottoman region into the interempire war.[3] After attacking the Algerian ports and moving north close to Messina, Sicily, the two ships were originally to head west to join the German fleet in the Atlantic. Aware that superior Allied naval forces in the Mediterranean had been put on notice to intercept the German vessels, Souchon changed the order: the *Breslau* and *Goeben* instead sailed as fast as possible east from Italy to Istanbul. A dramatic cat-and-mouse chase ensued, with the two German boats narrowly evading British vessels and making it to the entrance to the Dardanelles narrows five days later. They were met by an Ottoman pilot boat that guided them through mine barriers to Istanbul.

The arrival of the German ships at the Ottoman capital on August 10, 1914, set off a major controversy. Unlike the other European imperial powers, which had declared war against each other in a domino progression over the previous two weeks, the Ottomans still remained officially neutral in mid-August. According to international naval law, they had to either confiscate the German cruisers or openly declare war, a conundrum that seemingly forced their hand to declare whether they were for or against Germany and the other Central Powers. The Ottoman's ingenious delaying tactic was to announce that they had bought the two vessels.

The *Breslau* and *Goeben* were rechristened the *Yavuz Sultan Selim* and the *Midilli*, and they and their German officers and crews were incorporated into the Ottoman navy. Just weeks before, the British had canceled an Ottoman order for two long-awaited dreadnoughts, requisitioning them for the Royal Navy. Gaining the state-of-the-art German warships was retribution: it also gave the Ottomans naval superiority over the Russians in the Black Sea and strengthened their hand against the Greeks in the Aegean Sea.

In August 1914, the Ottoman leadership was understandably reluctant to engage in the escalating European conflict, having only just gotten a short break from an exhausting three-year war footing against Italy and the Balkan states. Though buying the German ships gave lie to the alliance they preferred, the Ottoman Empire resisted German pressure to officially declare war. Stalling for time, they hoped to remain out of the conflict long enough for it to run its course, an understandable expectation given the widespread belief among the belligerents that it would be "over by Christmas." Throughout the summer and even well into September, the Ottoman government also remained divided between pro-British and pro-German factions. Though they had signed a secret pact with the Germans against Russia on July 28, on the eve of the war, they were not fully committed to the Central Powers. In early August, Enver Pasha, himself part of the pro-German block among the CUP leadership, put out diplomatic feelers to the Russians about a nonaggression pact, and the option of joining the Allies remained viable well into September. By the end of the month, though, the British recalled their naval mission, which had advised the Ottoman navy since 1908.[4] The German admiral, Souchon, just weeks after directing the *Breslau* and *Goeben* from the Algerian coast to Istanbul, took command of the Ottoman fleet.

He soon ended the Ottoman Empire's equivocation. In late October, having been given permission by Enver Pasha to sail an Ottoman flotilla including the two German-cum-Ottoman cruisers into the Black Sea, the German admiral ordered an attack on Russian ports including Odessa, Sevastopol, Feodosia, Yalta, and Novorossiysk on October 29. Despite frantic diplomatic attempts by the Ottoman government to send an apology and forestall full entry into the war, the Russian Empire declared war on November 2, immediately attacking the easternmost Ottoman provinces in Anatolia. On November 3, under orders from Winston Churchill,

First Lord of the Admiralty, the British navy started shelling Ottoman positions on the Aegean coast and the Dardanelles. On November 5, the British and French both officially declared war on the Ottoman Empire. On November 6, the British Indian Expeditionary Force landed at the head of the Persian Gulf to secure the Abadan oil complex and began advancing on Basra. The Ottoman Empire reciprocated almost a week later, officially declaring war on the Entente Powers on November 11, 1914.

Since the 1870s, the fate of the Ottoman Empire had been in the balance: the Eastern Question created a tenuous equilibrium in which the threat of a European land war partially restrained unilateral moves to seize territory in the greater Ottoman sphere. In 1911, French, Spanish, and Italian advances into Morocco and Tripolitania threatened that equilibrium. The escalation of the Balkan conflict into a Europe-wide continental war in the summer of 1914 completely upended it. With all of Europe now at war, including the Ottomans after November 1914, the empire's territories were viewed among the war's choicest spoils, particularly by the Allied British, French, and Russian Empires.

Because of its central geographic position, the Ottoman Empire had to fight a multifronted, defensive interempire war over the next four years. From the beginning, the action on and fate of these fighting fronts—eastern Anatolia and the Caucasus, Mesopotamia, Northern Africa, southern Syria, and the Dardanelles approaching Istanbul—would be interlinked. As many scholars of the Great War have emphasized, "total war" entangled fighting and home fronts. Communities across the Ottoman Empire were more and less exposed to direct fighting, but massive mobilization, victories and losses, and horrific civilian and military casualties exacted deep economic, cultural, gendered, public health, and political effects across every region.[5] In comparison to the European theater, the relationship between fighting and home fronts in the Ottoman Empire was unique. Most of the European powers—Britain, Germany, France, Russia—fought the war on one or, at the most, two fronts, typically with a spatial distance delineating "home" from war front. The Ottoman Empire fought the Great War in at least five directions, and these disparate fighting fronts had varying impacts on the internal "home" areas with which they were intimately linked.

This chapter focuses specifically on how this interplay among multiple fronts over the course of the 1914–1918 interempire phase of the Long

Great War reshaped different regions of the Ottoman Empire.[6] I first look at the factors influencing the Ottomans' entry into the European conflict on the side of Germany and the Central Powers, the sultan's official declaration of jihad, and the empire-wide mobilization for war during the fall of 1914. The subsequent sections address the course of the Ottoman's Great War on the Caucasus, Mesopotamia, Northern Africa, and Southern (Syria/Arabia) fronts. With each, I examine the links between the various fighting fronts and how the war's progress drove internal transformations on the home front that included total mobilization, partisan and paramilitary activity, forced population transfers, famine, and genocide. The course of the Great War disrupted the status quo in specific ways across these various fronts, setting up divergent conditions for how local populations and the European powers would begin to reimagine various parts of the post-Ottoman order.

THE OTTOMAN MOBILIZATION OF THE HOME FRONT AND ENTRY INTO THE WAR

For months after the 1914 July Crisis, the Ottoman leadership wavered over whether and, on whose side, to enter the war. Since the 1890s, Germany had viewed the Ottoman Empire as an important ally through which to drive a wedge between the rival British and Russian imperial spheres and project its own interests from the eastern Mediterranean through the Middle East to the Indian Ocean. Following his celebrated tour of the empire in 1898, Kaiser Wilhelm II approved a joint German-Ottoman project to construct a rail line linking Berlin, Istanbul, Baghdad, and Basra. The Baghdad railway would open up an overland route bypassing British naval dominance in the Mediterranean and the British-controlled Suez Canal, allowing an alternate Europe-to-India connection through the Persian Gulf. Construction proceeded over the next two decades and, on the eve of World War I, only two sections remained unfinished.[7] In addition to infrastructural investment, German-Ottoman relations had also been cultivated through the second half of the nineteenth century through military liaisons, the most recent of which was the assignation of General Otto Liman von Sanders as a senior adviser to the Ottoman military in 1913, along with a German military mission that included thirty officers and forty soldiers.

Despite these dense ties, it was still not a foregone conclusion in August 1914 that the Ottomans would side with the Central Powers or enter the war at all. The previous century's experience of losing more and more territory to Russian, British, French, Italian, and Balkan states' expansionary desires made it clear to Ottoman strategists that the costs of losing were incredibly high. They rightly worried the unfolding conflict in Europe posed an existential threat to the empire. At this juncture, the upper echelons of the Ottoman hierarchy, including the CUP triumvirate that had taken control of the government in 1913—Talaat Pasha (interior minister), Enver Pasha (war minister), and Cemal Pasha (naval minister and mayor of Istanbul)—had to weigh the cost-benefit merits of neutrality versus joining either the Entente (Britain, Russia, and France), each of whom had occupied various Ottoman territories over the past four decades, or acting on their secret alliance with Germany.

When the rest of Europe went to war in early August 1914, the Ottomans declared their official neutrality, but they also announced an empire-wide general mobilization that began to dramatically transform the "home front" across the empire. On August 2, the war ministry gave instructions to hang posters in public places and sent out town criers accompanied by drums and trumpets to announce *seferberlik*, the term used for general mobilization and one that came to be associated, particularly in Greater Syria, with the broader trauma of World War I, including enlistment, bounty hunters pursuing young men, forced resettlement, and starvation.[8] All men between twenty-one and forty-five years of ages, both Muslim and non-Muslim, were given five days to report to a recruiting office. From early August to November, the Ottomans increased their number of standing troops from two hundred thousand to nearly half a million, though this total was dwarfed by numbers from some of the other countries.[9] General mobilization also involved building up the Ottoman Empire's war-making capacity, including large amounts of war materiel—artillery, guns, ammunition—shipped by rail from Germany.

By late September, the Germans began placing more intense pressure on the Ottomans to officially enter the war. Germany's rapid gains in the first weeks of the war on the Western Front came to a halt at the First Battle of the Marne (September 6–12), and in the east, their dramatic early success against the Russians at the Battle of Tannenberg (August 26–30) slowed to a stalemate later in September. For the German Empire, getting the Ottomans to attack anywhere—against Russia in the Caucasus or the Crimea or against the British in Egypt—would help shift the balance of power on these European fronts. Ottoman entry into the war would also help get Bulgaria to engage against Serbia and take pressure off the Austro-Hungarian Empire. Perhaps most importantly, the Germans believed a declaration of jihad by the Ottoman sultan would have a significant symbolic impact, rallying the large Muslim populations under Allied control—in the Russian, French, and British Empires in Asia and Africa—to revolt.

In early October, Ottoman delaying tactics finally triggered a German ultimatum. In response to Enver Pasha's request for a loan for five million Turkish pounds, Germany stipulated it would be extended only if the Ottoman Empire intervened in the war. On October 11, at a meeting at the German embassy, Talaat, Enver, and Cemal agreed to authorize Admiral Souchon to enter the Black Sea and attack Russia, once the Germans deposited a first installment of two million pounds. The Germans would release the remainder of the loan once the Ottomans fully engaged in the war.[10] On October 25, Enver instructed Souchon to sail into the Black Sea and, though much of the Ottoman leadership, including Enver himself, still preferred neutrality up to the last minute, the German admiral's intention was clearly to provoke war.[11] On October 29, Souchon's fleet, including the rechristened *Goeben* and *Breslau*, opened fire on multiple Russian ports on the north Black Sea coast, definitively bringing the Ottomans into the war.

In early November, the Ottomans issued official fatwas, drawn up by a council of religious authorities and blessed by the sultan, calling for jihad against the Allied Powers. The German Kaiser had long been fascinated with the potential for using jihad strategically, an idea championed by Max von Oppenheim, a German diplomat, archaeologist, and intelligence officer who had spent the decades before the war in the Middle East and would serve as a chief propaganda adviser to the Ottoman Empire. Von Oppenheim's scheme was to rally Muslim populations in British Egypt and India, French North Africa, the Russian Caucasus and Central Asia, in addition to the Muslim Arab, Kurdish, and Turkish populations of the Ottoman Empire, against the Allied powers.[12] Beyond the Ottoman

Empire, German agents were sent out during the course of the war to Iran, Afghanistan, and Northern Africa to try to fan the flames of jihad against the Allies, though these attempts were almost a complete failure.[13] While much has been written about this so-called "Holy War Made in Germany," Aksakal has shown that the call for jihad in November 1914, rather than being solely concocted in Germany, was consistent with long-running Ottoman strategies to mobilize troops and increase public sentiment.[14]

The Ottoman Empire's full mobilization, declaration of jihad, and eventual entry into the war significantly expanded the interempire conflict's geographic scope to include multiple theaters beyond Europe's Western or Eastern Fronts. Though marginalized in much of the European historiography focused on the Western Front, the greater Middle Eastern region was one of the most strategic theaters of the war because it

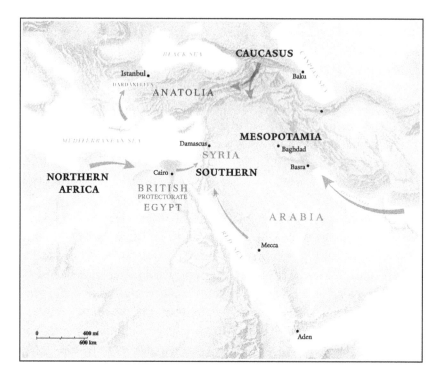

FIGURE 2.1 Fighting fronts in the greater Ottoman region (1914–1918).

Source: Author adaptation from public domain.

was situated at the intersection of multiple imperial spheres of power and strategic interest. These included the British Empire's latitudinal lifeline to and from India, Australia, and New Zealand and its oil reserve at the head of the Persian Gulf. They also included Russia's desperate need for access through the Bosphorus and its desire to open up an outlet through the Caucasus and Persia to the Indian Ocean. These geopolitical priorities would determine the major fighting fronts of the Ottomans' Great War.

THE CAUCASUS FRONT: ANSWERING THE OTTOMAN EMPIRE'S OWN EASTERN QUESTION

The Ottoman Empire's Great War started on its long-contested eastern frontier with the Russian Empire. Just two days after the Ottoman-German attacks on Russian Black Sea ports at the end of October 1914, the Russian general Georgy Bergmann ordered an offensive from Kars into eastern Anatolia on November 2, crossing the border in the direction of Erzurum, the Ottoman's major regional stronghold seventy-five miles to the west. The southern Caucasus and eastern Anatolia region over which Ottoman and Russian troops would battle the next four years consists of high plateaus and more than sixty peaks reaching close to 10,000 feet (the highest, Mount Ararat, reaches 16,854 feet). This area also serves as the headwaters for several of the region's largest rivers, the Euphrates, Çoruh, and Aras, which respectively flow to the Persian Gulf, Black Sea, and Caspian Seas. Warfare across this terrain would extend from the Black Sea southeast to the Lake Van region. Russian forces would advance westward across almost half of Anatolia in 1916 then withdraw following the October Revolution in 1917, allowing the Ottomans to sweep eastward all the way to the Caspian Sea in 1918 by the time of the October armistice. Fighting across this volatile front would fundamentally upend the social and political order in eastern Anatolia, the Caucasus, and Northwest Iran, and it would exact tragic human costs.

For the Ottoman Empire, the onset of yet another war with Russia on the Caucasus Front activated an internal Eastern Question: namely, their long-standing structural insecurity about the eastern borderlands and the loyalties of the Armenian, Assyrian, and Kurdish groups that comprised the majority population. The "shatter zone" encompassing eastern Anatolia, the Caucasus, and the northwestern Iranian Plateau for centuries constituted the critical buffer space between the Ottoman Empire and the Persia-based Safavids.[15] At the 1514 Battle of Chaldiran (in present-day northwest Iran close to the Turkish border), the Ottomans, wielding superior artillery and muskets, routed the Safavid armies, checking their westward expansion and establishing a frontier zone roughly defining their separate spheres, though both sides periodically pressed for gains across that boundary.[16] During the decades following the victory, the Ottomans consolidated control over eastern Anatolia and northern Mesopotamia. Like the Safavids on their side of the border, they cultivated opposing local Kurdish statelets over the next centuries to secure their interests rather than imposing direct rule.[17] In the late eighteenth century, the Russian Empire began to also intervene in this shatter zone, pushing over the Greater Caucasus range to annex Georgia in 1801 then expanding its reach over the next decades into Azerbaijan and Armenia. In the 1877–1878 Russo-Ottoman War, the Russians seized the Ottoman Empire's easternmost provinces of Batum, Kars, and Ardahan.

It was from Kars that Bergmann, commander of the Russian forces on the Ottoman front, ordered an offensive the first week of November 1914 into the Eleşkirt valley. Believing the Ottoman army not ready to mount an offensive before winter, his initial goal was to contain the Hamidiye units, irregular light cavalry formed two decades earlier by the Sultan Abdülhamid II as auxiliary forces. Modeled on the Russian Cossacks, these mostly Kurdish forces were intended to shore up the empire's vulnerable eastern Russian border in the aftermath of the 1878 war, though they also served an internal function to brutally police internal minorities including the Armenians.[18] The Russian units moved swiftly, reaching the town of Köprüköy, twenty-five miles east of Erzurum, by November 4. By mid-month, though, the Ottomans had stalled the Russian advance and by the beginning of December they had pushed them back toward Kars.

Heading into the brutal cold and snow of winter, the Ottoman Third Army commanders planned to dig in to hold their defensive positions then go on the offensive when spring came. The Ottoman war minister, Enver Pasha, however, wanted to push forward immediately. Enver was under pressure from the Germans to move against the Russians in the Caucasus to divert troops from the Eastern Front in Europe. He also sought the glory of a dramatic victory like the Germans had achieved against the Russians at Tannenberg at the end of August. Enver believed the Third Army could similarly encircle and destroy the Russians at Sarıkamış, a village in a strategic pass that controlled movement from the plain surrounding Kars through the mountains westward on the main road to Erzurum.

Overriding his own generals' warning that it was foolish to mount this kind of offensive in mountainous terrain in winter, Enver ordered the attack, arriving personally at Erzurum on December 21 to direct what would prove one of the most catastrophic Ottoman defeats of the war. At the start, Enver had three Ottoman units numbering around 120,000 troops to stage in battle against 65,000 Russian forces. His three-prong strategy was to send the Tenth Corps in the north through the town of Oltu over the Allahüekber Mountains to cut the road and railroad connection from Kars to Sarıkamış. The Eleventh Corps would attack to hold the Russian main group in place, while the Ninth Corps would move to take Sarıkamış. The three units would then converge to destroy the Russian forces in the Aras Valley to the east. Over the three weeks of the battle that followed, from December 22, 1914, to January 17, 1915, this plan would fall apart and more than four-fifths of the Ottoman troops sent to fight would perish.[19]

The most horrifying Ottoman losses did not come from Russian fire but from marching tens of thousands of ill-equipped, undersupplied troops, many of whom did not even have boots, through snow and devastating cold. On December 25 and 26, the Tenth Corps sustained a 90 percent casualty rate—most because of freezing to death on the high mountain passes. Despite these setbacks, Enver pushed the offensive on. Thinking the Russians were retreating, he sent the Ninth Corps in to take Sarıkamış. In fact, the Russian units had circled around to envelop the three Turkish battalions. In mid-January, the Ottoman troops were forced to withdraw all the way back past their lines on the road to Erzurum. Enver himself rushed back to Istanbul to suppress news of the catastrophe.

The devastating Sarıkamış defeat had dire ramifications on the military front and, even more consequentially, on the home front. Enver's Caucasus offensive had been a total disaster for the Ottoman army, with official Turkish reports putting the number of causalities at sixty thousand, with an additional ten to twenty thousand troops being lost behind

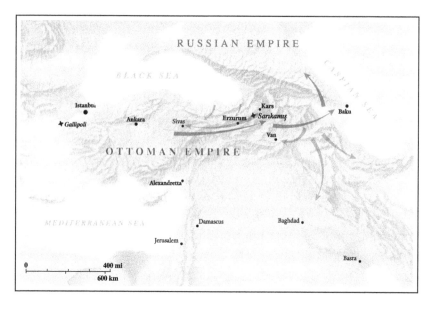

FIGURE 2.2 The Caucasus front.
Source: Author adaptation from public domain.

the battle lines. During and after the campaign, he and other commanders, in addition to lower-ranking officers, tried to shift blame to Armenians, Greek, and Georgian groups that had joined the Russian Caucasus Army, a unit formed the previous summer in advance of the war. The defeat at Sarıkamış made the perceived threat that Armenian coethnics on the Ottoman side of the border would serve as a fifth column for Russian aggression more acute. Long-standing fears about the empire's suspected internal ethnic and religious enemies and their separatist political aspirations, exacerbated throughout the nineteenth century by external European imperial intervention in the Balkans and eastern Anatolia, were amplified in February, when the Allies launched the Gallipoli campaign to take Istanbul. For the Ottoman high command, existential threats at these two fighting fronts were linked to deep insecurities within the home front. That spring, the interior minister, Talaat Pasha, and two advisers, Dr. Mehmed Nazim and Dr. Bahaeddin Şakir, started deliberating on a set of directives laying the groundwork for the

Armenian genocide and massive attacks against the Assyrian community in southeast Anatolia.

In the immediate aftermath of Sarıkamış, the Russian and Ottoman armies on the Eastern Front withdrew to recover. That winter, a typhus epidemic and other diseases decimated the weakened troops and local populations in the eastern provinces. With the arrival of summer, the Russians made another effort to take Erzurum, this time from the northeast, but they were repulsed by the Ottoman forces. In the southeast, however, the Russians were much more successful, pushing far into the Lake Van region. This offensive catalyzed a series of Armenian revolts in 1915, including in the town of Van.

Elsewhere in the empire, Talaat ordered the relocation of Armenians in Cilicia away from the Mediterranean port, Alexandretta, in February 1915, because of fears they would aid and abet an Allied landing there. On April 24, he ordered the arrest of most of the Armenian intellectual and political leadership in Istanbul. Then, in May and June, reacting swiftly to the Russian invasion in the Van region, he issued orders to provincial and district governors to announce the immediate deportation of the entire Armenian population in the six eastern Anatolian provinces away from the front. At the time, secret orders were also communicated orally commanding the extermination of the Armenian deportees.

The goal was to solve the Ottoman Empire's Eastern Question by eliminating Armenians and Assyrians from eastern Anatolia, or at least by reducing their number in any given location to no more than 5 to 10 percent of the population. The mode for these mass murders was to mobilize, with the assistance of Enver's secret intelligence service (consolidated in Libya during the Italo-Ottoman War), armed local gangs consisting of released violent prisoners, Kurdish armed bands, recently arrived Muslim refugees from the Balkans and Caucasus, and ordinary Turkish villagers to pillage and kill the unarmed and ill-supplied Armenian groups being forced to march southward toward the Syrian desert.[20] The Ottoman military had successfully repelled the Russian incursion by the fall of 1915, leaving the southeast front quiet for the rest of the year. But, the Ottoman-CUP genocide of the Armenian population in the empire continued, killing between 800,000 and 1.5 million people between 1915 and 1917. An additional 250,000 Assyrians and Chaldeans were also killed between 1915 and 1918.[21] The genocidal ethnic cleansing of virtually the entire non-Muslim population on this front of the war devastatingly reshaped eastern Anatolia's demography, with long-term effects on the fate of this region.

Militarily, the CUP's drastic "solution" to the empire's Eastern Question did very little to secure the Eastern Front. In early 1916, the Russians launched a surprise offensive toward Erzurum, catching the wintering Ottoman Third Army off guard. The devastating fall of Erzurum in February 1916 and other losses in the east quickly deflated the euphoria of the Ottoman's January victory in the west over British and French allied forces at Gallipoli. The Russian army continued to press westward, reaching Sivas by the summer, halfway across the Anatolian plateau toward Ankara. The only part of the front the Ottomans held was in the southeast, where Mustafa Kemal had been reassigned after Gallipoli to command a division. The arrival of severe winter shut down most military operations and finally gave the Ottomans a reprieve.

In 1917, the dynamics on the Eastern Front completely changed with the onset of the Russian Revolution. With the overthrow of the Tsar in March and the October Revolution that fall, Russian troops rapidly withdrew from Anatolia. On December 16, the Bolsheviks and Ottomans signed an armistice at Erzincan. The next spring, a reinforced Third Ottoman Army quickly moved on the offensive to roll back their losses and reclaim the three provinces lost in the 1877–1878 war. By March 1918, they had pushed east into Kars, ousting the Armenian forces left in place after the Russian army withdrew. On March 3, 1918, the new Russian communist government signed the Treaty of Brest-Litovsk, officially ending hostilities with the Central powers. According to its terms, the Ottoman Empire was given back Kars, Ardahan, and Batumi provinces. The Ottomans also entered negotiations with the Transcaucasian Federation (Armenia, Georgia, and Azerbaijan) formed that year. In the midst of these negotiations, Enver continued to push the Third Army through the Caucasus to achieve further expansionary goals in Central Asia. The Ottomans helped create the Army of Islam by drawing on Muslim recruits in the Caucasus, with the goal of continuing to fight toward the Caspian Sea before pushing southward through Persia to put pressure on the British in Mesopotamia. By July 31, 1918, Enver's forces had taken the city of Baku, on the Caspian coast, and by the early fall, the Ottomans were in control of virtually all of Transcaucasia and parts of northwestern Iran and were moving into the northern Caucasus at the time of the Armistice of Mudros in October.

During the course of the 1914–1918 conflict on the Caucasus front, the Ottoman Empire went from its most devastating loss at Sarıkamış to its most dramatic successes with the expansion into Transcaucasia, the latter in large part because of the exogenous windfall of the Russian Revolution. Setbacks and advances on the eastern fighting front had drastically transformed eastern Anatolia: the Armenian population had been physically eliminated, the Assyrian population nearly so, and relations among Turks and Kurds and other groups had been reshaped in ways that would become increasingly important in the 1920s. Though advancing across the Caucasus Mountains in the fall of 1918, the Ottoman Empire was, at the same time, reeling in the south as British forces advanced on the Mesopotamian and Syrian fronts.

THE MESOPOTAMIAN FRONT: FROM BASRA TO MOSUL

Mesopotamia, the "land between two rivers" stretching from the Taurus Mountains to the Persian Gulf, constituted a second major Ottoman front in the Great War. The four-year struggle between the Ottomans and British up the riverine courses of the Tigris and Euphrates from Basra to Baghdad to Mosul radically transformed the Ottoman, British, and local perspectives on and future plans for the three provinces. The early Ottoman collapse in Basra in the first month of the conflict shifted the stakes all around: the Ottomans let go of aspirations to retain a Persian Gulf foothold and regrouped for a tenacious defense of Baghdad province while the British, having easily gained their initial limited objective, aggressively expanded their mission to include the conquest of Baghdad and beyond. The various communities caught up in the conflict had to navigate life on the battlefront, under British or Ottoman wartime rule, or, in several cases in the Middle Euphrates region, declared their own local independent rule.

In late September 1914, more than a month before the official Anglo-Ottoman declarations of war, the British Empire's London and India

Offices began planning an invasion to secure the Basra and Khuzestan regions at the head of the Persian Gulf. After oil was discovered in southwest Iran in 1908, the Anglo-Persian Oil Company had opened a refinery at Abadan, on the left bank of the Shatt al-Arab (the outlet of the combined Tigris and Euphrates Rivers into the Persian Gulf), in 1913. With the decision to transition the Royal Navy from coal to oil, Abadan and other potential oil supplies in the Basra region were a preeminent priority for the British from the very beginning of the war. The British Empire's interest in the Persian Gulf, however, long predated the discovery of oil.

British involvement in the region stretched centuries back to the East India Company navy's first incursion to oust the Portuguese from this strategic area in 1622. In the nineteenth century, the British Empire entered into a series of treaty relationships with local rulers on the southern shores of the Persian Gulf to protect shipping interests and project and maintain the British Raj's influence as a regional hegemon in the Indian Ocean sphere. This included a protectorate agreement with the Sabbagh family, south of Basra in Kuwait, which guaranteed Kuwait's autonomy from Ottoman oversight and taxation and helped the British block Germany from putting the terminus of the Berlin-Baghdad railway on the shores of the Persian Gulf. In southwest Iran, the British had been similarly active since the 1890s in negotiating alliances with the powerful Bakhtiyari tribal confederation that enabled the construction of a road through the Zagros Mountains to Isfahan and the development of the oil fields in Khuzestan province.[22] For their part, the Ottomans launched several reform attempts in the 1870s under Midhat Pasha to develop the economic potential of the three provinces in Iraq, which became even more important following the devastating territorial losses in the Balkans and Anatolia during the 1877–1878 Russo-Turkish War, and to buttress their influence along the southern littoral of the Persian Gulf and the Arabian interior to counter British power.[23] The signed, but not ratified, 1913 Anglo-Ottoman Convention papered over, but did not resolve, tensions related to the two empires' competing claims to Kuwait, Qatar, and Bahrain.

With this background, the British, anticipating the Ottoman Empire's entry into the war in the fall of 1914, were keen on securing Basra to protect their oil supply and their larger sphere of influence in the Persian Gulf, southern Persia, and the Indian Ocean. Toward this end, the Sixth Division of the India Expeditionary Force (IEF), under secret orders, preemptively set out from Bombay on October 16, 1914, and docked in Bahrain less than a week later.[24] On November 6, the day after the British Empire declared war on the Ottomans, these Indian Army troops immediately attacked Ottoman units at the mouth of the Shatt al-Arab, landing on the al-Faw peninsula.[25] They then quickly occupied the Abadan complex and moved upriver toward the city of Basra. On November 11, the British engaged Ottoman forces in and around Basra then occupied the city on November 21 after the Ottomans withdrew. By the end of November, the IEF had progressed forty miles further upstream from Basra to Qurna, the juncture where the Tigris and Euphrates Rivers come together.

The Ottoman military command had been caught completely off guard with the Indian Army's campaign in Mesopotamia in November 1914. During the general mobilization that summer and fall, Ottoman troops from Iraq had been redeployed to two higher-priority fronts: the Caucasus, to make the ill-fated push against the Russians at Sarikamiš, and Palestine, to prepare for an offensive across the Sinai against the British-controlled Suez Canal. Not expecting an attack in Basra province, very few Ottoman troops were garrisoned there or elsewhere in Iraq. For their part, the British had not expected to make such rapid progress and faced a strategic quandary in early 1915. The Indian Army had quickly secured the initial objectives of safeguarding access to the oil fields, protecting the Abadan refinery, and blocking Ottoman-German access to the Persian Gulf. They now had to decide whether to proceed further up into the "land between the rivers."

In early 1915, a fateful decision was made in London that would have far-reaching implications affecting the subsequent history of Iraq: rather than sticking with the limited objective of securing a Persian Gulf bulkhead, the British decided to press further into Mesopotamia toward Baghdad, 550 miles up the Tigris from Basra. The major difficulty for forward operations for this and later offensives was supply lines. Basra had primitive port facilities, and a sizable fleet of river steamers able to navigate the Tigris and Euphrates was needed to supply troops sent north. Once a reinforcement of eighteen thousand British Indian troops from the Twelfth Indian Division, rechristened the Tigris Corps, arrived, the expeditionary army moved upstream later in the spring. Under the command of Sir John Nixon, formerly in charge of the Northern Army in India, the British expeditionary forces took key points over the summer including

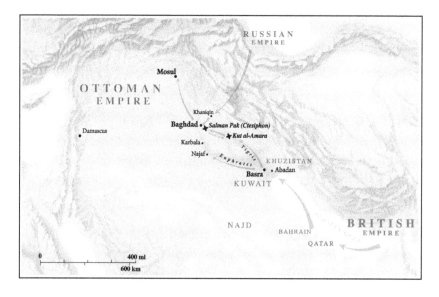

FIGURE 2.3 The Mesopotamia front.
Source: Author adaptation from public domain.

Nasiriyya on the Euphrates and Amara and Kut on the Tigris. That fall, the leading edge of the British forces was two hundred miles south of Baghdad.[26]

Having strategically withdrawn from Basra province, the Ottomans fought a rearguard action up the Tigris and Euphrates. In the Middle Euphrates, however, Ottoman attempts to clamp down on deserters provoked a rebellion in Najaf, Karbala, and several other towns, which declared their independence. On the Tigris, the Ottomans reorganized their forces, sending divisions from the Caucasus in October for reinforcement and creating the Sixth Army to anchor the defense of Baghdad. Under the command of Nurettin Bey, the Sixth Army spent several months preparing positions twenty miles to the southeast of Baghdad, laying out a network on both sides of a bend in the Tigris River of trenches and earthworks for artillery and machine guns at the ancient ruins of Ctesiphon, the seventh-century Sasanian capital, near the town of Salman Pak.

In early November 1915, Nixon ordered General Charles Townshend, the new commander of the British Sixth Division, to march on toward

Baghdad, overriding Townshend's concerns about overextending British supply lines to frontally assault the well-prepared Ottoman defensive fortifications at Salman Pak. On November 25, Townshend sent his fourteen thousand Anglo-Indian troops up against the twenty thousand Ottoman defenders. Both sides made some tactical gains but both also suffered heavy losses. By the first week of December, having no reserve troops, Townshend ordered a strategic withdrawal of the British Indian Army to Kut al-Amara, a town more than 125 miles back down the Tigris. The Ottoman Sixth Army had finally turned back the British surge in Mesopotamia, and the Tigris Group, under the command of Halil Bey, pursued Townsend's retreating forces, encircling Kut and digging in earthworks to lay siege.[27]

Between January and April 1916, the British command in Basra made four unsuccessful attempts to break the siege at Kut al-Amara. With his troops and the city's civilians on the brink of starvation, Townshend surrendered to Halil Bey on April 29, 1916. The defeat was considered the "greatest humiliation of the First World War" for the British Empire, with 272 British officers, 204 Indian officers, 2,952 British soldiers, 6,988 Indian soldiers, and 3,248 noncombatant support troops being taken captive, many of whom were extremely malnourished.[28] For the Ottomans, the victory on the Mesopotamia front restored confidence following the string of losses to the Russians that spring in eastern Anatolia. That summer, Halil Bey, now in charge of the Sixth Army, responded forcefully to a Russian assault through Persia toward Baghdad, defeating them at Khaniqin in June and pressing through to Kermanshah and Hamdan in July and August.[29] For the British, the Kut disaster came close on the heels of their defeat and withdrawal from Gallipoli in January 1916, following an eight-month failed attempt to move up the peninsula to Istanbul. That summer, the British greatly feared their string of defeats contrasted with the Ottomans' successive string of victories might generate increased momentum for the sultan's call for jihad within their own and in French Muslim-majority colonial possessions. They were desperate to score a victory in the Middle Eastern theater of the Great War.

The British command thus still viewed the taking of Baghdad as a critically symbolic if not strategic priority. No campaign could be attempted through the summer, though: the temperatures were too high and it was still too logistically difficult to sustain the long supply lines. In the early fall, a new British commander, Major General Stanley Maude, reorganized and retrained the British Expeditionary Force, integrating reinforcements from India. The British Indian Army also worked on the road and rail infrastructure in Basra province and purchased a large fleet of watercraft to increase their capacity to resupply forward forces upstream. In early December 1916, Maude launched a new offensive. Again, British and Ottoman troops met at Kut, but this time the British switched to the other side of the river and bypassed the Ottoman lines. By March 1917, the British Indian Army had reached Baghdad, entering the city on March 11 and taking fifteen thousand Ottoman soldiers prisoner. The British forces took Samarra, up the Tigris, and pushed to Ramadi, up the Euphrates, in April. In May, Halil Pasha was forced to tactically withdraw his thirty thousand remaining troops north to Mosul. That summer, Maude halted the British advance because of the heat and the logistical challenges of stretching his resupply lines further from Basra.

The British plan in 1918 was to press their advance into upper Mesopotamia, but this offensive was put on hold because troops were needed for the Palestine campaign and to defend British positions in Persia. Throughout 1918, British war planners were preoccupied with other fighting fronts in Europe and the Middle East and had little interest in moving beyond Baghdad. That fall, however, the start of armistice negotiations with the Ottomans in early October catalyzed a final British push on the Mesopotamia front. The goal was to grab as much territory in Mosul province as possible. In two days, the British moved seventy-five miles north, reaching the Little Zab River north of Kirkuk. Even after the armistice was signed, the British pushed north for fifteen more days, occupying the city of Mosul before they stopped in mid-November.

Over four years of fighting on the Mesopotamia front, a total 890,000 troops had been involved on both sides and close to 100,000 had lost their lives. The shared experience on this front of mobilization, fighting, famine, disease, and the end result of British occupation—from 1914 in Basra and later for the other provinces—had transformed the urban and rural communities in this region of the Ottoman Empire. It had also transformed the conditions in which they and the British would imagine post-Ottoman Iraq in the early 1920s.

THE NORTHERN AFRICAN FRONT: THE OTHER ARAB REVOLT

The southern shores of the Mediterranean and the coastlines of the Red Sea represented lower-profile strategic fronts where the Central and Allied Powers vied with one another to mobilize local forces against their enemies. The most well-known of these movements was the Arab Revolt. This internal anti-Ottoman uprising, covered in the next section, was mobilized in the Hejaz and led up the Red Sea coast toward Syria by Faisal, son of Sharif Husayn of Mecca, with British support. Though unique in its relative success, relevance to the postwar negotiation of the status of Greater Syria, and the exceptional coverage it received through the writings of T. E. Lawrence, the British-instigated Arab revolt was not an isolated case. The Central Powers also tried to foment anti-Allied local revolts throughout the war, sending out agents to Persia, Afghanistan, and Northern Africa to try to rally the jihad declared by the Ottoman sultan.

The earliest rounds of the Great War conflict had been waged in Northern Africa in the 1911–1912 Franco-Spanish and Italian military invasions of Morocco, Tripolitania, and Cyrenaica. Though "pacification" operations were largely put on hold in these areas, German agents actively tried to instigate anti-French resistance, particularly in Morocco where they enjoyed relative freedom of operation in Spain's barely conquered northern zone. German intelligence officers freely distributed gold and arms throughout the war to incite tribal leaders in the Rif and Jibala regions of northern Morocco to attack the French zone, though these efforts bore little to no fruit.[30] They were much more successful in Cyrenaica. This other Arab revolt—instigated through existing Ottoman liaisons reinforced in the Italo-Ottoman War and materially supported by the Ottomans and Germans—was carried out by the Sanusi forces of Sayyid Ahmed al-Sharif, who launched an attack from eastern Libya in the fall of 1915 toward Egypt.

From the very beginning of the Great War, Egypt represented the strategic node and ultimate prize of this southern theater. Starting in the fall of 1914, Germany pressured the Ottomans to attack the Suez Canal zone, the primary artery of the British Empire for troop movement, to relieve pressure on the Western Front. Since occupying Egypt in the early 1880s, the

British had exercised increasingly direct control, declaring Egypt a protectorate in 1914 and exacting exhausting requisitions of agricultural production, animals, and human labor for the war effort.[31] Ottoman forces under Cemal Pasha's command crossed the Sinai in January 1915, expecting their advance to catalyze a popular Egyptian revolt, but the mass uprising failed to materialize. The Ottoman's Suez assault was decisively turned back, and Cemal Pasha withdrew the troops back across the Sinai Peninsula to Palestine to consolidate defenses on the Ottomans' southern flank.

It was at this point that the Ottomans and Germans switched to a western strategy: the goal was to incite tribal groups in Cyrenaica to attack through Egypt's Western Desert. The critical parallel figure to Sharif Husayn (Britain's Hejaz ally) for the Ottomans and Germans in Cyrenaica was Sayyid Ahmed al-Sharif al-Sanusi (1876–1923). Sayyid Ahmad's grandfather, Muhammad ibn Ali al-Sanusi, founded the Sanusiyya, a Sufi order, in Cyrenaica in the 1830s. By the early 1900s, the Sanusi network of lodges had spread to Tripolitania, to Egypt's western oases, across the Saharan trade routes to the south, and to the Red Sea coast of the Arabian Peninsula. In 1902, Sayyid Ahmad al-Sharif became leader of this state-like religious movement, and during the Italo-Ottoman War, he actively coordinated military operations with Enver Bey and Mustafa Kemal. After the Ottoman officers withdrew from Libya in 1912 with the outbreak of the First Balkan War, the Italian army made limited headway in Tripolitania and Fezzan. Eastern Libya, however, remained functionally independent, as Sayyid Ahmad and his Sanusi forces easily defended the autonomy of their core Cyrenaican and Saharan strongholds.

With the outbreak of the war in 1914, the Sanusi's military potential in the southern Mediterranean theater became strategically important. From Al-Sallum, a small Egyptian coastal village closest to the ill-defined boundary between Egyptian and Sanusi territory, British officers serving in the Egyptian Coast Guard maintained cordial relations with Ahmad, who was encamped a few miles to the west.[32] Sir John Maxwell, the British commander of forces in Egypt, also carried out an extensive correspondence from Cairo with Ahmad, striving to convince him to maintain Sanusi neutrality. At the same time, German agents including Otto Mannesman and Ottoman advisers including Nuri Pasha (Enver Pasha's brother), Jafar Bey al-Askari (an Ottoman Arab officer from near Mosul), and Sulayman al-Barani (a Libyan Ottoman officer) were present within or near the Sanusi camp. They tried to convince Ahmad to act on the Ottoman sultan's declaration of jihad against the Allies, urging him to order his Sanusi fights to attack the British in Egypt. As the Gallipoli quagmire drew increasing numbers of British forces out of Egypt month after month in 1915, the Ottoman and German military advisers lobbying the Sanusi saw an increasingly urgent opportunity to strike while the British position was vulnerable.

Like multiple other Arab civilian and military actors caught up in the war, Ahmad faced strategic and emotional dilemmas in determining whether to support one side or another or to try to remain neutral. In practical terms, the Sanusi were caught between the Italians' coastal enclaves of control to their west, French expansion in the Sahara to the south, and the British in Egypt to the east. Most of his supply lines came through Egypt, as did increasing amounts of aid during the war. To replace these, the Ottomans and Germans had tried to land military equipment and other supplies to the coast, using submarines and boats. The Ottoman-Arab officer

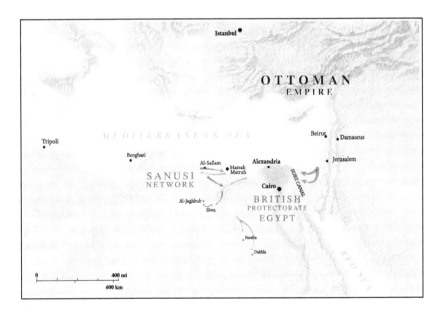

FIGURE 2.4 The Northern Africa front.

Source: Author adaptation from public domain.

sent to help coordinate the Sanusi offensive, Jafar al-Askari, had himself completed two daring supply runs, one from Greece and another from Lebanon, slipping through the Allied blockade, but the quantities could not compare to that available overland from Egypt.[33]

Up through the summer of 1915, Ahmad carefully maintained a neutral position between the British and the Ottomans. That summer, Italy's official entry into the war on the side of the Allies in June and Ottoman successes at Gallipoli began to shift the equation. Finally, in September 1915, Nuri Pasha's unit of Sanusi-Ottoman forces launched an attack on Sidi Barrani, a small Egyptian settlement fifty miles past the border. The action forced Ahmad's decision to draw the Sanusi into an active military campaign along the Egyptian Mediterranean coast and into the interior oases of Egypt's Western Desert. Initially, the British staged a strategic withdrawal from outlying coastal posts including Al-Sallum. That fall, Sanusi

FIGURE 2.5 Ahmad al-Sharif leading Sanusi troops to fight the British in Egypt's Western Desert.

Source: Bain Collection, Library of Congress.

forces under the command of Nuri Pasha and Jafar al-Askari advanced steadily along the coast toward Marsah Matruh, 125 miles inside Egypt and halfway to Alexandria, before the British-Egyptian forces mounted a counteroffensive. British-Egyptian troops decisively defeated the Sanusi forces at the Battle of Aqaqir on February 26, 1916, taking their injured commander, Jafar al-Askari, to Cairo as a British prisoner, where he was recruited to flip sides and join the Arab Revolt being organized against the Ottoman Empire in the Hejaz. By March, the Sanusi troops on the coast had been pushed back across the border into Cyrenaica.

Following the defeat of his coastal forces, Ahmad withdrew his main group of Sanusi troops south to Egypt's Western Desert oases, moving them among Siwa, Bahariya, Al-Fayyum, Farafra, and Dakhla to evade the British and keep fighting. That spring, he and his nephew Sayyid Muhammad Idris nominally divided the leadership of the Sanusiyya, with the former claiming the political and military and the latter the spiritual roles. Throughout 1916, Ahmad tried to survive and keep raiding in the Western Desert, as the British refined a mode of desert warfare (first experimented with by the Italians in the 1911–1912 war in Libya) that combined aerial reconnaissance and bombardment with rapid overland movement across long distances using armored Rolls-Royce vehicles, "light cars" (mainly Ford Model Ts), and motorbikes to hit Sanusi forces with machine-gun fire and light artillery.[34] By early January 1917, Ahmad had decided to withdraw back to the Sanusi stronghold, the Jaghbub oasis in the deep Sahara south of Cyrenaica, to which he successfully returned, despite intense British-Egyptian operations to intercept his force, in early February. In April 1917, Sayyid Idriss (who after World War II would be independent Libya's first king), concluded negotiations with the British and Italians to end hostilities and signed a treaty at Akramah. Ahmad left Cyrenaica in August 1918 on a German U-boat and was dropped off on the Austro-Hungarian-controlled Adriatic coast at Pola; via Trieste and Vienna, he traveled to Istanbul, where he was given a ministerial position by the CUP leadership.[35]

In terms of overall war objectives, the Sanusi operations against the British had a much more limited impact compared to the Arab Revolt in the Hejaz against the Ottomans. Like Faisal's British-supported Arab Army, the Sanusi received limited material supplies (some artillery and machine guns) and advisory support from the Ottomans and the

Germans. But, unlike the Arab Army, they had no Ottoman equivalent of Allenby's British regular forces advancing as a parallel prong of attack, no air support, and no robust supply lines from their rear. Nevertheless, despite their limited strategic success in 1915–1917, the Sanusis (like the Hashemites and Arab officers who led the Arab Revolt, including Jafar al-Askari—who played such a prominent role in both revolts) would emerge after 1918 as a major player in struggles to redefine post-Ottoman Northern Africa. Later in the 1920s, the Sanusi, under the command of Omar al-Mokhtar, would pose the primary obstacle to Italian plans to conquer Cyrenaica and consolidate rule over Libya.

THE SOUTHERN FRONT: THE OTTOMAN GALLIPOLI DEFENSE AND THE BRITISH-ARAB PUSH FROM SINAI AND THE HEJAZ TOWARD DAMASCUS

The final front of the Ottomans' Great War was the empire's southern flank. As has been demonstrated thus far, the Ottoman Empire faced a multifronted struggle, on their own territory, to a degree unique among the belligerents in World War I, most of whom only had one or two active military theaters. On almost all of these fronts, the Ottomans were able, remarkably, to hold their own. They blocked the Allied assault on Istanbul through the Dardanelles for months and gained the Gallipoli victory in January 1916. In the Caucasus and eastern Anatolia, they held on just long enough for the 1917 Russian Revolution to eliminate that threat, and the next year the Ottomans went on the offensive and pushed all the way to the Caspian Sea in 1918. In Mesopotamia, the Sixth Army repulsed the British Indian Expeditionary Force multiple times, deflected a Russian assault through Persia, held on to Baghdad until March 1917 and kept Mosul almost to the end of the war. In Northern Africa, the Ottoman-German support to the Sanusis helped keep the Italians under siege on the coasts and generated a western threat against British-controlled Egypt.

The front on which the Ottoman Empire eventually broke down was in the south. Here they faced a steady Allied assault starting from 1916 into Greater Syria (modern-day Syria, Lebanon, Jordan, and Israel/Palestine). One prong of this offensive came up from Egypt across the Sinai Peninsula in the form of the expeditionary forces under the command of General Allenby; the other came up from the Hejaz region of the Arabian Peninsula in the form of the Hashemite-led, British supported Arab Revolt. Across this front, the turmoil of sustained wartime mobilization, *seferberlik*; widespread famine caused by locust infestations in 1915, an Allied blockade, and military requisitioning; strict martial law meted out by the CUP governor, Cemal Pasha; the violence and destruction of aerial, artillery, and trench warfare as the British advanced against the Ottoman defenses; and the ravages of disease before and including the 1918 influenza pandemic, all deeply marked communities from Palestine to Aleppo. Wartime experiences forced them to begin thinking of various political futures as the Ottoman status quo was destroyed, colonial designs were formulated, and local aspirations were kindled.

The Southern Front was one of the first to see activity in the war. Just months after the official onset of hostilities in November 1914, the CUP triumvirate of Enver, Jamal, and Talaat and their German advisers began planning an attack on the lifeline of the British Empire, the Suez Canal, hoping to also rally the Egyptian public to revolt. The Ottoman-German offensive was mounted between January 26 and February 4, 1915. Diversionary attacks were sent to the northern area of the canal around Qantara and south to the city of Suez, while the main attack was launched at the midpoint of the canal, Ismailiya, during the night of February 3–4. The Ottoman Suez Expeditionary Force was able to cross the canal, but, though surprised, the British put up a stiff defense. The Ottomans were forced to withdraw halfway back across the Sinai to a predetermined fortified line stretching from El Arish, on the Mediterranean coast, down to Nekhel, a key crossroads at the center of the peninsula. The offensive had failed to spark an Egyptian revolt, and the Ottomans settled for a Sinai position from which to harass and harry the Suez Canal. Cemal Pasha and the Ottoman-German planners shifted to a defensive strategic posture in southern Syria. A second Ottoman defensive line was set up between Gaza and Beersheba, with a rail line extended to Beersheba to facilitate supply lines. From these positions, the Ottomans kept up small raids on the canal through the spring and summer of 1915 to try to disrupt shipping traffic. The British responded by moving their fortifications to the east side of the canal. Their goal was also defensive, to protect Suez; an offensive across the Sinai desert buffer protecting Syria was not yet viewed as necessary or feasible.

Instead of southern Syria, the British offensive strategy on the Southern Front in 1915 was to launch an amphibious assault from Egypt more directly toward Istanbul. In late 1914, an initial plan to seize the northern Syrian coastal city of Iskanderum (Alexandretta) and effectively cut the Ottoman Empire in half by taking control of the connection point of the Ottoman railway network and severing Greater Syria, the Hejaz, and Mesopotamia from Anatolia, was tabled because of French worries about British forces gaining control of areas they wanted for themselves after the war. Russia, heavily engaged on the Eastern Front with Germany and in the Caucasus with the Ottomans, remained desperate to have Black Sea access to the Mediterranean reopened (the Ottomans mined the Dardanelles when they entered the war in November 1914). Here the interdependence of the war's fighting fronts came into play. Under Russian and French pressure, the British planners shifted to a new strategy: a massive naval assault to force open the Dardanelles and occupy the Bosphorus region. Faced with a static Western Front, the Allies viewed a war of movement in the east focused on the prize of Istanbul as a way to shake up the stalemate.

In February and March 1915, British and French war vessels spent two months shelling the Dardanelles from the sea, but they could not advance because of stubborn Ottoman-German defensive artillery and skillfully laid mines in the narrows. Ground forces, including large numbers of Indian, Australian, and New Zealand troops, were built up in Egypt. On April 25, 1915, they made an amphibious landing on the Gallipoli peninsula with orders to knock out the Ottoman artillery controlling the waterway and to secure overland access to Istanbul. By the time the land invasion was launched, Ottoman units on both sides of the straits had had months to dig in, with the assistance of German advisers and materiel, and they tenaciously repelled the initial wave of attacks. The Gallipoli struggle shifted quickly to static trench warfare that persisted for eight months. In January 1916, the British command in London finally accepted their inability to progress toward Istanbul and evacuated the Anzac expeditionary forces on January 9. The Ottoman Gallipoli victory, which saved the core of the empire, was one of their most significant of the war.

For the British, the failure of the Dardanelles offensive in January 1916 and the embarrassing loss in Mesopotamia with the disastrous surrender at Kut al-Amara three months later in April forced a reassessment of strategy. That spring, planners in Cairo and London began discussing an offensive against the Ottomans' southern flank in Syria. One prong of this strategy included launching an invasion across the Sinai against Ottoman defensive positions in southern Palestine. The other was to try to activate secret contacts that had been cultivated in the Hejaz (the Ottoman province on the west coast of Arabia including the holy cities of Mecca and Medina) to mobilize a local revolt that would strike up from Arabia toward Damascus. A year earlier, the British and the Sharif of Mecca, Husayn, had begun communicating about rallying the Arab tribes of the Hejaz against the Ottomans. In a series of letters starting in the summer of 1915 between Husayn and the British high commissioner in Cairo, Henry McMahon, this nascent collaboration began to take shape. For the British, Gallipoli and Kut raised the stakes of achieving some kind of victory in the Middle East. For Husayn, the stakes were also high; Cemal Pasha, governor of Syria and commander of the Ottoman's southern forces, was intensely pressuring him to provide auxiliary forces to aid another assault on the Suez. Sharif Husayn had to carefully weigh the potential rewards and risks of the British alliance.

Husayn was also in regular communication with the leadership of a handful of secret societies, including al-Fatat and al-Ahd,[36] which had been formed in the years after the 1908 Young Turk revolution by a small network of Arab urban elites and officers, the latter of whom had developed relationships at Ottoman military academies. In prewar Damascus, Beirut, Baghdad, Istanbul, and in Paris, members of these societies had begun to reimagine the Ottoman Empire. The goal for most was not separatist independence, in the vein of the Balkan nationalist movements, but a dual Turkish-Arab Ottoman configuration along the lines of the Austro-Hungarian Empire. The exigencies of war—mass conscription, a devastating locust plague in 1915, increasing food shortages exacerbated by the Allied blockade, and Cemal Pasha's brutal attempts to sustain Ottoman rule—however, shifted perceptions within the Greater Syrian home front through the 1914–1918 period. This was particularly true as the possibility of Ottoman defeat became increasingly probable.

One of the early Arabist formulations of a post-Ottoman regional political order was articulated in what became known as the Damascus Protocol, which representatives from al-Fatat and al-Ahd communicated to Husayn in January 1915 in an effort to persuade him to lead an Arab revolt. The leaders wanted Husayn to pass on the protocol to the British, the terms of which included independence for the Arab countries lying south of the Taurus Mountains and bounded within the Arabian Peninsula, the abolition of capitulations, and a defensive and economic alliance with Great Britain. In late May 1915, Faisal, Husayn's son, had a meeting in Damascus with representatives from the societies on a trip back from Istanbul, during which this basic outline of aspirations was reiterated. Months later, the CUP governor, Cemal Pasha, brutally cracked down on suspected Arabist notables and executed eleven by hanging in Beirut in August 1915. The next spring, as the British reinitiated the idea of an Arab revolt, Husayn and his sons had to calculate their chances if they allied with the British, whose fortunes in the Middle East theater were at their nadir after the Gallipoli and Kut defeats, against the danger of Ottoman reprisals. This threat was underlined in May 1916, when Cemal Pasha executed another round of twenty-one suspected Arab nationalist leaders in Beirut and Damascus.

In ten letters of correspondence with McMahon, Husayn pressed the British to clarify the terms of a quid pro quo for carrying out a revolt against the Ottomans. Husayn wanted British support for the creation of an Arab Kingdom, tweaking the Damascus Protocol to ensure his own dynasty encompassing Syria, Mesopotamia, and Arabia. The boundaries of this entity, however, ran up against French expansionary ambitions in the region. In November 1915, in the midst of the Gallipoli campaign, the French, British, and Russians had begun negotiating their respective interests in the region. That spring, Mark Sykes, for the British, and Georges Picot, for the French, hammered out an agreement of respective zones of influence in the post-Ottoman Middle East in the event of an Allied victory. Russia was assured control of the Bosphorus and its interests in eastern Anatolia were recognized; the French claimed southern and southeast Anatolia (Cilicia), Greater Syria, and the Mosul province; and Britain claimed southern Iraq and the whole of the Arabian Peninsula. Palestine, a point of contention among the parties, would be declared an international zone. To square these terms with their emerging commitments to Husayn, the British left open a core area of indirect control to accommodate an Arab Kingdom encompassing the Arabian Peninsula (sans Aden), the interior of Syria (leaving the coasts to the French and leaving Palestine ambiguously defined), and parts of Mesopotamia (leaving Basra under

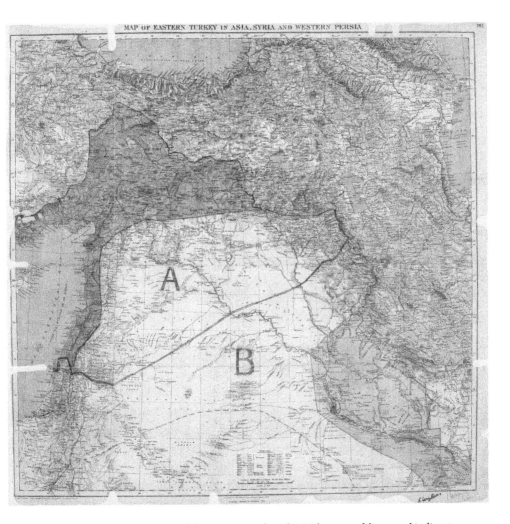

FIGURE 2.6 Sykes-Picot map delineating French and British zones of direct and indirect control and an international zone in Palestine.

Source: Wikimedia Commons.

British control). By the end of the spring of 1916, these (still ambiguous) terms were accepted by Husayn, who pledged to launch an uprising.

The Arab Revolt commenced in June 1916 with Hashemite attacks led by Husayn's sons on Mecca and Jeddah, both of which had small Ottoman garrisons.[37] The key Red Sea ports of Jeddah, Yanbu, and Rabegh fell almost immediately, while the Ottoman forces in Mecca held out three weeks. By September, the Arab Army had taken Taif, sixty miles inland from Mecca, and begun to attack Medina, over two hundred miles north of Mecca, where a large Ottoman contingent was based. Medina was also the terminus point for the Hejaz railway. This subline of the Baghdad railway linked the Ottoman Empire southward through Damascus to Amman, Ma'an, and reached Medina in 1908. The railroad was the lifeline of support for the Ottoman Fourth Army. It also had well-constructed stations along its length that functioned well as forts.

Neutralizing the Hejaz railway through sabotage and by taking key points along the line was the major objective set for the Arab Revolt by the British command in Cairo. The plan was to siege Medina, trapping the twelve thousand troops sent there as reinforcements, while another group of Arab forces skirted north along the Red Sea coast, where British ships would provide supplies. By the spring of 1917, this plan had been successful, and Arab forces under the command of Faisal, with the help of a British liaison officer, T. E. Lawrence, had moved up to take the port of Wejh and begun launching raids on the rail line north of Medina.

In Egypt, the British Sinai Expeditionary Force, swelled in number by Indian, Australian, and New Zealand troops returned from Gallipoli, had been laying the groundwork during the fall of 1916 to push across the peninsula against the Ottoman defensive lines in southern Palestine.[38] Key water sources—oases and wells—the Ottomans would need in order to counterattack were first seized or filled up. A railroad line and water pipelines were also extended from Qantara to provide the infrastructure for the leap across the Sinai desert that winter. In December 1916, British forces took El Arish, on Sinai's Mediterranean Coast, and pressed forward toward Rafah, where they won a victory in January 1917. The British Expeditionary Force was poised to continue north into Gaza, but a concurrent major offensive on the European Western Front siphoned off troops and stalled their momentum, delaying the advance by several months.

The First Battle of Gaza between the British and the Ottomans commenced on March 26, 1917, along the Ottoman's twenty-mile-long defensive line stretching from Gaza inland to Beersheba. The Ottomans successfully repelled this first assault by Allied troops under the command of General Allenby. When Allenby renewed the attack in mid-April, the British were again decimated in a second battle, and both

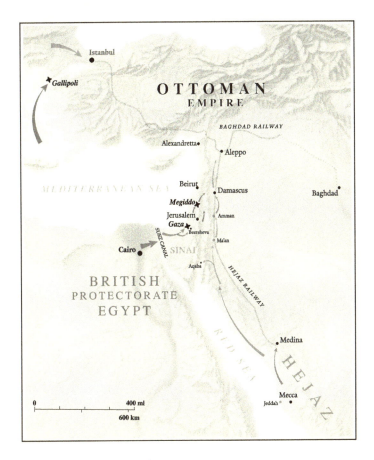

FIGURE 2.7 The Southern front.

Source: Author adaptation from public domain.

sides dug entrenchments along the line. Over the next six months, from April to October, the Palestine front remained static. One of the only advances on the Southern Front for the British was the surprise attack led by T. E. Lawrence and a group of forty Arab mounted camel cavalry, who cut west through Wadi Rum to surprise the Ottoman garrison at Aqaba and take the key port on July 6, 1917. Aqaba was the last Ottoman outlet to the Red Sea, and, with the port secure, the British and French were able to freely land supplies for the advancing Arab Army at a forward location.

FIGURE 2.8 Enver Pasha and Cemal Pasha visiting the Dome of the Rock in Jerusalem in 1916.

Source: American Colony Photo Department, Library of Congress.

Action resumed on the Palestine front in late October, when the British flanked the Ottoman line at Beersheba, forcing them to withdraw further north up into the Hebron Hills. That November, with the Egyptian Expeditionary Force pushing rapidly toward Jerusalem, the British government in London made a related move to leverage their territorial gains in Palestine. Days after the Beersheba victory, on November 2, the British government, in what became known as the Balfour Declaration, promised the Zionist movement that it supported the creation of a Jewish national homeland in Palestine after the war, with a proviso that the civil and religious rights of the non-Jewish inhabitants not be prejudiced. Unable to contain the British advance, the Ottoman forces, commanded by the German general Erich von Falkenhayn, withdrew from Jerusalem in late November northward to Nablus, partly because of concerns about the damage the Holy City might sustain during a prolonged siege. The Ottoman-German strategy was to dig in in Northern Palestine to continue to protect the rest of Greater Syria and the imperial core in Anatolia. That December 11, 1917, General Allenby entered Jerusalem, on foot out of respect for the city's sacred history, through the Jaffa Gate.

On a parallel trajectory on the eastern bank of the Jordan River, the Arab Northern Army continued to operate against the Hejaz railway. Jafar Pasha al-Askari was one of the key Ottoman Arab officers-cum-Arab Army officers leading this campaign. After being injured and captured by the British while leading the Ottoman-Sanusi attack in Egypt's Western Desert, al-Askari had been approached while convalescing in Cairo by his fellow Iraqi, Nuri al-Said, and convinced to flip sides and join the nascent Arab Revolt. Al-Askari was deployed in the northern Hejaz and put in command of the Arab Regular Army, with British and French officers in command of two accompanying detachments. These forces gained increasing tribal support throughout 1918, particularly after it became clear the tide had turned against the Ottomans, and they moved steadily northward up the Hejaz railway.

In the West Bank, Allenby's forces also continued to make progress, taking Jericho and moving up the Jordan Valley with one prong and proceeding north out of Jerusalem past Nablus with another. The British forces faced stiff resistance, however, in northern Palestine from the Ottoman Army of Palestine, over which the German general Otto Liman von Sanders had taken command in February 1918. The pivotal engagement on the Southern Front came at the Battle of Megiddo, on September 19, 1918, when Allenby took the Ottomans by surprise, enveloping their flank with cavalry, after which the Seventh Army had to flee north into Syria in retreat. From this point forward, the Ottoman army in Greater Syria ceased to function as a fighting force.

On October 1, Australian and Indian advance cavalry, and the Arab Army, entered Damascus, with Faisal entering the city officially on October 3. The Hejaz flag had already been raised by remaining local Arabists in Damascus, and Faisal and his group of Arab Army officers immediately began coordinating the administration of the city and surrounding areas. By October 25, 1918, Aleppo (over two hundred miles north of Damascus) had also fallen to British forces, and the Ottomans had lost their last foothold in their Syrian province. As with each of the other fronts, years of mobilization and fighting on the Southern Front had profoundly remade the political landscape of both Greater Syria and the Arabian Peninsula, forcing new political actors and perceptions forward that would greatly influence the struggle to shape the post-Ottoman order.

The simultaneous collapse on the Ottomans' Syrian front and in Macedonian, where the Allied campaign in mid-September pushed through Bulgarian lines and opened a path toward Istanbul, forced the Ottoman Empire—by this point exhausted militarily, economically, and politically—to move quickly to the negotiating table. By mid-October 1918, Ottoman and British officials had begun talks to arrange a cease-fire within the Middle East theater of the war. On October 30, at Mudros, the Lemnos port from which the Gallipoli campaign had been launched, Allied and Ottoman commands signed an armistice ending a period of interempire war that had started almost exactly four years earlier with Russia's attack on the Caucasus frontier and Britain's landing at the head of the Persian Gulf in early November 1914. Over the next two weeks, the Austro-Hungarian and German Empires also signed armistices with the Allies.

In the Middle East, the war had required total mobilization of the general population, which had suffered tremendously because of food shortages exacerbated by the Allied blockade and the horrific purges of suspect populations, forced resettlement, and genocide of Armenian and Assyrian populations within the empire. On each of the fighting fronts discussed—in the Caucasus and eastern Anatolia, Mesopotamia, Northern Africa, and in Arabia and Syria—the way the war played out transformed political horizons. Rather than being fixed, these boundaries of collective political solidarity were in tremendous flux within the fluid post-armistice environment. The first phase of the Long Great War had completed the unmaking of an Ottoman political order that had largely structured the greater Middle East for the previous four centuries. The chapters in part 2 trace how local and colonial actors reimagined the post-Ottoman future and began to mobilize competing political projects to shape it.

II

REIMAGINING THE POST-OTTOMAN MIDDLE EAST

3

THE MIDDLE EAST'S SO-CALLED WILSONIAN MOMENT, 1918-1920

At 9:30 a.m. on Wednesday, June 11, 1919, the members of an American delegation led by the Oberlin College president, Henry King, and a Chicago businessman, Charles Crane, sat down at a hotel in the port city of Jaffa, Palestine, for the first meeting of a six-week fact-finding mission focused on the political future of the region. World War I had ended seven months earlier, but the postwar settlement remained far from settled. Since January 18, 1919, the "Big Four" Allied heads of state—British prime minister David Lloyd George, U.S. president Woodrow Wilson, French premier Georges Clemenceau, and Italian premier Vittorio Orlando—and their large retinues of advisers, other state delegations, and a slew of groups from around the world lobbying for self-determination had been gathered to deliberate the peace in Paris. The negotiations would last eighteen months, extending through the next summer. Between July 1919 and August 1920, five treaties were signed, setting out terms to the defeated Central powers.[1] The very last of these, the Treaty of Sèvres, dealt out terms regarding the former Ottoman lands.

One reason for the delay was that the British and French, despite their wartime Sykes-Picot Agreement, were at an impasse over the "Syrian Question"; namely, what zones of control would be delineated in the Arab-majority, former Ottoman provinces for the French, the British, and potentially for an Arab government. To move the issue forward, President

Wilson, in late March 1919, floated the idea of sending a commission to the Middle East to assess local preferences regarding their post-Ottoman future. In his January 1918 "Fourteen Points" speech outlining why the United States was entering the Great War, he had included a fifth point promising "a free, open-minded, and absolutely impartial adjustment of all colonial claims," giving equal weight to the interests of the concerned populations, as well as a twelfth point specifically addressing the Ottoman lands. The latter stated that the Turkish portion of the Ottoman Empire should be assured "secure sovereignty" but that the other "nationalities" should be granted "an unmolested opportunity of autonomous development" after the war.[2] For Wilson and the other Americans at the Paris Peace Conference, it seemed obviously necessary to inquire what these "nationalities" wanted in the peace settlement.

The French, then the British, begrudgingly agreed, but two months later, neither had named representatives. An exasperated Wilson decided to unilaterally designate his own emissaries and send what was officially known as the "Inter-Allied Commission on Mandates in Turkey" to the region that June.[3] King and Crane were joined by experts drawn from the American mission at the Paris conference. One of these was Albert Lybyer, a historian of the Ottoman Empire who had taught at Robert College in Istanbul and then at Oberlin, Harvard, and the University of Illinois. The other was William Yale, a Standard Oil man sent on the eve of the war to do surveying work in Palestine, who had stayed on in Jerusalem then been recruited as an American intelligence officer in the Middle East when the United States entered the conflict.[4]

The American commission was well aware that the British and French occupation authorities had orders to try to influence their findings. They thus purposefully made a surprise landing at Jaffa instead of Beirut on June 10. Yale, already familiar with the area, was charged with setting up meetings with local figures and delegations to hear their preferences about Greater Syria's postwar future. That first day in Jaffa started off with a meeting with B. M. Nasir, an Episcopal priest representing local Protestant opinion, who communicated that this constituency leaned toward a separate Palestine under British supervision. Next, a Christian-Muslim committee expressed support for a united Syria, including Palestine, under British supervision but also protested against the threat of Zionism and Jewish immigration; a local Zionist committee explained how Jewish colonists could mix with and help the Arabs; and a Greek Catholic delegation indicated a preference for a French mandate over Greater Syria and worries about the British. The last meeting brought the Grand Rabbi of Jaffa and the Jewish manager of the Anglo-Palestine Bank, who defended Jewish claims and reassured the Americans that they would also protect the interests of the six hundred thousand Arabs in Palestine.[5]

That afternoon, the commission met with a delegation of Muslim men from Al-Ludd, Ramleh, and their surrounding villages (about ten miles inland from Jaffa) that consisted of ten Muslim dignitaries including Sulayman al-Tagi al-Faruqi, Shaykh Said Al-Khasi, Haj Abd al-Latif Kayah, Shaikh Montafa Al-Khasi, Shaykh Saleh Subuh, Said Al-Hinadi, Shaykh Ramzi Hamad, Ahmed Shukri Omari, Ibrahim Haki Tagi, and Hassan Khaha. This group told the committee that the great majority of their cities and villages strongly opposed separating Palestine from Syria. Their first preference was to have an independent Syria that unified the "northern Arabs" economically and politically. They also expressed worries about Jewish domination of a separate Palestine. When asked about the security of Christian and Jewish minorities in the larger Syrian state they envisioned, they assured the commission that religion would be separated from a "democratic government, and that freedom of worship would be guaranteed." The Palestinian Muslim delegation's second preference was for an American mandate over a unified Syria that would be under the supervision of the League of Nations. When probed about the possibility that Palestine would be separated from Syria at the Paris peace negotiations, they responded bluntly: "It makes little difference to a man condemned to die, whether he be shot or hung." At the end of the meeting, they turned the questioning back toward the American commission members, pointedly asking them "if Mr. Wilson still held to his fourteen points and the right of a people to self-determination; if the Peace Conference had decided definitely against an independent Syria; and if it was possible to send to the commission the desires of the people through petitions or a quiet plebiscite." The delegation also warned the Americans that the occupying British military governors were seeking to prevent the local populations from freely expressing their opinion.[6]

Before heading from Jaffa up for a longer stay based in Jerusalem, Lybyer wrote up the tentative conclusions from the commission's first three days of fact-finding. The first was that the non-Jewish population in the area, numbering around 80 percent of the whole, unanimously opposed Zionist political aspirations and increased Jewish immigration. This majority overwhelmingly supported creating a unified Syria that geographically encompassed all the lands, including Palestine, between the Mediterranean and the Syrian Desert, stretching from Aleppo province in the north down to the port of Aqaba on the Red Sea. Politically, they preferred that this state be constituted as a federated democracy that protected religious freedom and full political equality. Lybyer's second conclusion was that, if there had to be external oversight, the majority favored a single mandatory power over all of Greater Syria (the United States was preferred, followed by Britain) rather than a partition under two powers.

Lybyer also noted that the British were actively trying to suppress local support for independence: the Foreign Office had communicated to its interim occupying administrators that British or French mandates—not independence—would be imposed in Syria and Palestine (the latter of which would have some form of official support for Zionism) and that the local population should be kept quiet long enough for the Paris conference to announce these decisions. Lybyer pointed out that the British had made contradictory promises in the November 1917 Balfour Declaration, which promised a Jewish homeland to the Zionist movement, and the November 1918 Anglo-French Declaration, which affirmed support for "indigenous governments and administrations in Syria and Mesopotamia." Neither the British nor French were making any effort to consult the local populations. And, the locals the American commission had thus far consulted were incensed that the Paris conference was leaning toward endorsing the Balfour Declaration and ignoring wartime promises made to the Arabs. This strong majority preference for an independent, unified Greater Syria and a widespread awareness of and concern about the international state of play regarding the Syrian Question at the Paris conference would be reiterated over and over in meetings held from Beersheba to Mersin over the next five weeks as the commission visited thirty-six towns and cities and met with 442 delegations representing 1,520 villages.

As the King-Crane interviews in the summer of 1919 clearly reveal, the political future of the former Ottoman territories was a pressing question for a wide range of the public across the Middle East. Over the previous eighteen months, the global dissemination of rhetoric emphasizing self-determination, articulated by Vladimir Lenin in writings just before the war in 1914 then adopted by Wilson in 1918, opened up what Erez Manela has described as a "Wilsonian Moment" of raised political aspirations and anticolonial mobilization as the conflict in Europe drew to a close.[7] In line with the thinking of Manela and others, this chapter moves beyond the much-studied Paris diplomatic nerve center for the postwar negotiations to ask how local communities imagined and fought for new forms of political community in the post-armistice period.[8]

But, this chapter also directly challenges how this so-called Wilsonian Moment is understood to have worked out. First, it looks not just outside of Paris but also outside major urban centers like Cairo or Damascus to ask what was really happening on the ground across the Middle East in other cities, villages, and, crucially, in the countryside and more remote areas from Northern Africa to the Iranian Plateau. In the wake of the October 1918 Armistice of Mudros, rural actors also formulated post-Ottoman political projects and mobilized what would prove the most significant and sustained military campaigns to realize these visions in the 1920s.

The second intervention is to argue that this "moment" in the Middle East needs to be considered beyond 1919 with more attention to the nuances of how Wilson was invoked over time. The following discussion distinguishes between two important phases. During the initial, highly fluid, first stage (summer 1918 through summer 1920), a wide array of forms of local aspirations for independent self-determination including kingdom, republic, emirate, autonomy within empire, and others were formulated and reformulated in tension with simultaneously shifting European colonial aspirations for direct and indirect rule in the region. From Palestinian representatives before the King-Crane Commission in Jaffa to the previously discussed Kurdish leader, Shaykh Mahmud, in Sulaimaniya, local actors instrumentally used Wilsonian logic in their arguments and appeals, particularly when addressing international audiences in hearings, petitions, and presentations. But, it is important to note that they were in no way constrained by these or by any other single mode of "national" self-determination: multiple idioms and an array of solidarities were evoked, often in overlapping ways, to mobilize and defend local political autonomy and independence.

The crystallization, formalization, and first stages of implementing European colonial projects in the wake of the April 1920 San Remo conference signaled a transition to an important second stage of this "moment." By early summer 1920, the European powers were effectively ignoring even the pretense of honoring self-determination (the King-Crane commission's report itself was immediately buried and not published publicly until 1922) and clashes between rival local and colonial visions for the post-Ottoman Middle East escalated into large-scale conflicts in Syria, Iraq, Anatolia, Iran, Arabia, and Northern Africa. By the end of the year, several local *and* colonial projects that had emerged during the initial flush of the post-Ottoman moment had been violently crushed. This second phase narrowed down a set of still-viable post-Ottoman polities that would compete for survival.

THE OTTOMAN EMPIRE AT THE PARIS PEACE CONFERENCE

Among the three defeated Central Powers, the fate of the Ottoman Empire was a delayable priority for the victorious Big Four Allied leaders (Britain, France, Italy, and the United States) gathered to deliberate the postwar settlement in Paris in January 1919. Their principal concern during the first sixth months of the conference was to set stringent peace terms for Germany—including reparations, the Franco-German border, and the apportionment of its colonial overseas possessions—then deal with Eastern and Southeastern Europe in similarly severe treaties with Austria, Bulgaria, and Hungary.

Though it took a year and a half to finalize the treaty dealing with the Ottoman Empire, the Great Powers did, after convening in January 1919, immediately begin debating the post-Ottoman Middle East's future. There were four key issues on the table in Paris. One was control of the strategically important Straits zone (the Dardanelles, the Sea of Marmara, the Bosphorus, and the city of Istanbul and its environs). The second was the future of the rest of Anatolia: namely, what would be left under Turkish control, what might be constituted as Armenia, whether a Kurdistan should be created, and what zones of control would be awarded to European powers (British, French, Greek, and Italian). The two other areas of contention concerned the future of the former Arab provinces of the Ottoman Empire in Greater Syria and Mesopotamia. Two tracks of discussion—about Great Power and local interests—were carried out in tandem. With regards to the latter, as was the case for other global regions whose geopolitical futures were at stake, numerous delegations from the Middle East made their way to Paris to publicly and privately make a case to the Big Four decision-makers about their claims regarding the post-Ottoman future.

The conference first heard a series of delegations present cases about the future of Greater Syria. The first of these was made on February 3, 1919, by Chaim Weizmann, who represented the Zionist Organization. Building off the pledges made in the 1917 Balfour Declaration, Weizmann argued for a Jewish homeland to be created in a British-administered mandate over a Palestine separated from Syria. He recommended the borders of this entity be set just south of Sidon in the north and encompass all the territory (on both sides of the Jordan Rift Valley) to the west of the Hejaz railway down to Aqaba. Weizmann buttressed these claims by appealing to the Jewish people's historical connection to the land, their suffering from pogroms and other antisemitic persecution in Eastern Europe, and by highlighting the "civilizing mission" the Jews could accomplish in developing a "desolate" Palestine.[9]

Three days later, the Arab claims regarding Greater Syria were put forward by Faisal, the son of Sharif Husayn of the Hejaz and leader of the Arab Revolt. Faisal had traveled to France from Damascus in late 1918 accompanied by officers who had served in the Arab Army including Rustum Haidar, Nuri al-Said, and Tahsin Qadri, and by T. E. Lawrence, who served as translator for the Arab delegation.[10] Dressed in embroidered white robes, Faisal stated that the Arabs wanted self-determination and that, with special exceptions for Lebanon and Palestine, the Arab world should be independent.[11] Woodrow Wilson probed whether the Arabs preferred one mandate or several. In response, Faisal diplomatically responded that the Arabs preferred unity and independence but would, if mandates were imposed, prefer American supervision.[12] A week later, the conference heard petitions from two other parties, both groomed by the French delegation. Shukri Ghanim, representing the Central Syrian Committee, expressed support for a French mandate over a federally organized Greater Syria that included Lebanon. Dawwud Ammun, heading a Lebanese delegation, lobbied for a separate

Lebanon, affiliated with a Syrian entity, with France the appointed mandatory power over both.[13]

Trying to block French designs on Greater Syria, Faisal and Lawrence cultivated American support, reaching out to Howard Bliss, the president of the Syrian Protestant College (later renamed the American University of Beirut), to arrange a meeting with Wilson. In the meeting, they convinced Wilson of the need to send out a commission of inquiry to study the Syrian question (which eventually took the form of the King-Crane Commission in the summer of 1919). After this series of meetings in Paris, Faisal, seeing that the British and French were locked in a stalemate over Syria, left the conference on April 23 to return to Damascus to prepare for the inter-Allied commission he expected Wilson would organize.

Following the sessions related to Greater Syria, the Supreme Council heard presentations related to the future of Anatolia and the Caucasus. On February 26, 1919, an Armenian delegation headed by Boghos Nubar Pasha, representing Ottoman Armenians, and Avetis Aharonian, representing the Armenian Republic (formed in the Caucasus in May 1918), presented a case for a unified Armenian state under the protection of a European mandate power. This plan would incorporate the six easternmost Ottoman provinces and Cilicia (roughly the Adana province), the region stretching inland from Anatolia's southeastern coastline, into a unified Armenian Republic that stretched from the Mediterranean to the Black Sea. In their speeches to the council, Nubar Pasha and Aharonian emphasized the sacrifices made by the Armenian Legion in fighting alongside the Allied powers and the tragic massacre and deportation of hundreds of thousands of Armenians during the war. The Armenian case elicited great sympathy at the Paris conference, and two months later, Lloyd George proposed a draft resolution to the Council of Four on May 14, 1919, which would appoint an American mandate over this greater Armenia. Wilson accepted, but the provision was subject to Senate approval, which never came.[14] Despite widespread sympathy for the Armenian project, little political and less military will would be exerted on the ground by external powers, despite Armenian pleas, to make it a reality in subsequent years.

In a similarly quixotic manner, Kurdish national aspirations were also represented in Paris. General Mehmet Şerif Pasha, who had served in the Ottoman military and as foreign affairs minister (1876–1909) but gone into exile after disagreeing with the direction taken by the 1908 Young Turk revolution, headed a delegation to Paris on behalf of the Society for the Advancement of Kurdistan (Kürdistan Teali Cemiyeti), an association organized in December 1918 in Istanbul.[15] Before coming to Paris, he had attempted to establish a network with Shaykh Mahmud Barzinji in northern Mesopotamia, Sayyid Taha Gilani in eastern Anatolia, and Simqu Shikak in northwest Iran to promote an independent Kurdistan, but, in reality, he had virtually no local ties in the region. Nevertheless, on March 19, 1919, he had an opportunity to make the Kurdish case to the Supreme Council. In "Memorandum on the Claims of the Kurdish People," he argued for the creation of a free and independent Kurdish state within the following borders: "The frontiers of Turkish Kurdistan, from an ethnographical point of view, begin in the north at Ziven, on the Caucasian frontier, and continue westwards to Erzeroum, Erzindjian, Kemah, Arabkir, Behismi and Davick; in the south they follow the line from Haran, the Sindjihar Hills, Tel Asfar, Erbil, Kerkuk, Suleimanie, Akk-el-man, Sinna; in the east, Rvandiz, Bash-Kale, Vizir-Kale, that is to say the frontier of Persia as far as Mount Ararat."[16]

This proposal notably excluded the Van region and aroused suspicions among other Kurdish nationalist groups that Şerif Pasha, with British involvement, had coordinated these boundaries with the Armenian nationalist Nubar Pasha. Another competing Kurdish leader, Emin Ali Bedirhan, proposed an alternative larger Kurdistan map that not only included Van but also an outlet to the Mediterranean Sea through Cilicia. Like the Armenian project, the idea of carving out a Kurdish polity in former Ottoman lands gained a sympathetic hearing in Paris and was eventually included in the provisions of the Treaty of Sèvres. But, it also never received sufficient tangible support from the Great Powers to translate a treaty clause into a concrete reality.

Several other delegations made their case to the Paris assembly about the future of the shatter zone region in eastern Anatolia and the southern Caucasus. The fledgling Georgian and Azerbaijani Republics, formed, like the Armenian Republic, in May 1918 after the collapse of the Russian Empire, both sent delegations to Paris to get recognition as independent states. The delegations had months of meetings in Paris in 1919 with various committees, as the unfolding Russian civil war provided a constantly evolving backdrop. Finally, on January 10, 1920, the Supreme Council, with British prompting, dedicated a session to the question of the southern Caucasus republics, after which their de facto independence was recognized.

With less success, the Persian government also made a play in Paris to expand its territory. Before the outbreak of the war, a mixed Ottoman-Qajar commission, with British and Russian arbitrators, had surveyed the length of the Iran-Ottoman border from the Persian Gulf to Mount Ararat in 1914.[17] In 1919, the Persian foreign minister, Prince Firuz Nosratdoleh, submitted several territorial claims to the Supreme Council in Paris, boldly asking that Iran be given Mosul province and even Diyarbakir province, but these aspirations were summarily rejected because of strong British opposition.[18] That spring and summer, Lord Curzon, British foreign secretary, and Qajar representatives secretly hammered out a provisional Anglo-Persian agreement instead; although never ratified by the Iranian Majlis, it would have given Britain control over financial and military affairs, effectively making Iran a British protectorate.

The official representatives of the Ottoman government were among the last delegations to meet with the Supreme Council members—Clemenceau, Lloyd George, and Wilson—who received them on June 17, 1919. The representatives' strategy was to make a case for leniency by appealing to Wilson's Twelfth Point, which stated that the postwar peace should guarantee "the secure sovereignty of the Turkish portion of the present Ottoman Empire." Before the Supreme Council, the Ottoman representatives asked for direct rule in these Turkish zones in Anatolia and Thrace. They also asked that the Arab provinces formally remain under Ottoman sovereignty but be given high levels of local autonomy (as had been the case in Egypt and Tunisia before French and British intervention). These appeals fell on deaf ears, however. The Allied leaders deemed these demands ludicrous and instead moved quickly toward a formula to partition Anatolia and the Arab lands under different European mandates.[19]

The first big treaty of the Paris Peace Conference was signed on June 28, 1919, at Versailles, a couple of weeks after that session with the Ottoman representatives. The Treaty of Versailles dictated peace terms to the German empire, but it also first included twenty-six articles setting out the covenant of the newly formed League of Nations, which had been President Wilson's overarching goal. For the Middle East, the critically relevant section of this League covenant was Article 22, which devised a mandate system for the colonies and territories formerly belonging to the defeated German and Ottoman Empires. It stated that these territories were "inhabited by peoples not yet able to stand by themselves under the strenuous conditions of the modern world" and would need to be under the "tutelage" of "advanced nations" who could act as "Mandatories on behalf of the League." The mandates would vary depending on the "state of the development of the people, the geographical situation of the territory, its economic conditions and other similar circumstances."

The League of Nations deemed the communities formerly under the "Turkish Empire" to have reached a developmental stage at which their existence as "independent nations" could be "provisionally recognized," subject to the administrative advice and assistance provided by a Mandatory power until the point they could stand alone. The article stated, "The wishes of these communities must be a principal consideration in the selection of the Mandatory."[20] On paper, the mandate system devised in Paris combined Wilson's twelfth point and the Anglo-French Declaration of November 1918. Wilson had asserted that the "Turkish portion" of the Ottoman Empire would be assured sovereignty but that "other nationalities" would be granted an "absolutely unmolested opportunity for autonomous development." The Anglo-French declaration proclaimed the wartime goal was "the complete and final liberation of the peoples who have for so long been oppressed by the Turks," with the important rejoinder that France and Great Britain would "further and assist in the establishment of indigenous Governments and administrations in Syria and Mesopotamia" and "recognize them as soon as they are effectively established."[21]

While publicly hearing numerous delegations' cases for self-determination in 1919, however, the Great Powers were at the same time meeting to negotiate their own conflicting colonial claims in the region behind closed doors. The preamble to Wilson's Fourteen Points had castigated "secret understandings" and "secret covenants" that "upset the peace of the world" in January 1918. A year later in Paris, Wilson himself was trying to mediate the conflicting British, French, Italian, and Greek secret understandings and covenants that would upset the peace of the Middle East in the coming years. The mandate system had been agreed to that summer in the Treaty of Versailles, but *how* it was going to actually be allocated remained a source of deep division: the French and British were at loggerheads over the allocation of mandates for Greater Syria and Mesopotamia; the Italians had already withdrawn from the Paris conference for several weeks that spring because of disputes related to their interests in the Adriatic and in western Anatolia; and the Americans themselves vacillated over potential mandate commitments in Armenia, the Straits zone, and elsewhere. These tensions would not be resolved until the San Remo conference the next year, in April 1920.

LOCAL POSTWAR POLITICAL PROJECTS

As the Great Powers and a myriad of global delegations convened in Paris in 1919, a range of local players were also mobilizing thousands of miles away behind new visions of political order and independence. On the ground, these local movements and occupying Western powers vied over the future shape of various parts of the post-Ottoman Middle East.

REIMAGINING GREATER SYRIA

The area of the former Ottoman Empire at which the most competing colonial and local claims intersected was the Arabic-speaking region known since the first Muslim conquests as Bilad al-Sham. This term means the "land to the north" or, more literally, the land to the left of someone standing in the Hejaz region of the Arabian Peninsula facing east. Stretching from the Taurus Mountains in the north to the Sinai Desert in the south, this area now encompasses Syria, Lebanon, Jordan, and Israel-Palestine. From the 1870s, it was organized into three Ottoman provinces including the vilayets of Aleppo (extending north to the Taurus), Damascus, and Beirut and a number of special administrative units including the sanjak of Zor (to the east of the Aleppo Provinces) and the Mutasarrifates (Governorates) of Mount Lebanon, Jerusalem, and Karak. As a whole, the region was knit together by social, cultural, and economic ties linking primary urban centers such as Aleppo, Damascus, and Beirut; secondary urban centers such as Jerusalem, Nablus, and Salt; and the villages and tribes in the countryside.[22]

From 1914 to 1918, this area was governed as a single unit under Governor Cemal Pasha, who drew extensively on Greater Syria's resources, through requisitioning and recruitment, to launch the two failed Suez invasions. Southern Syria then served as the Ottoman Empire's bulwark on the Southern Front when the British moved on the offensive across the Sinai into Palestine and up from the Hejaz into the East Bank of the Jordan Rift Valley. Greater Syria's local population suffered extensively during the war because of famine, which was exacerbated by the Allied blockade of the coast, and disease, which was compounded by the flu pandemic in 1918 and 1919.[23] During this period, Cemal became known as al-Saffah, "the Blood Shedder," after he executed dozens during a severe crackdown on Arab nationalists, publicly hanging them in the squares of Beirut and Damascus.

From early in the war, multiple ideas began to emerge in this region about what the postwar order might (or should) look like. Salim Tamari's discovery of and work on wartime journals help us see how this future was being envisioned within Greater Syria. On March 2, 1915, a young Jerusalemite Arab serving in the Ottoman military, Private Ihsan Hasan al-Turjman, recorded his recollections of a visit with the friends Khalil Effendi Sakakini, Hasan Khalidi, and Omar Salih Barghouti. That night, the group talked mostly of the war, how long it would continue, and about the "fate of this [Ottoman] state." Turjman writes at length about their thoughts about the future:

> We more or less agreed that the days of the [Ottoman] state are numbered and that its dismemberment is imminent. But what will be the fate of Palestine? We all saw two possibilities: independence or annexation to Egypt. The last possibility is more likely since only the English are likely to possess this country, and England is unlikely to give full sovereignty to Palestine but is more liable to annex it to Egypt and create a single dominion ruled by the khedive of Egypt. Egypt is our neighbor, and since both countries contain a majority of Muslims, it makes sense to annex it and crown the viceroy of Egypt as king of Palestine and the Hijaz.[24]

This remarkable sense of open possibilities and speculation about what might replace the Ottoman status quo—in this case the expectation that Palestine and the Hejaz would likely be incorporated into a British-controlled Khedival Egypt—accelerated in the months leading up to and just after the October 1918 armistice.

In early 1919, as they considered new political possibilities, Greater Syria's local population, from the coastal areas to the inland villages and cities, was well-informed about the international politics entangled with their future, including the British and French postwar designs on the region. A year and a half before, news of the Balfour Declaration had been published widely in the Arabic press after it was announced in London on November 2, 1917. Three weeks later, news also spread rapidly about the Sykes-Picot Agreement, when the Bolsheviks published the full-text of the secret accord in the Russian newspapers *Izvestia* and *Pravda*, on November 23, 1917. The *Manchester Guardian* republished these on November 26, and the story was put out on the international newswires. Many were also familiar with the locally formulated Damascus Protocol, the British pledges to Sharif Husayn about an Arab kingdom, and the Anglo-French Declaration about Syria and Mesopotamia in December 1918.

In early 1919, this wider Syrian region, Bilad al-Sham, was caught in a fluid and volatile moment: British and French occupation forces had only partially asserted control within their respective zones, and the local population knew the postwar settlement was not yet a done deal. That spring, developments at the Paris Peace Conference were followed closely throughout the region through reporting in the Arabic press (which had been allowed to flourish again after the armistice), and many were dismayed with the inclusion of Article 22 in the Covenant of the League of Nations, which set out a mandate solution in the former Ottoman Empire. They thus knew that some form of European or American oversight, or "tutorial" involvement, was likely but that there was still room to maneuver to forestall, negotiate, or prevent it from happening. In this unsettled period immediately after the armistice, local opinions and aspirations regarding the postwar political order were in flux and had to quickly be recalibrated as the context evolved.

It was into this moment that the American delegation of the Inter-Allied Commission on Mandates in Turkey was sent out from the Paris Peace Conference over the summer of 1919 to assess public opinion.[25] The

Americans' social scientific, democratic optimism shaped their goal to get a quantitative measure of the populist pulse. Various critical appraisals have since been written about the King-Crane Commission, its methodology, and the value of its findings, but it nevertheless represents the best, and in many respects the only, window we have into public opinion from the Syrian provinces of the former Ottoman Empire about what should replace it.[26]

As they conducted their six-week survey, the members of the commission were well aware of the political context and the competing colonial and local interests in play in the region. Physically, Greater Syria had been divided after the armistice into separate Occupied Enemy Territory Administrations (OETA) including the southern region under British control (Palestine encompassing both sides of the Jordan) and a northern area under French control (the coast stretching north from Tyre to Alendretta). A third area, under the Arab administration of the Damascus-based Amir Faisal, included the inland cities and their surrounding hinterlands from Aleppo south to Amman. To mitigate against undue outside influence, the commission tried to get an accurate reading on local political views by receiving any delegation or petition presented to them.

They also planned an ambitious six-week itinerary that took the eleven-man party through most of the proposed mandate areas in Palestine, Syria, Lebanon, and Cilicia—traveling by car, train, and yacht—to receive delegations and conduct interviews:

Itinerary of the King-Crane Commission, June 10–July 21, 1919[27]

June 10–13	Jaffa
July 2–3	Damascus
June 13–16	Jerusalem (by auto)
July 4–5	Baalbek
June 17	Bethlehem, Hebron
July 6–9	Beirut
June 18	Beersheba (including Gaza delegations)
July 9	Jebeil, Batrun, Bkerke
June 19–20	Jerusalem
July 10	Sidon and Tyre
June 21	Ramallah and Nablus

July 11	Ainab, Baabda, Zahle
June 22	Jenin
July 12	Tripoli (by yacht)*
June 23	Nazareth and Haifa
July 13	Alexandretta (by yacht)
June 24	Acre
July 14	Ladikiya (by yacht)
June 25	Travel to Damascus via Tiberias and Capernaum
July 15	Homs (by auto)
June 26–30	Damascus
July 16	Hama (by train)
July 1	Amman and Deraa
July 17–19	Aleppo
July 20–21	Adana, Tarsus, Mersina

*General Allenby gave the commission use of his private yacht, the *Maid of Honor*, to get up and down the coast.

On July 21, they boarded the U.S. destroyer *Hazlewood* to return to Istanbul. During this month and a half in the summer of 1919, the commission met with 442 delegations representing 36 cities and 1,520 villages across the breadth (as this grueling itinerary underscores) of Greater Syria.

In these inquiries, the key questions the commission asked concerned what form of government and what territorial boundaries the population preferred within the space of Greater Syria. In their findings, four major projects came into focus. The first, and the one with the most support by far, was a unified Syria, with an independent Arab monarchy under Faisal, that extended from the Taurus Mountains south to Aqaba and the Sinai and encompassed the lands from the Mediterranean coast inland to the Syrian Desert. This framework was articulated early on by multiple Muslim and Christian groups in Palestine, and, by early July, it had crystallized into a formal program backed consistently in meetings between the commission, Amir Faisal, and Syrian notables in Damascus.[28] When they pressed delegations and interviewees to state preferences about different mandate scenarios, the commission discovered a definite consensus that, after first choosing an independent unified Syria, the second preference was for a unified Syria under American supervision, while the third was for a unified Syria under a British mandate.

The three other political projects, which had much less support, imagined a different political system and territorial configuration within Greater Syria, namely dividing off a separate Palestine and Lebanon. The Zionist project envisioned a separate Palestine, under a British mandate, that provided for a Jewish state and continued Jewish immigration in line with the pledges made in the 1917 Balfour Declaration. With regard to Lebanon, there was an array of different plans. Some envisioned a Greater Lebanon that was independent while others wanted it under French control; some included the Bekaa Valley in this entity while others did not; and some put forward plans for a Lebanon affiliated with Syria but maintaining a level of autonomy.

Three things became very clear during the summer of 1919 from the hundreds of interviews the commission carried out and petitions it received during the six weeks it traveled from southern Syria up to Cilicia. First, it was evident that the local populations in Greater Syria had a range of configurations in mind for the post-Ottoman political order—unified versus partitioned Greater Syria, independence versus mandate control—and that they had ranked preferences among these imagined futures. Second, it became clear that these preferences shifted over the weeks the commission traveled through the area to assess public opinion. This evolution was catalyzed by the spread of awareness about the commission's purpose and by concerted efforts by organized groups including Zionists, proponents of a Greater Lebanon, and the official representatives of Faisal's Damascus-based Syrian proto-state to mobilize public opinion.[29] Third, the Commission's interactions and findings during the summer of 1919 revealed that the local populations of the Middle East were highly aware of the international context and audience for their political claims. They knew the Paris Peace Conference's role in deliberating the postwar order and that the Wilsonian ideals of self-determination had become part of the equation. The unfortunate limitation of the commission's scope, however, was that the group did not travel in Anatolia, with the exception of a number of cities in Cilicia, nor in Mesopotamia. But, in both of these regions, local populations were also reimagining the postwar order and mobilizing political projects as actively as groups in Greater Syria.

REIMAGINING MESOPOTAMIA

Political conceptions within the three Ottoman provinces compromising the "land between the rivers"—Basra, Baghdad, and Mosul—were already in flux even before the war. Basra's historic orientation through the Persian Gulf out to the Indian Ocean, and increasing integration into British imperial circuits linking it to India and Egypt, meant local elites had been in contact with active nationalist movements from the early 1900s. Groups like the Reform Society founded by Sayyid al-Talib al-Naqib in 1913 had begun to emphasize a stronger separate Arab identity within the Ottoman Empire, particularly in response to the CUP's increased Turkification and centralization policies after the 1908 revolution.[30] In Baghdad, similar associations like the National Scientific Club and a branch of the Al-Ahd (The Covenant) were founded following the 1913 CUP coup against Abdülhamid. Their goal was also to protect Arab cultural and linguistic identity. Politically, very few wanted full independence; instead, they imagined some kind of a federal relationship with Istanbul.

With the British invasion in the fall of 1914, some of the tribes in the south responded to the Ottoman proclamation of jihad and Ottoman military commanders' entreaties to serve as auxiliary forces. These alliances were fragile, however, and tensions quickly mounted between these groups and the Ottoman army. In the Middle Euphrates region, the population in Najaf rose up and drove out the Turkish garrison in the summer of 1915 (with Karbala following suit shortly thereafter), declaring independence and flying the Arab flag until the British arrived in 1917.[31] Later in the war, multiple secret societies were formed in early 1918 in Najaf, Karbala, and Baghdad among Shi'i and Sunni urban notables, military officers, and rural chiefs, who began discussing the region's political future. In February 1919, a national organization, the Haras al-Istiqlal (Guardians of Independence) was founded in Baghdad in reaction to the British blocking a Mesopotamia delegation going to the Paris Peace Conference. Branches were created in Hilla, Kut, Karbala, and Najaf. This organization combined a broader cross-section of sectarian communities, the ulama, and military officers. Al-Ahd also formed a branch in Mesopotamia, which, as in Syria, was comprised primarily of Sunni officers who had joined the Arab Revolt after leaving the Ottoman army. Well aware of the political developments happening in Paris and the proposed mandate system, many of these groups in Basra and Baghdad provinces opposed a British mandate and supported some form of an independent Iraq unifying the provinces, potentially with one of Sharif Husayn's sons as ruler. In Basra, however, there was also a growing preference, among many of the business elites, for the creation of a separate republic, which would be articulated in a petition in 1921.[32] In Mosul province, Kurdish leaders, who had been given wide latitude by British intelligence officers who had arrived in 1918 in Kirkuk and Sulaimaniya and other northern cities, were intent on preserving their autonomy, if not aspiring to outright independence.

The British themselves were undecided about the political future of the three Ottoman provinces they had occupied since 1914. Following the occupation, they had initially laid the groundwork for direct rule, replacing elected municipal institutions from the Ottoman period with British political officers partnered with local notables. Using the Tribal Criminal and Civil Disputes Regulation developed in India, the British administration designated tribal shaykhs, who were given authority to arbitrate disputes in their tribes and were obliged to collect taxes. In early 1919, Arnold (A. T.) Wilson, the civil administrator over Mesopotamia, spent two months surveying local notables across the three provinces about their preferences for their political future, and the skewed sample (which disregarded nationalist opinion) supported continued British rule, either direct or with an Arab amir under British protection. Within the British administration itself, a division was also deepening between advocates for direct rule on the India model, championed by Arnold Wilson, and those supporting indirect rule, with some form of Iraqi self-government under British oversight. The latter camp was advocated by Gertrude Bell, who increasingly pushed for the British to partner with Sunni nationalist elites drawn from the Arab officers around Faisal to modernize the country.[33]

Linked to the British tug-of-war about direct and indirect rule, and the role, if any, for local self-determination, was a parallel ambivalence about the future of the northern Mosul province. Though British officials quickly presumed Baghdad and Basra would merge to form a united Iraq, debates continued about Mosul. The demography of this region was much more diverse, with a majority Kurdish population, largely in the highlands, mixed with Sunni Arabs, Turks, Jews, and Christians, and its topography— transitioning from the Nineveh plains into the Zagros Mountains—also contrasted strongly with the riverine valleys, plains, deserts, and delta wetlands of Baghdad and Basra. The British administration's initial idea was to implement a form of indirect rule in parts of Mosul province on the model of India's northwest frontier zone, partnering with Kurdish chieftains in the regions bordering Iran and northward toward the still-to-be-defined Armenian and Turkish states. Toward this end, soon after occupying Kirkuk, the British made the Kurdish leader, Shaykh Mahmud, a governor in Sulaimaniya. In early May 1919, though, he declared the independence of Kurdistan, kicking out the British administrators and military detachment, citing, as the anecdote in the introduction noted, Woodrow Wilson's Twelfth Point and the Anglo-French Declaration in his justification for this action.[34] The British military expedition sent from Baghdad quickly put this down, defeating Shaykh Mahmud's forces and capturing him that summer, after which he was eventually exiled to India. This move, however, did not resolve the basic fact that the British did not have the military capacity to completely subdue the Kurdish highlands ringing Mosul.

In these regions, Kurdish tribal leaders themselves were calculating what to do in the political vacuum created by the Ottoman defeat and the general fluidity of the immediate postwar period. Four years of war on this fighting front had transformed the political topography of the north Zagros Mountains region and local, subnational, and Wilsonian-like national forms of autonomy were simultaneously being considered and rapidly adjusted. Many were also simply waiting to see whether the British or another power would try to rule them. To their east, Qajar power had severely waned in northwest Iran, and a Kurdish leader, Simqu Shikak, had begun to carve out an expanding area of autonomous rule around Lake Urmia starting in March 1918. To the north, in Anatolia, the ambitious plans proposed in Paris by the Big Four powers for an independent Kurdistan and independent Armenia were very far from the actual realities emerging on the ground in 1919.

REIMAGINING ANATOLIA

In negotiating the armistice ending hostilities between the Ottoman Empire and the Allied powers in October 1918, Hussein Rauf, newly appointed Ottoman minister of the navy, trusted the goodwill of the

British admiral Arthur Calthorpe. Meeting in the harbor of the Greek island of Lemnos on the admiral's flagship, the *Agamemnon*, Calthorpe officially pledged that Britain would treat the Ottoman rump area left after the war fairly: a military occupation would not happen in Istanbul and a sphere of control in Anatolia would be preserved.[35] These assurances that the Ottomans would be allowed to retain some territorial integrity quickly proved specious. Less than two weeks later, Allied military personnel—French, British, Italian, American, and later Greek—began to pour into Istanbul, as did thousands of displaced persons—Armenians, white Russians, Bulgarians—from around the region. On February 10, 1919, an Allied military commission divided the Ottoman capital into French, British, and Italian occupation zones.[36]

Much of the Anatolian peninsula was also being parceled up that spring among the Allied powers. The French landed in November 1918 in Alexandretta and immediately began occupying cities (Antakya, Mersin, Tarsus, Ceyhan, Adana) in the Cilicia region in southeast Anatolia in December, with the aid of the Armenian Legion. Late in 1918, British forces had occupied the key areas in the Caucasus between the Black and Caspian Seas, securing the oil pipeline from Baku to Batumi. Italy landed occupation forces on the southwest coast in Antalya and other cities in January 1919, and in early May they made preparations to land in Smyrna (Izmir) on the west coast of Anatolia. On May 6, Eleftherios Venizelos, the Greek prime minister, rushed to get British, French, and American support for a Greek occupation, and less than ten days later Greek forces landed, beating the Italians to the punch, and began to spread out into Smyrna's immediate hinterland.

As with the other areas of the former Ottoman Empire, the Western powers' partition plans for Anatolia and the Caucasus clashed directly with how local groups imagined the post-Ottoman order. In the Transcaucasus, a series of ephemeral polities were formed over the winter in early 1919 including a Pontian Greek Republic in Trabzon and a Kars Republic, in addition to the fledgling Georgian, Armenian, and Azerbaijani states. In Anatolia, the postwar priority for recently decommissioned Turkish military officers and for large numbers of the Muslim population was to defend a core homeland from the threats of French, British, and Italian colonial occupation, Greek expansion in the west, and the possibility of an Armenian state seizing provinces in the east. This vision was defined and then mobilized around the leadership of Mustafa Kemal. In May 1919, the day after the Greeks landed in Smyrna (Izmir), Kemal shipped out from Istanbul for a posting in Central Anatolia. The Ottoman caretaker government, instructed by the British, had ordered Kemal to bring order to the interior. Instead, after landing at the Black Sea port of Samsun, he began networking a resistance movement to challenge the postwar diplomatic settlement being hammered out in Paris.

On June 22, 1919, a group of former Ottoman government and military officials, including Kemal, sent out a joint circular from the town of Amasya in the Sivas province. Distributed to cities across Anatolia, the document declared that the "unity and independence" of the nation was at risk, that the caretaker government in Istanbul was powerless to defend it, and that a national committee was needed to defend the people's rights. A congress would therefore be convened in Sivas in September, to which representatives from the provinces should be sent. At a preliminary congress held between July 23 and August 4 in Erzurum, the eastern Anatolian city that had been a major pivot point on the Caucasus Front during the war, Kemal and the nascent nationalist leadership gathered with fifty-six delegates, including both Kurds and Turks, from the Bitlis, Erzurum, Sivas, Trabzon, and Van eastern provinces to lay the groundwork for resistance against the Allied occupation. The congress affirmed these provinces' desire to remain in the Ottoman Empire and rejected any form of mandate scheme or privileges for Greek or Armenian political entities.[37] At the Sivas Congress convened in early September, thirty-eight delegates gathered from all over Anatolia, declaring that the Erzurum principle applied to all of Anatolia and Rumelia (the European portion of the empire).

On January 28, 1920, the Ottoman Parliament voted to acknowledge the decisions made at Erzurum and Sivas in what was called the Misak-i Millî, the National Pact. The platform distilled the nationalist agenda down to five principles. These included independence for the Turkish majority territories and referendums for the easternmost three provinces (Kars, Ardahan, Batum), western Thrace, and the Arab majority territories of the empire. They demanded Turkish control over the Straits. They assured protection for ethnic and religious minorities but conditioned this on Muslim minority protections in neighboring countries. Finally, they called for an end to all economic, judicial, and political capitulations that had applied to the Ottoman Empire.

Beyond political mobilization, the nascent Turkish resistance movement was also active militarily. Local autonomous groups, or with loose connections to Kemal's movement, took matters into their own hands. In the fall of 1919, the residents of Maras and Urfa rose up against French troops who had arrived to replace British occupation forces in the interior areas of Cilicia. Two months later, in January 1920, French colonial forces and the Armenian Legion faced uprisings in Antep and Maras.[38] In Maras, the French had to withdraw in February, but the Antep battle would last for over a year. From the spring of 1920 forward, the Muslim-majorities of the local communities in Cilicia, having initiated revolts against the occupying French forces, would continue to make gains as they were later aided by the former Ottoman units that Kemal had begun to reorganize and deploy from the interior provinces of Anatolia.

MANDATES AND REVOLTS IN SYRIA AND MESOPOTAMIA

In the spring and summer of 1920, the Middle East's so-called Wilsonian Moment transitioned fully into a second, more violent phase as the populations of Syria and Mesopotamia, like those in Anatolia, also rose up politically and militarily in an effort to reject the mandates proposed for these regions and determine their own political futures. In Syria, Faisal returned to Damascus in January 1920, frustrated and disappointed with the progress of the Paris Peace Conference. Before leaving, he had been forced to acquiesce to a *modus vivendi* stipulating that the French would accept a Syrian state in the interior and not station troops there on the condition that he accepted the French as the exclusive advisory power for this entity. The Pan-Syrian Congress that had convened in May 1919 ahead of the King-Crane Commission's visit, however, unanimously supported a unified, independent Syria. The congress was vehemently anti-French, opposed the compromise, and pressured Faisal to break the commitment. On March 8, 1920, the Syrian Congress unilaterally declared independence, proclaimed Faisal as the king of the Arab Kingdom of Syria, and set about drafting a democratic constitution over the next two months.[39]

FIGURE 3.1 Book of the Independence of Syria (Dhakra istiqlal al-suriyah) with aspirational borders used in the March 8, 1920, Declaration of Independence.
Source: Wikimedia Commons.

Days after the independence declaration in Damascus, a revolt led by Ibrahim Hananu broke out in northern Syria in and around Aleppo, coordinated loosely with an Alawite revolt in the coastal highlands of Latakia led by Shaykh Saleh al-Ali that had already been active for over a year. In late 1918, French forces had landed in Latakia, disbanding local provincial councils that had been organized in the coastal towns and affiliated with the Damascus government, then pushing inland up into the Alawite-dominated highlands. Shaykh Saleh's forces engaged the French throughout the spring of 1919, achieving almost complete control over the Jabal Nusayriyya (the massif inland from the Latakia coastline) by July. The outbreak of the Hananu revolt to his northeast in March 1920 created a band of active resistance against the French occupation that extended from the inland areas of Cilicia near Antep south through Aleppo to the Latakian highlands. These movements had links to Damascus, but they were tied more closely to the military resistance and uprisings to the north in Anatolia, with Turkish supplies and weapons being actively distributed into northern Syria.[40]

A month after Syria declared independence, the European powers with stakes in the post-Ottoman Middle East met for a week in San Remo, Italy, in late April 1920. Their task was to finally hammer out how to apportion the mandates proposed by the League of Nations charter and to determine, at least roughly, their boundaries. At the conference, the French received the mandate for Syria, Britain was given mandatory authority in Palestine and Mesopotamia, and Italy's interests in southern Anatolia and Libya were registered.

News of the terms negotiated at San Remo reinforced and fueled intense local opposition in Syria and Mesopotamia. The Syrian Congress denounced it, putting pressure on Faisal to take a stronger stance on independence, as he tried to steer a course that would prevent further French occupation. Faisal's administration, like the Turks, had also already begun to materially support the revolt in northern Syria, and, in May, the Arab Kingdom began to conscript soldiers to mount an armed defense of Damascus. That summer the Franco-Syrian crisis came to a head. The French commander in Lebanon, General Henri Gouraud, called on Faisal to clamp down on the northern rebellion, and on July 14, issued the Syrian king an ultimatum demanding that he demobilize his army and recognize the French mandate. A little more than a week later, French forces pushed inland to occupy Aleppo on July 23, stationing more than eighteen thousand troops in and around the city in two days. The French Army of the Levant also moved toward Damascus. On July 24, they met and easily defeated the cobbled-together Syrian army at the Maysalun Pass, northeast of Damascus on the road from Beirut.[41] The French occupied Damascus the next day and ousted Faisal, who initially moved down to Daraa in the Hawran Plain southwest of Damascus but then had to leave by ship from Haifa after the French threatened to bomb any community sheltering him.[42] That September, Gouraud announced the creation of the French mandate and the partition of the short-lived Arab Kingdom into six administrative units, including a separate Greater Lebanon state.

In the southern part of Greater Syria, under British control, resentment at the impending Anglo-French mandate terms had also activated resistance in Palestine. As discussed with regard to the findings of the

FIGURE 3.2 Anti-Zionist demonstrations at Jerusalem's Damascus Gate on March 8, 1920 in solidarity with the Syrian National Congress's Declaration of Independence.

Source: Matson Collection, American Colony Photo Department, Library of Congress.

King-Crane Commission, Arab, Muslim, and Christian aspirations to be included in the Arab Kingdom or for an independent Palestine clashed directly with Zionist goals for a Jewish state. Palestinian delegates participated in the Syrian-Arab Congress from its initial convening in Damascus in June 1919, and several Muslim-Christian associations and nationalist clubs were formed in major cities to advocate for political goals. In the spring of 1920, tensions broke out in two episodes of violence. The first was in upper Galilee north of Lake Hula, in the liminal zone between British and French occupation zones. In early March, the four Jewish settlements in this area, including Tel Hai, came under attack from Arab-Bedouin groups, loosely affiliated with Faisal's Damascus government and engaged in banditry and anti-French raiding. There were other minor skirmishes with other settlements in the north through the summer. From early March, following the Syrian Congress's declaration of independence, there were also a number of Palestinian-Arab demonstrations in cities. In early April, large crowds gathered in Jerusalem for the annual Nabi-Musa festival protested against the British mandate plan and against the Balfour Declaration support for Zionism, with three days of violence breaking out in the city with five Jews and four Arabs killed and hundreds injured.[43]

Parallel to these developments in Greater Syria, opposition also began to steadily increase in late 1919 against British rule in Mesopotamia. The al-Ahd al-Iraqi association convened in tandem with the Syrian Congress in March 1920 in Damascus and intrepidly declared the independence of Iraq. They named Amir Abdallah, Faisal's brother, as king, though few actually recognized this nomination, including Abdallah himself. In April, some of these former Ottoman Iraqi officers moved to Deir el-Zohr, a city in far eastern Syria upstream from Haditha on the Euphrates River. In January, Ramadan al-Shallash, an ex-Ottoman officer, had returned to Deir el-Zohr to kick out the British political officer assigned there and capture it in the name of the Arab government.[44] Al-Ahd planned to use it as a forward base of operations to launch a revolt in Iraq against British rule. In May 1920, a group of these Arab Army soldiers and tribal allies attacked and captured the town of Tal Afar, east of the Sinjar Mountains, then moved on to Mosul. They intended to arrive at Mosul at the same moment as a planned uprising in the city, but the British were able to disperse both.

In the mid-Euphrates region, too, resentment against the British had also reached a critical mass in the spring of 1920.[45] In Karbala, the Ayatollah al-Shirazi published a fatwa declaring service in the British administration unlawful and meetings among the Shi'i ulama, tribal sheikhs, and members of the Independence Guard were convened to plan anti-British action. In Baghdad, large Ramadan gatherings were held throughout May, alternating between Sunni and Shi'i mosques, protesting the British mandate over Iraq announced after the San Remo conference. In these gatherings, nationalist poems, songs, and speeches reinforced solidarities across sectarian boundaries. Fifteen representatives were nominated to present a petition calling for Iraqi independence to the British authorities. In early June 1920, they met with the British commissioner, Arnold Wilson, who himself had gathered twenty-five Baghdadi notables to counter their demands. Later in June, Wilson announced that elections for a constituent assembly would soon be held, but the British administration simultaneously cracked down severely on demonstrations and made several arrests early that summer.

In May 1920, printing presses in Najaf and Karbala had begun producing tracts that actively incited tribes to prepare to revolt, and Arab flags were manufactured and widely distributed. At the end of June, al-Shirazi issued another fatwa; this time encouraging rebellion. The first shot of the Iraqi revolt happened in the Diwaniya province in June, when a British effort to put down unrest by arresting tribal chiefs backfired and armed bands attacked the jail to free them. The revolt spread rapidly in the Shi'a-majority mid-Euphrates area between Karbala and Najaf. The British soon lost control, and a provisional revolutionary government was set up in Najaf after the British governor withdrew. This early success caused the revolt to spread rapidly into the Basra province to the south. In the north, Kurdish chiefs also opportunistically grabbed control, particularly in the towns near the Persian border.

It took until the early fall for the British to regroup and begin a counteroffensive. To retaliate, Winston Churchill, then the British war secretary, mobilized sixty-five thousand troops, including reinforcements from British-controlled areas of southern Persia and two air squadrons. The Royal Air Force bombed the mid-Euphrates and other areas extensively, using fire bombs and phosgene gas, the latter a lethal chemical weapon first deployed by the Germans in December 1915 at Ypres.[46] During this campaign, the British also used Assyrian refugees as auxiliary troops. These groups had fled attacks on them in the Urmia region of northwest Iran by the Kurdish leader Simqu Shikak. Their alliance with the British in the 1920 Iraqi revolt created tensions that later erupted in the early 1930s in severe anti-Assyrian sectarian violence. Facing a shortage of supplies and unable to sustain a coordinated cross-regional movement, the Iraqi rebellion started to flag in the autumn. In the mid-Euphrates, the British cut the water off to Karbala and were able to capture that city and Najaf by the end of October. These British successes, and the RAF's brutal air campaign, effectively brought the revolt to a close by the end of 1920. The cost of imposing the mandate in Iraq had been high, with six thousand Iraqi lives lost and five hundred British and Indian soldiers. Monetarily it cost the British one hundred million pounds in direct and indirect costs, five times the budgeted annual allotment for the whole mandate administration.[47] On the Iraqi side, the experience of mobilization, military confrontation, and brutal suppression up and down the Tigris and Euphrates, though still largely local, also strengthened a nascent larger collective solidarity.

COLONIAL VISIONS AND POLITICAL AUTONOMY IN ARABIA AND NORTHERN AFRICA

Though most of the attention in the Paris negotiations was focused on Anatolia and the former Ottoman Arab provinces in Syria and Mesopotamia, the liminal moment from 1918 through 1920 of heightened expectations for self-determination also had ramifications in further peripheries including the Arabian Peninsula and Northern Africa. In contrast to the clashes between the competing claims of multiple European and local powers in the eastern Mediterranean, in the Arabian Peninsula, there was functionally only one interested colonial power after the 1914–1918 conflict: the British Empire.[48] The British themselves, though, were internally divided between the competing interests of the India Office and the Cairo Office in Arabia. The overall British policy was to support a plurality of local leaders rather than betting exclusively on one, but, in practice, Delhi and Cairo (with London's support) backed rival local proxies.

In the decades before the war, British India officials had concluded trucial agreements with shaykhs in the Persian Gulf, and, during the war, they had courted alliances in the Arabian Peninsula's interior. In the Najd region, a British India political officer, Percy Cox, signed a treaty agreement on December 26, 1915, with the chieftain, Abd al-Aziz Ibn Saud, that recognized his independence and in which he pledged to not move against Gulf principalities. During this same period, as was discussed in the previous chapter, the Cairo Office was conducting negotiations with Sharif Husayn about an alliance in the Hejaz region on the western Red Sea coast, which developed into the Arab Revolt led by Faisal. As the war began to draw to a close in 1918, these two primary British clients in the Arabian Peninsula, Ibn Saud and the Hashemites, began to come into direct conflict. The Paris Peace Conference recognized the Kingdom of the Hejaz, and it would be a signatory to the 1920 Treaty of Sèvres. Ibn Saud's position within the Arabian Peninsula was not recognized by the international community, though, despite the fact that he was rapidly strengthening his power on the ground.

In 1919 and 1920, the Hashemites and Ibn Saud had distinct aspirations. Sharif Husayn assumed the British wartime promises guaranteed that his Kingdom of the Hejaz would rule over all of the Arabian Peninsula and affiliated polities in Syria and perhaps Mesopotamia, with his sons on those thrones. Ibn Saud, for his part, was consolidating his position in the interior, expanding into Ha'il to the northwest. Ibn Saud's priority was that the British clarify the boundary between the Kingdom of the Hejaz and his own domains, particularly with reference to the al-Khurma and Utayba tribes, who were under his patronage and were being raided by the Hejaz.

These aspirations clashed over the summer of 1919 in the First Najd-Hejaz War. In April 1919, Ibn Saud again pressed the British to force the Hashemites to recognize a permanent boundary between the Najd and Hejaz polities. In May, Husayn sent his son Abdallah with troops to take the strategic oasis, al-Khurma, which was located between the Najd and the Hejaz and had shifted allegiance to al-Saud. The Hashemite forces took the Turaba oasis to the west of al-Khurma but were then defeated soundly on May 25–26 by a contingent led by a Khurma tribal leader, Khalid ibn Mansur ibn Luway, which included fifteen hundred supplemental forces sent by Ibn Saud. In early July 1919, Ibn Saud arrived in Turaba with an army of ten thousand men, prepared to move west against the Kingdom of the Hejaz, but he agreed to turn back after the British threatened him on July 4, 1919. The conclusion of the conflict brought a temporary end to the tensions on that border, as al-Saud shifted his attention to expanding his power base into other areas of the peninsula. The basic tension between the rival Najd and Hejaz polities emerging during this period was not resolved, however, and would break out into war again in 1924.[49]

In Northern Africa, as in the Arabian Peninsula, there was ample room to mobilize local, autonomous post-Ottoman polities after the armistice because these areas were not occupied by significant Allied forces. In the former Ottoman provinces of Cyrenaica and Tripolitania, though the Italians had nominal claims, local groups were largely in control on the ground outside of a few Italian-controlled coastal enclaves. In the east, the Anglo-Sanusi settlement in the aftermath of the Ottoman-Sanusi campaigns in Egypt's Western Desert in 1916–1917 had required the abdication of Sayyid Ahmad al-Sharif al-Sanusi, who was replaced by his cousin, Idris al-Sanusi, as the head of the order. Idris then concluded agreements with the British and Italians in April 1916 and again in April 1917 that acknowledged Sanusi autonomy in the Cyrenaican interior. After the war, the Italians, first for Tripolitania in June 1919 and then for Cyrenaica in October 1919, issued a set of decrees known as the Legge Fondamentale (Basic Law) that allowed each province to convene a parliament and governing council and offered the local population joint Libyan-Italian citizenship. In October 1920, the Italians and the Sanusi signed another accord recognizing the de facto dual sovereignty in place in Cyrenaica. It formalized Idris's title as Amir, delineated the extent of his administrative control, and guaranteed him a regular subsidy from the Italian administration. Idris also pledged to disband most of the Sanusi military forces, but this was never honored.

In the west, local notables proclaimed the independence of a Tripolitanian Republic (Al-Jumhuriyya al-Tarabulusiyya) on November 1, 1918, immediately after the armistice, with two capitals at Aziziyyia and Gharyan. A council of four prominent notables and a parliament of twenty-four notables and chiefs were elected, and a judicial and religious council, police force, and army were formed. Attempts to gain recognition at the Paris Peace Conference in the spring of 1919 failed, however, because the Tripolitanians had no Great Power backer: the British, French, and American governments had already acceded to Italian claims in the region.[50] In negotiations with Italy, the nascent Tripolitanian Republic was able to reach an agreement, though, on April 18, 1919, that established the Basic Law (al-Qanun al-Asasi) mentioned above. On the ground, Tripolitania in 1920 had a plurality of political orders interacting, with the Italians and local political leaders in coastal and inland cities and villages and the Berber-majority Jabal Nafusa vying for control. The fragile coalition drawn together under the banner of the Tripolitanian Republic itself struggled with factional infighting encouraged by the Italians.[51]

Further west in Morocco, the French and Spanish had simply tried to hang on during the 1914–1918 conflict to the limited territorial control they had thus far achieved in their respective zones. Most of the French forces in the country, including large numbers of recently recruited Moroccan colonial troops, had been deployed to the Western Front. Both colonial powers were content to hold on to coastal and lowland zones of control and leave the mountainous hinterland alone. This state of affairs shifted in 1919, as both the Spanish and French reactivated military campaigns to "pacify" the still-autonomous tribal groups in the Rif and Atlas Mountains. The Spanish, from enclaves on the Atlantic and Mediterranean coasts, plotted an ambitious two-pronged military campaign. In the west, from Larache and Tetouan, one group would press eastward into the Jbala hill country; in the east, another would move westward from Melilla into the Rif Mountains. Over the next eighteen months, these Spanish operations would catalyze a massive resistance movement and lead to the founding of a new political entity, the Rif Republic, which would end up challenging both the Spanish and French emerging colonial states in Morocco.

As was the case across other parts of Africa, Asia, and Eastern Europe, the armistice ending the interempire hostilities in the fall of 1918 and the convening of the Paris Peace Conference in January 1919 opened up a period in the greater Middle East in which it was possible for colonial and local actors to imagine a wide variety of possible political futures in the region. In the heady early days of this so-called Wilsonian Moment, local visions of political self-determination were expressed in a range of forms—a constitutional Arab monarchy in Syria, a Tripolitanian "republic," a Kurdish kingdom statelet in Sulaimaniya, sultanates and kingdoms in Arabia, and many others; this was happening at the same time that European empires were planning a range of colonial frameworks—mandates, protectorates, zones of influence—for the region's future. Several of these projects, local and colonial, were eliminated in early violent clashes. In the next longer and critical "moment," the set of surviving, still viable polities that had emerged across the region would compete in a period of warfare that continued through the 1920s.

4

EMERGING POLITIES IN THE EARLY 1920S

On January 18, 1923, several dozen leading chiefs and notables from the Rif region of northern Morocco assembled on a small hill overlooking the beautiful sweep of Al Hoceima Bay's turquoise Mediterranean waters.[1] The group had gathered to perform the *bay'a*, an oath of allegiance officially recognizing the rule of Mohamed bin Abd el-Krim. The ritual symbolically affirmed the political and religious legitimacy of the Republic of the Rif (Arabic, Jumhuriyyat al-Rif; Tarifit, Tagduda en Arrif) that Abd el-Krim and tribal forces had established by repeatedly repelling the Spanish army's attempts to expand control in the northern zone of Protectorate Morocco.

Over the previous two years, Abd el-Krim's troops had pushed the Spanish out of the Central Rif back to a handful of coastal enclaves the Spanish had held since the seventeenth century. One of these was a presidio down in the bay below, just three hundred yards off the shore, on the tiny Alhucemas islet.[2] Since 1673, Spanish soldiers standing on the whitewashed ramparts of the Peñon de Alhucemas had stared south across the water at the fertile Nekor valley and at the wall of Tamsaman mountain peaks (many reaching over 6,500 feet) that surrounded this one small break in the formidably rugged coastline between Spain's two other North African footholds, Ceuta and Melilla.[3] That January morning, everything on the opposite shore was under the control of the upstart Rif Republic, whose flag (red background, white diamond, and green star and crescent) waved over Abd el-Krim's headquarters in Ajdir, visible on a hillside just to the southwest.

In the late nineteenth century, Spain, like France and Italy, had become increasingly interested in colonial expansion in North Africa and had attempted a couple of lackluster military excursions into northern Morocco from Ceuta (during the Spanish-Moroccan War, 1859–1960, they briefly occupied Tetuan) and from Melilla (when the expansion of Spanish fortifications in 1893 sparked an intense military conflict with nearby Rif tribes). The humiliating loss after defeat in the 1898 Spanish-American War of Cuba, Puerto Rico, and the Philippines, among the last remnants of Spain's once vast empire, raised the stakes across the Straits of Gibraltar: Morocco became the African terrain in which Spain would attempt to regain its standing among the European powers. This view was born out in the early 1900s in the diplomatic wrangling over the Moroccan Question, as Spain's strategic position as a weaker buffer of colonial power on the southern shore of the Straits of Gibraltar was reiterated in successive agreements about Morocco among the British, French, Italians, and eventually the Germans.[4]

In February 1908, Spain actively relaunched its own scramble for Africa, using a Rif tribal attack on mining interests and a railroad running south from Melilla to Wiksan as a pretext to begin more aggressive expansion inland.[5] In 1911, they landed troops on the Atlantic coast at Larache and slowly proceeded inland toward the Jbala hills. In 1912, the French, having imposed a protectorate treaty on the Moroccan sultan in March, officially delegated a subprotectorate zone of control in November to Spain in the north, while also recognizing Spain's prerogative in the Saharan south. In 1913, the Spanish occupied Tetuan, making it the capital of the northern zone, but then made little further progress inland. During the 1914–1918 conflict, the Spanish stood pat, but tacitly allowed German agents, industrial representatives, and diplomats freedom to distribute arms, payments, and anti-French propaganda to the autonomous interior tribes.[6]

The end of the war in Europe in November 1918, however, was viewed by Spain, like European colonial counterparts active elsewhere in the Middle East, as an opportunity to restart colonial conquest. Madrid initiated a policy in 1919 to complete the military "pacification" of the northern protectorate zone. Spanish forces made significant progress, moving up into the Jbala and Ghomara mountain ranges in the west, and in the east, moving up the Wadi Kart into the foothills of the Rif Mountains. In the summer of 1921, however, the eastern campaign hit a wall: the large Ait Waryaghar tribe that dominated the Central Rif region south of Al Hoceima Bay.

The previous fall, a coalition of the Ait Waryaghar and neighboring tribes had been rallied by Mohamed bin Abd el-Krim, the son of a prominent Ait Waryaghar leader, who himself had previously served as a chief Islamic judge, *qadi qudat*, for the Spanish administration in Melilla and as a newspaper editorialist for *El Telegrama de Rif*. Abd el-Krim's vision, even at this very early stage of anticolonial mobilization, was to fundamentally reshape the political order of the Rif and create a country "with a government and a flag."[7] In June 1921, Abd el-Krim's forces skirmished with the forward edge of Spanish posts, which General Silvestre had strung out in an overextended line westward from Melilla up into the eastern Rif Mountains. In early July, Abd el-Krim ordered a coordinated full assault, overwhelming the Spanish principal position at Anwal, then routing their entire eastern front. The battle devolved into a chaotic retreat with the Spanish units fleeing to try to find refuge in Melilla: in the rout, the Spanish lost over 13,000 lives, 20,000 rifles, 400 machine guns, 129 cannons, and large quantities of ammunition and canned food.[8] Abd el-Krim, however, refrained from pressing the attack to the coastal Mediterranean enclave of Melilla, allowing the Spanish to reoccupy the lowland areas to his east while his troops dug defensive breastworks in the Rif foothills that September.

Anwal, modern Spain's worst military defeat (and one of the worst ever by a European colonial power), was a pivotal moment marking the rise of a Rif-based military-political movement catalyzed by the expansion of the Spanish colonial state. This initial success in 1921 gave Abd al-Krim the symbolic and material capital needed to consolidate a nascent state apparatus over the next year and a half. As early as December 1921, the Rif Republic began making appeals to the League of Nations contesting the legitimacy of the protectorate framework and urging it to recognize Rif independence. The financial foundation for this project was reinforced January 27, 1923, when the Spanish paid the Rif government four million pesetas in exchange for Spanish prisoners captured during the Anwal battle. The first *bay'a* ceremony held the week before the ransom reinforced the symbolic foundation for the state-building project. Over the next several weeks in early 1923, a wave of similar declarations spread across the Rif. On February 2, a large delegation of tribal chiefs from further east and west—Ghumaris, Walshakis, and Timsamanis—arrived at Ajdir to offer the *bay'a* to Abd el-Krim. Three weeks later, Abd el-Krim officially accepted these oaths combining the religious, military, and political legitimacy of his rule and declared the creation of the Emirate, or the Republic, of the Rif, on February 21.[9] Over the next eighteen months, his army would continue to steadily expand control, eventually encompassing close to 90 percent of the northern protectorate zone allotted to Spain. By the end of 1924, Amir Abd el-Krim's de facto state rule stretched from the walls of Tangier to the outskirts of Melilla and was admired worldwide— even inspiring one of the biggest Broadway hits of the 1920s, *The Desert Song*, which opened in New York in 1926—as an anticolonial David versus Goliath story.

The Rif Republic's explosive emergence in the early 1920s as a de jure, sovereign, territorial polity was not an isolated case in the post-Ottoman greater Middle East. From Morocco to Iran, as the previous chapter examined, a wide spectrum of visions about what should replace former political structures proliferated across the region. That range of political futures imagined by the local populations and by the colonial powers steadily narrowed, however, between late 1918 and 1920, when several colonial (like French Cilicia) and local (like Faisal's Damascus-based Arab Kingdom covering Greater Syria) projects were militarily eliminated by the end of 1920. Other political projects taking shape across the region proved viable in the early 1920s. This chapter turns to this set of colonial and local polities that emerged across the greater Middle East; to the factors contributing to their mobilization, momentum, and consolidation; and to the internal and external struggles shaping their formation and the increasingly contentious interactions among them.

In analyzing the colonial and local political projects, the new technologies, and the new competitive dynamics that gained momentum in the early 1920s, this chapter emphasizes an essential point: the region neither entered nor exited the 1914–1918 phase of the Great War as an evenly patterned political space. This fact strongly shaped the trajectories and fates of emerging polities. Priot to the war, certain parts of the greater Middle East had historically been more and less under central Ottoman, Qajar, or Alawite state control, with shatter zones buffering rival empires and less legible ecologies like desert or highland zones typically enjoying higher levels of local autonomy. Similarly, prewar colonial state formation varied, as areas including Algeria, Tunisia, and Egypt had been occupied by

European powers four to eight decades before 1914, while Morocco and Libya had just begun to be conquered in 1911. Finally, the course of the 1914–1918 conflict took different paths across the multiple fighting fronts in the Ottoman theater. All three of these factors influenced the degree of political fluidity expressed in different regions in the early 1920s.

Keeping this variation in view, the next section critically assesses the 1920 Treaty of Sèvres, pointing out the gaps between the Paris conference's judicial peace terms set out on paper and the sociological reality of ongoing armed conflict and violent contestation across the very different types of political spaces expressed from Morocco to the Iranian Plateau. Working back from the periphery of the former Ottoman system to its core—from Northern Africa to Arabia to Greater Syria and Mesopotamia to Anatolia—these sections inventory the European colonial and local state-building projects emerging and interacting in the early 1920s. This developmental period set the stage for the climactic violent clashes, dealt with in part 3, among these emerging polities in the middle and late 1920s.

SETTLED AND EMERGING POLITIES IN THE 1920 TREATY OF SÈVRES

Eighteen months after convening in Paris in January 1919, a group of dignitaries gathered at the Manufacture nationale de Sèvres porcelain factory in a Paris suburb to sign the final treaty of the peace conference in August 1920. Over the previous year and half, the Allied powers—the heads of state and their accompanying delegations—had hashed out the various postwar territorial, political, military, and economic questions, hearing from delegations from regions of the defeated Central powers, to negotiate the postwar settlement. In June 1919, the Paris conference set out the terms for the defeated German Empire with the signing of the first of the Paris treaties, the Treaty of Versailles. Over subsequent months, three more were signed in other Parisian suburbs, setting terms for Austria (Treaty of Saint Germain, September 1919), Bulgaria (Treaty of Neuilly, November 1919), and Hungary (Trianon, June 1920). The final treaty of the Paris Peace Conference, signed on August 10, 1920, in Sèvres, settled terms among the remaining defeated Central power, Turkey; the principal Allied powers" (the British Empire, France, Italy, and Japan); and other powers (Armenia, Belgium, Greece, the Hejaz, Poland, Portugal, Roumania, Kingdom of Serbs, Croats, and Slovenes, and Czechoslovakia).[10]

The hundred-page Treaty of Sèvres set out the international legal terms of the peace settlement, not only for the Ottoman Empire but for the breadth of the greater Middle East, from Morocco to Persia and from the Black Sea to Sudan.[11] Much more than the infamous Sykes-Picot Agreement, it was in the League of Nations–ratified Sèvres treaty that the European powers actually drew lines on the map, negotiated which colonial power got what, and determined which local claims were recognized over others. As a "final" settlement, however, the article-by-article peace terms set out on paper and signed that August glossed over the complex, continuing wartime interactions in the region that were, even at the moment the treaty was being signed, rapidly making the treaty terms a dead letter.

The most important aspect needing to be unglossed is that, despite the undifferentiated way the treaty referenced the territories being divvied up, the post-Ottoman map was neither flat nor blank nor homogenous. There was a crucial distinction between what need to be understood as *settled* versus *emergent* polities referenced in the treaty. These two categories correlated closely to parts of the map occupied *before* versus *during* the war by various European powers. The first group, the more or less "settled" polities, comprised the former Ottoman territories taken de jure and de facto decades before 1911. These included Algeria (occupied by the French in 1830), Tunis (occupied by the French in 1881), Egypt (occupied by the British in 1882), Sudan (occupied by British in 1899), and Cyprus (occupied by the British in 1878). To clarify, "settled" refers to the boundaries of the polities, not politics within them. In these units, decades of pre–Great War military conquest, occupation, and colonial state formation had already consolidated dominant modes of rule and political boundaries. Though there was relatively little contention over the boundaries of units like Algeria, Tunisia, or Egypt after the Mudros armistice, it is important to note there was significant protest and contention mobilized over control *within* these units, including the massive popular revolt in 1919 in Egypt against British protectorate control.[12]

The emergent polities referenced in Sèvres, in contrast, are those where both political boundaries *and* control were in tremendous flux at the time of the treaty signing and the years afterward. These include the territories taken by European powers *at the onset* of the Long Great War, such as

Libya and Morocco in 1911; during the 1914–1918 conflict, such as Syria and Palestine (occupied in 1917–1918), Mesopotamia (Basra, Baghdad, and Mosul, occupied progressively between November 1914 and November 1918), and the Hejaz and other parts of Arabia (not occupied but with varying levels of British involvement); and those occupied in the months after the 1918 Mudros armistice such as Constantinople and the Straits (occupied in late 1918), Smyrna (occupied by Greece in May 1919), southern Anatolia (occupied partially by Italy and France in late 1918 and early 1919), and parts of eastern Anatolia and Transcaucasia (lightly occupied by British forces in late 1918). Each of these regions destabilized by the war saw continued conflict through the next decade among rival colonial and local efforts to remake the post-Ottoman map.

The following sections begin with the settled and emergent polities referenced in Northern Africa then spiral back toward the core of the former Ottoman system, examining the complex and interconnected

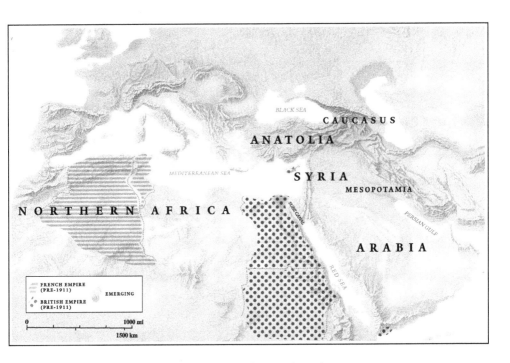

FIGURE 4.1 Map of settled and emerging polities in the early 1920s.

Source: Author adaptation from public domain.

TABLE 4.1 Emerging polities in the early 1920s

Region	Colonial Projects	Local Projects
Northern Africa	French protectorate in Morocco Spanish protectorate in Morocco Italian colonial state in Libya	Atlas jihads Rif Republic Tripolitanian Republic Sanusi state
Anatolia/Caucasus	British Straits Commission Greek, Italian, and French presence in regions of Anatolia (all removed by 1923) Soviet creation of Transcaucasian Federation in 1923	Turkish Republic Kurdish polities mobilized from the mid-1920s Greater Armenian Republic Transcaucasian Republics
Syria	French mandate (splitting Lebanon and Syria and subdividing Syria) British mandate for Palestine (splitting Palestine and Transjordan)	Arab Kingdom, Great Syrian Revolt Zionist proto-nation/state Emergent Palestinian nation Hashemite emirate
Mesopotamia	British mandate	Hashemite kingdom Kingdom of Kurdistan, tribal autonomy
Arabia	British sphere of indirect influence British Aden Colony Italian indirect influence in Yemen	Saudi Sultanate of Najd Hashemite Kingdom of the Hejaz Idrissi Emirate of Asir Imamate in Yemen

emerging political projects catalyzed by the war in Arabia, Greater Syria, Mesopotamia, and Anatolia. I contrast the treaty terms formally set out in Sèvres with an inventory of the actual local and colonial political projects gaining traction in each region (see the figure 4.1 map and table 4.1). These sections also highlight connections among subregions and how interdependent these projects were with respect to neighboring contexts (i.e., how the French state-building projects in Greater Syria and Cilicia, Mustafa Kemal's Turkish state-building project, and Syrian state-building projects intersected).

SETTLED AND EMERGENT POLITIES IN NORTHERN AFRICA

Though the Sèvres treaty dealt primarily with the former territories of the Ottoman Empire in the eastern Mediterranean (Anatolia, Thrace, and the Arab provinces), the victorious Allied powers (Britain, France, and Italy) also included numerous clauses related to Northern Africa and the Mediterranean (Egypt, Sudan, Cyprus, Libya, and the Aegean Islands) they had occupied before or on the eve of the war. In this respect, the treaty retroactively cleaned up a variety of nineteenth and early twentieth century colonial faits accomplis, legally inscribing these protectorates and colonies in the postwar international order being created by the League of Nations. The Part III treaty sections dealing with Northern Africa were grouped according to the interested colonial power: Britain (Section IX on Egypt, Sudan, and Cyprus), France (Section X on Morocco and Tunis), and Italy (Section XI on Libya and the Aegean Islands).

SETTLED POLITIES: EGYPT, SUDAN, CYPRUS, ALGERIA, AND TUNISIA

The Khedivate of Egypt had been under various forms of British control since 1882, when British forces put down the Urabi Revolt and occupied the Suez Canal Zone. Administratively, the British imposed a form of indirect rule that retained the Mehmet Ali dynasty but paired it with a British consul general, a position filled by Lord Cromer from 1882 to 1896. During this period of de facto British rule, the Ottomans still retained a legal right of sovereignty over the Khedivate of Egypt and Sudan, with the sultan the official ruler in international law.[13] On December 18, 1914, a month after declaring war on the Ottomans, the British proclaimed Egypt to be a protectorate. In the Sèvres treaty, Article 101 legally recognized this new status, stipulating that Turkey renounced "rights and title in or over Egypt." Turkey also relinquished any claims on Sudan, being forced to recognize the 1899 Anglo-Egyptian Condominium established after the suppression of the Mahdist revolution. With regard to Cyprus, which Britain had occupied after the 1878 Conference of Berlin, the Sèvres treaty recognized Britain's annexation of the island on November 6, 1914 (a day after declaring war on the Ottoman Empire), and stipulated that the Ottoman sultan relinquish any right of tribute formerly paid by the island and that Turkish nationals residing in Cyprus would acquire British nationality.

The Sèvres peace terms referencing Egypt, however, glossed over the previous twenty-four months of tumult the British had faced there since the 1918 armistice. From 1914 to 1918, Egypt served as a huge staging base for British operations in the eastern Mediterranean, first for Gallipoli and then for the campaign into southern Syria across the Sinai. Egyptian labor had been key in the transport of Indian and ANZAC troops between the Indian Ocean and Mediterranean theaters, Egypt had supplied tons of food and supplies, and over 1.5 million Egyptians had been conscripted. Having borne these heavy costs, Egyptians had high expectations for independence after the war, which Saad Zaghlul and a delegation of other nationalist sought to present before the Paris Peace Conference. The delegation's arrest and exile to Malta in March 1919 provoked a massive popular response in late March and April that included demonstrations and strikes and mobilized a broad spectrum of society across classes, both Muslims and Christians, and in urban and rural contexts. In the countryside, Egyptians attacked military and civilian installations, escalating the violence and leading to over eight hundred Egyptians being killed that summer. The Milner Commission was sent to study the situation that December. It took until 1921, however, for their report, recommending the abolition of the protectorate, to be published. On February 22, 1922, that advice was finally acted on when Britain declared Egypt's nominal independence.

In 1920, there were two other relatively settled polities in Northern Africa, Algeria and Tunisia, both of which had been incorporated into the French Empire in the nineteenth century. In 1920, the status of French Algeria, occupied ninety years before when the French invaded and abolished the Ottoman *deylik*, was not in question and not mentioned in the Sèvres treaty. Tunisia, however, was mentioned, with Article 120 stipulating that Turkey had to recognize the French protectorate, retroactive to its initiation in the 1881 Treaty of Bardo with the Hafsid bey. Though anticolonial mobilization and contention increased greatly in both Algeria and Tunisia throughout the 1920s and 1930s, the struggle centered, as in Egypt, on challenging control within, rather than over defining, a settled polity.

EMERGENT POLITIES IN MOROCCO AND LIBYA: THE RIF REPUBLIC AND THE SANUSI NETWORK

The remaining entities in Northern Africa referenced in the Sèvres treaty, Morocco and Libya, however, were far less settled. The treaty's brief references to them completely glossed over the fact that French, Spanish, and Italian colonial designs and various local mobilizations were dynamically evolving and interacting. Though Morocco had never been part of the Ottoman territorial sphere, it was referenced alongside the other former Ottoman provinces in articles 118 and 119, which stipulated that Turkey recognize the political and economic status of France's protectorate treaty with the Moroccan sultan, retroactive to its signing on March 30, 1912. The Spanish zones in the north and Saharan south presumably fell under these provisions, but the special international status for Tangier created in the 1906 Algeciras Treaty was also not mentioned and had to be dealt with three years later in the 1923 Lausanne negotiations. Most of the Allied powers had already diplomatically recognized France's status (and Spain's secondary position) over Morocco, with Italy (1912), Great Britain (1914), and the United States (1917) all signing agreements about this with France during the war. The provisions in the Treaties of Versailles (1919) and Sèvres (1920) forcing Germany and Turkey to recognize the protectorate set up in Morocco further enshrined its legal status in the new international order being constructed in Paris.[14]

Though settled in international law, Morocco was far from a settled polity on the ground. The French, Spanish, and Alawites (the Moroccan dynasty) were all far from exercising much actual state control, and Morocco itself was far from even being a clearly defined territorial entity. The "Morocco" cursorily referred to in the Sèvres treaty had been split up in 1912 in complicated ways among French, Spanish, and international (around Tangier) zones, but these zones' actual boundaries remained fuzzy. In the east, the 1845 Convention of Lalla Marnia constituted the first and last time the frontier with Algeria had been negotiated, with the border relatively clearly demarcated southward from the Mediterranean coast one hundred miles inland to the southeast of Oujda. The frontier further south and southwest was left undefined until 1912, when a line proposed by the French high commissioner in Oujda, Maurice Varnier, was extended beyond Figuig to administratively delineate between Moroccan and Algerian.[15] Here, and even more so further southwest, the French, ostensibly in control of both sides of the border, had no urgent need to parse a boundary in an area officially designated *confins algéro-marocaines* through the protectorate period. The frontier between the Spanish and French zones in the north was also only vaguely spelled out in the 1904 and 1912 agreements between the two countries (following the Moulouya River south from its Mediterranean outlet inland about forty miles then along the Ouergha River going west and then northwest toward Ksar el-Kebir and west along the Loukkos River to the Atlantic coast) but had never actually been surveyed. The zone around Spain's fishing port foothold at Ifni on the southern Atlantic coast was relatively well defined, but its Saharan territory was only very loosely marked as south of the Draa River.

Within the roughly sketched out and subdivided space of the Sharifian Alawite dynasty, two colonial states and multiple nodes of local autonomy were emerging in the early 1920s. The French and Spanish colonial states had thus far only made limited progress in "pacifying" (the euphemism used for military conquest and occupation) and extending state administration in their respective zones. From 1907 to the outbreak of the war in 1914, the French military had extended control over much of the Atlantic plain inland from Rabat and Casablanca and through the corridor passing through Meknes, Fes, and Taza toward the border with Algeria. The Middle and High Atlas Mountains ranges, the southern reaches of the Rif Mountains that extended into the French zone, and the Saharan and southern Jabal Saghro range, however, remained fully self-governing. Between 1914 and 1918, France kept a skeleton military crew in the protectorate to preserve the status quo, as most of the French and colonial soldiers in Morocco were redeployed to the Western Front. The Spanish made no further progress in their zone. On the Atlantic coast, they had occupied the inland plain from Larache, made Tetuan (twenty-five miles south of the Spanish enclave in Ceuta) the capital of the zone, and occupied limited territory south of Melilla. All of the mountainous interior—the Jbala, Ghomara, and Rif ranges—remained autonomous, though the Spanish (and Germans) put many of the tribal chiefs on their payroll in an attempt to mollify them.[16]

After the end of the war in Europe, both France and Spain restarted "pacification" operations in 1919. Facing the economic constraints of postwar French austerity and a reluctance to shed more French blood in Morocco after horrific losses during the Great War, the French resident-general Hubert Lyautey prioritized securing and developing what he termed *le Maroc utile* (useful Morocco)—the economically profitable lowland areas with cities, arable land, and phosphate deposits. *Maroc inutile* (useless Morocco)—the relatively autonomous highland and desert areas, which were logistically much harder to conquer and whose populations were militarily stronger—was deemed a lesser priority. The French administration in Rabat was content to maintain a mixed topography of state and self-governed spaces in their zone in which the colonial state controlled the lowlands and strategic access routes through the mountainous interior but left blocks (*zones de dissidence*) of tribal autonomy in place around the Taza Gap (through which the route to Algeria passed between the Rif and Middle Atlas ranges), in much of the central High Atlas, and in the desert south. This status quo began to shift in the mid-1920s when warfare related to the Spanish zone began to spill over and forced a change in French policy.

In Morocco's northern zone, the Spanish also reinitiated military operations in 1919. With the war's conclusion, the Spanish Army of Africa officers convinced the civilian leadership in Madrid to give them financial, material, and troop support, including several air squadrons, to complete the "pacification" of the northern zone and link their widely separated enclaves. A military general, Damaso Berenguer, was appointed high commissioner in Tetuan. In the western Jibala region, Berenguer's forces made considerable progress against the local strongman al-Raisuli between 1919–1920, who they pushed toward his stronghold in Tazrut; against the Anjera tribes around Tangier; and they occupied Chaouen in October 1920. In the east, the commandant general appointed in 1920 in Melilla, Manuel Fernandez Silvestre, quickly occupied the lowland plains south of Melilla before turning southwest up the Wadi Kart toward the Rif foothills.

It was here that the Spanish ran into trouble. Between 1920 and 1921, Silvestre's forces advanced further and further into the central Rif area south of the bay in Alhucemas, where the strongest tribal group, the Ait Waryaghar, was based.[17] Silvestre's military strategy was to establish a string of blockhouses and small military posts at key points to hold the territory. By April 1921, over 140 posts had been constructed with more than 25,700 men garrisoned in them. The forward front line extended eighty miles to the west of Melilla and stretched south from Sidi Driss, on the coast, down to Anwal then Zoco el Telata de Metalsa.[18] These rapid gains would prove ephemeral. In the summer of 1921, the Ait Waryaghar tribe responded to this advance with the attack at Anwal that led to the stunning Spanish defeat described earlier in the chapter. Five more years of war and a joint Franco-Spanish force of more than two hundred thousand troops would be required to suppress the Rif Republic that emerged and evolved in response to the expansion of the Spanish colonial state.

Before this, the Rif tribes had rarely acted in concert. They typically recognized the Moroccan sultan as a religious-political leader, but the *makhzan*, or central state, had little capacity to tax the populace or interfere militarily, and the functionally autonomous Rif tribes adjudicated relations among themselves. Some, including the al-Khattabi family, initially thought the Spanish might install a beneficial collaborative form of protectorate rule; one Khattabi son, M'hammad, went to school in Melilla, then Malaga, before studying engineering at the College of Mines in Madrid, while Mohammed, another son, studied Islamic law at the Qarawayn University in Fes before working for the Spanish administration in Melilla as a judge. Mohammed also edited the Arabic sections of *El Telgrama de Rif*, one of the principle newspapers in the Spanish zone.[19] These hopes were dashed, however, when the Spanish generously supported military pacification operations but provided virtually nothing to the local population reeling from drought conditions and widespread famine in 1919–1920.[20] Anti-Spanish resistance gained momentum in the Rif and collaborationist elites like the al-Khattabis eventually severed relations with the colonial state.

With the death of the elder al-Khattabi, Mohammed bin Abd el-Krim assumed command, consolidating his own authority and beginning to centralize and rationalize a core governing structure during the spring of 1921. He instituted a paid police force and army, carried out a census counting 19,600 able-bodied men, purchased guns, and dug defensive trenches.[21] After an abundant harvest in June, Abd el-Krim was ready to strike. In late July, he ordered a coordinated attack across the overextended Spanish lines, decimating the forward units at Anwal and routing the Spanish retreat back to Melilla. His forces gained weapons, munitions, and food supplies in the victory. The Anwal success made it possible for the Ait Waryaghar and other eastern Rif tribes to imagine Abd el-Krim's vision for a Rif polity "with a government and a flag."

Throughout 1922 and 1923, Abd el-Krim and his core nucleus of commanders—many related by kinship and intermarriage—developed the administrative structures of al-Jumhuriyya al-Riffia, or Republic of the Rif. These included establishing courts; enforcing disciplinary mechanisms to undercut tribal autonomy (imposing *shari'a* forms of individualistic justice instead of collectivistic customary law); economic regulation, including the collection of customs duties and Islamic taxes; and creating a regular army. In early 1923, the financial foundation for this project was reinforced when the Spanish paid the Rif government four million pesetas in exchange for Spanish prisoners captured during the Anwal battle. The symbolic legitimacy of the Rif state was also consolidated in early 1923 as tribal leaders gathered to sign the *bay'a*, or oath of allegiance document, in the Rif capital, Ajdir. Across Morocco's northern zone, Abd el-Krim was increasingly recognized as the *amir al-mu'iminin*, "commander of the faithful," in charge of mobilizing a political-religious struggle, or *jihad*, against the Spanish Christian invader.

There was a similar juxtaposition of emerging colonial and local polities in the former Ottoman Tripolitania, Cyrenaica, and Fezzan provinces in the early 1920s. The Treaty of Sèvres cleared up Italian claims in Libya and the Aegean Sea that were left unsettled after the 1911–1912 Italo-Ottoman War. Though Italy had grandiosely declared Tripolitania and Cyrenaica to be under the full sovereignty of the Italian kingdom in November 1911, the Italo-Ottoman War continued for another year in Tripoli and Cyrenaica then eventually spread to the Aegean Sea, where Italy occupied a number of Ottoman islands. When Montenegro and the other Balkan League states also declared war on the empire, the Ottomans settled quickly with Italy, pledging in the Treaty of Lausanne (signed October 18, 1912) to withdraw Ottoman officers and soldiers from Tripolitania and Cyrenaica on the condition that Italy also withdraw from its occupied Aegean Islands.

Two days before the treaty signing, however, the Ottomans preemptively granted Tripolitania and Cyrenaica formal independence to undercut Italy's claims in Libya. As chapter 2 detailed, the Ottomans and Germans continued to liaise with the Sanusi in Cyrenaica, providing advisers, weapons, and supplies to support an attack on British-controlled Egypt in 1916. To remove any ambiguity over the legal status of these former Ottoman provinces, Section XI of Part III of the Treaty of Sèvres tersely states that "Turkey definitely renounces all rights and privileges which under the Treaty of Lausanne of October 18, 1912, were left to the Sultan in Libya" and that Turkey acknowledged Italy's right to fourteen islands in the Aegean that had been taken during the Ottoman-Italian War.

As with Morocco, the Paris Peace Conference's terse, blanket legal recognition of Italy's claims in northern Africa did not reflect the meager reality of their actual physical control. Between 1914 and 1918, the Italians were pushed back to just two coastal cities (Tripoli and Khums). Several statelets were formed in the liberated areas of Tripolitania, including an independent republic at Misurata in 1915. At the war's end, leaders in the province, including Sulayman al-Baruni and Ramadan al-Suwayhili, declared the formation of a single government in 1918: the Tripolitanian Republic. The Italians themselves concluded a treaty in 1919 with this entity, recognizing spheres of control and the autonomy of the Tripolitanian parliament.

In the east, the Italians and British also negotiated the April 1917 Akramah treaty with the Sanusi leader Sayyid Muhammad Idris. In this agreement, the Sanusi pledged to sever their alliance with the Ottomans, expel Ottoman military advisers, and monitor the frontier with Tripolitania to prevent pro-Turkish infiltration and agitation in return for the Italians accepting the status quo of Sanusi autonomy. The Sanusi, no longer under nominal Ottoman suzerainty, now received diplomatic recognition as an independent polity. This was reinforced in the October 1920 Accord of al-Rajma in which the Italians acknowledged Idris as amir, recognized Sanusi administrative autonomy, and agreed to an annual subsidy. In a follow-up agreement, the 1921 Bu Mariam treaty, Italy formally recognized the presence of two sovereignties, themselves and the Sanusi, in Cyrenaica.

In late 1921, however, Italy shifted modes in Libya. Having tacitly and explicitly accepted the coexistence of the colonial and local polities, the Italians, like the Spanish in northern Morocco, shifted to an aggressive policy of total military conquest to eliminate local autonomy. Under directives from the newly appointed governor, Giuseppe Volpi, Italian forces began to expand control outward from Tripoli in the fall of 1921. Misurata was taken in January 1922 and, in April, troops under Rodolfo Graziani secured most of the Tripolitanian coastline. When Mussolini became prime minister in October 1922, pacification operations in Libya were prioritized even more by Rome and expanded southward. By the end of 1923, the Italian forces had overcome the factionalized resistance in the Tripolitania province. In 1924, they subdued much of the more remote Fezzan region south of Tripolitania, though ongoing resistance continued there until 1930. By the mid-1920s, the Italian colonial state had succeeded in consolidating control over virtually all of western Libya.

In the east, however, they were less successful. In 1923, the newly installed Fascist government abrogated the previous treaty arrangements with the Sanusi and went on the attack. The Italians made quick gains along the Cyrenaican coast by the end of 1924, but, like the Spanish, their attempts to move up into higher elevations—in this case, the upland areas of the Jabal Akhdar—faced stiff resistance from the decades-old Sanusi network anchored there. By 1925, the status quo in Cyrenaica looked very much like what had emerged in the Rif. An expanding colonial state was in a standoff with a strong local autonomous polity, the Sanusi proto-state, which it could not overcome. It would take the Italians seven more years of brutal colonial war to finally destroy the Sanusi polity rooted in Cyrenaica, a story to which Chapter 6 returns.

CONTENDING EMERGING POLITIES IN ARABIA

As much as anywhere else on the post-Ottoman map, the Arabian Peninsula was far from a settled political space in the early 1920s. But, as with Morocco and Libya, the relevant Treaty of Sèvres's political articles (Part III, Section VIII) relayed simplistic terms that selectively acknowledged certain political realities while completely ignoring others. The Arabian Peninsula was one of the few places in the greater Middle East in which there was no European colonial state in formation attempting to *directly* reshape the postwar map. A British zone of influence in the peninsula was internationally accepted (though Italy made a play for influence in Yemen), yet within this zone, outside of the Aden Protectorate (established in 1839), the British acted more as a referee than an active player in struggles amongst multiple local emerging polities.

The single post-Ottoman Arabian polity recognized in the 1920 Sèvres treaty was the Kingdom of the Hejaz. Sharif Husayn declared the entity's independence within the western coastal region of Arabia, including

Mecca and Medina, when he launched the Arab Revolt with British backing in 1916. In the Sèvres treaty, the Hejaz was recognized as a "free and independent state." Its king, Sharif Husayn, was himself not a signatory to the Sèvres treaty, though the Hejaz was a founding member of the League of Nations. Three brief treaty articles dealt with the kingdom. Article 98 stated "Turkey, in accordance with the action already taken by the Allied Powers, hereby recognises the Hedjaz as a free and independent State, and renounces in favour of the Hedjaz all rights and titles over the territories of the former Turkish Empire situated outside the frontiers of Turkey as laid down by the present Treaty, and comprised within the boundaries which may ultimately be fixed." Article 99 affirmed that the king was obliged to assure pilgrimage access to Muslims from all over the world and to protect the religious foundations, *awqaf*, established there by global Muslims. Article 100 ensured trade access in the Arabian Peninsula for Allied powers. Article 98 concluded with a statement that the territories of the Hejaz would be "comprised within the boundaries *which may ultimately be fixed*" (emphasis mine), which proved to be a telling foreshadowing of political transformations to come. These would be forced on the Hashemite polity by other Arabian actors, not recognized in the treaty, who had also begun mobilizing during and after the 1914–1918 hostilities.

The new Arabian political order that emerged in the 1920s was shaped by several factors including the region's geostrategic importance, the internal dynamics of contending local state building projects, and the interactions between these Arabian emerging polities and neighboring emerging polities in greater Syria and Mesopotamia. As a landmass, Arabia sits between the two waterways linking the Mediterranean Sea to the Indian Ocean. The British were the European empire most invested in this lateral linkage (which was vital for transport and communication lines to India, Singapore, Australia, and New Zealand). From the nineteenth century, they implemented a littoral strategy aimed at securing the Suez Canal, Red Sea, Bab al-Mandab, Gulf of Aden, to Indian Ocean and Persian Gulf, Strait of Hormuz, to Indian Ocean pathways. Coasts were to be secured—which was done through the annexing of Aden as a Crown colony in 1839, the imposition of indirect rule in Egypt in the early 1880s and in Sudan in the 1890s, trucial agreements with local chiefs in the Persian Gulf through the nineteenth century, and indirect British rule in southern Persia—but interior hinterlands were left more or less alone. In the greater Red Sea to Horn of Africa area, however, the British were not the only European colonial power with strategic interests: Italy had staked a claim by going into Eritrea and Somaliland in the 1880s and 1890s while France also grabbed a foothold in Somaliland (Djibouti) opposite Aden in 1894. Throughout the 1920s and 1930s, the British were wary of Italian interference in Arabia, particularly in Yemen, where Italy developed a patronage relationship with the Imam Yahya.

It is telling that the only references to Arabia in the Treaty of Sèvres were to the Hejaz. Implicitly, the League of Nations assumed Britain's prerogative as the sole Great Power hegemon in Arabia. In fact, its Arabian policy was torn between three competing camps: one based out of Delhi and expressing the foreign policy interests of the British Raj, one based out of British Aden (under Delhi but with its own priorities), and one based out of Cairo and by extension London. During the 1914–1918 conflict, each of these poles pressed for different policies. The British Raj's priorities centered on the security of the Persian Gulf and the related extension of British power into Mesopotamia. British Indian forces fought the bulk of the Mesopotamian campaign and British India administrators laid the initial groundwork for British rule in Iraq. British India also pursued its own policies in eastern Arabia, cultivating, through the work of agents Shakespear and St. Jean Philby, relations with Ibn Saud in the interior, whom they tried to mobilize against the pro-Ottoman Rashidis in the Ha'il region. One of the India Office's overriding concerns was to contain Arab nationalist and pan-Islamic sentiments. In contrast, Aden's sole priority was to keep this critical node of the London to India Suez route secure.[22] Here, the policy was to encourage Muhammad al-Idrissi, a leader in Asir (a region up the Red Sea coast from Aden) to rebel against the pro-Ottoman Imam Yahya, who ruled in northern Yemen. From the Cairo Office, the British Arab Bureau's focus was to cultivate the relationship with Sharif Husayn in the Hejaz and foment the anti-Ottoman Arab Revolt. Following the 1918 armistice, these camps' divergent priorities fragmented Britain's vision for the future of Arabia.

The onset of the war, the defeat of the Ottoman Empire, and the increase of revenue and support streams from external sources had made new political visions thinkable for multiple local actors in the Arabian Peninsula. These included the Hashemites in the Hejaz, the Rashidis in Ha'il, the Saudis in the Najd, the Sabbagh family in Kuwait, the various emirates between Kuwait and Oman, the Idrissid amir in Asir, and the Imam in Yemen. In stark contrast to other regions where local emerging polities (like the Rif or Sanusi proto-states) had to compete against European colonial states, in Arabia they had to compete with each other. The primary struggle in the early 1920s was in the center of the peninsula between the Hashemite Kingdom of the Hejaz and the Saudi Sultanate of the Najd.

Since the Husayn-McMahon correspondence in 1915–1916, in which the British promised Sharif Husayn a post-Ottoman Arab Kingdom, the Hashemite political imaginary had been rapidly adapting to a changing political landscape through the course of the Arab Revolt, the post-armistice British and French military occupations in Greater Syria and Mesopotamia, the peace negotiations, and the ultimate demise of Faisal's Damascus-based Arab Kingdom in July 1920. The Hashemites nevertheless continued to make claims for parts of Syria and Mesopotamia, which bore fruit when the British installed Abdullah, another of Husayn's sons, as amir over the eastern half of a partitioned Palestine, Transjordan, in the spring of 1921 and made Faisal king of Iraq in August 1921. During this period, their father, Husayn (king of the Hejaz from 1916 until his abdication in 1924), and older brother, Ali (king from October 1924 through December 1925), attempted to consolidate control within and beyond the Hejaz in Arabia.

As the Sèvres treaty language indicated, the boundaries of the Kingdom of the Hejaz needed to be "ultimately fixed" in virtually every direction other than the Red Sea coastline in 1920. The core consisted of the urban areas of Mecca and Medina—the two holy cities that were pilgrimage destinations and commercial and educational centers—and Jedda, the Hejaz region's primary seaport. Outside these urban areas, the Hashemites had forged links with tribal groups during the Arab Revolt, extending loose administrative control to areas of southern Syria, particularly the Ma'an province and other areas south of Amman along the Hejaz railway, as they progressed toward Damascus. To the south of Mecca, Sharif Husayn aspired to control the coastline down to Asir.

The most problematic territorial claim of the Kingdom of the Hejaz was to the east, toward the interior, where it ran into the Najd polity being forged in Central Arabia by Ibn Saud. The House of Saud had a long history of state formation and political expansion from its tribal base anchored in the town of Riyadh. In the eighteenth century, a reformist Islamic jurist, Mohamed bin Abd al-Wahhab, gained a strong following in this area and established a religio-political alliance with the dominant chieftain, Mohamed bin Al-Saud. The Saud-Wahhab alliance created an expansionary state that unified the peninsula politically in the mid-1700s under the Emirate of Diriya, which waxed until it was defeated by Ottoman-Egyptian forces deployed in the 1810s to take back the Hejaz. Following this defeat, a truncated Saudi state, ruling over Najd and part of Ha'il, survived through the late nineteenth century. This second Saudi state was defeated by Ottoman-backed forces of the Rashidi dynasty of Ha'il in the early 1890s, after which the Saud family took refuge in Kuwait.[23]

In 1902, Abdul Aziz bin Abd al-Rahman Al-Saud successfully took back Riyadh and, over the next decade, reconsolidated Saudi control over the Najd. He also expanded eastward into al-Hasa (a massive oasis complex south of Kuwait), gaining a port outlet to the Persian Gulf in 1913.

FIGURE 4.2 Ibn Saud's Ikhwan Army on the March near Habl, 1911 (W. Shakespeare, Royal Geographical Society)

Britain's invasion of Basra in November 1914 opened up more possibilities for expansion and resources. Ibn Saud and the British signed the Treaty of Darin in December 1915, recognizing Saudi lands as a British protectorate and pledging financial support for Saud to attack the pro-Ottoman Rashidis in the Ha'il region.

The 1918 Allied-Ottoman Mudros armistice did nothing to dampen the intra-Arabian tensions primed by the conflict, particularly in the transition zone between the Hejaz and the Najd, where Husayn and Ibn Saud's forces clashed repeatedly. By the summer of 1919, as the peace negotiations were at full steam in Paris, Ibn Saud stood poised to invade the Hejaz, after key victories over the Hashemites in Khurma and Turaba. The British intervened, though, instructing Ibn Saud to back off and withdraw to the Najd. With tacit British acceptance, Ibn Saud instead turned to expand his reach to the north, east, and south from the summer of 1921.

Ibn Saud's first priority was to eliminate the threat of the Rashidi power base four hundred miles to the northwest of Riyadh in the Jabal Shammar region and around the town of Ha'il. The Rashidi-Saud rivalry in Central Arabia stretched back to the mid-1800s and had escalated during the Great War with Ottoman and British patronage of the rivals. By the fall of 1921, Saud's forces had overcome the Rashidis and taken Ha'il. Ibn Saud now had a power base in Northern-Central Arabia from which to access the Jawf date palm oasis and the Wadi Sirhan, a shallow depression that serves as the primary corridor connecting central Arabia to southeast Syria.

The nascent Sultanate of the Najd's northern push brought it up against and into conflict with the two other emerging Hashemite polities, the British-backed colonial states in Transjordan and Iraq, where Abdullah and Faisal had just been installed as rulers in 1921, and the French and Arab polities competing in Syria. In the desert spaces where Arabia transitioned into southern Syria and Mesopotamia, the transhumant groups that traversed these areas proved key actors driving state formation and territorialization through the 1920s. One of these groups was the Ikhwan, partially sedentarized groups drawn largely from the northern Mutayr and Ajman tribes; from the early 1900s, they had adopted a strict Wahhabi code and lived in garrison villages called *hujar*.[24] The Ikhwan formed the backbone of Ibn Saud's military power, but they also repeatedly exacerbated international tensions by raiding incessantly across still-undefined frontier zones into eastern Transjordan, southern Iraq, and Kuwait.

Across this northern frontier, Saudi state expansion was the primary driver of border making and territorialization throughout the 1920s and into the 1930s. In the northwest, the key area of contention was the Al-Jawf region and the Wadi Sirhan, which lay between the emerging Saudi, Transjordan, and Syrian spheres of control. In this region, the Ruwalla tribe was the strongest group, which made them strategically important to Ibn Saud, Abdullah, the British, and the French. The Ruwalla, led by Nuri al-Sha'alan, played off these interested powers, though they were frequently in conflict with the Ikhwan, who were pushing to extend Saudi control toward Syria. In August 1922, the British annexed the Ruwalla territories to Transjordan, but the Ikhwan continued to raid into this territory, including several excursions reaching the outskirts of Amman. To the north and northeast, Ibn Saud's Ikhwan pressed against southern Iraq, where the Mutayr and Ajman groups continued regular raiding into the Muntafiq region, and Kuwait, where Ibn Saud had a long-running territorial dispute with the amir, al-Sabbagh. The Saudis, having earlier gained Persian Gulf access through the ports at al-Qatif and al-Jubail, added extra pressure on Kuwait by imposing a trade blockade to ensure all the customs on all goods headed into the Arabian interior went into the Najd sultanate's coffers.

Ibn Saud also expanded control southward, exploiting tensions between the Hejaz, Asir, and Yemen. In Asir (the region between Yemen and the Hejaz), a leader in the city of Sabya, Sayyid Muhammed al-Idrissi, had signed a treaty with the British and revolted against the Ottomans in June 1915, creating a semi-independent Asir emirate. After the 1918 Mudros armistice, however, the Idrissid Emirate in Asir was severely at odds with Britain's other client, Sharif Husayn's Kingdom of the Hejaz. Earlier, in 1911, Husayn put down an Asir revolt on behalf of the Ottomans, pointedly disparaging al-Idrissi's North African origins (his grandfather was from Fes and al-Idrissi himself studied with the Sanusi in Kufra), and in 1919–1920, Husayn focused on turning local tribal chiefs against him. In the spring of 1920, al-Idrissi reached out to Ibn Saud to aid him against Husayn, and in the summer of 1922, Ibn Saud responded by sending his son Faisal down with a contingent of four thousand Ikhwan fighters. The gradual increase of Saudi involvement in the early 1920s led to the de facto incorporation of Asir into the Sultanate of the Najd.

Throughout this period of Saudi expansion, the British attempted repeatedly to arbitrate among their various clients in the Arabian Peninsula—in the Hejaz, Najd, and Asir—and Transjordan, Iraq, and Kuwait. One of the first efforts, the 1922 Treaty of Muhammara forestalled British-Saudi conflict over Ikhwan incursions into southern Iraq. The resulting Uqayr Convention, convened by the British high commissioner in Iraq, Percy Cox, recognized Saudi territorial gains and attempted to define boundaries among Iraq, Kuwait, and the Kingdom of the Najd, including a buffer zone in which no military posts or other permanent buildings and nomadic groups could enter to access grazing lands. As Chapter 6 discusses, persistent Ikhwan refusal to abide by these emerging boundaries, and those with Transjordan, would prove pivotal for Saudi state formation in the late 1920s and early 1930s, precipitating a civil war within the Saudi polity over fundamentally different notions of the polity's boundaries.

In 1923, the British convened the Kuwait Conference to again try to resolve persistent borderland disputes involving the Najd and its Hashemite neighbors in the Hejaz, Transjordan, and Iraq. Tensions had come to a head that summer because Najdi tribes kept raiding into Transjordan, Kuwait, Bahrain, and southern Iraq, where the Saudis were also collecting taxes among tribes over whom Faisal claimed jurisdiction. King Husayn refused to join the Kuwait Conference, but he finally sent his son Zayd in January 1924. From Ibn Saud's perspective, the Hashemite ring of British-backed emerging states that surrounded the Najd was a critical threat.[25] That spring, despite a ceasefire, Saudi forces continued to raid, including an attack in the Diwaniyya region of southern Iraq in March that killed seven hundred. By May 1924, it was clear that the conference would not succeed in negotiating a regional system of territorial boundaries; the tension between the Sultanate of the Najd and the Kingdom of the Hejaz was unresolvable.

In July 1924, Ibn Saud consulted with the Wahhabi ulama and Ikhwan leadership and decided to attack the Hejaz. Saudi forces were sent against Transjordan and Iraq in August as a diversion, while a main force attacked Taif, massacring much of the population of this city just east of Mecca, on September 5. That fall, the British Colonial Office officially adopted a policy of nonintervention in the escalating Najd-Hejaz War, informing Husayn on September 24, 1924, that they would not intervene on his behalf. Though the British had cut off Ibn Saud's subvention in May 1924, they decided to let the conflict play out. In early October, Husayn abdicated, putting his son Ali on the throne, as the Wahhabi-Saudi forces entered Mecca on October 18. Ali withdrew to Jedda, where Saud's forces arrived on January 5, 1925, to lay siege.

Through 1925, Ibn Saud pursued a policy of "crawling" into the Hejaz, putting enough pressure on the Hashemite kingdom to make it collapse while also maintaining good relations with European and Muslim countries concerned about the management of the *haj* and with the local Hejazi population, many of whom had grown tired of Hashemite rule. Ibn Saud also pushed into the still undefined northern areas of the Hejaz and southern Transjordan. In April 1925, Ibn Saud sent forces to Aqaba, where Husayn had fled after abdicating (he would be exiled to Cyprus that June), but the British firmly warned him not to attack the critical Red Sea port. That summer, Ibn Saud also withdrew Najdi troops from the disputed Ma'an province, where they had skirmished with Abdullah's forces. On December 6, Ibn Saud's son, Muhammad, finally took Medina, after besieging it for over a month. The last Hashemite stronghold in Jedda was held by Ali, with the support of mainly Palestinian mercenaries. On December 16, 1925, Ali informed the British vice-consul in Jedda that he wished to abdicate, and on December 26, Ibn Saud entered the city. By the end of 1925, Ibn Saud had defeated the Hashemite polity and unified the newly christened Kingdom of the Hejaz and Najd.

EMERGING COLONIAL MANDATES AND LOCAL OPPOSITION IN GREATER SYRIA AND MESOPOTAMIA

The most complicated, and most contentious, Sèvres peace terms were imposed on Syria and Mesopotamia, both of which had been occupied by the British during the course of fighting on these fronts between 1914 and 1918. Uniquely among the former Ottoman territories, the treaty made both subject to the supervision of a Permanent Mandates Commission set up by the League of Nations. Article 94 of the Sèvres treaty stated that both were "provisionally recognised as independent States" but "subject to the rendering of administrative advice and assistance by a Mandatory until such time as they are able to stand alone." The subsequent clause, Article 95, specified that Greater Syria would be split up, completely disregarding the majority sentiment for a unified Greater Syria expressed to the King-Crane Commission the previous summer. Palestine, boundaries still to be determined, would be administered as a separate mandate, enacting the paradoxical provisions of the British-backed Balfour Declaration: support for creating a "national home for the Jewish People" while maintaining "that nothing shall be done which may prejudice the civil and religious rights of existing non-Jewish communities in Palestine."

The "Mandatories" to whom these territories would be entrusted had been fiercely debated over the previous months, as the British prime minister, David Lloyd George, and French president, Georges Clemenceau, hammered out tensions related to the Sykes-Picot terms, each country's relative wartime sacrifices, and their respective deserved Ottoman spoils. The assignation of mandates was finally determined at the April 1920 San Remo conference: France would get Syria, Britain Palestine and Mesopotamia. But, Franco-British imperial rivalries and tensions remained unresolved with respect to three questions: the fate of Faisal and the Syrian National Congress's Arab Kingdom; conflicting French and British interests, including oil and the Kurdish question, in Mosul province; and finally, the question of Palestine, including its still-to-be-determined boundaries and British pledges to the Zionist movement.

In the early 1920s, as the mandate system took shape, the trajectories of Greater Syria and Mesopotamia went in two directions. Mesopotamia was unified, with Basra, Baghdad, and eventually the Mosul province joined together in the newly christened mandate state of Iraq. Syria went the opposite direction, being repeatedly partitioned and fragmented. First, southern Syria was split off and put under British control in Palestine, which was then subdivided on both sides of the Jordan into Palestine and Transjordan. Northern Syria was put under French control and subdivided into Lebanon and Syria. Syria was then subdivided into five separate administrative units: the Sanjak of Alexandretta, the Alawite State, the Aleppo State, the Damascus State, and the Jabal Druze State.

SEGMENTARY FRENCH MANDATE STATE-BUILDING AND LOCAL RESISTANCE IN GREATER SYRIA (1920-1924)

In the early 1920s, the French set about shaping the mandate they had been assigned by the League of Nations. Ostensibly, the goal was to tutor a "Syrian" state to the point that it could "stand alone." In July 1920, the Arab state already constructed over the previous twenty months by the Damascus-based Syrian National Congress and King Faisal was ironically, and tragically, crushed militarily by the tutorial mandate power. At the Maysalun Pass just west of Damascus, the French Armée du Levant defeated the Arab Kingdom's army, forcing Faisal to flee southwest through the Hawran toward British-controlled Palestine. Having demolished the local democratic constitutional political architecture that had emerged in Greater Syria between October 1918 and July 1920, the French set about constructing their own authoritarian colonial apparatus.

This first phase of the French colonial political project in mandate Syria was shaped by several factors: commitments and ties to Lebanese Christian populations; long-standing suspicion of Arab nationalist aspirations for a united Syria and of the Hashemite connection to this dream through Faisal; local resistance movements in the uplands of Latakia, Aleppo and its environs, and in the Jabal al-Druze in the south; and Syria's security position relative to cross-border developments. This last factor encompassed the spillover of the Turkish independence struggle into northern Syria, French suspicions about British intentions in Transjordan, and fears and hopes related to Saudi expansion up the Wadi Sirhan toward the confluence of the emerging Syria, Transjordan, and Iraq political units.

Limited numbers of French troops had been active in the Middle East theater between 1914 and 1918, outside of the Gallipoli campaign and later offensive in Thrace, as France bore the larger burden on the Western Front while the British deployed troops to the fighting fronts in Mesopotamia and greater Syria. After the armistice in October 1918, the British and French began a handover process in areas the British occupied following the withdrawal of the Ottoman Army. The French military occupation progressed from the coastal ports of Syria and Cilicia, where troops were landed, eastward toward the interior urban centers—Aleppo, Homs, Hama, and Damascus—which were under the administrative control of the Damascus-based Arab Kingdom. While French power was quickly established in coastal Syria (and Lebanon) in late 1918 and early 1919, they faced military resistance inland.

Within weeks after the signing of the Treaty of Sèvres, the French announced multiple administrative reorganizations subdividing their Syrian mandate. The first was to separate and enlarge Lebanon. The French had encountered no local resistance as they landed in Beirut and other ports on the Mediterranean coast in the last weeks of the war with the Ottomans in October 1918. After crushing the Arab Kingdom in July 1920, General Gouraud signed Arrêté 318 on August 31, 1920, which created a separate State of Greater Lebanon that encompassed the core area of the Ottoman *mutasarifiyya* of Mount Lebanon plus eastern *cazas* including Hasbaya, Rachaya, Maallaka, and Baalbek. Though designed to benefit their Maronite clients, France's construction of Greater Lebanon transformed the demography of the earlier, smaller autonomous unit, adding a plurality of Sunni, Shi'i, and Druze groups to its population that permanently altered its political dynamics. Two other French decrees divided the rest of Syria into separate administrative units. On August 31, Gouraud signed a decree creating an Alawite State in the Nusayriyya Mountains, with the coastal port of Latakia designated as its administrative capital. The next day, September 1, Arrêté 330 created the State of Aleppo in northern Syria, attaching the autonomous sanjak of Alexandretta (including the port city and its hinterland) to this entity. Finally, on September 3, 1920, the French issued a decree creating the State of Damascus in the center-south, roughly corresponding to the Ottoman vilayet of Damascus minus the Beqaa Valley and some other areas of southern Lebanon.

The fact that the French issued these decrees dividing up mandate Syria's territory did not mean they actually were in control of all of these areas in September 1920. In the Jabal al-Nusayriyya, the Alawite-majority highland area inland from Latakia, a coalition of Alawite groups led by Shaykh Ali Al-Saleh had consolidated control over virtually the whole northern Syrian coastal range by the end of that summer. Al-Saleh's movement was boosted by the simultaneous anti-French resistance coordinated by Ibrahim Hananu in and around Aleppo. Since the spring, Hananu had mobilized a network in northern Syria—establishing the institutions of a proto-state including a legislative council, tax and weapons collection, and a judicial apparatus—that intensified its struggle following the French occupation of Aleppo on July 23, 1920. Hananu and Al-Saleh, with Turkish military supplies and logistical support, coordinated anti-French resistance throughout the fall, extending a Syrian zone of effective local autonomy between Aleppo and the Mediterranean.[26]

On November 29, 1920, Gouraud and the French Army of the Levant launched a campaign to retake Jabal al-Nusayriyya from Shaykh Saleh's Alawite forces and also gained several victories over Hananu-led forces that December. On February 10, 1921, Shaykh Badr, a key Alawite city, fell to the French. During the spring of 1921, the rapprochement between the French and Mustafa Kemal in Cilicia meant a cutback in Turkish aid. Turning abroad, Shaykh Saleh and Ibrahim Hananu sent a joint petition in March 1921 to the League of Nations, making a case for Syrian independence. That summer, the Syro-Palestinian Congress was also formed in Geneva just before the convening of the second League of Nations assembly to argue the same point, but both attempts failed to generate an international response to the Syrian Question.[27]

With no international support forthcoming, both groups lost ground. The French overran Saleh's forces on June 15, though he escaped, went into hiding, and finally gave himself up a year later. Hananu's revolt also was dealt a final blow with the taking of Jabal Zawiya, their last stronghold, in July 1921. By this point, the Franco-Turkish conflict in Cilicia had also been resolved; France withdrew southward, and a more settled Syrian-Turkish border began to crystallize. The end of the military conflict in Cilicia and northern Syria and solidification of a Turkish-Syrian frontier signaled the start of a deeper shift reorienting the Aleppo region's historic economic, cultural, and political primary ties from southern Turkey southward to Damascus.

The French also faced challenges to their control in the early 1920s in the upland areas of the Jabal Hawran, south of Damascus, where they created a separate State of Suwayda in May 1921. This region was also known as the Jabal al-Druze because large numbers of Druze had migrated there, mostly from the Mount Lebanon area, in the seventeenth through nineteenth centuries. In 1909, the Ottomans had to put down a major Druze revolt in Jabal Hawran; during the 1914–1918 hostilities they tried to leave it alone to avoid trouble. This laissez-faire policy left Sultan Atrash, one of the primary Druze leaders, free to send one thousand men to join Faisal's

Arab Revolt forces when they reached Aqaba in 1917. Later, Atrash himself joined Faisal with three hundred more men, and Atrash and his troops were among the first to enter Damascus in late September 1918 and to raise the Arab flag over the city. Atrash supported the Arab Kingdom up to its fall in July 1920. Following the 1921 Franco-Druze agreement creating a separate administration, Atrash continued to wage a guerrilla war against the French, exploiting his ability to use the northern reaches of British-controlled Transjordan as a base, but, in May 1923, the British finally forced him out. Sultan Atrash accepted French authority, at least temporarily.

By 1924, the Syria mandate the League of Nations had assigned the French had taken shape. Within weeks after destroying the Arab Kingdom in the summer of 1920, the French administratively subdivided the "Syria" mentioned in the Treaty of Sèvres into five separate units, systematically segmenting the Greater Syria polity preferred by the majority of the region's inhabitants. They then had to forcibly put down local politico-military movements for autonomy in Latakia and the Jabal al-Nusayriyya, in Aleppo and its hinterland, and in the region of Damascus and the Jabal Druze. In the north, a key to the French success in snuffing out emergent local polities had been the deal they struck with Mustafa Kemal to withdraw from Cilicia in which the Turks agreed to cut off cross-border aid. In the south, Franco-British tensions over frontier between Syria-Lebanon and Palestine-Transjordan remained unresolved. The temporary calm finally established in the Jabal al-Druze, Hawran plain, and other areas of the Damascus state, however, would only last a matter of months.

BRITISH MANDATE STATE-BUILDING IN IRAQ AND PALESTINE: THE HASHEMITE SOLUTION, AMBIVALENCE ABOUT ZIONISM, AND LOCAL ASPIRATIONS

In the Treaty of Sèvres, the League of Nations delegated the mandate authority for Palestine (southern Syria) and Mesopotamia to the British Empire. The British had functionally been the sole Allied power active in the Ottoman theater, apart from a few French auxiliary forces, and it had been British troops—largely from India, Australia, and New Zealand—that advanced on the Mesopotamian and Syrian fighting fronts. In the weeks following the Mudros armistice in October 1918, British forces continued northward, occupying Mosul and a line of cities in southern Anatolia. In 1919 and 1920, the British and French negotiated control of northern Syria and southern Anatolia, with the British handing over control after the two empires agreed the French would take the Syrian mandate, with Palestine and Mesopotamia staying under British control.

Though assigned Mandate Palestine and Iraq, the British did not know yet exactly how they envisioned the post-Ottoman political future of these territories. British Middle East strategy in the fall of 1920 was in turmoil because of intense local resistance to their rule. They had put down a revolution in Egypt the previous spring and summer, provoked by the British arrest of the nationalist Saad Zaghlul on his way to make the case for Egyptian independence at the Paris Peace Conference. In April 1920, the British faced an outbreak of Palestinian pro-independence and anti-Zionist demonstrations during the Nebi Musa festival in Jerusalem. And, from the summer through the fall, the British had brutally put down a massive revolt in the Baghdad, Basra, and Mosul provinces. The revolt had prompted London to shift administrative responsibility for the Iraq mandate from the India Office, which had been in charge since the initial invasion in 1914, to the Colonial Office in early 1921.

In March 1921, the newly appointed colonial secretary, Winston Churchill, convened the Cairo Conference, drawing in the British colonial administrators from across the Middle East including A. T. Wilson (from Persia), Percy Cox (high commissioner for Mesopotamia), Herbert Samuel (high commissioner for Palestine), and Gertrude Bell (Oriental secretary for Cox in Mesopotamia) to deliberate the future of the Palestine and Iraq mandates.[28] The two-week meetings convened at the Semiramis Hotel in Cairo from March 12 to 20 then continued in Jerusalem from March 24 to 30 at Government House, the repurposed German-built Augusta Victoria complex that had previously served as Cemal Pasha's headquarters. The Cairo Conference's main task was twofold: to sort out the conflicting trajectories set in motion by promises to the Hashemites (Husayn-McMahon correspondence), the French (Sykes-Picot Agreement), and the Zionists (Balfour Declaration) about post-Ottoman Syria and Mesopotamia, and to clarify their own priorities for these mandates and in the Arabian Peninsula. Churchill had convinced T. E. Lawrence to join the Colonial Office as assistant for Middle East affairs two months beforehand, and the two came with a basic regional policy sketched out.

Mesopotamia, where the 1920 revolt had exposed the fragility of the British occupation, was taken up first. The British India officials initially in charge after the invasion had envisioned Iraq as an extension of the Raj's sphere of influence, planning to annex Basra and make Baghdad province a protectorate;[29] they had only slowly adjusted to the postwar Wilsonian discourse in which colonial rule had to be cloaked with a nod to self-governance. The acting civil commissioner in Mesopotamia from September 1918 through June 1920, A. T. Wilson, was blamed for not adjusting India-style direct administration, not successfully coopting key Arab and Kurdish intermediaries, and thereby exacerbating anti-British resentment that broke out in revolt in the summer of 1920.[30]

By the time of the revolt, and certainly afterward, the British had two priorities in Mesopotamia, or Iraq, the historic Arabic name of this area now being used for the mandate: (1) transforming the government, or at least its façade, from a British to an Arab administration; and (2) reducing the cost to the treasury, which had skyrocketed to put down the revolt. A new high commissioner, Percy Cox, was installed in October 1920; he quickly put together a provisional government, or "Council of State," ahead of the Cairo Conference. Along with T. E. Lawrence, Gertrude Bell, and Winston Churchill, Cox supported installing Faisal, Sharif Husayn's son, as king over the Arab administration in Iraq. This move assuaged British guilt for abandoning Faisal to the French in Damascus. They also saw advantages to the fact that Faisal was a third party outside existing Iraqi power centers, but he came with Sharifian legitimacy (tracing genealogical descent from the Prophet Mohammed) and had a proven track record collaborating with the British. At the Cairo Conference, Faisal was affirmed as the preferred choice, and, after being confirmed by a British-organized popular referendum that summer, he was crowned king of Iraq on August 21, 1921. The 1922 Anglo-Iraqi treaty signed the following October formalized a dual form of rule split between British and Hashemite administrations. The exact territorial parameters of this entity, however, remained hazily defined. South of Iraq, the British maintained the separate autonomy of Kuwait on one border, but the long desert stretches from Baghdad and Basra toward the Najd and Ha'il regions were left undelineated.

The other pressing issue in Iraq was the fate of Mosul province and what southern Kurdistan's position should be in the newly created Iraq mandate. On one side, Lawrence and Churchill, along with Major Noel, who had been serving as special enjoy in Kurdish regions, supported the creation of a largely autonomous Kurdistan that could serve, similar to the Northwest Frontier Province of India, as a buffer zone with Turkey. On the other side, Cox and Bell supported a policy integrating southern Kurdistan firmly in Mosul province, and thereby to Baghdad and Basra in a single, unified Iraq.

In the early 1920s, as an active, pluralist Iraqi public sphere began to debate the contours of political participation within the hybrid Anglo-Hashemite political and administrative structure being constructed,[31] many Kurds were ambivalent about their political future. The rapid mobilization and success of the Turkish state-building project launched by Mustafa Kemal in late 1919 contributed to this uncertainty. Having ousted the French from Cilicia by the end of 1921, the emerging Turkish Republic aspired to also retain Mosul province. Through the next decade and beyond, the plight of Northern and Southern Kurdistan, the Kurdish majority areas falling in the emerging containers of Mandate Iraq and the newly forming Turkish Republic, continued to be unsettled.

Palestine was the other major item on the Cairo Conference's agenda, and, on March 20, Churchill and the other British officials boarded a train to Jerusalem to discuss it. More than anywhere else in the post-Ottoman Middle East, Britain's overlapping wartime pledges to the French, the Zionist movement, and to the Hashemites (and to Arab self-determination more generally) came into direct conflict in southern Syria. With regards to the French, as the British army occupied western Palestine in 1916–1918 and set up the Occupied Enemy Territory Administration, the Sykes-Picot provision that Palestine west of the Jordan would be designated an international zone fell by the wayside. The French accepted de facto British control and the awarding of the mandate in post-armistice negotiations, but the northern boundaries of Palestine with Lebanon and Syria were left undefined. Across this boundary, both sides would distrust the other's designs on their respective mandates and be wary of efforts to undermine each other through the 1920s.[32]

The pro-Zionist Balfour pledges incorporated in the Treaty of Sèvres begged two questions. The first was the political dimension with regard to what the British were to do with opposing Jewish and Arab aspirations. Despite wording that assured British support for Zionism would not infringe on the rights of the local inhabitants, the Balfour pledge was viewed by these inhabitants as precisely that: a fundamental threat to their own right for self-determination. The King-Crane Commission data from 1919 clearly indicated that the vast majority of the local non-Jewish population supported the idea of an independent Greater Syria and adamantly opposed a separate Palestine in which Jewish in-migration was backed by the mandate power. When the British conference moved from Cairo to Jerusalem, Churchill received Arab (the Muslim-Christian Haifa Congress) and Jewish (the Jewish National Council) Palestinian delegations that presented conflicting claims for the mandate. In the end, though, Churchill dismissed the Palestinian Arab concerns, arguing the language of the mandate charter did not imply the creation of an exclusive national home for the Jewish people or that it would dominate non-Jews.

The territorial dimension was the second question addressed in Jerusalem: What constituted the space of Britain's mandate in Palestine? Namely, did it include both sides of the Jordan Rift Valley? While the western side had been occupied from 1917 by the British, the eastern bank, Transjordan, had been under Hashemite control since the Arab Revolt. The northern territories had been administered, albeit loosely, from Damascus, and the Ma'an province and the rest of the south was ostensibly under the control of Husayn's Kingdom of the Hejaz. Following the Arab Kingdom's defeat at Maysalun, Transjordan's status had remained undetermined: the British high commissioner, Herbert Samuel, requested it be brought under the Palestine administration, but this request was rejected. Instead, a few British political officers were charged with coordinating with local leaders, who were given assurances that Transjordan would not come under the Palestinian administration. The Zionists, for their part, continued to hope for a greater Palestine territory in the mandate that would encompass both banks of the Jordan.

In November 1920, this fluid status quo was disrupted when Abdullah arrived with a group of Hejazi forces en route to avenge the ouster of Faisal from Damascus by the French. Abdullah settled in Amman, one of the villages at which a depot had been built for the Hejaz railway south of Damascus. The British priority was to keep Abdullah in their orbit (they were worried the French would offer him a position replacing his brother

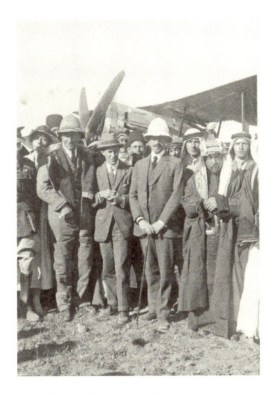

FIGURE 4.2 Amir Abdullah, Herbert Samuel, T. E. Lawrence, and Gertrude Bell at the Amman aerodrome following the British proclamation about Transjordan, April 1921.

Source: American Colony Photo Department, Library of Congress.

in Damascus) and to preserve British control over the strategic corridor between Palestine and Iraq. Rail lines and eventually an oil pipeline were planned to run through this route, connecting the Kirkuk oilfields to the Mediterranean port of Haifa. Transjordan was also a key territorial puzzle piece blocking Ibn Saud from direct contact with the French.

On March 28, 1921, Churchill, Abdullah, and Herbert Samuel met in Jerusalem at Government House on the Mount of Olives. In these meetings, the British proposed to Abdullah that he be provisionally appointed amir over Transjordan. Though technically part of the Mandate for Palestine, Transjordan would be set off as a separate Arab country not under the mandate provisions supporting the creation of a national home for the Jews. Abdullah agreed and was appointed amir in April. British legal advisers amended the Palestine mandate document they were preparing for the League of Nations. Article 25 was added differentiating Transjordan. While the boundary between Palestine and Transjordan was relatively clearly demarcated by the Sea of Galilee, the Jordan River, and the Dead Sea, none of Transjordan's other frontiers were set in 1921. The French and British had roughly sketched the border with Syria (though it would not be finalized until 1931). The southern reaches of Transjordan were more ambiguous, given the Hejaz claim on Ma'an and Aqaba. The eastern border, where Saud's Ikhwan forces would soon begin projecting their influence, was left completely undemarcated.

EMERGING POLITIES IN ANATOLIA AND THE CAUCASUS: FROM SÈVRES TO THE TREATY OF LAUSANNE

Having worked back from its peripheries, we now focus on the gap between rapidly changing realities on the ground and the territorial and political terms the Treaty of Sèvres applied in August 1920 to the Ottoman Empire's core in Anatolia. In contrast to other sections of the treaty where few if any boundaries were referenced (Morocco, Libya, Egypt, Sudan, and the Hejaz) or boundary commissions were proposed (Syria and Mesopotamia), the "Frontiers of Turkey"[33] section much more explicitly delineated the greatly reduced boundaries set for the Ottoman rump state.

The treaty first assured the Turkish government its rights and title over Constantinople (Istanbul), including its role as capital and residence of the sultan, but these assurances were juxtaposed with the fact that, within six months of the armistice, Istanbul had been occupied by and split up into different spheres of Allied control.[34] Authority over the Straits (the Dardanelles, Sea of Marmara, and Bosphorus) was put under an International Commission, with its own police and customs duties administration, to ensure the critical waterway remained free and open. In the west, almost all of the European Turkish territory in Thrace, reaching to the Çatalca line just outside Istanbul, was given over to Greece. Greece also gained several islands in the Aegean, and the League of Nations awarded it control of Smyrna and its hinterland.[35] In the east, the Sèvres treaty kept most of the Turko-Persian boundary established between the Ottomans and Qajars in the 1913 Constantinople Protocol. In the northeast, the treaty referenced the "former frontier between Turkey and Russia," not specifying whether this referred to the 1878 border but nevertheless making it subject to later treaty clauses regarding an expanded Armenia.

In the south, the Allies drew a border giving French-controlled Syria a generous portion of southern Anatolia. This included the Cilician plain up to the Taurus Mountains; then the frontier stretched east on a line ten to forty miles north of the present-day border, putting key cities including Aintab, Urfa, and Mardin, and the whole stretch of the Baghdad railway from Adana to Nusaybin, under French mandate control. The boundary between Turkey and Mesopotamia was much less precisely defined, simply continuing "in a general easterly direction to a point to be chosen on the northern boundary of the vilayet of Mosul" and thence on to the point where it "meets the frontier between Turkey and Persia." A boundary commission was to be formed to survey and determine the border.

Two political terms in the treaty—regarding the creation of Kurdistan and expansion of Armenia—had radical implications in eastern Anatolia. Section III charged an Allied commission with drafting a "scheme for local autonomy for the predominantly Kurdish areas lying east of the Euphrates, south of the southern boundary of Armenia as it may be hereafter determined, and north of the frontier of Turkey with Syria and Mesopotamia."[36] The Kurdish autonomous area, a year later, could petition the League of Nations for independence. In that event, Turkey would renounce its rights over Northern and Southern Kurdistan, the latter of which had the option to join this new polity. The Sèvres treaty terms also forced Turkey to recognize an expanded Armenia as a free and independent state (the strong sentiment at the Paris Peace Conference was for Turkey to be punished and the Armenians recompensed for the Armenian genocide). The president of the United States was to arbitrate the frontier, including the fate of the eastern provinces (Erzurum, Trebizond, Van, and Bitlis) that had gone back and forth between Russia and the Ottomans since 1878.

Almost none of these territorial or political provisions in the Treaty of Sèvres would ever become reality, however, in Anatolia or the Caucasus. By 1920, colonial and local actors had already long been actively reshaping the post-Ottoman map on the ground. Soon after the Mudros armistice in October 1918, France, Italy, Greece, and Britain started to move in to agreed-upon separate zones of economic, military, and political administrative influence in Anatolia and the Caucasus. The French landed troops in November 1918 at Alexandretta and at Mersin, moving quickly inland to Tarsus and Adana to secure the fertile Çukurova plain. France's main focus in Anatolia was Cilicia, where they planned a mandate setup partnering with Armenians who had joined with France to fight during the war. Franco-Armenian forces moved inland in 1919 to take over the cities of Antep, Marash, and Urfa as British troops evacuated. On the Black Sea coast, the French also landed troops in March 1919 at two important coal exporting ports, Zonguldak and Karadeniz Ereğli. And they stationed troops—alongside the British, Italians, and Greeks—in an occupation zone in Constantinople in the early 1920s.

The Italians began to carve out their own zone of control on the southwest coast of Anatolia, occupying Antalya on January 21, 1919. They expanded to other coastal cities including Marmaris, Kuşadası, Bodrum, and Konya and appointed a high commissioner, Eugenio Camillo Garroni.[37] These moves in the southwest grew from their occupation of the nearby Dodecanes Islands at the close of the Ottoman-Italian War back in 1913. Worried the Italians would also take Smyrna, the Greeks preemptively landed on the Aegean coast in May 1919. In October 1920, Greek troops began to rapidly extend their zone of control in western Anatolia far beyond the Smyrna enclave delineated in the Treaty of Sèvres.

The British had also scrambled as fast and far to the north as they could in the last weeks of the war with the Ottomans, occupying Mosul province, northern Syria, and key cities in Anatolia on the southern slopes of the Taurus Mountains, most of which they handed over to the French in 1919–1920. Further north, in the Caucasus, the British also took over after the Ottomans withdrew, moving troops from northern Persia into Azerbaijan to secure the rich Baku oil fields on the western shore of the Caspian Sea. Additional British forces landed at Batumi, on the Black Sea coast, to occupy the rest of the Caucasus, and from 1918 to 1920, the British administration tried to negotiate among the emerging proto-states of Georgia, Azerbaijan, Armenia, and Kars in this region.[38] In the west, the British took charge of the international Straits zone set up to secure passage from the Black Sea into the Mediterranean.

None of these colonial aspirations survived for very long. Instead, local movements remade Anatolia in the early 1920s, with the prime mover among these the Turkish state-building project launched in late 1919–early 1920. This was led by the former Ottoman officer Mustafa Kemal, who reconsolidated demobilized Ottoman army regiments and police forces in Central Anatolia to launch a military campaign to liberate Turkish territory. As was discussed in the previous chapter, in January 1920, the Ottoman parliament voted to affirm the National Pact's reimagining of a postwar polity. In its early phase (before shifting to a secular, modernist, Turko-centrism), the vision was national self-determination for the Turko-Kurdish Muslim majority and the urgent necessity of a *jihad* to defend against the "Christian" Armenian, Greek, French, Italian, and British attempts to take parts of Anatolia.[39] From the beginning, after landing in Samsun in 1919, a major part of Mustafa Kemal's mobilization in Central and Eastern Anatolia involved reaching out to Kurdish chiefs, notables, and shaykhs, many of whom he had developed relationships with during his posting in Diyarbakir in 1916.[40] This was almost completely successful among the Sunni Kurdish groups, but the Alevi populations in the Dersim region in Central Anatolia rejected these overtures, asserting and defending their own autonomy in the Koçgiri uprising that started in July 1920 and continued through 1921. Though this was brutally put down by the commander of the Central Army, Nurettin Pasha, it represented a harbinger of future Turko-Kurdish conflicts.[41]

Kemal's first priority in 1920 was to reestablish control over the eastern provinces—Kars, Ardahan, and Batumi—and stabilize the Caucasus frontier. Though the Ottomans had swept into this area following the Russian withdrawal in 1917, the Mudros armistice required them to withdraw, allowing Armenian forces to reoccupy most of the major towns. With the dissolution of the Ottoman, Russian, and Qajar Empires at the end of the war, numerous political entities emerged in the eastern Anatolia-Southern Caucasus shatter zone. The Transcaucasian Democratic Federative Republic briefly unified Georgia, Armenia, and Azerbaijan in 1917, but it fell apart with the advance of Ottoman forces into the region the following year. In May 1918, all declared their own independence, with the newly arrived British occupation forces attempting to sort out boundaries as they successively went to war with each other.[42]

In 1920, the Russian Soviet and Turkish armies began to move back into the southern Caucasus to impose control. In April, Soviet Russia invaded Azerbaijan. In September, the Turkish general Kâzım Karabekir moved to retake the Kars and Ardahan provinces from Armenia. By that November, the Turks were threatening the Armenian capital, Yerevan, prompting Armenia to agree to an armistice. Soviet Russian forces then entered Yerevan unopposed and forced the Armenian Republic to join the Soviet Union. Months later, the Red Army also advanced into Georgia and brought a Bolshevik government to power in February 1921. That March, Vladimir Lenin and Mustafa Kemal agreed to the Treaty of Moscow. The treaty established a friendly peace between Soviet Russia and the emerging Turkish state, with Turkey ceding the northern half of Batumi to Georgia but having its claim to Kars and most of Ardahan recognized by the Bolsheviks. In October 1921, the Treaty of Kars reiterated these same terms and was signed by the three Caucasian Soviet Republics: Georgia, Armenia, and Azerbaijan.

Having secured its eastern frontier against the threat of a Greater Armenia and signed a treaty with Soviet Russia that settled the rest of the Caucasus frontier, Kemal was free to turn back to the liberation of other parts of Anatolia from French, Italian, Greek, and British occupation. This effort initially focused on repelling Franco-Armenian forces in Cilicia. In Cairo, the French had helped create an Armenian Legion in 1917–1918. As with their patronage of the Maronites in creating Greater Lebanon, the French, with British support, intended to back an Armenian polity in Cilicia, and, after the armistice, they encouraged over 170,000 Armenian refugees to return or to resettle in this region.[43] The retreating Ottoman army, however, had left multiple caches of weapons and ammunition that were hidden by local population and officers who melted into the civilian administration.

Drawing on these resources, a strong local movement immediately resisted France's attempt to control Cilicia. From early 1920, the Kemalist units joined them in sustained operations that resulted in Turkish forces taking Marash in February 1920, Urfa in April 1920, and Antep in February 1921. Though an initial attempt to negotiate a Franco-Turkish peace failed in March 1921, by October both parties agreed to the Ankara Treaty, by which France agreed to completely withdraw from Cilicia. France and Turkey also agreed to revise the Sèvres boundary with Syria, moving the frontier to the south and giving Turkey control of the Baghdad railway. By January 5, 1922, the French had completely withdrawn from Cilicia, leaving the region firmly under Kemalist control. As the previous section discussed, the rapprochement between Turkey and France had direct impacts on the northern Syrian resistance in Latakia and Aleppo, as Kemal shut down the aid flowing to aid the anti-French revolt. With the Turkish military successfully consolidating power, the Italians also began negotiating with the Kemalists, allowing arms smuggling through their zone of control on the southern coast around Antalya and their zone on the Anatolian side of Istanbul. The Italians soon withdrew completely from Anatolia.

The most brutal phase of the Turkish struggle for the new polity's independence was against the Greeks in western Anatolia. In the fall of 1920 and spring of 1921, Turkish forces retreated rapidly in the face of British-supported Greek expansion from the Smyrna enclave. The Greeks launched a major offensive in June 1921, occupying the cities of Afyonkarahisar, Kütahya, and Eskişehir (on the main rail line), and forcing the Turkish forces under Ismet Inönü to withdraw east of the Sakarya river, less than sixty miles from the interior city of Ankara, the nascent Turkish Republic's capital. In August the Greek army pushed again against the Turkish lines, aiming to occupy Ankara. However, during the twenty-one-day Battle of Sakarya, they were stymied by the Turkish defense, and the front settled into a stalemate that lasted almost a year.

The international situation shifted, though, that fall. Turkey signed the peace treaties with the Soviet Union and France in October 1921, allowing the Turkish generals to redeploy large numbers of troops to the western front. With the upper hand, Kemal rejected an Allied-proposed armistice, knowing he could maximize his gains, particularly after Soviet Russia sent significant military arms and a gold supplement to the Turkish Republic in April and May 1922. That summer, the Turks launched a counterattack, overrunning the Greek army at the Battle of Dumlupinar in late August; Eskişehir fell on September 2, and the Greek forces fled back to the Aegean coast. Turkish troops entered Smyrna on September 9; four days later a fire broke out and burned down the city, killing tens of thousands of Greek and Armenian refugees trapped in the city and unable to get on ships at the waterfront.[44] Within two weeks, on September 18, 1922, the Greek army had been completely expelled from Anatolia.

The last task for the Turkish liberation army was the Straits zone, stretching from the Dardanelles to Constantinople, which was occupied by British, French, and Italian troops. The Turkish threat to the zone provoked what became known as the "Chanak Crisis," referencing the strategic point (Çanakkale) on the Anatolian shore controlling the entrance to the Dardanelles. After British appeals that September for help from the Commonwealth countries (Canada, South Africa, Australia, and New Zealand), France, and Italy to repel the Turkish offensive were met with silence (Italy and France actually withdrew forces from Chanak), the British themselves were forced to back down. They averted direct hostilities with the Turkish army by convincing the Greeks to withdraw behind the Maritsa River in Thrace, and all of the parties signed the Armistice of Mudanya on October 11, 1922.

That November, representatives from Great Britain, France, Italy, and Turkey convened in Lausanne, Switzerland, to negotiate a new treaty to replace the defunct Treaty of Sèvres. To eliminate any ambiguity about who represented sovereign power in Turkey, Kemal and the Turkish parliament abolished the sultanate, separating it from the caliphate, on November 1, days before the conference began. The negotiations continued for over seven months, with Turkey determinedly asking for important revisions to Sèvres. The renascent Turkish state needed to normalize relations with the European powers to rebuild after more than a decade of continuous war, but victorious Turkish forces also stood poised to advance on Istanbul, giving them leverage at the negotiating table.

On July 24, 1923, the Treaty of Lausanne was finally signed by the various parties with interests in Anatolia. As with Sèvres, the first section dealt with territorial clauses establishing Turkey's borders with Bulgaria, Greece, and Syria. Greece lost all legal claims to the zone around Smyrna (Turkish, Izmir). Turkey regained control over Constantinople (now Istanbul) and the Straits (though these remained demilitarized and an international commission was retained), and Turkey also gained more of Thrace at Greece's expense. The capitulations, which had allowed Europeans to have their own legal systems, post offices, and extraterritorial rights in the Ottoman Empire, were also abolished. For its part, Turkey relinquished claims on Syria, Palestine, and Iraq, with the exception of the Mosul province, which the British and Turks agreed to submit for arbitration at the League of Nations. Turkey also relinquished claims on

Dodecanese Islands (Italian), Cyprus, Egypt, and Sudan (British). Lastly, a separate Greco-Turkish agreement, concluded at Lausanne earlier in January 1923, formalized the relocation of Greek Christians and Muslim Turks who remained in the opposite country. By this point, tragically, many of the Greek and Turkish minority populations in the respective territories had already been killed, expelled, or had fled during the upheaval of the Balkan Wars, World War I, and the Greco-Turkish War (1919–1922).[45]

By the mid-1920s, the Middle East's political landscape, initially flush with an array of imagined futures, had coalesced around a more limited inventory of viable emerging colonial and local polities. In Northern Africa, these included the French, Spanish, and Italian colonial states in Morocco and Libya as well as the Rif Republic, Atlas nonstate zones of tribal autonomy, and the Sanusi state-like network anchored in Cyrenaica. In Arabia, the British played the role of imperial referee over a set of emerging rival local polities. In the early 1920s, the Najd-based Saudi state expanded to absorb much of the peninsula, including the Hashemite Kingdom of the Hejaz and the Idrissid emirate in Asir. Greater Syria was subdivided into French and British mandate spheres, with the French further fragmenting northern Syria into five separate administrative zones while the British divided southern Syria into Palestine and Transjordan. Within and across these emerging units, varying degrees of local resistance struggled against mandate rule in places ranging from Latakia, Aleppo, Jabal al-Druze, to Palestine.

Elsewhere, the British consolidated the three provinces in Mesopotamia—Basra, Baghdad, and Mosul—to create a unified Iraq mandate, with Faisal appointed king in August 1921. As the next chapter covers, the Mosul Question, however, remained open. Finally, in Anatolia and the Caucasus, an array of imagined political futures—including independent Kurdistan, Armenia, Georgia, and Azerbaijan; Greater Greece; and French, Italian, and British colonial zones of control—were eliminated by Soviet and Turkish military successes in the early 1920s.

Though the 1923 Treaty of Lausanne seemed to finally mark the judicial settlement of a new Middle East order, ending the region-wide period of warfare that had started with the Italo-Ottoman War in 1911, the next part of this book shows how this was not, in fact, the case. Local and colonial polities continued to clash over the next decade in two climactic waves of conflict that would remake the region's political order and the contours of its political boundaries. The next chapter examines the first wave of these Great Revolts in the middle 1920s, starting with Kurdish mobilization against the Iraq Mandate and the Turkish Republic.

III

REMAKING THE MODERN MIDDLE EAST

5

KURDISH UPRISINGS, THE RIF WAR, AND THE GREAT SYRIAN REVOLT, 1924-1927

On March 2, 1925, a Kurdish force numbering close to seven thousand descended from the eastern Taurus Mountains to the Tigris plains to besiege Amed (Diyarbakir), an ancient walled city nestled in a bend in the Tigris River and the principal urban center of southeastern Anatolia. Four days after arriving at Diyarbakir, Shaykh Said, the leader of the Kurdish army, ordered a simultaneous attack on the night of March 6 on all four of the city's gates, while seventy special forces attempted to enter by sneaking through tunnels under the southern wall. Though outnumbered, the Turkish troops defending the city used their superior vantage points on the imposing basalt walls to direct machine-gun fire against the advancing Kurds below. Quickly, the Turkish commanding general, Hakki Mürsel Bake Pasha, also redirected troops on the north side to repel the Kurdish forces that had breached the southern wall. By morning, the city remained securely under Turkish control: Shaykh Said's assault had been repelled and dead bodies lay strewn around the fields surrounding the walls.

The Kurdish uprising that reached Diyarbakir in early March had begun among the Zaza-speaking mountain dwellers thirty miles to the north three weeks earlier. But, Turkish-Kurdish tensions had been building since the end of the War for Independence. Having abolished the sultanate in November 1922, just before the start of the Lausanne negotiations, the Ankara government abolished the Ottoman Caliphate in March

1924. In October 1924, the Turkish National Assembly ratified a new constitution that declared Turkey a republic and banned the use of Kurdish. In response to this hard secularizing, Turkish nationalistic turn taken by the Kemalists, a group of military and religious leaders involved in a Kurdish nationalist organization, Azadî (Freedom), met to plan a large-scale uprising to try establish an independent Kurdistan.[1] Though the main revolt was planned for May 1925, a premature, failed Azadî mutiny among Kurdish regiments stationed in Hakkari province in September 1924 led to a massive crackdown that eliminated much of the Kurdish organization's leadership.

Shaykh Said, a prominent Sufi leader in the Naqshbandiya order and one of the most prominent surviving Azadî figures, was eventually persuaded in January 1925 to mobilize a widespread revolt that spring. In early February, a skirmish between his forces and Turkish gendarmes in the small village of Piran prematurely set off the uprising. Said's men retaliated by attacking the post office in Lice, the district's administrative center. In mid-February, Said issued a fatwa calling for a jihad against the newly formed Turkish Republic. Said declared himself the Amir al-Mujahidin, leader of the holy fighters, and announced that the town of Darahini would be the temporary headquarters of a Naqshbandi caliphate, to which taxes and captured Turkish soldiers should be sent. He and his key leaders set out a five-prong military plan radiating outward from the Zaza Kurdish base: one group was sent north and northeast to open up the path to Erzurum, another went northwest toward Harput and Elâzığ, a third was sent west toward Ergani, a fourth was directed south toward Diyarbakir, and a fifth was deployed eastward toward Silvan. The Kurdish uprising had numerous successes against Turkish forces during the last two weeks of February, consolidating control of the northern areas of Diyarbakir province and extending the front southwest toward Siverek and east to the city of Mus.[2]

In early March, Said moved his main force against Diyarbakir. Though they failed to breach the city's walls, the Kurdish *mujahidin* kept the city under siege through the end of March, when they had to retreat upon the approach of a large Turkish relieving force. Elsewhere, his troops continued to advance westward toward Elâzığ and to the east in March and April. By May, around fifty thousand Turkish troops (more than half of Turkey's entire standing army) had been deployed to the region. This superior force was finally able to contain and defeat Said's main group and capture him by the beginning of the summer, but Kurdish rebel groups kept fighting across the southeast.

The Said-led Kurdish revolt in eastern Anatolia against the Turkish Republic's internal colonization was one of three powerful uprisings in the spring and summer of 1925 that seriously challenged colonial state-building projects in the region: the other two were in Morocco and Syria. In April, the Rif Republic launched a massive assault on the French protectorate zone in Morocco. The Riffis had expanded since 1921 to encompass most of the northern Spanish zone, but during the winter of 1924–25 the French protectorate state began to encroach on their southern flank, cutting off desperately needed food supplies. Internally, the Rif leadership also faced pressures from their own tribal coalition to direct the successful jihad they had waged against the Spanish toward the French. After much deliberation, Abd el-Krim and his generals finally decided to go on the offensive into the French zone, occupying Banu Zerwal villages on April 12 and crossing the Ouergha River on April 25. Over the next weeks, the Rif army completely overran French military posts guarding the northern reaches of their protectorate zone, forcing a strategic French withdrawal at the end of May. On June 5, 1925, the village of Biban, the "gateway to Fes," fell to the Riffi forces, bringing them to within twenty-five miles north of Fes's earthen walls. Through the summer, Abd el-Krim stood poised to capture one of Morocco's imperial cities and cut the critical lateral corridor connecting Casablanca and Rabat to Algeria. The French were petrified the Rif Republic would link up to the "dissident" tribal areas of the Middle and High Atlas, creating a massive autonomous bloc independent of French control that could threaten their whole colonial position in northern Africa.[3]

That same summer, the French Empire's foothold in the Middle East was threatened by a massive revolt in Syria. In July 1925, tensions that had been building up in southern Syria exploded into armed revolt in the Jabal al-Druze, a highland area south of Damascus. In early June, the duplicitous French high commissioner, Maurice Sarrail, arrested a number of Druze leaders he had invited to Damascus for negotiations, prompting Sultan al-Atrash, one of the most prominent Druze clan heads, to begin mobilizing. In the third week of July, Druze fighters began to skirmish with French forces, shooting down an airplane and taking control of Salkhad, one of the Jabal's main towns. The Druzes' decimation of a French column sent to retake the city on July 22 sent shockwaves not only in Jabal al-Druze but, as word quickly spread, throughout the rest of Syria. By the end of the summer, the whole of the Jabal al-Druze was independent of French control. That fall the revolt spread across the mandate, including the cities of Hama and Damascus, rebuffing the French segmentary mandate system and fighting for an independent unified Syria.

These nearly synchronic Kurdish, Riffi, and Syrian jihads—the term most of their participants used to refer to these struggles—launched in the spring and summer of 1925 gave lie to any presumption that the 1923 Treaty of Lausanne had finally crystallized the post-Ottoman political order of the modern Middle East. The Lausanne treaty officially recognized the dramatic transformations the Turkish Republic had achieved, but, as with Sèvres, there still remained a huge gap between the treaty terms and still unsettled political realities in eastern Anatolia, Greater Syria, and Northwest Africa. At friction points across the region, viable colonial and local polities that emerged in the wake of the fall of the Ottoman Empire continued to clash in crescendoing waves of large-scale military conflict in the mid and late 1920s. The book's last part traces out a transregional history of this final phase of the Long Great War during which the modern Middle East's political order was violently remade.

This chapter covers a first wave of clashes that climaxed in the mid-1920s: large-scale revolts in Kurdistan; the Rif War in northern Morocco; and the Great Syrian Revolt in the French mandate. Though highly asymmetrical, pitting the military power, resources, and technologies of stronger centralized states (the Turkish Republic and French and Spanish Empires) against local movements with varying levels of organization and coordination, these conflicts involved some of the most significant troop deployments and fiercest conventional fighting, anywhere in the world, since the 1914–1918 hostilities ended. Each of these struggles seriously threatened the political projects, respectively, of the post-Ottoman Turkish Republic, the British mandate in Iraq, the Spanish and French protectorates in Morocco, and the French mandate in Syria. The following sections emphasize key internal and external interconnected factors relevant to how these struggles played out. These include levels of organizational, administrative, and military capacity; cross-border and transnational flows (or blockages) of movement and support; geographic positioning and terrain; and the contingencies of local and colonial decision-making that influenced their outcomes.

THE PERSISTENCE OF THE KURDISH QUESTION

The signing of the Treaty of Lausanne on July 24, 1923, marked what seemed to be the culmination of the program that Turkey's nationalist movement had outlined in the National Pact regarding the reconsolidation of a post-Ottoman Turkish polity and its territory. From the fall of 1919 to the fall of 1922, the Turko-Kurdish army steadily forced the French, Italians, Armenians, Greeks, and British out of Anatolia and eastern Thrace, redrawing the map the European powers had planned in the Sèvres treaty. The northeastern frontier was stabilized with the signing of the Treaty of Kars in October 1921 with the Soviet Union and the southern border with Syria was settled with the signing of the Treaty of Ankara with France that same month.[4] Two years later, the 1923 Lausanne treaty restored the western border in the Balkans with Greece and Bulgaria and officially recognized the other territorial adjustments forged by the Turkish nationalists over the past three years in international law.

The glaring still-undefined part of Turkey's border was in the southeast. Here, the Lausanne treaty punted the Mosul Question, leaving the fate of the former Ottoman province undetermined where the boundaries of Turkey, Iraq, and Iran were tangled up. Article 3 of Section I stated, "The frontier between Turkey and Iraq shall be laid down in friendly arrangement to be concluded between Turkey and Great Britain within nine months" but included the realistic proviso that if no agreement was reached, "the dispute shall be referred to the Council of the League of Nations." Nine months later, Turkey and the British remained far from concluding a "friendly arrangement," and the Mosul Question was indeed referred to the League of Nations, which formed a commission to study the issue. The Mosul Commission reached the region in January 1925 to begin a survey and interviews in the province.

The hotly contested status of Mosul province was a manifestation of a deeper structural tension in the region: the Kurdish Question. For centuries, the mountainous shatter zone where the Ottoman, Romanov

(Russian), and Safavid-Qajar empires came together had been a geostrategic flashpoint, with local Armenian, Assyrian, and Kurdish populations serving as proxies for Great Power aspirations and insecurities. During the 1914–1918 hostilities, the entire area, from Sarıkamış in the north to Khaniqin in the south, had been a major war front between the Ottomans, Russians, and British, and the local populations had been drastically affected by military service, disease, displacement, and death. After the CUP leadership ordered the genocidal ethnic cleansing in 1915 and 1916 of the area's indigenous Armenian and Assyrian communities, the Kurds constituted the largest remaining demographic group astride this mountainous region.

In the early 1920s, this liminal zone between Mesopotamia, Anatolia, and the Iranian Plateau remained a fault line where multiple emerging state spheres of influence overlapped, including the Transcaucasian Soviet satellites (Georgia, Armenia, and Azerbaijan), Ataturk's Turkey, Reza Shah's Iran, and British-mandate Iraq. On paper, the Allied powers had carved out a Greater Armenia and a Kurdistan from this space in the Sèvres treaty, mostly out of the former far eastern Ottoman provinces. On the ground, Kemalist forces, including large numbers of Kurdish soldiers, were already forging the contours of the Turkish Republic in this area. Turkey's military operations blocked the westward reach of the Greater Armenia project, limiting Armenian rule to a rump state in the southern Caucasus. The Turkish national project also seemed to quash the idea of an independent Kurdistan. Tellingly, the 1923 Lausanne treaty made absolutely no mention of Armenia nor did it include a word about Kurdish autonomy, much less independence (or even use the word Kurd or Kurdistan a single time).[5]

Irrespective of Kurdistan's nonstatus in international law, the Kurdish Question endured long after the Treaties of Sèvres and Lausanne. In an autonomous zone between multiple emerging state-dominated polities, the Kurds, a large ethnolinguistic block loosely networked by tribal and religious ties, remained staunchly resistant to state controls being imposed from Ankara, Baghdad, Tehran, or Damascus. For emerging state powers like Turkey, Iraq, Iran, and Syria, the Kurdish Question was both local and regional, with internal and cross-border dynamics. This was true for the Kurds, too, as different local groups had varying levels of political awareness and institutional infrastructure, and their attempts to define and mobilize political aspirations within any of the emerging state polities were connected to the potential for (and difficulty in) cross-border coordination and resistance with other Kurdish groups in neighboring states.

For the two emerging state powers with the largest Kurdish populations, Turkey and British-mandate Iraq, the idea of Kurdistan represented both internal and external threats that had to be neutralized. Though the British had initially backed Kurdish self-determination in the Treaty of Sèvres in 1920, they completely ignored it three years later at the Lausanne peace talks. Having installed a Hashemite Arab monarchy following the 1921 Cairo Conference, the British insisted Southern Kurdistan (a large portion of Mosul province) remain firmly part of the Iraq mandate, though internal autonomy remained an option. Turkey had also shifted dramatically on the Kurdish Question. During the initial mobilizing of Turko-Kurdish Muslim solidarity against Armenian, Greek, and Allied occupation in Anatolia from 1919 to 1922, the Kurds had been promised autonomy and ethnolinguistic recognition. From 1922 to 1923, however, the Turkish leadership shifted to an integralist Turkish nationalism that precluded any recognition of Kurdish linguistic, cultural, or political identity.

The Kurds themselves were caught in a vise between rival state-building projects, facing a constantly evolving context of political opportunities and constraints through the 1920s. In this complex moment, divergent priorities were expressed among various rural and urban Kurdish groups about local autonomy, regional autonomy, and independence. In the early 1920s, Turkey and Britain tried to play off these ambivalent Kurdish desires to foment uprisings against the other state and to bolster their own claims to the disputed Mosul province. From below, the slow burn of tensions across the breadth of Kurdistan burst out throughout the 1920s in local and regional jihads against both of these state powers.

THE TURKISH REPUBLIC AND THE KURDISH QUESTION

For the nascent Turkish Republic, the Kurdish problem in the 1920s was intertwined with the internal Eastern Question that had perennially plagued the Ottoman Empire: how to maintain a secure position in the highland areas of the eastern frontier, which now butted up against emerging rival states including Georgia, Armenia, Iran, and Iraq. For Mustafa Kemal and other elites forging a Turkish nation-state out of the wreckage of the Ottoman Empire, the obsessive concern was how to assimilate a cohesive national community when their most vulnerable flank was populated by a majority Kurdish ethnolinguistic group that had never been easily brought under state control, valued local autonomy, and already had the seeds of self-determination growing.

The Kurdish Question was also entwined more broadly with the question of Turkey's territorial boundaries. The 1920 National Pact stated that the goal was to reconstitute a polity in the non-Arab parts of the empire where Turks formed a majority. In this formulation, the Kurds, whom Kemalists would later refer to as "mountain Turks," were subsumed within a Turko-Kurdish solidarity; the Turks and Kurds belonged to the same Muslim *watan* (homeland) whose territorial boundaries included Kurdistan beyond the Mudros armistice line, that is, Mosul province. The cement binding this solidarity in the early 1920s was Muslim unity against the imminent threats of rival Christian polities encroaching from the east through Armenian expansion and the west through Greece's invasion of Anatolia.

Early on, Turkish state-builders, including Kemal, frequently used language about a unified Turkish, Kurdish, and Circassian Muslim identity to mobilize resistance against the Allied (Christian) occupation of Anatolia. To this end, Kemal also often emphasized the *khilafa*, or caliphate, as a unifying rallying symbol, stating in September 1919, "As long as there are fine people with honour and respect, Turks and Kurds will continue to live together as brothers around the institution of the *khilafa*, and an unshakeable iron tower will be raised against internal and external enemies."[6] Kemal successfully galvanized Kurdish support for the nationalist military effort, securing the allegiance of over seventy Kurdish tribes in southern and eastern Anatolia by the fall of 1919.[7] During these years of national anticolonial resistance, he and other Turkish leaders emphasized a national vision recognizing Turkish, Kurdish, and other "national" identities unified by Islam. In a speech in late April 1920 to the national assembly, Kemal declared, "Do not imagine there is only one kind of nation within these borders. There are Turks, Circassians, and various Muslim elements within these borders. It is the national border of brother nations whose interests and aims are entirely united.... The article that determines this border is our one great principle: around each Islamic element living within this homeland's borders there is a recognition and mutual acceptance in all honesty to their race, tradition, and environment."[8]

This more pluralistic vision of Turko-Kurdish Muslim solidarity, framed from 1919 to 1922 to mobilize against Christian rival states, began to evolve rapidly toward an exclusive ethnonationalist Turkism in 1923. Over the course of 1923 and 1924, the Ankara government increasingly pivoted toward explicit and more rigid Turkification policies. Turkish administrators were sent to replace Kurdish officials in Northern Kurdistan. A systematic naming policy replaced Kurdish and other local place names with Turkish alternatives. Turkish was declared the only official language to be used in courts and in schools. And, on March 4, 1924, Kemal announced the abolition of the caliphate, eliminating the crucial religious symbol of Turko-Kuridsh unity, and, at the same time, announced the closure of all religious schools, which represented the only educational option in most Kurdish regions. In April, the Grand National Assembly ratified a new constitution in which Turkish was declared the official language (Article 2) and Turkish identity was equated with citizenship (Article 88), with absolutely no reference to Kurds or the Kurdish language.[9]

By the spring of 1924, the Turkish state had shifted completely from a multiethnic imagined national polity articulated in the War of Independence and 1921 constitution to a homogenizing Turkish ethnonationalism that left no room for Kurdish identity: Kurds (and any other Muslims) were to be completely assimilated as Turks. Three interconnected factors contributed to this shift. First, after expelling the Greek army from western Anatolia and signing the Mudanya armistice in October 1922, the Ankara leadership had space and time to think beyond military strategy to nation-building. The second related factor was that, with the independence struggle over, many leadership members had had time to read and internally adopt the prescriptions offered by the Turkish sociologist Zia Gökalp.[10] These included his 1920 publication *The Principles of Turkism*, in which he advocated the social engineering of a Turkish nationalist identity by a strong state that implemented Turkish cultural-linguistic assimilation policies. The third factor was internal Kurdish revolts in the summer of 1920 among the Alevi Kurds in Dersim and Kharput and smaller-scale uprisings in southern cities including Diyarbakir, Nusaybin, and Mardin during the War for Independence that troubled Ankara's confidence about its hold over the Kurdish majority regions of Anatolia. As a result, the Turkish delegation in Lausanne was extremely sensitive about Great Power meddling, particularly with respect to proposals offering the Kurds autonomy in either Turkey or Iraq.

The Anglo-Turkish struggle over the future of Mosul province was deeply entwined with these unresolved questions about Kurdish political aspirations and loyalties. Turkish policy since the articulation of the National Pact had been revanchist. Though willing to part with the "Arab" former Ottoman provinces, the Turkish nationalists believed Mosul, because of its Kurdish and Turkmen populations, constituted an integral part of "Turkish" territory. From the beginning of the War for Independence (1919–1923), Kemalists were active in the province, trying to undermine the British and rally the Kurds. A platoon of Turkish soldiers was sent in June 1921 to Rawanduz, about a hundred miles to the northeast of Mosul, and more troops were added that August. The next summer, Kemal assigned Colonel Ali Shafaq (better known by the alias Oz Demir) to mastermind the Turkish conquest of the Mosul vilayet. Turkish propaganda was spread throughout the province emphasizing pan-Islamic solidarity and anti-Arab sentiment to undermine the newly formed Sunni-led Iraqi government. Given the Turks' dramatic success in western Anatolia against the Greeks in the fall of 1922, after they had already successively defeated the Armenians and French, it seemed not improbable that Mosul province would fall next.

SHAYKH MAHMUD, SIMQU SHIKAK, AND THE KURDISH QUESTION IN BRITISH-MANDATE IRAQ AND PAHLAVI IRAN

As was the case for Turkish state-builders, the Kurds posed a quandary for the British colonial project in Mesopotamia. In the final weeks of the war against the Ottomans, and portentously in the weeks *after* the October 1918 armistice (having pressured the Ottoman army to withdraw), British imperial forces raced north into Mosul province to claim as much territory as possible in the postwar settlement, setting up the long-running tensions with Turkey over this violation of the Mudros terms. British officials in Baghdad, Cairo, and London remained ambivalent, though, about what policy to pursue in Southern and Northern Kurdistan. One view supported Kurdish autonomy and perhaps even independence, particularly for the north. In this scheme, the Kurdish highlands were viewed like the Sandeman System in Baluchistan or the Northwest Frontier model in India, where autonomy could be granted to local chiefs to create a buffer zone with Turkey, the Soviet Caucasus, and Iran.[11] Others firmly advocated integrating all of Mosul province, including Kurdish-majority areas, with Baghdad and Basra provinces under King Faisal's Hashemite monarchy, though debates continued over whether autonomy should be granted in Southern Kurdistan in terms of administration, language, and education.

As with Turkey, the internal dimensions of the Kurdish Question in Iraq were imbricated with cross-border concerns about developments in Anatolia and on the Iranian side of the Zagros Mountains. The British were well aware that the Kemalists were actively attempting to undermine the British position in Southern Kurdistan. Initially, after signing the 1920 Sèvres treaty, the British hesitated to actively encourage Kurdish mobilization to the north, hoping the treaty would work out with the nominal Ottoman state in Istanbul. But, as the Kemalists continued to have military success, the British became more open to the idea, particularly after Turkish troops were deployed to Rawanduz in the summer 1921 expressly to launch a Kurdish revolt against British rule.

The threat of a Turkish invasion of Mosul became more tenable after the French withdrew from two key areas around Nusaybin and Jazira bin Umar, following the signing of the October 1921 Ankara treaty. That fall, the British entertained a proposal from Abd al-Rahman of Shirnakh to create a Kurdish buffer state to the northwest of Iraq.[12] They also received an offer from Khalil Badr Khan to stage simultaneous uprisings in Dersim, Diyarbakir, Bitlis, and Van—more or less across the entire southeast of Anatolia—if the British would give him mountain artillery, machine guns, rifles, ammunition, and advisory support. A similar plan was proposed the next March by a British officer, Rawlinson, to mobilize Kurdish tribes to take Erzurum, Bayazid, and Erzinjan in eastern Anatolia. All of these proposals to foment revolt in Northern Kurdistan were eventually shot down, however, by the colonial secretary, Winston Churchill, because of concerns about the diplomatic and military risks involved.[13]

Throughout the early 1920s, the British, Turks, and Kurdish groups also closely tracked developments on the eastern slopes of the Zagros, where a Kurdish polity was emerging in the Lake Urmia region where Iran, Turkey, Iraq, and the Transcaucasian Republics came together. Simqu, leader of the Abudi Shikak Kurdish confederacy (the second largest Kurdish tribal coalition in Iran), had carved out an autonomous area of rule in this area during the 1914–1918 conflict. He had also solidified alliances across the Zagros range with Kurdish leaders in eastern Anatolia, including Shaykh Taha of the Shamdinan (Shikak married the sister of this grandson and successor of the Shaykh Ubedydullah, the famous leader who had tried to carve out an independent Kurdish polity in the 1880s) and in the mountains above Sulaimaniya, including Jafar Sultan in Nawsud.[14] In 1919 and 1920, Simqu steadily expanded a Shikak zone of control from north of Lake Urmia down to Bana. In the fall of 1921, he seized the city of Sawj Bulaq (Mahabad), on the southern end of this zone, and made it his capital.

General Reza Khan Pahlavi, who had seized power from the Qajars in Tehran in 1921 and begun to consolidate and modernize an Iranian state, sent repeated expeditions against Simqu Shikak but was unable to subdue the Kurdish polity. Faced with numerous local revolts elsewhere as he attempted to consolidate his rule, it took Reza Pahlavi until August 1922 to redeploy forces to the region and finally defeat Simqu's army.[15] Though short-lived, Shikak's success in eastern Kurdistan gave pause to Turkish and British policy makers and hope to other Kurdish groups.

In the fall of 1922, the British and Turks signed the Mudanya armistice and staved off a war in Thrace and the Straits zone, but in Mosul they remained at the brink, as the Kemalists continued to make inroads into the Kurdish highlands to the north and east of Mosul. After arriving in June 1922, Oz Demir, in coordinating the reconquest of the province from Rawanduz, quickly began assembling a coalition of Kurdish tribes across the Arbil, Sulaimaniya, and Kirkuk districts. That fall, a joint Turko-Kurdish force, numbering in the hundreds, made progress to the south, routing a British unit sent to retake Raniya, and forcing them to evacuate personnel by air from Sulaimaniya.[16] The British responded with an intense aerial bombardment of Rawanduz and other areas in northeast Mosul province in October.

The British also decided to pardon Shaykh Mahmud, the Kurdish leader they had exiled for declaring an independent Kingdom of the Kurds back in 1920. They hoped to co-opt Shaykh Mahmud's appeal as

FIGURE 5.1 Shaykh Mahmud with his fighters, ca. 1919.
Source: Archives Benke Jin / The Photo Library of Kurdistan.

a Kurdish nationalist to offset and undermine the Turkish propaganda in northern Iraq. On December 20, 1922, the Baghdad government also announced a proposal to establish a regional Kurdish government within Iraq. Mahmud, however, was interested in resurrecting his Kurdish kingdom and reached out to Oz Demir to try to negotiate better terms for the autonomy of Southern Kurdistan over the winter.

All eyes in the region were focused on the Lausanne negotiations through winter 1922–23 (a British field officer reporting from Kirkuk in January 1923 remarked that "even the most unsophisticated tribesmen constantly ask after the progress of the European conference").[17] The British and Turks continued to fight in Mosul, even while negotiating a peace treaty thousands of miles away in Switzerland. In late February 1923, fed up with Shaykh Mahmud's blatant efforts to create an independent Kurdistan, the British suspended his administration and began to bomb Sulaimaniya. In March, Oz Demir visited him near Sulaimaniya to discuss a Turkish offer for Kurdish autonomy. Seeking to establish facts on the ground ahead of the second round of the Lausanne conference, the British pushed hard, retaking key cities including Sulaimaniya, Koi, and Rawanduz on April 22, the day before negotiations restarted.[18] These gains slipped away, though, over the summer, as the British were overstretched and had to withdraw troops. On July 11, 1923, Mahmud triumphantly reentered Sulaimaniya, just two weeks before the Treaty of Lausanne was signed.

The postwar status of Kurdistan, which the treaty did not mention, and of the Mosul province, for which the treaty delayed a final resolution, clearly remained hotly contested. During the fall of 1923 and spring of 1924, the period in which they were supposed to resolve the Mosul Question, Britain and Turkey actively worked against each other in Northern and Southern Kurdistan to try to shape the outcome. For leverage in the negotiations, the British demanded that Hakkari province, in far southeast Anatolia, with its remaining and recently exiled Assyrian population, be joined to Iraq. British-trained Assyrian levies were used to push back the Turkish-led Kurdish forces in Rawanduz then sent northeast toward Hakkari to pressure Turkey. Elsewhere, the British began to have more success turning Kurds to their side. In May 1924, the Royal Air Force intensified the bombing campaign, destroying Shaykh Mahmud's headquarters and forcing him to withdraw up into the mountains.

The nine months stipulated in the Lausanne treaty for the British-Turkish negotiation of the Mosul Question expired in the summer of 1924 with no bilateral agreement in sight. The two parties submitted the issue to the League of Nations in August. Early that fall, Turkey refused Britain's demand to withdraw Turkish troops completely from the disputed territory. Open war was averted only when a League of Nations commission drew up a temporary border—named the Brussels Line after the city in which the committee was meeting—to hold the peace on October 29, 1924. In mid-November, the Mosul Commission was formed in Geneva, consisting of Swedish, Hungarian, and Belgian members, and sent to the region. After stopping in London, Ankara, and Baghdad, they reached Mosul in January 1925. As they toured the disputed province for the next three months, the Kurdish regions just to the north erupted in a massive anti-Turkish revolt.

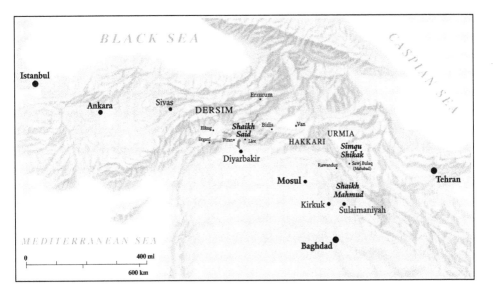

FIGURE 5.2 Shaykh Said and other Kurdish movements in the mid-1920s.
Source: Author adaptation from public domain.

SHAYKH SAID AND KURDISH JIHAD AGAINST THE TURKISH REPUBLIC

Tensions in the Kurdish-majority regions of eastern Anatolia had steadily increased since the onset of the Lausanne negotiations over Turkey's post-Ottoman boundaries. On the eve of the treaty negotiations, on November 1, 1922, the Grand National Assembly abolished the Ottoman sultanate, and it declared Turkey a republic less than a year later, on October 28, 1923. On March 4, 1924, the Turkish Republic took the final step of severing ties with the House of Osman by abolishing the Ottoman caliphate and the last vestiges of the dynasty's symbolic power. During this period, the Ankara government also increasingly implemented secularizing and Turkifying policies, ratifying a Turkish ethnonationalist constitution in October 1924 that banned the use of Kurdish. This sequence of policy shifts steadily frayed the ties holding together the Turko-Kurdish Muslim solidarity framed earlier, alienating an array of Kurdish groups in Anatolia that had supported the Turks in the 1914–1918 conflict and the 1919–1923 Turkish War of Independence.

In 1923, an alliance of urban Kurdish nationalists (from Istanbul and various European capitals), officers and soldiers in Kurdish-heavy army regiments (including many former Hamidiye), and rural tribal and religious notables came together in the city of Erzurum to form the Azadî (Freedom) party.[19] The network spread quickly through central and eastern Anatolia, mostly among the Zaza and Qizilbash Kurdish tribes. At a congress convened in 1924, the Azadî leadership began planning for a mass uprising in May 1925 to establish an independent Kurdistan.[20] That fall, the organization took a heavy blow, however, when a planned Kurdish mutiny among the Eighteenth Regiment of the Seventh Army Corps was discovered. The regiment had been deployed to Hakkari province in early August 1924, to the city of Bayt Al-Shabab, to deal with British-backed Assyrian attacks in the border area where Turkey, Iran, and Iraq come together. Two of the commanders, Ihsan Nuri and Riza, were directed by a telegram from an Azadî leader in Istanbul, Yusuf Zia, to stage a mutiny the night of September 3, 1924. The hope was to spark a large-scale uprising including most Kurdish officers and soldiers in the Turkish army. The plan was leaked, however, and the local Turkish commander began arresting the mutiny leaders, though five hundred pro-Azadî Kurdish soldiers and officers escaped across the Iraq border. This loss, coupled with subsequent purges in the Turkish military, stripped the Azadî movement of much of its military leadership and support.[21]

This shifted the balance toward the religious Azadî leaders, who now combined religious and nationalist elements in framing the Kurdish struggle as a jihad to restore the caliphate. In the winter of 1924–25, Shaykh Said, a prominent Naqshbandi Sufi leader, emerged as the Azadî figurehead. The plan was still to stage a mass uprising in May, now starting from Said's Zaza-speaking core constituency in the Palu district north of Diyarbakir. In early February, however, a skirmish between a group of his followers and Turkish gendarmes escalated and forced an early launch of the revolt. Said's forces made rapid progress in mid-February in the Palu region, defeating local Turkish units in Lijja, Hani, and Chabaqchur and attracting numerous Kurdish defectors from the army.

In late February, he issued a manifesto stating the movement's aims. These included a Kurdish government, the restoration of the caliphate, and support for one of the late Sultan Abdülhamid's sons to be declared king of Kurdistan. In this statement, Said emphasized the priority of the religious political dimension of the movement over its Kurdish ethnic identity, stating, "Jihad is an obligation for all Muslims without distinction of confession or tariqa." But, he also built off the concept of Kurdish *asabiyyet*, or ethnic group solidarity, claiming the Kurds had a special obligation to take up the cause of *da'wa*, or the Islamic propagation. As Bozarslan explains, "In Sheikh Said's discourse, Kurdishness was explicitly understood as *the* force that could and should save Islam, whose flag 'has been abandoned' by the Turks, who not only betrayed their promises to the Kurds, but also Islam as a religion, and its *umma*."[22]

Under this banner, Said led a seven-thousand-strong force south during the first week of March 1925 against Diyarbakir, the primary administrative center and one of the largest cities in southeast Anatolia. The night of March 6, Said's troops launched a coordinated assault, moving against all four main city gates but were repelled by Turkish machine-gun fire and mortar grenades. Over the next week, Said's forces continued to lay siege to Diyarbakir, briefly making headway into the Zaza quarter but were again repelled. The Kurdish *mujahidin*'s calls for public support from the Milli Paramount in Diyarabkir, Mahmud bin Ibrahim, and other religious and civic leaders sympathetic to the Azadî movement were resolutely ignored. On March 11, 1925, a second major assault on the city failed. Said's forces besieged the city through the end of the month but could not penetrate its medieval basalt walls.

The Kurdish jihad did make progress elsewhere. In early March, they reached Malazgirt to the northeast but encountered stiff resistance to the north among the Kurmak and Lawlan tribes. To the west, Said's forces advanced, taking and sacking Elazig on March 24, 1925, and to the east they made rapid progress across the plains in Bitlis province, though they were unable to proceed further toward Van.

It took several weeks for the Turkish government to mobilize a response to the uprising. First, Ankara declared martial law for Kurdish areas on March 4, 1925. The reinstated prime minister, Ismet Inonu, also reestablished the Tribunals of Independence used during the War of Independence to prosecute those deemed threats to the nascent government. One tribunal was established in Ankara and another in Diyarbakir, and both were given the power to sentence capital punishment in the crackdown against the Kurdish revolt. By the end of February, close to thirty-five thousand troops had been mobilized and were being transported to the southeast, with France allowing Turkey the use of key southern railway lines that traversed Syria.[23]

By the end of April, more than half the Turkish army, close to fifty-two thousand troops, had been deployed in southeast Anatolia to put down the Kurdish jihad, along with the seven airplanes the Turkish air force had in operation. This numerically superior force defeated most of the Kurdish contingents by the end of March, and they captured Shaykh Said and his close advisers on April 14, 1925. The crackdowns continued for months, with trials and executions of many of the jihad leaders. Said himself was publicly executed at Diyarbakir's Dağkapı (Mountain Gate) on June 29, 1925; his body was thrown in a mass grave to prevent his followers from making it a pilgrimage site.[24]

RESOLUTION OF THE MOSUL QUESTION

During the same three months Said's revolt peaked in Turkish Kurdistan, the League of Nations' Mosul Commission was in the field just to the south carrying out a survey studying whether the province should belong to Turkey or Iraq and to what extent its Kurds should have autonomy.[25] By the spring, the commission members came to several conclusions. In Mosul province as a whole, they deemed it impossible to draw a line between "Arab" and "Turkish" areas or apply the logic of ethnonational self-determination in the province. The Kurdish-majority highlands were economically interdependent with the Arab-majority city of Mosul, and the commission found the Kurdish population highly heterogeneous. Those living north of the Great Zab River tended to be oriented toward Hakkari and Mardin in Turkey, those living south of the Little Zab to the Iranian side of the border, and the rest were tied to other parts of Iraq. With no overwhelming Kurdish majority and no clear Kurdish political program, the committee concluded there was no pressing reason for a Kurdish state to be created in part or all of the Mosul vilayet.

The vast Kurdish uprising that spring against Turkish rule in Northern Kurdistan could not have helped Turkey's argument to the League of Nations that the Mosul Kurds wanted to be incorporated into the republic. In the final report submitted in July 1925 (and in that of a second commission sent to investigate Turkey's deportation of Assyrians from

Hakkari south into Iraq), the consensus recommendation was for the League of Nations to give the province to Iraq and use the Brussels Line as the Turko-Iraqi border. They recommended Kurds be given administrative, legal, and educational positions in the provincial government and that the Kurdish language be officially used, but these clauses had no force. A Turkish appeal of the decision failed at the Permanent Court of International Justice, and the League of Nations officially accepted the recommendation giving Iraq the Mosul province and using the Brussels Line border on December 16, 1925. The next summer, on June 5, 1926 (six years after the Sèvres treaty and three years after the Lausanne treaty), Britain, Iraq, and Turkey signed an agreement finally settling the Mosul Question—though it took over fifty-five more meetings between Turkish, Iraqi, and British officials from April to October 1927 to actually demarcate the boundary.[26]

The underlying Kurdish Question, however, remained far from resolved in either Iraq or Turkey. In Turkish Kurdistan, the resistance launched with Shaykh Said's call for a jihad in the spring of 1925 was not eradicated with the crackdowns in southeastern Anatolia or with his execution. For the next two years, Kurdish groups in the countryside and numerous eastern Anatolian cities continued to rally around a Kurdish notion of solidarity aimed at fighting the Turkish state and reinstating the caliphate. In 1926 Kurds attacked Turkish troops in the Van vilayet, which had not been involved in the Said revolt; the Dersim region was turbulent; and in 1927, there was continued unrest from Diyarbakir to the Bitlis provinces, including an attack on the Turkish regiment in Batman, an uprising in Bayazid by the Jalali and Haydranli tribes in June, and a revolt in Bitlis in December. The Turkish military responded by expanding its brutal counterinsurgency, which involved razing villages, mass executions, destruction of property and livestock, the abolishment of Sufi orders, and the forced deportation of large numbers of Kurds and their replacement with Turks, Balkan Muslims, and Circassians.[27] In Iraq, though the British position was strengthened with the final allocation of Mosul, the integration of the Kurdish highland areas in the province under the administration would also prove exceedingly difficult. In the early 1930s, another wave of Kurdish uprisings and Kurdish-Assyrian violence roiled the mandate. The next chapter returns to these last stages of the Long Great War involving Syrian, Turkish, and Iraqi Kurdistan.

THE RISE AND FALL OF THE RIF REPUBLIC

At the same moment the Turkish Republic was buffeted by Kurdish uprisings in southeast Anatolia in the spring of 1925, the French colonial state in Morocco was shaken by a massive southern offensive launched by the Rif Republic from its mountain fortifications in late April. This final expansionary burst marked the apex of the local polity that had emerged in the 1920s in northern Morocco. As described in the previous chapter, the formation of the Rif Republic was catalyzed by the Spanish decision in 1919 to relaunch the conquest of their allotted northern zone. Facing a pincer movement of Spanish forces moving eastward from Tetouan and westward from the Spanish Mediterranean enclave, Melilla, the Ait Waryaghar leader, Abd el-Krim, mobilized the Central Rif tribes and achieved a massive victory over the Spanish in late July 1921 in the Anwal battle. The symbolic power of the victory and the material gains in weapons (rifles, machine guns, artillery), ammunition, and prisoners (later ransomed to the Spanish government for significant payments) gave Abd el-Krim the resources to consolidate the building blocks—administration, judicial system, bureaucratic infrastructure, and, importantly, a professional army—of a nascent Northern African state.

In early 1924, with his eastern frontier stabilized at the Rif foothills, where his forces kept pressure on the Spanish lines, Abd el-Krim turned westward to expand into the Ghomara and Jibala regions. In September, the Rif army forced the Spanish to begin withdrawing from the Oued Lau area, and in November, to completely withdraw from Chaouen, the western Rif's only major city. In the Spanish retreat from Chaouen, Rif forces decimated the withdrawing troops, with the Spanish sustaining losses almost on the scale of Anwal. By early 1925, Abd el-Krim's Rif Republic had almost reached the city gates of Tetouan and Tangier. The capture of his chief rival in the Jbala, El-Raisuni, in January 1925, eliminated a major internal threat in the west.

By early 1925, Rif forces had consolidated control over more than 80 percent of the territory ostensibly designated as the Spanish northern zone of the Moroccan protectorate. Within this emerging polity, the main physical presence of the Rif state was a system of primary and secondary *mahkama-s*, or military command posts, similar to the indigenous affairs posts the French and Spanish established as they expanded into rural areas. The Riffis also constructed a network of roads, in reality rough tracks, linking these posts and the major towns, as well as a telephone system, providing both a means and symbol of Abd el-Krim's rule.[28]

The extension of the Rif state's institutional and military infrastructure developed an unprecedented sense of political identity and territorial boundedness. Very concretely, in terms of the latter, the Rif state actually threatened to shoot anyone crossing over to trade in Spanish areas, erected customs stations on the border with French Morocco and French Algeria, and required travel permits to move across from neighboring zones into Rif areas.[29] Non-elite Riffis experienced these disciplinary measures in numerous ways. For example, in a sung poem from the period, the author castigates his uncle and aunt for betraying the cause by engaging in clandestine trade with the Spanish across the front lines:

> Have you filled your silo with grain, my aunt? / Your husband is an insolent man
> When he is out of work / He rushes to rejoin the *rumi* [Christians]
> The face colored / He goes out to steal
> On his back he carries bread and tea
> His wife waits to bring him something to eat
> Him, he loves wine / Be sure he will be pierced like a dog!
> What have you gained? / Oh you who spies on your village?
> Have they given you a salary / So that you exploit the reaper?[30]

On the opposing side, the Spanish, unable to militarily advance into the Rif Republic, resigned themselves to blockading it, stationing thirty thousand troops on the eastern front—a move that also concretized, in an unprecedented way, a spatial boundary between Spanish and Riffi territory. They also, as the song above describes, tried to undermine Abd el-Krim's control through cross-border trade, propaganda, and attempts to bribe tribal leaders to revolt against him.

THE RIF STRUGGLE'S GLOBAL REACH

The local Rif struggle to defend and extend an independent Northern African polity had closely entwined regional and international dimensions.

Though isolated because of its forbidding mountain topography, Rif society—both elite and non-elite—was also linked closely to nearby regions. From the late nineteenth century, its surplus population provided a ready labor force for large farms in French Algeria's Oran region.[31] The Rif also maintained important economic and cultural ties southward toward Taza and Fes, and, because of its proximity to Melilla and the Mediterranean, Riffis interacted extensively with the Spanish.

The two brothers at the head of the Rif Republic, Mohamed and M'hammed bin Abd el-Krim, exemplified these connections. Mohamed, the elder, had been sent by his father at the age of twenty to study for two years at the Qarawayn University in Fes (1902–1904) before going to work in Melilla as a teacher (1906–1907), for the Spanish administration as a caid, and then as the editor of the Arabic section of the Melilla-based paper, *El Telegrama de Rif*.[32] His younger brother, M'hammed, was educated in Spanish schools in Melilla before being sent in 1917 to study at the School of Mines in Madrid. Beyond these elite trajectories, the broader Rif population, even in remote areas, also had a fair amount of knowledge of world events.[33] During the 1914–1918 conflict, the Spanish northern zone had been an active staging area for German anti-French propaganda and agitation, and through the mobilization against the Spanish in the early 1920s, the Rif public was aware of the Spanish and French colonial tensions centered on the Rif War.

Popular songs from the period demonstrate this international sensibility, teasing the airplanes passing by on bombing routes:

> Oh my dove / Oh plane that flies
> And deposits no more
> Pass on a greeting to the president of the nations
> Tell him to drop bombs on us
> Abd el-Karim is very strong
> Omar N Rmadani / Is a fighter without equal
> He fights with his pistol / And his sword.[34]

Another similar song tells the plane to pass on a message encouraging the French president to agree to a treaty with the Rif Republic:

> Oh my dove / Who flies where he wants
> Pass on my greeting / To the president of France

Tell him to agree to a link of friendship with Abd el-Karim
Otherwise, be sure that Abd el-Karim is dangerous!"[35]

Here, the lyrics refer to diplomatic overtures by Abd el-Krim to ensure French neutrality, which was imperative for maintaining the Rif's vital supply links to the east into Algeria and south into the French zone and because he was, unsurprisingly, not eager to open up another fighting front against a major European power. A clear awareness of the international implications of the anticolonial struggle is combined with a dismissive bravado when confronting European colonial powers.

As the Rif state was consolidated, its leaders, including Abd el-Krim, his brother M'hammed, and the foreign affairs minister, Mohamed Azarqan, carried out a diplomatic campaign to make the international case for Rif independence within the discursive framework of national self-determination opened up during the early 1920s. In December 1921,

FIGURE 5.3 Abd el-Krim and officials at Ajdir, capital of the Rif Republic.
Source: Albert Harlingue, Granger.

just five months after the Anwal victory, Azarqan sent a petition to the diplomatic delegations in Tangier including England, France, America, and Italy, notifying them of the proclamation of the Rif Republic and asking them to pass on their request to have the Rif's independence recognized at the League of Nations.[36]

In September 1922, the Rif leadership sent a set of documents directly to the League of Nations. One was a letter titled "To the Civilized Nations," which was from the "President and Commander in Chief," Abd el-Krim. In it, he critiqued the whole premise of Spain's civilizing state-building mission enshrined in the protectorate treaty, arguing they had only brought destruction, warfare, aggression, and dispossession. He argued the Riffis had defended themselves and set about creating the structures of self-rule the Spanish were ostensibly charged with instituting: "[The] Riff is anxious to set up a system of government for herself, dependent on her own will; and to found her own laws and commercial treaties so as to be the protector of her own internal and foreign rights. Europe could not refuse such a government so long as it does not oppose European rights and reforms and civilization in any way."[37]

An accompanying statement to the General Council of the League of Nations was signed by two members of the Rif parliament, Mohamed Ben Bujibar and Mohamed Abd al Krim ben Haj Ali, stating the Rif had a "duly elected representative government comprising deputies from forty-one tribes in the Rif and Ghomara." In twelve points they expressed their desire for a peace treaty with Spain that recognized "a delimitation of geographical limits between ourselves and Spain," asked the League to press Spain to allow the Rif free access by sea, assured the League of the integrity of the Rif parliament as a representative body elected to three-year terms, guaranteed that the Rif state would "open our country to the commerce of all nations," and assured the League that the Rif state could govern the country "in the interests of peace and international commerce."[38]

In August 1923, an agent acting for the "Government of the Riff Republic" in London, C. Gardiner, delivered another communiqué from the Rif cabinet, which was titled "Declaration of State and Proclamation to All Nations." This document gave historical background on Morocco's political history before and after the 1906 Act of Algeciras, claiming the Rif, though acknowledging the religious prestige of the Alawite sultan, had functionally been independent. Since June 1920, it had established a government that had negotiated with the Spanish as an equal, including the 1923 prisoner exchange.[39] The notice declared that the Rif Republic "intends to preserve its political independence absolutely and that she will continue to fight for official recognition as perseveringly as necessity demands." The petition concluded by stating the Rif had an open door for industrial and commercial investment and encouraged all countries to establish consular and diplomatic services at Ajdir, the capital of the Rif.[40]

Beyond diplomatic channels, the emerging Rif polity also garnered strong international support from numerous sectors of global civil society. Abd el-Krim's anticolonial victories captured the imagination and support of individuals and groups in unlikely and far-flung sites. The Rif Republic received material and symbolic expressions of support from across the Muslim world, with funds raised by communities in Egypt, Tunisia, Algeria, Palestine, Lebanon, New York, Buenos Aires, India, and Indonesia. Numerous petitions and proclamations supporting the Riffis were extended from Muslim groups and covered extensively in the press in India, Palestine, Syria, and Arabia. The French consul in Iraq reported that the Baghdad papers had been extensively covering the Rif War, that prayers for the Riffis were being said in mosques in Basra, and that secret meetings were being convened across the mandate to raise money and support the Rif fighters.[41]

Non-Muslim groups were also active in expressing support for the Rif. A "Committee of the Rif" was formed by a British group, enamored by the Rif struggle, who set up branches in London and Edinburgh. Other far-flung expressions of support included a group of Ukrainian students distributing flyers displaying a portrait of Abd el-Krim and a song in his honor sung in St. George's Cathedral in Lviv.[42] Marcus Garvey, the Jamaican pan-Africanist leader, hailed the Rif success as an example for other African peoples; the American Negro Labor Congress hung a portrait of Abd el-Krim up next to Nat Turner and Sun Yat-sen as an example of a "resister of white imperialism," and petitions from the Chicago-based National Association of Colored Women's Clubs were sent to the League of Nations in support of Rif Independence.[43] Much like Mustafa Kemal Atatürk during and after Turkey's War for Independence, Abd el-Krim became a global sensation in the 1920s as an underdog triumphing over European military power. A Broadway musical loosely based on

Abd el-Krim and the Rif War, *The Desert Song*, even became a smash hit when it debuted at the Casino Theatre in New York on November 30, 1926.

TOTAL COLONIAL WAR AND THE ENDGAME FOR THE RIF REPUBLIC

From early on, the struggle between this local polity and rival colonial powers moved toward total war, with the Spanish and later the French deploying massive numbers of troops and modern weaponry (artillery, machine guns, and airplanes) to destroy the Rif Republic. The Spanish, to avenge the devastating August 1921 Anwal defeat, quickly ramped up an aerial bombing campaign targeting the civilian population and infrastructure, using chemical weapons extensively against the Rif tribes.[44] By late spring 1922, the Spanish air force was dropping TNT, incendiary bombs, and chemical gas bombs against enemy positions. Hundreds of incendiary bombs were dropped on Rif villages and also specifically on the forests to destroy these zones of refuge.[45] A request to the General Command in Melilla from May 16, 1922, discussed how to maximize delivering these at night or early morning, partly because the chemical bombs were sensitive to the heat of the day:

> It has been requested to the superior [officer] to allow night flights to the bombing sites where there are enemy concentrations. Shortly it will also be possible to also launch gas-laden shells shortly before dawn. So that the effectiveness of one or the other of these means may be maximized, it is requested, if possible, that the intelligence service provide information about the sites where the enemies, gathered as a *harka* [military grouping], sleep, detailing if this is the same place they stay during the day or if they return to lodgings closer to the *harka* camp.[46]

Starting in June 1922, the Spanish began assembling phosgene and teargas bombs at a facility in Melilla, with assistance from the French-owned armaments firm, Schneider. These bombs were first launched by artillery then dropped from airplanes, starting in November 1923. The Spanish government also negotiated a contract with the German chemical manufacturer Hugo Stoltzenberg to build chemical weapons factories in Spain and in Morocco, which began production in 1923. From July 1923, the Spanish started using the much more pernicious mustard gas—which in addition to its immediate and long-term direct effects on the human and animal body (including intense internal and external burns and cancer) also contaminated water supplies, crops, and orchards—shooting it first by artillery and then dropping it the next summer from airplanes.[47] Bombing raids were carried out daily, weather permitting, particularly during the harvest season between mid-April and mid-May. The Spanish also prioritized hitting weekly markets, which were the few times the population would be concentrated together.[48] While they initially procured the chemical weapons from German sources, and continued to import these from Hamburg, the Spanish also set up production facilities in Melilla.[49]

Though devastating in terms of human and environmental costs, Spain's chemical war from the air was not able to effectively project the colonial state's power on the ground. The Rif forces adapted quickly to these threats, strategically moving encampments, using underground shelters, changing the patterns of the weekly markets, and devising ways to protect civilian populations. The status quo was ultimately shifted, not by Spain, but because Abd el-Krim and his commanders made a strategic decision over the winter of 1924 to expand southward into the French zone in the spring.

From the beginning, the spatial configuration of the Rif Republic was fundamentally inflected by its position vis-à-vis the French protectorate zone. Abd el-Krim prudently prioritized nonprovocation to the south. The Rif state, while creating territorializing infrastructure, like customs checkpoints, was also fundamentally dependent on the porosity of that border, allowing economic exchange and the supply flow of food and weapons. Through 1922 and 1923, however, French "pacification" operations steadily pushed northward, bringing autonomous tribes on the Rif Republic's southern fringe under French control and threatening flows across what was becoming a hardened border.

By the fall of 1924, several factors tipped the balance toward opening a southern front. One was ideological: Abd el-Krim had galvanized this political project through the rubric of a defensive jihad against the Spanish "Christian" invader, he achieved spectacular success in this endeavor, and the Rif state's legitimacy was, in part, predicated on continued spatial expansion against the other "Christian" invader in Morocco, the French.

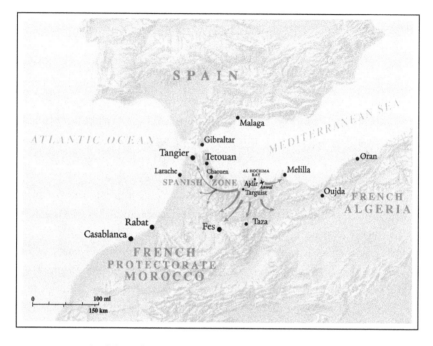

FIGURE 5.4 Peak of the Rif Republic's expansion in the summer of 1925.

Source: Author adaptation from public domain.

This cause was particularly important after the French conquered several tribes, including a number from the Middle Atlas, who had sent men to fight in the Rif army. Another factor was material: the Rif, a marginal zone at best, had a bad harvest in 1924–1925, and they needed the agricultural riches of the Ouergha Valley to their south.

The Riffis began preparing for the offensive in the early spring of 1925, digging in defensive positions to fall back to if needed. On April 11, they moved south to occupy the Banu Zerwal tribe, and on April 25, they crossed the Ouergha River and overran multiple French military outposts. This momentum continued the next month, and by the end of May, they had gotten within twenty-five miles of Fes, one of the major interior cities in the French protectorate zone. Abd el-Krim's agents in Fes appealed to the ulama and other urban leaders to rise up in support, but they were reluctant to do so given the French hold on the city. For their part, the French staged a strategic withdrawal southward to stabilize a defensive line. Hubert Lyautey, the founding resident-general, was forced into retirement and Marshal Pétain, the "Lion of Verdun" and hero of the Great War, took over military command. Early that fall, the Rif Republic was at the height of power, having defeated and pushed back two European colonial powers to establish an independent state encompassing most of the Spanish territory in the northern zone and parts of the French zone.

During the summer, French and Spanish diplomatic and military strategists coordinated efforts restricting arms transfers into the Rif and developed an armistice proposal that recognized Rif autonomy, guaranteed amnesty and prisoner exchange terms, and created a native police force to control arms and munitions. Abd el-Krim rejected the proposal, though, making a counteroffer to refrain from interference in the French zone in return for France recognizing Rif independence, which the French refused. While negotiating with the Riffis, the French and Spanish were also holding their own discussions over the exact territorial boundary between the two zones, which had never been surveyed, and plotting a military counteroffensive.

The Franco-Spanish campaign began on September 10, 1925, with a large-scale Spanish amphibious assault at Alhucemas Bay, landing over sixteen thousand troops. These troops proceeded inland very slowly, taking a month to break through Rif defensive installations and seize the evacuated capital of Ajdir (the Rif command had relocated to Targhuist, high up in the mountains). From the south, the French moved much more quickly to reoccupy the Banu Zerwal area and meet up with the Spanish troops, effectively sealing off the southern and eastern border before winter. Hundreds of reconnaissance flights, in addition to bombing raids, were flown by the French that fall, taking photographs to map the topography of the Rif and plan out angles for attack. Building up the total troop numbers to over two hundred thousand and using extensive air power, artillery, mechanized transport, and machine guns, the combined Franco-Spanish forces launched a final assault in the spring of 1926 that overwhelmed the Rif core army of five to six thousand with overpowering force.

Abd el-Krim, acknowledging the Rif Republic no longer had the capacity for warmaking, sent out a message encouraging each tribe to resist on its own. Rightly worried about what the Spanish would to do him if captured, he negotiated his own surrender to the French on May 26. Abd el-Krim, his brother, his uncle, and their families were taken to Fes, then Casablanca, where they boarded a ship for Marseille. They were later exiled on Réunion Island in the middle of the Indian Ocean. Back in northern Morocco, smaller-scale resistance continued on for many months. By the time the last holdouts surrendered in 1927, the destruction of the upstart Rif Republic had required thousands of hours of flight time by French and Spanish pilots, extensive bombing with chemical weapons, hundreds of thousands of boots on the ground, total war on the Rif population, and the human cost of fifty-two thousand Spanish-French casualties and ten thousand Riffi casualties.[50]

The war drove transformational state, collective identity, and boundary-making processes for all the parties involved. The extended wartime experience has for generations since shaped notions of collective identity. The Rif resistance also fired the imagination of urban and rural communities elsewhere in Morocco for anticolonial struggle that would take various forms over subsequent decades. For the Spanish and French, the threat of the Rif Republic forced massive mobilization and massive expenditures to extend the reach of the colonial states in their respective zones. It was also in and through the exigencies of total colonial war that spatializing technologies like cartography, surveying, aerial photography, physical occupation, and scientific surveying had to be deployed to delineate and monopolize state space in the rugged interior terrain of northern Morocco.

For Spain, the reverberations of the war continued directly into the 1930s, as General Francisco Franco and other Army of Africa officers, soldiers, and the Moroccan *régularé* colonial troops that had fought in the Rif returned from Spanish Morocco—on German Nazi-provided transport planes and Italian Fascist-protected merchant ships—to lead the Nationalists against the Republicans in the Spanish Civil War in 1936. For the French, the Rif War catalyzed a paradigm shift toward total territorial control, or *pacification totale*, in their own protectorate zone. Over the next seven years following the end of the war in 1927, France staged military campaigns each summer, coordinating operations in the Atlas Mountains, the Jbel Sahro, and the Sahara Desert to eliminate any remaining autonomous zones, a process that took until 1934 to complete. By the mid-1930s, the territorial boundaries of the partitioned Moroccan protectorate (French, Spanish, and international Tangier zones) had been forged through three decades of military conflict, and anticolonial mobilization over control of that unit shifted toward a dominant mode of more urban nationalist protest.[51] The memory of the Rif polity, however, would remain potent in uprisings in 1957 and 1958 and more recently in the 2017 *hirak* protests against the Moroccan state.

THE GREAT SYRIAN REVOLT AND THE DEMISE OF THE GREATER SYRIA DREAM

With Abd el-Krim perched on the hills overlooking Fes, the Rif Republic posed an existential threat to the French colonial state in Morocco in the summer of 1925. The Rif War was shaking the broader French position in North Africa and began to create reverberations across the empire. At this very moment, the French were blindsided at the other end of their Mediterranean colonial sphere by a massive uprising in the Syrian Mandate. The summer revolt led by the Druze chieftain, Sultan al-Atrash, ousted the Armée du Levant from the south, and the uprising spread through the rest of the Syrian mandate territory that fall.

The Great Revolt between 1925 and 1927 constituted the final major military mobilization in the Long Great War around the imagined polity of an independent Greater Syria. As discussed in chapter 3, the 1919 King-Crane Commission found overwhelming public support for a unified Greater Syria—from Aleppo to Aqaba and encompassing all of present-day Syria, Lebanon, Israel-Palestine, and Jordan—with a constitutional monarchy led by Faisal as king. Against these widespread local preferences and stated desires for self-determination, the British and French had split Greater Syria into two spheres of control: the British then split southern Syria again, into Palestine, west of the Jordan, and Transjordan, to the east, while the French systematically dismembered northern Syria into six separate administrative units: Greater Lebanon, Damascus, Aleppo, Alexandretta, Latakia, and Jabal al-Druze.

The French colonial project in northern Syria had been resisted fiercely in the Alawite highlands of Jabal al-Nusayriyya in Latakia and in the

Aleppo district, but by 1922 local resistance had been largely quelled, particularly after Turkey stopped facilitating supply chains across the northern border after France withdrew from Cilicia. It seemed the French had completed the conquest of Syrian territory, isolating and placating rural, ethnically distinct subregions like the Alawite mountain areas and the Jabal al-Druze with degrees of local autonomy and leaving no rural base from which to challenge the colonial state. The French mandate officials' primary worry shifted instead to the urban Syrian nationalists. Ironically, a massive Syrian nationalist revolt originated shortly thereafter in the countryside before spreading to the cities.[52]

In the summer of 1925, the Druze uprising reactivated widespread military mobilization against the French colonial political vision for Syria. For those participating in the Great Syrian Revolt, Mustafa Kemal in Anatolia and Abd el-Krim in the Rif were models of successful resistance, giving them hope that it was possible to challenge colonial aspirations and create an independent Greater Syria within the post-Ottoman Middle East. Like the Kurdish and Riffi movements taking place at the same moment, the Syrian revolt started in a rural, mountainous area—the Jabal al-Druze— that had long enjoyed a high degree of autonomy from state control. It differed, though, in how the rural Druze resistance was also linked to Syria's cities. While neither Diyarbakir nor Fes rose up with Shaykh Said or Abd el-Krim, Hama and Damascus did eventually rise up with Sultan al-Atrash. This revolt brought together veteran ex-Ottoman Arab officers and soldiers who fought in the Great War and the post-1918 uprisings, rural and urban leaders, and thousands of volunteer fighters.

DEFENDING GREATER SYRIA FROM THE JABAL AL-DRUZE

The Hawran plain stretches 150 miles south from Damascus, flanked to the west by the Jawlan (Golan Heights) and to the east by the Jabal Hawran (also known as Jabal al-Druze). To the south, it extends into what is now northern Jordan. At an elevation ranging from sixteen hundred to twenty-six hundred feet, the plain's fertile volcanic soils have long made it a major grain-producing region. To the east, the Jabal Hawran, a massif of black basalt, rises more than three thousand feet to its highest point at Tell Qeni (with an elevation of almost six thousand feet). The Hawran mountain is strategically protected to the north by the Laja, a desiccated lava field with countless caves and ravines providing protective cover; to the east by the Syrian desert; and to the south, by the fact that, in the 1920s, both the plain and upland Hawran areas extended down into the loosely governed northern edge of British-mandate Transjordan, which offered strategic depth to which Druze fighters could withdraw.

In the mid-nineteenth century, the Jabal Hawran had offered a natural refuge for Druze migrating out of Mount Lebanon in the wake of Maronite-Druze violence. By the early 1900s, the Druze on the Hawran plain and the mountain, which became known as Jabal al-Druze, had developed a symbiotic relationship with the merchant class in the Maydan quarter of Damascus, linked to grain production and trade. In 1910, the Ottomans brutally put down a Druze rebellion, sending in thirty-five battalions and killing close to 10 percent of the population.[53] Worried about another Druze uprising, the Ottomans left Jabal al-Druze largely alone between 1914 and 1918.

In 1916, Druze communities sheltered Arab nationalists fleeing crackdowns in Damascus by the Ottoman governor, Cemal Pasha, and with the start of the Arab Revolt that year, Sultan al-Atrash, whose father had been executed by the Ottomans after the 1910 Druze rebellion, actively supported Faysal's army; he sent a thousand men to Aqaba after it fell, supplying the army with bread, then brought three hundred more men to join the main force when they reached Bosra. In 1918, he was at the head of the contingent entering Damascus.[54] After the 1918 armistice, he continued to support the Syrian Arab Kingdom founded by Faisal. In 1920, he mobilized Druze fighters against the French advance into the interior, but his forces did not reach Maysalun before the devastating defeat of the Arab forces. After the dissolution of the Arab Kingdom, he continued sporadic anti-French attacks in the early 1920s.

The proximate factors that led al-Atrash and other Druze leaders to relaunch a widescale revolt in the summer of 1925 traced back to early French policies in Jabal al-Druze. The League of Nations' formal mandate for Syria and Lebanon was finally given to the French in July 1922 and went into effect in September 1923. As discussed in the previous chapter, the French subdivided Syria into statelets, including a Druze state with an elected council (*majlis*) and elected Druze governor, under French military supervision.[55] In 1923, the first governor, Salim al-Atrash (a relative of Sultan al-Atrash) resigned, then died, and was replaced by a French officer, Major Trenga, not another elected Druze governor.

After the French Left took power in Paris the next year, a new high commissioner, General Maurice Sarrail, was appointed over Lebanon and Syria in November 1924. In contrast to the Lyautey-influenced initial generation of French administrators in Syria oriented toward the so-called associationist, indirect rule used in Protectorate Morocco, Sarrail was a staunch republican anticlericist with no previous colonial experience, who prioritized reformist policies that broke down rather than preserved,

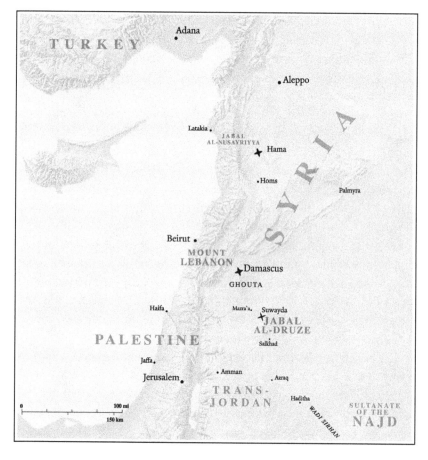

FIGURE 5.5 Key terrains of the Great Syrian Revolt.

Source: Author adaptation from public domain.

local hierarchies.⁵⁶ In the Jabal al-Druze, he replaced Major Trenga with his own man, Captain Gabriel Carbillet, to break down the Druze "feudal" order, including a decision to equally impose the corvée on peasants and shaykhs (the latter as punishment) to build roads and canals that was particularly unpopular. Sarrail rebuffed Druze leaders' attempts to convey their displeasure and continued to disregard provisions for local rule in the Druze charter. Stressed by four successive years of drought, poor harvests, high taxes, the devaluation of the Syrian pound (which had been pegged to the weakening French franc), and Carbillet's vexing administration, the Jabal al-Druze was pushed to the brink of revolt.

In early summer 1925, the Druze resentments reached the breaking point. In June, al-Atrash and others founded a "Patriotic Club" (al-Jam'iyya al-Wataniyya) that drew up a list of demands, including a request that the interim local governor, Raynaud, be kept in place rather than Carbillet, who had been put on temporary leave. On June 15, 1925, a delegation of twenty-nine Druze leaders tried to get a French response to their situation by presenting a petition to a visiting French senator. The petition combined claims related to local and regional grievances but situated them in a national Syrian framework; the Druze clearly envisioned a unified urban and rural Syrian framework in which Damascus and other areas had an equal partnership.⁵⁷

In early July, the conflict escalated into violence. After al-Atrash arrived at a council meeting in Suwayda, the principal city in the Jabal, accompanied with four hundred mounted men on July 3, shots were fired at a French officer and gendarmes, though there were no casualties. French mandate authorities ordered Suwayda to pay an indemnity of one hundred Ottoman gold pounds and to hand over twenty youths for detention. The next week, General Sarrail invited the five most prominent Druze leaders to Damascus for negotiations, but the offer was a trap: Sarrail arrested the three who came, imprisoning them in Palmyra to try to blackmail the Druze into settling down. The plan had the exact opposite effect. News of the arrests traveled almost instantly around Damascus and then to Jabal al-Druze, where al-Atrash, who had ignored Sarrail's invitation, immediately began mobilizing. He called on the villagers to join the resistance, using a multivalent term *watan*, or homeland, as a call for unification. Al-Atrash evoked the defense of one's home village, the Jabal al-Druze, the Hawran, and Greater Syria at the same time, saying, "The French are only seven thousand in all of Syria. With the support of Damascus, which will rise up, we will liberate our *watan* from the foreigner."[58]

The next week, the Druze shot down a French reconnaissance plane flying over the village of Urban on July 19 and took control of Salkhad, the second largest city in the Jabal, which the French garrison surrendered without firing a shot.[59] The French immediately sent a column of 250 troops from Suwayda to retake Salkhad. On June 21, al-Atrash sent an advance party to try to negotiate with the commanding officer, Normand, but Normand refused to return to Suwayda. Al-Atrash's Druze and Bedouin forces attacked and decimated the column the next day, killing some 115 out of 120 soldiers near the village of al-Kafr.

Up to this point neither the French nor the Druze fully knew the extent of the uprising. The al-Kafr victory forcefully tipped the balance, drawing the whole mountain over to war. News quickly spread throughout the Hawran and up to Damascus that the Druze controlled the Jabal and were threatening the Hejaz railway line at al-Mismiyya, a station just thirty miles south of Damascus. The last week of July, Druze forces took Suwayda, the administrative capital, and also destroyed the railway and road linking Suwayda to Azru, blocking the easiest route up into the Druze mountain territory. Destroying the main road, recently built with the hated corvée labor, had additional symbolic importance.

Over the next month, the Druze army repeatedly defeated the French Armée du Levant units sent south to put down the revolt. On July 25, General Roger Michaud arrived in Damascus from Beirut, commanding a column of three thousand troops. Slowed by the destruction of the railway and roads, it took them until August 2 to reach the village of Mazra'a, where the plain rises up into the Jabal. As they began the ascent toward Suwayda, the completely exposed column was immediately attacked by five hundred Druze and Bedouin horsemen and had to halt. With no water left and suffering from the intense heat, Michaud ordered a retreat back to Azru, but not before the column was routed and the Malagasy colonial troops comprising the rear guard were completely annihilated. In a smaller-scale version of Abd el-Krim's triumph over the Spanish at Anwal, the Druze rebels killed more than six hundred French soldiers and captured two thousand rifles, in addition to ammunition, supplies, machine guns, and artillery.[60]

In mid-September, the disgraced Michaud was replaced by General Maurice Gamelin, who arrived with several thousand reinforcements, including troops from the French Foreign Legion. Gamelin ordered an advance on Suwayda, transporting his force of eight thousand troops by rail down to Azru, and marching up the mountain with significant air support, which pummeled the villages on the Hawran plain and mountain with near-constant bombardment. On September 15, after a fierce battle in which forty-seven French and three hundred Druze soldiers were killed, the French columns took the town of al-Musayfira. Two days later they reached Suwayda, facing little resistance from the Druze fighters, who had withdrawn to the smaller villages, sending their families south to Transjordan for refuge.

After relieving the garrison, however, Gamelin withdrew from Suwayda back to al-Musayfira, deciding it was too difficult to hold the capital of the Druze state. Though technically a Druze defeat, the French withdrawal from Suwayda made it symbolically seem like a Druze victory, leaving the Jabal still a de facto independent region. That fall, the Druze revolt swept the entire southern portion of the French mandate, scoring numerous victories over the occupying army and raising hopes throughout the rest of Syria.

FROM JABAL AL-DRUZE TO HAMA AND DAMASCUS

In late August 1925, the Hawran Druze and Damascene rebel leaders began to plan an attack on Damascus that would take place at the end of September. Two of the prominent Arab nationalists from Damascus, Dr. Shahbandar and Jamil Mardam, had traveled to Transjordan in August to ask for support and received promises from the prime minister for King Abdullah, Ali Rida Basha al-Rikabi, a former Ottoman Arab officer who had served in Faysal's government. Though not fully confirmed to be from Transjordan or Iraq, French intelligence reported "Sharifian" artillerymen were manning cannons captured in the Mazra'a battle to fire on the French garrison still holed up in the citadel at Suwayda.[61] Having fought alone for two months, the Druze were impatient for the Damascus-based nationalist leadership to come through on promises to spread the revolt.

That help would come in the first week of October, not in Damascus, but in the city of Hama.

The Hama revolt was masterminded by Fawzi al-Qawuqji, a former captain in the Ottoman army. Born in Tripoli on the Syrian coast in 1890, al-Qawuqji was studying in the military academy in Istanbul at the time of the 1908 CUP revolution. He fought in Tripoli and Cyrenaica during the Italo-Ottoman War in 1911–1912 then served on the Mesopotamian front during the 1914–1918 conflict. In the summer of 1920, he fought with Faisal's Arab army at the defeat at Maysalun. After the French established their administration in Damascus, he joined France's Syrian Legion, commanding a cavalry squadron in Hama, the third largest city in Syria, known for its Islamic conservatism and strong anti-French sentiment. During the summer of 1925, Al-Qawuqji's attempts to get approval from Damascus to create a branch of the People's Party in Hama and his queries about spreading the revolt were rebuffed by Dr. Shahbandar and other nationalist leaders.[62] Instead, he created his own group, the Hizb Allah (Party of God), to coordinate anti-French activity with the end goal of Syrian independence.[63]

Al-Qawuqji also reached out in the early fall to the Druze leadership, where he received a much more positive response than from Damascus. His delegates Mohamed al-Rayyis and Mazhar al-Siba'i (the latter of which had fought with Mustafa Kemal in Anatolia and then with Hananu in Aleppo) asked the Druze to keep the pressure up on General Gamelin's forces in early October to help divert French attention from Hama. Throughout September, al-Qawuqji also reached out to Hama's religious and commercial leadership, the native police, and the Bedouin tribes surrounding the city, planning to use his Syrian Legion forces and take the city.

From the time news of Abd el-Krim's spring offensive against the French zone in Morocco reached Syria, al-Qawuqji had closely followed the Rif conflict; that fall, he was well aware that the French had diverted regular and colonial forces to Northern Africa to begin the joint counteroffensive with the Spanish against the Rif Republic. In his memoirs he writes: "The French army had gotten entangled in the fighting with the tribes of the Rif under Abd el-Krim's leadership. News of his victories began to reach us. We also began to receive news of French reinforcements sent to Marrakesh."[64] His strategy was to escalate the Syrian revolt precisely at the moment the Rif War occupied most of France's colonial military capacity in Protectorate Morocco. His goal was to make holding the mandate too costly and force the French to abandon Syria.

The Hama uprising started in the evening of October 4, 1925, when al-Qawuqji's cavalry unit and affiliated irregulars from the Mawali tribe entered and occupied the city around seven in the evening, cutting off telephone connections and blocking the main thoroughfares. Before midnight, they had taken the Sarrail government building, and the city was fully under rebel control. The next morning the French responded with brute force: airplanes started bombing the city continuously from the morning into the early afternoon. The destruction decimated several sectors, including the bazaars and homes of leading notables, and killed around 350 civilians and 76 rebel soldiers (according to the petition the Hama citizenry later submitted to the League of Nations to refute the French assertion that just 76 rebels had been killed).[65] Two companies of French troops were rushed to Hama from Rayak and Aleppo. On October 5, the major landowning families in Hama, worried about further destruction, turned against the uprising. Two notables, Najib al-Barazi and Farid al-Az, negotiated with the French commander, Eugéne Coustillère, to end the bombardment on the condition that al-Qawuqji and his forces withdraw from the city. Al-Qawuqji did so, leaving Hama to join up with Ramadan al-Shallash, another former Ottoman and Sharifian officer who had fought with al-Qawuqji in Cyrenaica and the Balkans, and who eventually joined the Arab Revolt in 1916, serving under Faysal until the French crushed the Arab Kingdom in 1920.[66]

Though the Hama uprising was quickly put down, the French hold on the Syrian countryside and its cities progressively slipped through that fall. In late October, the field of action shifted to Damascus itself and its environs, which remained the primary front of the Great Syrian Revolt over the subsequent year. After the Druze's initial victory over Normand's column at al-Kafr in July, Sultan al-Atrash had immediately reached out to the two major leaders of the nationalist People's Party in Damascus, Nasib al-Bakri and Dr. Shahbandar, writing to ask for their support in the revolt. The Damascus elites, however, were split. Many landowners did not support armed resistance against the French, but the Maydan quarter just outside the southwest walls of the Old City did. The road heading south to the Hawran and Transjordan passed right through the Maydan, and the quarter had long served as the link connecting Damascus economically and in terms of information to the grain-rich Hawran.[67] Earlier that summer, the French columns sent to subdue the Jabal al-Druze had gone down this road, and the remnants of Michaud's column had returned on it after being routed at Mazra'a. Despite the mandate's attempted news blackout of both French and Arabic newspapers, updates on the French setbacks in Jabal al-Druze traveled quickly to the Maydan and thence to the rest of Damascus.

Early that fall, several rebel bands formed on the southern and northern outskirts of Damascus. The southern band active in the Maydan quarter and the Ghouta oasis complex was commanded by Hasan al-Kharrat, a former chief night watchman in the Shaghur quarter, while the northern group, carrying out raids on the Beirut road heading out of the city into the Barada river valley, was commanded by the Akash brothers. Increasing rebel activity around Damascus provoked the French to launch a massive assault on October 12—using airplanes, tanks, and artillery—on the Ghouta, to try to capture al-Kharrat's group. Failing to flush the rebel forces out, the French destroyed two villages, taking civilian prisoners and executing them in Marja Square back in Damascus. Al-Kharrat's group responded by hanging twelve Circassian soldiers they had captured from the Syrian Legion from another Damascus gate.

The next week, on October 18, 1925, a combined Syrian force of Druze, Bedouin, and other fighters under the command of Hassan al-Kharrat and Nasib al-Bakri attacked from the southwest and took control of Damascus. Working through the al-Shaghur quarter, Al-Kharrat's group aimed to capture the new high commissioner, Maurice Sarrail; finding he had left the city, they instead pillaged and burned his residence within the Azm Palace.[68] Al-Bakri's group worked from the Maydan quarter through the Bab al-Jabiya, disarming and pillaging police stations on their way. Many Damascus residents joined in by throwing up barricades with paving stones in various quarters as the rallying cry of "The Druze are coming!" spread quickly through the city. The rebels soon controlled the city; the French military was only able to move haltingly through the streets in armored vehicles.

That evening, however, the French responded with force. Having withdrawn their troops from the Old City that afternoon, they launched a massive artillery and aerial bombardment at 5 p.m. For two days, from

October 18 to 20, the French systemically shelled many of Damascus's quarters, killing 1,416 civilians, displacing over 15,000, and destroying whole swaths of the Old City (137 French soldiers were killed in the uprising). Seeing no end to the wholesale French devastation of the city, the rebel forces withdrew on October 20, leaving the Damascus notables to reach out to the French to negotiate a ceasefire to the bombardment. The French ordered the city residents to pay one hundred thousand Turkish gold lira and to hand over three thousand rifles, threatening they would recommence the bombing on October 24 if the terms were not met. Declaring martial law, the French reoccupied the city over the next few days. They captured one of the attack's primary leaders, al-Kharrat, and publicly executed him on October 22. Much of the rest of the nationalist leadership remaining in Damascus were imprisoned by the French, while others fled to Jabal Hawran or out of Syria.[69]

THE GHOUTA FRONT

After the French bombardment and recapture of Damascus, the Great Syrian Revolt's main field of action shifted to the city's hinterland to the east and south: the sprawling Ghouta oasis. The examples of Hama and Damascus had taught the rebels the lesson that dense, urban areas were too vulnerable to massive bombardment from the air or from artillery, and no further uprisings occurred in major Syrian cities. Instead, the operations were carried out in more open terrain, particularly in the strategically illegible refuge of the Ghouta, which was functionally under rebel control through the fall of 1926.

The Ghouta constituted a fairly well-populated area in which irrigation using the Barada River allowed for a highly productive mixed form of agriculture. This terrain of small villages, palm groves, orchards, and small-scale plots also constituted an ideal environment for the Syrian rebels to maximize guerrilla tactics. From the Ghouta, small rebel bands were able to cut telephone lines, cut off railroads, and destroy roads, isolating Damascus. They could also penetrate fairly easily through the Maydan quarter into the Old City at night.

Despite the brutal October setback in Damascus, the Syrian revolt maintained momentum in the Ghouta and elsewhere through the winter.

Ramadan al-Shallash encouraged villagers, telling them the situation was like Ankara in 1920 and that their jihad in Syria was like that waged by the "Ghazi" Mustafa Kemal in Turkey.[70] Through the winter, al-Shallash and other leaders rallied Syrian opinion with appeals to a composite identity combining patriotism, Muslim solidarity, and tribal honor. Rather than a fully articulated or rigid definition of national identity, the common denominator appealed to was an Arab-Islamic polity encompassing Greater Syria, with Damascus as its capital.

Pragmatically, as Abd el-Krim had done in the Rif, the anticolonial revolt needed to engage in state-building activities, particularly taxation, to purchase weapons, ammunition, and supplies and to mobilize manpower for the armed struggle. Toward those ends, the leaders made appeals in the name of the Arab Army for material support for the anti-French jihad. Provence relates an example in his definitive study of the revolt, with al-Shallash sending a letter requesting gold in late November from the Shihkali family, one of the wealthiest in the town of Duma: "God requires Muslims who follow Him and his Prophet to make *jihad*, 'Undertake jihad *with your possessions and your person*'; it follows then that you should conform to the requirements of God and that you should send 2,000 (Gold pieces) for the maintenance of the army of the *mujahidin*."[71] Jihad provided the discursive framework for the armed anticolonial mobilization, implicitly synthesizing a Syrian Arab-Muslim solidarity against the French occupier. This solidarity did not mean the resistance did not suffer, though, from personal rivalries. In early December, al-Shallash was accused of personal profiteering at a joint meeting of the commanders of the rebel groups fighting in the Ghouta—including Nasib al-Bakri, president of the council, and other leaders from Hama, Jabal al-Druze, and Damascus—after which al-Shallash was arrested by the resistance's leadership, who also confiscated his personal goods.

That winter, the French adjusted their strategy. On December 23, 1925, Sarrail was replaced by Henry de Jouvenel as the high commissioner. One prong of de Jouvenel's new approach was reaching out to the Druze, but these attempts to arrange a truce were rebuffed. The other prong was a counterinsurgency plan devised by the French general, Charles Andréa, which entailed building a ring road around Damascus. Completed in February 1926, the barbwire-lined road separated Damascus from the surrounding Ghouta countryside. It also ran right through the Maydan district outside the city walls, splitting it in half.[72] This plan succeeded in securing the city center, but French control functionally still only projected outside of Damascus within the range of their artillery.

To extend that range, the French counterinsurgency tactics thus also included systematic, daily aerial bombardment of suspected pro-revolt villages and towns all over Syria including the Jabal al-Druze, the Hawran plain, the Anti-Lebanon range, and even Mount Lebanon. Here again, as seen with the British in Iraq and the Spanish in the Rif (and in the next chapter, the Italians in Cyrenaica and the Turks in Kurdistan), the new technologies of airpower were honed in the Middle East by colonial states struggling against rival local polities in these later stages of the Long Great War. In Syria, the French also sent punitive expeditions into these villages, machine-gunning downing anyone who refused to leave, looting goods, and burning all the structures to the ground. In these operations, the main shock forces the French used—in addition to colonial units drawn from Morocco, Senegal, and Madagascar—were local partisan forces including Circassians, Kurds, Armenian refugees, and other Christian minorities. This policy of arming non-Arab and non-Muslim minorities to counter the revolt was intended to deepen sectarian divides in the country. Resistance leaders, however, particularly al-Atrash and other Druze sensitive to their own minority status, explicitly reached out to Christian and other leaders to deny false allegations and apologize quickly for rebel misdeeds to try to mitigate these divide-and-rule colonial tactics.

THE DEFEAT OF GREATER SYRIA

Through the spring and summer of 1926, the French counteroffensive steadily made progress against the Ghouta and Jabal al-Druze centers of the resistance. The Armée du Levant aimed to first take out the Amer clan in the northern Jabal al-Druze then proceed against the Atrash strongholds in the south. On April 25, 1926, the French retook the Druze capital, Suwayda, but they had not quashed the Druzes' military capability; the first week of May, Druze forces clashed with the French on the outskirts of Damascus in the Maydan. In response, the French bombed the quarter systematically over the next several days, killing five hundred civilians and one hundred Druze fighters. With Abd el-Krim's surrender in Morocco in

FIGURE 5.6 Sultan al-Atrash and his Druze warriors at Azraq, 1926.
Source: Matson Collection, American Colony Photo Department, Library of Congress.

May 1926, the French were able to redeploy forces and their equipment to Syria as the Rif campaign wound down. By the end of June, the French general over the Army of the Levant, Gamelin, had ninety-five thousand troops under his command and could begin fighting on multiple fronts. Between July 18 and 26, the French forces launched a major offensive to drive the rebel forces out of the Ghouta. A massive artillery barrage on July 20 killed over fifteen hundred people. In the Jabal al-Druze, the French built a narrow-gauge railway to bring men and materiel up into the heart of the rebel stronghold.

Despite the French troop buildup, al-Atrash and al-Halabi continued to lead Druze raids from the Jabal while al-Qawuqji and al-As operated north of Damascus. One of the key shifts that finally sapped the Syrians' ability to sustain the revolt was Britain's decision to clamp down on the

Syria-Transjordan frontier. Up to this point, the British had functionally left Transjordan's northern boundary unpatrolled. The French and the British were mutually angry at and deeply suspicious of each other through much of the 1920s. The British believed the French more or less actively helped the Turks during the struggle for Mosul province, while the French believed rumors spread by al-Atrash and Dr. Shahbandar that the British were actively aiding the Syrian revolt. In late 1926, the mutual Anglo-French suspicions were finally overcome. Before taking up his post as high commissioner, de Jouvenel visited London in December 1925 to negotiate British support. The British pointed out that the French had aided Mustafa Kemal by allowing him to transport Turkish troops through French Syria to put down the Kurdish Shaykh Said revolt earlier in March. They then finally agreed they would help the French in putting down the Syrian Revolt but only as a quid pro quo for their support in the League of Nation's final ratification of the decision to award Mosul to Iraq.

When the Mosul Question was resolved in March 1926, Georges Catroux, head of the French intelligence service (Service de renseignements) in Syria, received confirmation that the British would crack down on Druze cross-border movement and shut down the Druze base at Azraq, in northwest Transjordan, where al-Atrash and others had moved in late 1926 to join families they had sent earlier for refuge.[73] The British expelled al-Atrash and the remnant of the Syrian resistance from Azraq in June 1927, moving them down the Wadi Sirhan to Haditha, in Saudi-controlled territory. On July 26, 1927, Catroux called a press conference to announce that the Syrian Revolt was over, that the Jabal al-Druze would be integrated into the Syrian state, and that the French had no intention to give up the mandate.[74]

After two years of the Great Syrian Revolt, the French had weathered the most serious threat against their imperial sphere of control in the Middle East. By the end of 1927, the key leaders of the revolt had been killed or captured or had fled across neighboring borders to find refuge in the Kingdom of the Najd and the Hejaz, Transjordan, or Palestine. From 1927 through the end of the mandate period in the mid-1940s, the basic structure of the French colonial state in Syria relied on a collaboration with the National Bloc (al-Kutla al-Wataniyya), a coalition of Syrian land-holding elites, mostly Damascus based, that had not participated in the revolt. Though large parts of the Syrian public would continue to imagine a greater Syria, particularly with regard to reabsorbing Lebanon, no other military mobilizations like the Great Syrian Revolt would challenge the reduced boundaries the French had imposed in partitioning the country. Politics from this point forward were carried out within the mandate unit brutally forged through the Franco-Syrian conflict—or, as was the case with the massive Great Palestinian Revolt a decade later (1936–1939), *within*, not over, the British mandate unit consolidated in southern Syria.

In the mid-1920s, the Turkish Republic, French and Spanish protectorate administrations in Morocco, and the French mandate regime in Syria faced significant, in some cases existential, threats from powerful local resistance movements. In highland areas including northern Kurdistan, the Rif, and the Jabal al-Druze, rural leaders such as Shaykh Said, Abd el-Krim, and Sultan al-Atrash used religio-political language appealing to amalgams of local, tribal, patriotic, and religious solidarity to mobilize powerful military challenges against these state centralization efforts. Each of these movements was largely understood by their participants as a jihad, a struggle to defend an imagined religio-political community against a colonial threat. In Kurdistan, this threat emanated from a secularizing, ethnocentric, expanding Turkish state bent on the "internal colonization" of Kurdistan; in Morocco, the Rif Republic was defending and liberating Muslim territory from the Spanish and French "Christian" colonial states; and in Syria, the more diverse movement, which included Druze, Sunni Muslims, and some Christian minorities, was defending the greater Syrian nation from French colonial dismemberment. Compared to Kurdistan and Syria, the Rif mobilization produced much more developed and resilient state structures and allowed the Rif Republic to continue for many more years. The Syrian Revolt was unique in how the rural and urban areas joined together far more than in Kurdistan and the Rif, where neither Diyarbakir nor Fes rose up like Damascus did in the revolt.

Each of these Great Revolts represented intensified periods of fighting in the Long Great War that accelerated state formation, territorialization, and boundary definition. Escalating warfare forced the Spanish, French, British, and Turks to worry about cross-border movement by rebel groups, to coordinate with each other, and to expend significant resources to enforce postwar boundaries. The end of the Rif War and the Great Syrian Revolt in 1927 signaled the close of a more fluid period in which locally defined polities could viably be imagined in northern Morocco (though resistance would continue in the Atlas for many more years in the French zone) or Syria. In Kurdistan, however, neither Turkey nor Mandate Iraq nor Iran had completely crushed the possibility of imagining an autonomous Kurdistan. The next chapter turns to this and two other struggles, in Arabia and Libya, in the last phase of the Long Great War that climaxed in the early 1930s.

6

ENDGAME STRUGGLES IN KURDISTAN, CYRENAICA, AND ARABIA, 1927–1934

On the night of March 28, 1929, near the hill of Sabila in central Arabia, Faisal al-Dawish snuck into the camp of Abdulaziz Ibn Saud to try to negotiate a compromise. Al-Dawish was head of the Mutayr tribe and one of the three main leaders of the Ikhwan tribal coalition that, since the early years of the Great War, had provided most of the military power with which Ibn Saud had dramatically expanded his nascent Riyadh-based state to encompass most of the Arabian Peninsula. The Ikhwan's and Ibn Saud's visions for this new Arabian polity steadily diverged, however, as it grew. In late March, they faced off, two hundred miles northwest of Riyadh, on the brink of civil war.

Over the previous decade, the major northern Ikhwan tribes—the Mutayr, Ujman, and Utayba—had raided repeatedly into the emerging British-backed polities of Transjordan, Iraq, and Kuwait. Saudi-Ikhwan military pressure provoked repeated British attempts—including the 1922 Treaty of Muhammara, the 1922 Uqayr Protocol, and the 1924 Kuwait Conference—to check the Najd state's steady expansion and negotiate boundaries among the Hashemite rulers—Abdullah and Faisal—in Transjordan and Iraq, Shaykh Ahmed al-Sabah in Kuwait, and Ibn Saud. These efforts included setting up a buffer zone between the Sultanate of the Najd, Kuwait, and the Kingdom of Iraq in which no military posts were to be constructed. Nevertheless, Ikhwan raiding—a jihad waged against and at the expense of internal and neighboring Muslim rivals—continued

ENDGAME STRUGGLES IN KURDISTAN, CYRENAICA, AND ARABIA 217

unabated in the late 1920s, flagrantly disregarding the post-Ottoman political boundaries the British and local rulers were attempting to consolidate.

Having together inexorably expanded the Najd-based Saudi polity to include al-Hasa, Jabal Shammar, the Hejaz, and Asir, Ibn Saud and the Ikhwan became increasingly at odds over the fundamental nature of the expansionary jihad they were pursuing: Was the Wahhabi polity they had consolidated to be bounded or not? The Ikhwan's ideological, economic, and political predilections were that the emerging polity should have no fixed, finite boundary but should continue to press outward: movement, interpenetration, overlap, and dynamic friction on the periphery were normal and to be expected. For the British, King Faisal, King Abdullah, Shaykh Ahmad, and, by the late 1920s, King Ibn Saud himself, the goal was to stabilize a more territorialized and static post-Ottoman regional order. In early 1929, the fundamental gap between Ibn Saud and the Ikhwan's political imaginaries reached the breaking point, with Ibn Saud caught between domestic pressures to do something about British military retaliation for cross-border raiding and external pressures from the British and neighboring local rulers to crack down decisively on the Ikhwan. In late March, Ibn Saud finally led out an expedition to crush the two main Ikhwan groups, the Mutayr and Utayba, at their base northwest of Riyadh.

Very early in the morning of March 29, 1929, after a full night of talks to reach a compromise, al-Dawish returned to the Ikhwan camp from his meeting with Ibn Saud. There are conflicting reports about whether a truce had been negotiated,[1] but that morning Ibn Saud's forces, wielding machine guns and superior cavalry, made a surprise attack and routed the forces of al-Dawish and Sultan Ibn Humayd. The defeat at Sabila severely hurt the Ikhwan, including al-Dawish himself, who was shot in the stomach, but it did not destroy the movement. For the next eight months, Ibn Saud had to keep pursuing the Ikhwan, as the Mutayr, Utayba, and Ujman tribes continued to resist his orders and raid deep into Kuwait and Iraq. Finally, in January 1930, al-Dawish was captured in Iraq and handed over by the British, after which Ibn Saud's forces were able to finally prevail over the remaining rebellious Ikhwan factions that spring. Renamed the Kingdom of Saudi Arabia in 1932, this new Arabian polity faced several further threats in the early 1930s, but by 1934, it finalized treaty agreements with neighboring countries that, with a few exceptions, settled its boundaries.[2]

At the moment Ibn Saud faced civil war with the Ikhwan in the late 1920s, the other independent post-Ottoman state to emerge in the Middle East, the Turkish Republic, was also dealing with a significant internal threat: a final wave of large-scale mobilization to create a separate independent Kurdistan. In 1927, Khoybun (literally "Be Oneself"), an amalgam of Kurdish nationalist organizations that had regrouped after the defeat of the Shaykh Said jihad, established an independent Kurdish state anchored on Mount Ararat (Çiyayê Agirîyê, in Kurdish, and Ağrı Dağı, in Turkish), on the far eastern edge of Anatolia. A flag was raised, three thousand trained Kurdish troops were deployed, and numerous military depots were set up in the area. In the summer of 1930, the Turkish state mobilized a massive military campaign—including over sixty thousand troops, more than one hundred airplanes, and numerous artillery and machine guns—to put down the upstart Kurdish state. Though the Turkish military declared victory by September 1930, they faced several more years of small-scale resistance, while also carrying out a massive ethnoengineering resettlement plan relocating Kurds to western Anatolia. Seven years later, the Turkish state's attempt to eliminate local autonomy in the Alevi Kurdish region of Dersim (renamed Tunceli by the Turkish state) triggered another period of revolt and brutal counterinsurgency that lasted close to two years, resulting in the deaths of tens of thousands of civilians in addition to wiping out local housing and infrastructure.

In the early 1930s, the last vestiges of local political autonomy were also stamped out in Northern Africa, by the French in the Atlas Mountains and Saharan regions of Morocco and by the Italians in eastern Libya. The Italian colonial state actively expanded its reach through brutal war in the early 1920s, first in Tripolitania and then in the Fezzan. Between 1924 and 1931, the Italo-Sanusi War in the east in Cyrenaica was the final stage of the decade-long struggle over the political future of post-Ottoman Libya. During this total colonial war, Italy physically delineated the Libya-Egypt border by extending hundreds of miles of barbwire fencing to contain the Sanusi resistance in the Jabal Akhdar and the Saharan interior to the south of Cyrenaica. They also forced over one hundred thousand civilians into concentration camps in which close eighty thousand died before victory was declared with the hanging of the Sanusi military leader, Omar al-Mokhtar, on September 16, 1931. The memory of this collective resistance effort and trauma of colonial total war imprinted itself deeply on communities in eastern Libya.

This chapter turns to these three sites—Arabia, Kurdistan, and Libya—in which the final major clashes of the Long Great War forged key contours of the modern Middle East in the late 1920s and early 1930s. Two of these cases—the Turkish Republic and the Kingdom of Saudi Arabia—involved the only local political projects to emerge in the decade after the 1918 Mudros armistice that have survived to the present. In the late 1920s, both of these polities faced strong internal resistance movements—the Kurdish nationalists and the Ikhwan—that forced critical junctures of state formation in which the polity and its boundaries were defined. In the case of Turkey, the Mount Ararat revolt signaled the final climax of the Kurdish-Turkish struggle to reimagine political space within and beyond Anatolia; this conflict forced the redefinition of the Turkish-Iranian boundaries and the beginning of a period of widescale state-sponsored Turkification in eastern Anatolia. In Arabia, the Ikhwan-Saud conflict constituted a civil war over the soul and trajectory of the Wahhabi state formation movement. Ibn Saud's plan for a territorially defined polity won out, while the Ikhwan threat gave him leverage in negotiations to finally delineate boundaries with Kuwait, Iraq, Transjordan, and Yemen. The final local project, the tenacious Sanusi state in Cyrenaica, challenged Italy's colonial project in post-Ottoman Northern Africa and intense warfare drove processes that defined the Libyan boundary with Egypt and in the Saharan south. The following sections trace the internal and translocal dimensions of these final stages of the Long Great War.

THE CONTINUING KURDISH QUESTION IN TURKEY: THE ARARAT AND DERSIM REVOLTS (1927-1938)

Though it seemed the Turkish military had crushed the Shaykh Said revolt in May 1925 then decapitated the movement in September, when Said and several other revolt leaders tried by the Independence Tribunal in Diyarbakir were hanged outside the old city's Mountain Gate and thrown in an unmarked mass grave,[3] Kurdish bands persisted in fighting from numerous pockets across eastern Anatolia. In 1927, a transnational network of

Kurdish activists, united under the name Khoybun, mobilized from Mandate Syria, linking up with the resistance bands in Northern (Turkish) Kurdistan to launch another major uprising. This movement founded a Kurdish microstate on the slopes of Mount Ararat (Çiyayê Agirîyê) in the Van province; from 1927 to 1930, it clashed with the Turkish Republic near the border with Iran. The high stakes of this struggle were whether any form of independent Kurdish polity would emerge and survive in the post-Ottoman Middle East.

From its turn toward Turkish ethnonationalism in 1922–1923, the goal of the Turkish Republic's social engineering policies in southeastern Anatolia was to destroy Kurdish ethnoreligious identity. The state's repertoire of anti-Kurdish repression built off earlier strategies used by the CUP leadership in the Armenian genocide.[4] Systematic deportation, the destruction of villages, and the implementation of a special legal regime of martial law in Turkish Kurdistan were used to try to erase Kurdish collective identity in eastern Anatolia. Later Kurdish reports claimed that, in crackdowns following the Shaikh Said revolt between 1925 and 1928, ten thousand houses were razed, fifteen thousand people were killed, and half a million Kurds were deported for resettlement in western Anatolia, with half of them dying on the way.[5] Ankara also established the Eastern Region Reform Commission, which developed a plan encouraging the Turkification of the eastern Kurdish regions through boarding schools and compulsory settlement of Kurds; banning the speaking of Kurdish in public; teaching Turkish to women; building police stations; carrying out a census; deploying Kurdish military conscripts outside the region; and resettling Turkish immigrants from the Balkans, Caucasus, and Iran in the east.[6]

On the Kurdish side, after the failure of the 1925 uprising, a network of Kurdish nationalists based as far afield as Paris, Cairo, Tabriz, Istanbul, Aleppo, Damascus, and Beirut came together to rethink their strategy. After a series of clandestine meetings in Northern Kurdistan, several of these figures met in Bhamdoun, Lebanon, on October 5, 1927, to create Khoybun, a unified Kurdish organization that would encompass multiple smaller ones.[7] It was composed of Kurdish nationalists who had been based in Allied-controlled Istanbul after the 1918 armistice but fled with the approach of Kemalist forces in 1922, as well as others who had participated in the 1925 uprisings and had to seek refuge outside of Turkey, going into exile in cities around the region, as well as Paris. The leaders, who included Memduh Selim and the president of Khoybun, Jaladat Badr Khan, learning from the failed Bayt al-Shabab mutiny in 1924 and short-lived Shaykh Said revolt in 1925, were committed to better planning and a tighter command structure. Khoybun focused on Turkey as its sole enemy, emphasizing good relations with other countries. One of Khoybun's distinctive qualities was that it succeeded in operating across, and drew support from, all four of the Kurdistan regions transected by the emerging states of Turkey, Iran, Iraq, and Syria.

Aleppo, northern Syria's main city, was chosen as the headquarters from which to plan the next Kurdish uprising. Ihsan Nuri Pasha, the former Ottoman officer who had led the failed Bayt al-Shabab mutiny, was appointed the operational commander, and he began training troops near Aleppo. Khoybun forged links with the Bolsheviks, trying to get funding from the International Minority Movement Front based in Odessa, reached out to the Armenian Dashnak Party, and also tried to recruit Italian and American mercenaries to help train the Kurdish army. Initially, French mandate officials tacitly allowed Khoybun to operate out of northern Syria until, under intense pressure from Ankara, they finally banned it in 1928.[8]

Across the border in Northern (Turkish) Kurdistan, Shaykh Said's brother, Shaykh Abdurrahim, continued to keep up pressure on the Turkish military in Diyarbakir province, attacking Turkish garrisons in Palu and Malatya in 1927. Kurdish fighters in southeastern Anatolia exploited their ability to take refuge in Mandate Syria, periodically returning back to Northern Kurdistan (Turkey) to keep fighting. Two of Shaykh Said's nephews, Shaykh Fozzi and Fahri, did this in late 1927, returning from refuge in Syria to take Çapakçur and the highlands between Palu and Kian that controlled the southern approach to the main urban center in eastern Anatolia, Erzurum.[9] Through the fall and winter of 1927–1928, these and other Kurdish fighting groups continued warfare against the Turkish in cities including Mus, Bitlis, and Van. A Kurdish force of four thousand attacked the city of Bayazid and occupied it before being driven out by Turkish units at the end of October. In this area, Ibrahim Haski Talu, who had sheltered the Jalali tribe on the high slopes of Mount Ararat to evade the deportation orders Ankara had issued for eastern Kurds, also led several attacks on Turkish battalions on the Zilan plain, capturing a large amount of supplies and weapons in September. In 1927 and 1928, Kurds effectively controlled, or at least had free movement, along the length of the Turkish-Iranian border.

It was in this topographically advantageous space in far eastern Anatolia, on and around Mount Ararat (elevation 16,854 feet), that the Khoybun leadership decided to set up an independent Kurdish polity. In addition to the high elevation areas from which to withstand the Turkish military, this area abutting Iran had the advantage of porous international boundaries across which to get supplies or take refuge. Khoybun declared the independence of Kurdistan, with Ararat as its provisional capital, on October 8, 1927, and the military commander, Ihsan Nuri Pasha, headed into the Ararat area with a nucleus of well-trained troops, joining up with the Jalali forces led by Talu. Together, they pushed back the Turkish again in December before breaking out to take the Mutki-Bitlis road in January 1928. From late 1927 to early 1928, Khoybun was also busy mobilizing

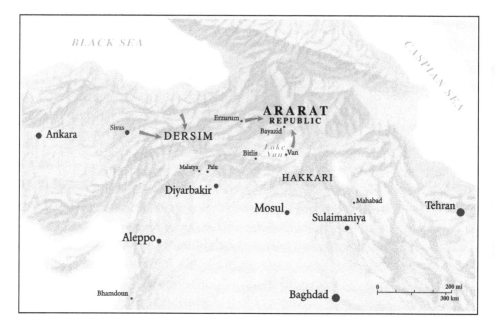

FIGURE 6.1 Turkish campaigns against the Ararat Republic and the Dersim Revolt.

Source: Author adaptation from public domain.

Kurdish and Armenian refugees in northeastern Syria to launch attacks across the border against Sasun, Botan, and Bitlis.

In the spring and summer of 1928, the Turkish government tried diplomatic tactics. Sensitive to the international reports about its anti-Kurdish aggression and the large number of refugees fleeing to Iraq, Syria, and Iran, Ankara issued a partial amnesty. The governor-general in the eastern provinces, Ibrahim Tali, also initiated limited investment in infrastructure. The process of Turkification of government positions continued, though, as did the extension of a cultural outreach program reinforcing Turkism as the basis of Turkish nationalism through the building of *ocaks* ("hearths") throughout eastern Anatolia.[10]

The Turkish state would not, however, accede to baseline demands from Ihsan Nuri and the Ararat leadership that Kurdish language be allowed and that the Turkish forces evacuate from Kurdistan, and the talks went nowhere. In early 1929, the Kurdish forces again had a string of military successes and were strengthened when Alevi tribes on the north side of Mount Ararat joined the movement. By the fall, the Kurdish state had carved out an autonomous zone stretching from Mount Ararat to south of Van, with a rear flank backed up against the Iranian border across which they had numerous supply lines. A poem composed by Kadri Cemilpaşa, an executive member of Khoybun, expresses the political hopes symbolized by the Ararat (Agrî) Republic: "Your chest is covered by a shadow / The Kurdish flag is flying / You became the *Kàbah* for the Kurds / Rise Agrî! Rise Agrî. Rise Agrî! Rise Agrî / Turks cry because they fear you / You've seen how Turks (Rom) run away / Rise Agrî! Rise Agrî!"[11]

The conflict climaxed in the spring and summer of 1930, when the Turkish military launched a major counteroffensive to crush the Kurdish polity. The two-pronged strategy was to push eastward from Erzurum with one unit and across the north side of Lake Van with another against the Kurdish defensive lines. Knowing the Kurds were being supplied from Iran and the Transcaucasian states, the Turkish government secured a pledge from Soviet Russia that they would seal that part of the border and allow the Turkish military the use of rail lines. Iran, however, made no commitments, and Turkish-Iranian relations grew tense through the course of the year.

As with the other colonial powers in the 1920s, air power had increasingly become a key part of the Turkish strategic arsenal in the "pacification" of mountainous autonomous areas of Turkish Kurdistan from 1927 to 1930. Two decades before, Mustafa Kemal and other officers stationed in Tripolitania and Cyrenaica in 1911–1912 had observed firsthand how Italy used air power to drop both bombs and leaflet propaganda; more recently, in the struggle with the British over Mosul province, Turkish officers had experienced how the Royal Air Force was used against them and their Kurdish allies. Turkish air power remained meager from the Balkan Wars through the War for Independence, but the 1925 Shaykh Said revolt, for which they still had few planes available, had been a wake-up call to build up the Turkish Air Force. The rapid expansion of Turkish air power can be directly attributed to the need to be able to respond to the Kurdish threat and strategic advantages in operating out of the difficult terrain and high elevations of the Eastern Taurus and Zagros mountain ranges.[12]

The first major battle took place on June 12, 1930; it involved fifteen thousand troops, artillery, and aircraft, and both sides sustained heavy losses. In July, the Kurds mounted a major counteroffensive trying to open up a corridor from Mount Ararat down to Diyarbakir. They were stopped by the Turkish forces on the Zilan plain to the southwest of Mount Ararat, which was a major setback and forced them to fall back up into the mountain for refuge. The Turkish forces continued to encircle the mountain, moving the main command center for the operation from Bayazid to the southwestern foothills of Ararat, where the Turkish general in charge of the campaign, Salih Pasha, also had a large airfield constructed.

Through July and August, Turkish planes pounded the Kurdish encampments and rebel villages while ground troops also tried to penetrate the Kurdish mountain fastnesses, forcing them to withdraw to higher elevations. Olson relates that the Turkish air force campaign entailed: "Taking off from airfields at Karaköse and Bayazid, every day at different times so that the Kurds would not know when to expect them, the planes were able to reach the heights of Mt. Ararat in 46 minutes, drop their incendiary (*yangin*) bombs and return to base."[13] Through the campaign, and particularly in these latter stages as the Turkish military surrounded the mountain, Kurdish fighters fled across the Turkey-Iran border to take refuge on Lesser Ararat (*Agiriyê biçÛk*), provoking the Turkish military to cross into Iranian territory.

In the early fall, three thousand Kurds were camped out on the mountain as over sixty-six thousand Turkish troops and over one hundred

FIGURE 6.2 Kurdish fighters at Mount Ararat, ca. 1930.
Source: Archives Benke Jin / The PhotoLibrary of Kurdistan.

aircraft were amassed for the final assault against them. In September, the Turks took the saddle between Lesser and Greater Ararat, cutting the Kurdish groups off from one another and forcing them to give up. On September 12, General Salih Pasha declared victory. The main force at Ararat had been defeated, but the Turkish military had to brutally suppress scattered local revolts that continued across southeastern Anatolia from Hakkari and Van to Diyarbakir for two more years, from 1931 to 1933.

The defeat of the Kurdish attempt to create and defend an independent polity in far eastern Anatolia, using Mount Ararat as a base, signaled the end of the formative phase through which the Turkish Republic emerged and defined a naturalized rectangular territorial "geo-body" for the Turkish nation-state.[14] In 1932, Turkey and Iran agreed to a border treaty (finally implemented in 1934) whereby Turkey gained all of Mount Ararat

(Greater and Lesser), to prevent another situation in which a Kurdish force could leverage that terrain, in exchange for giving Iran territory in two other places. In terms of territorial definition, this adjustment to the eastern border signaled the end of the major phase of post-Sèvres Turkish mobilization around the National Pact's territorial aspirations (the major final tweak of the Turkish Republic's borders occurred after the Franco-Turkish renegotiation of the status of the Sanjak of Alexandretta in the late 1930s, the culmination of which was its annexation by Turkey in July 1939).

The defeat of the Republic of Ararat, however, did not signal the end of Kurdish resistance to the Turkifying, centralizing policies of the Turkish Republic. The 1930s continued to be a tumultuous period in which dramatic transformation was attempted within Turkish territorial space.[15] In 1934, a resettlement law (number 2510) divided Turkey into three zones of habitation: regions with Turkish culture, regions for moving non-Turkish groups for assimilation, and regions to be emptied. In effect, this law was intended to reshape Kurdish settlement patterns in Anatolia, confiscate property, and abrogate previous titles and recognition of tribal rights. Villages or cities where Turkish was not the mother tongue were to be dissolved and inhabitants distributed to Turkish areas. Overall, just as the 1915 Unionist decrees for the Armenians had stated, the goal was to disperse the Kurds across Anatolia so that they did not constitute more than 5 percent of the population in any locality. Practically, however, though massive deportations were carried out, the law could not be implemented to that degree.[16]

These aspirations to erase the Kurdish Question in Anatolia proved to be an unremovable thorn in the side of the Turkish government, however, as resistance continued through the 1930s. The final major Kurdish uprising of the first half of the twentieth century happened in Dersim province, home to a major concentration of Alevi Kurds in central eastern Anatolia, which resisted the resettlement attempts and other policies aimed at consolidating central authority. In 1937, the Turkish military launched a massive assault on Dersim, assembling twenty-five thousand troops to completely destroy the rebellion. By the spring of 1938, over fifty thousand troops had been deployed; major artillery and aerial bombardment, including the use of mustard gas, were unleashed on the area, and then the military made systematic sweeps through the territory to kill the population and destroy villages. By that fall, the Dersim resistance had been quelled and the region was put under military rule.[17] Though briefly quelled in Anatolia, Kurdish political-military mobilizations to establish independent polities in the greater Zagros region recurred soon after with the brief establishment of the Mahabad Republic in 1946 in northwest Iran then in reorganized Kurdish movements' struggles against the Iraqi and Turkish states that started again in the 1960s and continue to the present.

THE ITALO-SANUSI WAR AND THE FORGING OF MODERN LIBYA (1924-1931)

In contrast to the Rif and Kurdish cases, where military mobilization and state formation were catalyzed by the respective expansion of the Spanish protectorate and Turkish Republic, the Sanusi's state-like Sufi religious network in Libya had already been consolidated decades before Italian colonial intervention. From the 1850s, the Sanusi had expanded inland, away from the push of the Ottoman Empire's Tanzimat efforts to strengthen their administrative reach from the coast. Later in the nineteenth century, French incursions into the central Sahara provided a pull, generating an ideological and military mobilization around a call to defensive jihad. This threat reinforced supratribal solidarity and catalyzed the consolidation of a state-like administrative apparatus that stretched from the Jabal Akhdar massif in Cyrenaica, or Barqa, across the Sahara to the Chadian basin.[18]

The institutional backbone of the Sanusi state was a network of religious lodges (*zuwayya*) that combined multiple functions including worship, guest lodging, storage, education, adjudication, economic exchange, and taxation (both in collecting the religious taxes—*ushr* and *zakat*—and collecting customs duties on trans-Saharan trade). In the early 1920s, the Sanusis had 146 of these lodges spread out in an interlinked network. Forty-five of them were in Cyrenaica and thirty-one were in western Egypt; to the west, there were eighteen in Tripolitania and fifteen in Fezzan; to the south deeper across the Saharan trade routes, there were six in Kufra and fifteen in the Sudan/Chad area; there were also seven lodges in the Hejaz on the Arabian Peninsula. The economic, cultural, and political links among these interconnected nodes gave the Sanusi polity a networked, rather than territorial, spatial logic. In this network, the Cyrenaican-Western Egyptian Desert nexus constituted an important core that, though somewhat self-sufficient agriculturally in years with good harvests, remained dependent on resource flows across the Sahara, from the Nile Valley, and, to an extent, from Tripolitania.

This framework of a functionally autonomous Sanusi state governing the interior of Cyrenaica remained in place, with few changes, through the 1911–1912 Italo-Ottoman War and the 1914–1918 interempire conflict. It was then externally ratified diplomatically as a state in postwar Italo-Sanusi treaties.[19] In 1922, the Italians abrogated these treaties and launched a war of conquest and occupation into Cyrenaica that opened up a split that had been emerging among the Sanusi leadership. One side, which included most of the coastal notables and many in the Sanusi family itself, urged a diplomatic accommodation with the Italians. The other block included scholars from lower socioeconomic backgrounds who had been field lieutenants for Sayyid Ahmad al-Sharif in the 1915–1917 jihad against the British, and this group urged military resistance. Omar al-Mokhtar was one of the latter group. Appointed as the Sanusi military commander in late 1922 by Sayyid Idriss al-Sanusi, the order's leader who had gone into exile in British-controlled Cairo, al-Mokhtar would be the pivotal leader galvanizing Sanusi resistance over the next decade.

By 1924, Italian forces had more or less reconquered all of Tripolitania. It is important to underline that by the mid-1920s there were almost twice as many Italian colonial soldiers, or *askaris*, from Eritrea, Somaliland, Ethiopia, and Yemen fighting in these campaigns as those from mainland Italy.[20] In Cyrenaica, which was still administered as a separate territory, Italian progress expanding from the limited coastal strip around Benghazi proceeded slowly. Al-Mokhtar was able to coordinate a remarkably successful guerrilla war against the Italians with around three thousand troops. British naval intelligence reports in 1920 estimate that the major tribes in Cyrenaica had more than forty-two thousand firearms, and the Sanusi administrative apparatus was also able to collect revenues through taxation and revenues on trade with Egypt.[21] Between 1924 and 1927, the Italians did make progress on a few fronts. Pushing south from Benghazi, they took one of the first Sanusi capitals, Agdabiya, in 1924. In February 1926, they pushed down to take

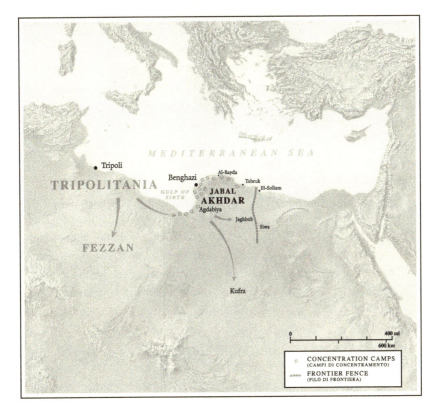

FIGURE 6.3 Italian campaigns against the Sanusi state.
Source: Author adaptation from public domain.

another former capital, the Jaghbub oasis. And, in 1927, they made gains inland from their coastal enclaves in Tobruk, Derna, and al-Bayda. Despite these advances, the Sanusi resistance was still connected to vital supply and reinforcement chains through the Sirte basin westward to Tripolitania and eastward to Egypt.

In contrast to the Rif or Arabia, where an expansionary threat provoked aggressive colonial attempts to eliminate or contain these emerging policies, it was simply the existence and persistence of the autonomous Sanusi polity based in Cyrenaica, or Barqa, that prompted the Italians to transition to total colonial war. Though Italians had partly surrounded it by the end of 1927, the Sanusi core in the Jabal Akhdar highland region was still viable and actively fighting. Its lifelines were resources drawn from the local population and from far-reaching supply chains.

In January 1928, the Italians launched operations to physically join together their separate spheres of rule in Tripolitania and Cyrenaica through a massive military campaign westward across the coastline and inland oases of the Gulf of Sirte. Using mechanized mobile units and aerial bombardment (including, like the Spanish in the Rif, the extensive use of phosgene and mustard gas) of both military and civilian targets, the Italian forces occupied 58,000 square miles in five months.[22] In December 1928, the Italian prime minister, Benito Mussolini, appointed General Pietro Badolgio as governor-general over both Cyrenaica and Tripolitania.

From 1929 to 1932, the Italo-Sanusi conflict entered a final phase of total colonial war, with disastrous human costs for the population of Cyrenaica. In late 1929, Badolgio gave Rodolfo Graziani, who had steadily risen in rank since being stationed in the Libyan territories in the early 1920s, command of operations to completely eliminate resistance in the Fezzan region, south of Tripolitania, which he completed by January 1930. Cut off now to the west, Omar al-Mokhtar and the Sanusi forces remained linked through their network east to Egypt and south to the Saharan oases, while also still drawing on their intimate local knowledge of Jabal Akhdar and its local resources. After failed summer negotiations between al-Mokhtar and Badolgio and the breakdown of a cease-fire in October 1929, Graziani, appointed vice-governor of Cyrenaica in January 1930, was given orders to complete the region's final "pacification." That spring Graziani began deploying a three-part strategy toward this end: the reorganization of the military in Cyrenaica, the construction of a road network through the Jabal Akhdar to enable the rapid transport of troops, and, finally, the "concentration of the populations."[23]

Viewing al-Mokhtar's persistent resistance as a "boil" manifesting from the "poisoned organism" of Cyrenaican society itself,[24] Graziani systematically targeted the local population, both men and women, who he saw as the key pillar of support for the Sanusi forces.[25] In an ominous June 1930 letter to the minister of the colonies, Emilio De Bono, also copied to Graziani, Badolgio underlines the importance of physically separating the subdued tribes from al-Mokhtar's forces, stating, "First of all, it is necessary to create a wide and precise territorial separation between the rebels

FIGURE 6.4 Omar al-Mokhtar and Pietro Badolgio at Sidi Rhuma Negotiations, June 1929. Source: Wikimedia Commons.

and the subdued population. I do not hide the extent and the gravity of this measure, which might mean the ruin of the so-called subdued population. But now the course has been set, and we must carry it out to the end, even if the whole population of Cyrenaica should perish."[26]

The plan was to physically remove virtually the entire civilian population of Jabal Akhdar to sixteen concentration camps built at a cost of thirteen million lira. Starting in the harsh winter of early 1930, Graziani ordered the deportation of two-thirds of the population of Cyrenaica, estimated at 110,832 people.[27] Many had to move to the camps across a distance of more than six hundred miles. Livestock outside the camps was confiscated and inventoried. Inside, most of the remaining livestock died off during that summer, exacerbating the problems of starvation and rampant disease already ravaging these populations. By the time the war was over and the camps were closed in 1933, the death toll from the forced march and time in the camps was over sixty thousand.[28]

The final phase of Graziani's "pacification" of Cyrenaica was to physically cut it off from supply chains into the Saharan oases and western Egypt. In February 1931, Graziani's mobile desert columns, with five thousand camels and twenty airplanes, took the Kufra oasis, the deep Saharan former Sanusi capital six hundred miles south of Benghazi. The Italians believed the Sanusis felt Kufra represented "the last support, their last refuge" and a final source of "prestige in front of the Cyrenaican population and the Muslim world."[29] Operating over a 550-mile supply line through the desert, the campaign was an impressive logistical and military success for the Italian forces. While it did deal a blow to Sanusi morale, al-Mokhtar's forces still remained autonomous and active in the Jabal Akhdar.[30]

The Italian colonial state's solution for cutting off the last Sanusi support lines, which traversed British-controlled Egypt's Western Desert, was a massive counterinsurgency infrastructure project: Graziani ordered the building of a fence down the entire eastern border. After negotiating the fence's relation to the proposed Libyan-Egyptian international border with the British in the fall of 1930, the Italians began construction in mid-April 1931 and completed the project in early September. At a total cost of over seventeen million lire, the project included a 167-mile, fifteen-foot-high barbed-wire fence stretching south from the Mediterranean coast past the Jaghbub oasis. Twelve guard posts were built along the fence, an airplane hangar was built at Jaghbub for patrols, and telephone wire was stretched along its length for communication.[31]

Al-Mokhtar still waged an incredibly active guerrilla campaign that year with over 250 attacks, but, by the end of the summer, his force of three thousand, cut off from cross-border supply lines, could no longer function. He and his close lieutenants were captured and hanged at the end of September in Benghazi, and the resistance was over. As in the Rif War and Turkey's campaign against the Kurdish Republic of Ararat, the Italian colonial state's ultimate success in Cyrenaica required physically isolating the Sanusi polity by surveying, physically hardening, and regulating a territorial boundary across which vital economic and military lifelines supplied these regions and made resistance sustainable. Here, too, the civilian population was targeted with chemical weapons but also physically removed and sequestered in concentration camps. These violent processes of state and boundary formation resulted in Italy's proclamation of the merging of the Tripolitanian, Cyrenaican, and Fezzan regions into a unified colony of Libya in 1934. Twenty years of brutal wartime had also deeply transformed notions of political identity across these regions.

FROM THE SULTANATE OF THE NAJD TO THE KINGDOM OF SAUDI ARABIA, 1926-1934

On December 23, 1925, King Ali ibn Hussein fled Jeddah via the Red Sea to seek refuge with his brother, Faisal, in Baghdad, surrendering the last enclave of the Kingdom of the Hejaz to Ibn Saud. A year earlier, the rest of the Hejaz had fallen to Ibn Saud's expanding Najd state: Najdi forces entered Taif, the key town controlling the route to Mecca in late August 1924 without a struggle, though the Ikhwan troops then went on a three-day rampage brutally massacring hundreds in the city. They occupied Mecca itself in mid-October, again without having to fight. Fleeing with a number of the Hejazi business elites to a final redoubt at the Red Sea port, Jedda, King Hussein abdicated in favor of his son, Ali, and left to take refuge in Transjordan with his eldest son, Amir Abdullah. Through much of 1925, King Ali made a last stand, hiring Palestinian mercenaries, pleading for arms and munitions from his brothers in Iraq and Transjordan, mining the area around Jedda, and purchasing five aircraft from Italy and several tanks from Germany. After a year-long siege, and with the neutral British ignoring repeated pleas to intervene, the last Hashemite ruler of the Hejaz capitulated. Najd forces entered Jedda on December 26, and Ibn Saud took the mantle of king of the Hejaz, creating a dual reign over the Sultanate of the Najd and the Kingdom of the Hejaz.

By the mid-1920s, Ibn Saud's conjoined state had emerged as the preeminent local power in the Arabian Peninsula. The question was when and where the Saudi state would stop expanding. For over a decade, Ibn Saud's rule had grown outward from the Najd to include the eastern al-Hasa and Qatif oases and access to the Persian Gulf in 1913, northwest to Ha'il and the Jabal Shammar mountains in 1921, and west to the Hejaz in 1924-1925. Despite multiple British-brokered attempts at arbitration and diplomacy, the Saudi state continued to press northward against Transjordan, Iraq, and Kuwait, and southward against Yemen in the late 1920s and

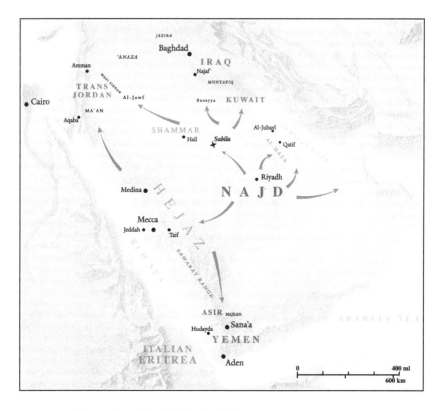

FIGURE 6.5 Expansion of Saudi polity in Arabia.
Source: Author adaptation from public domain.

early 1930s. Conflicts on these peripheries activated interlinked external and internal processes that transformed the nascent Saudi polity, effected processes of state-building in its neighbors, and ultimately produced the boundaries among them, in one of the last phases of the Long Great War.[32]

The regionally significant question of how far the Saudi state would expand was directly tied to an internal power struggle between Ibn Saud and the Ikhwan. The unification of the Kingdom of the Hejaz, the locus of the global Muslim *haj* pilgrimage to Mecca and Medina with a more sedentary, urban, and business oriented population, with Ibn Saud's more rural and transhumant Najd base in the mid-1920s, provoked an increasingly acute crisis about how Ibn Saud and the Ikhwan imagined the emerging polity's trajectory: Should it continue to have a dynamic, fluid periphery of outward proselytization, raiding, and expansion or settle into fixed territorial boundaries? This internal clash culminated in a civil war between the two parties in the late 1920s; Ibn Saud, who pivoted during these years to accepting a regional, territorialized, interstate order, emerged victorious. After this showdown, most of the frontiers between Transjordan, Iraq, Kuwait, and Saudi Arabia were finally settled in the early 1930s. Conflict erupted in the south, however, as Ibn Saud's consolidation of power in Asir provoked a confrontation with Yemen. During the Saudi-Yemeni War (1932–1934), both sides struggled back and forth across an ill-defined boundary stretching from the Tihama coastal plain up and over the Sawarat Asir mountains to the highland areas of the Najran. The war escalated regional tensions, almost provoking British (on behalf of Ibn Saud) and Italian (on behalf of the Yemeni imamate) intervention. A peace agreement was finally reached in 1934, in which the Saudi forces withdrew back to the Asir boundary, and the Yemen-Kingdom of Saudi Arabia boundary was settled.

NORTHERN EXPANSION: BORDERING TRANSJORDAN, IRAQ, AND KUWAIT AND THE SAUDI-IKHWAN CIVIL WAR

The Saudi state's inexorable northern expansion constituted one of the most volatile variables in Britain's Middle East policy formula throughout the 1920s. Political space in Arabia was being rapidly transformed by local state formation and expansion, not by Great Power colonial potentates drawing and imposing arbitrary lines in the sand. And, Ibn Saud and the Ikhwan were the primary drivers forcing the definition of post-Ottoman political borders during this period in the Arabian Peninsula and in southern Greater Syria and Mesopotamia. In this phase of the Long Great War, the British struggled to arbitrate conflict among its multiple client regimes emerging in the region, as repeated bilateral and multilateral negotiations and signed treaties failed to contain the Sultanate of the Najd's raiding and physical expansion into lands claimed by Transjordan, Iraq, and Kuwait.

During the Ottoman period, when these regions were under the jurisdiction of a single (if, at times, nominal) ruler, several powerful tribal groups freely traversed the northern regions of the Arabian Desert, the

Syrian Desert, the Jazira, and the Muntafiq. Political space and sovereignty were fluid, as these groups occasionally were subject to various local or Ottoman attempts to project state power, namely taxation, but more often functioned autonomously. In the 1920s, these spaces and their inhabitants fell between multiple emerging state centers (Mandate Transjordan, Syria, Iraq, and the Sultanate of the Najd). Attempts to increase each respective state's reach into these nonstate zones, to require mobile populations to fix their allegiance and tax revenues to a single sovereign, and to refrain from their own far-ranging raiding and pillaging economic activities, made these frontier zones on the eastern and northern edges of the Najd sphere of influence—bordering Kuwait, Iraq, and Transjordan—intense friction points where the British were forced to try to negotiate and delineate political boundaries.

Across this arc where Northern Arabia merges into Greater Syria and Mesopotamia, there were four strategic geographies contested among these emerging polities: (1) the southern and western reaches of Kuwait; (2) the southern reaches of Iraq; (3) the Wadi Sirhan (the primary corridor linking Central Arabia to Syria) and Jabal Unaza area (where the borders of Saudi Arabia, Iraq, and Transjordan eventually conjoined); and (4) the Ma'an/northern Hejaz region (including Aqaba, the Red Sea port). British diplomacy focused on reconciling overlapping claims to sovereignty over these spaces and over tribal groups that traversed them. In a first major effort at resolving these issues, and to put a check on Ibn Saud's claims in southern Iraq, the British brought together their Hashemite, Saudi, and al-Sabah clients between May and December 1922. In the Uqayr Protocol of 1922 that finally resulted, Percy Cox, the British high commissioner in Iraq, brokered a compromise map between the Najd, Iraq, and Kuwait, drawing a line that blunted Ibn Saud's ambitions in southern Iraq, giving Faisal control over the Amarat, Dhafir, and Muntafiq tribes; compensated Ibn Saud by giving him two-thirds of the Kuwait territory previously delineated in the 1913 Anglo-Ottoman treaty;[33] and, in another key concession, supported Ibn Saud's claims to the Wadi Sirhan. With regards to the last point, Ibn Saud's forces had taken control of the al-Jawf town and oasis complex controlling the southern end of the Wadi Sirhan and asserted claims over the powerful Ruwalla tribe in that area, bringing him into direct conflict with the Amir Abdullah and British officers making policy in Transjordan.

The protocol signaled a partial start toward juridically settling post-Ottoman borders. From east to west, Cox's map set out the Najd-Kuwait borders and the Najd-Iraq borders, from the Persian Gulf to the Jabal Anazah in the Syrian Desert, but along both borders the agreement built in polygonal neutral zones where wells and grazing were to be shared among tribes and where military installations were expressly forbidden.[34] The agreement settled nothing, however, about the boundary between the Najd and Transjordan. While providing a partial juridical definition of political space, it also did nothing to address, and in many ways aggravated, tensions among the state leaders and mobile tribal groups, particularly the key Ikhwan tribes, inhabiting and raiding across these desert zones. On the ground, boundaries remained far from settled: the Ikhwan continued to raid through 1924 and 1925 far into the ostensible territorial space of Iraq, Transjordan, and Kuwait, including attacks on Najaf, Diwaniyya, Amman, and Kuwait City, heedless of the warnings of Ibn Saud or the British. For his part, Ibn Saud also continued to press for a maximalist enclosure of the Wadi Sirhan directly abutting the French Syria mandate, making concerted efforts to get Nuri al-Shaalan, leader of the powerful Ruwalla tribe controlling the northern Wadi Sirhan region, to choose his side rather than Transjordan's Amir Abdullah.[35]

From November 1923 through May 1924, the British convened the Kuwait Conference in a concerted effort to secure a comprehensive settlement among the Hashemite states (Hejaz, Transjordan, and Iraq), Kuwait, and the Najd, but the rivalry between Ibn Saud and Husayn, both of whom refused intermittently to attend, prevented progress from being made. With the functional collapse of the Hashemite Hejaz state before Najdi advances in 1925, along with the outbreak of the Syrian Revolt over the summer, the British pushed hard again to broker a peace that fall. The negotiations bore fruit in the November 1 Bahra Agreement, in which Iraq and the Najd pledged to crack down on cross-border tribal raiding but not to launch a pursuit into each other's territory; they also agreed to set up a special tribunal to adjudicate when raiding had occurred. The next day, the Hadda Agreement between the Najd and Transjordan contained similar pledges about controlling raiding and arbitration. It also delineated a frontier that gave Ibn Saud the entire Wadi Sirhan but blocked Saudi access to the Syrian border.[36]

The following year, Italy's signing of a treaty in September 1926 partnering with the imam in Yemen internationalized internal Arabian tensions by increasing colonial competition for influence in the Red Sea-Southern Arabia-Horn of Africa sphere. After quickly reaching their own agreement with the Yemeni imamate, the British met with Ibn Saud to revisit terms initially set in the 1915 Pact of Darin. In the May 1927 Anglo-Saudi Treaty of Jeddah, the British officially recognized the unified Kingdom of the Hejaz and Najd; Ibn Saud, while not formally recognizing the British mandate position in Palestine, Transjordan, and Iraq or trucial relationships in the Gulf, pledged to respect the status quo (particularly with respect to the unresolved final status of Ma'an province and Aqaba) and maintain "friendly and peaceful relations" with Gulf principalities.[37]

Again, treaty terms on paper did not equal a political settlement on the ground, primarily because of the divergent priorities of Ibn Saud and the primary Ikhwan tribes across the northern borderlands. Through the late 1920s, Ibn Saud's strategic priorities were to contain but also wield the Ikhwan to achieve maximalist territorial goals, projecting influence into southern Iraq, laying claim to the southern and eastern reaches of Transjordan including the Ma'an province and the entirety of the Wadi Sirhan, and blocking a direct land connection between Hashemite Iraq and Jordan. Toward Kuwait, Ibn Saud also sought to both gain territory and capture the lucrative customs duties on Persian Gulf trade into the Arabian interior, building up ports at Jubayl and Qatif to bypass Kuwait and instituting a blockade on Najd tribes trading in Kuwaiti markets.

The Ikhwan's own economic interests were toward free movement—in terms of grazing, raiding, and trading—in and out of Kuwait, southern Iraq, and eastern and southern Transjordan, which dovetailed with their Wahhabi-shaped ideological motivation toward expansive proselytization and jihad, in this case against neighboring Muslim "apostates." Though the blockade on Kuwait directly hurt key Ikhwan tribes like the Mutayr (spurring increased raiding into southern Iraq) in the northern Najd, for most of the 1920s, the political imaginary of the Ikhwan and Ibn Saud more or less converged: the emerging Najd-Hejaz state would have a dynamic, flexible "tribal frontier" with its neighbors allowing the sphere of influence of the state to be determined by the movements and grazing zones of its tribes.[38]

In 1927 and 1928, this partnership began to break down. One factor building tension between the Ikhwan and Ibn Saud was the consolidation and strengthening of a central state apparatus under Ibn Saud's authority. In late December 1926, this was demonstrated in his foreign policy, as he sent his sons as emissaries to Egypt and to London and also to southern Arabia, where he, with no consultation with the key Ikhwan leaders, established a protectorate over the Idrissid emirate in Asir in response to strengthening Italian-Yemeni collaboration. As evidenced in a list of concerns the Ikhwan presented to him at the January 1927 al-Riyadh Conference, internal transformations following the conjoining of the Najd and Hejaz were also driving a wedge between the two parties: the Ikhwan complained about the use of telegraphs, telephones, and motor cars (state-controlled technologies they argued were against Islam); tolerance of the Shi'i minority in al-Hasa; the granting of grazing rights to Iraqi or Jordanian tribes in the Najd; custom duties on Muslims in the Najd; and an end to the ban on trade with Kuwait, or permission to wage jihad against them if they were not true Muslims.[39] Articulated within a Wahhabi interpretative framework, these points were deeply connected to the centralization of Ibn Saud's political power, what Kostiner refers to as the transformation of "the Saudi chieftaincy into an organized state," and resulted in a fatwa issued in February by the Wahhabi ulama. This decision affirmed Ibn Saud's authority to declare jihad (that is, conduct foreign policy), but the ulama declared his taxes illegal. They also called on him to fulfill several religious obligations as Wahhabi ruler: specifically, to destroy a mosque dome in Medina, ban an Egyptian pilgrimage group, and crack down on Shi'is.[40] In April 1927, Ibn Saud convened a follow-up conference in Riyadh to try to reconcile with the Ikhwan, which was boycotted by two prominent Ikhwan leaders, al-Dawish and Ibn Humayd, and had limited success.

THE IKHWAN-SAUDI CIVIL WAR

The crisis that ultimately ruptured the Saudi-Ikhwan alliance was provoked by an attempt to concretely territorialize the boundary between Iraq and the Najd. From February to November 1927, the mandate government in Iraq constructed a series of "posts" across the neutral buffer zone set up in the 1922 Uqayr Protocol, ostensibly as watch posts necessary for catching Iraq-based Shammar tribal raiding parties returning from excursions into the Najd. The northern Najd Ikhwan tribes, however, viewed these as military posts in clear violation of the treaty terms. Throughout that year, the issue emerged as the flashpoint around which Ibn Saud's intentions and loyalties regarding the trajectory of the Kingdom of the Najd and Hejaz were judged. Though he did lodge multiple protests with the Iraqi and British authorities, declaring the "military" (*qalʿa*) not "watch" (*makhfar*) posts obstacles to the Mutayr movement, the Ikwhan and many of the ulama pressed him further, urging him to authorize a jihad.

On November 5, the Mutayr chief, Faisal al-Dawish, forced the issue, leading an Ikhwan raid on the Busayya post, killing over twenty people, including six policemen, then proceeding further into Iraq and Kuwait for further raiding. The raiding party was pursued by the Royal Air Force, which made retaliatory bombing strikes on their camps back in the Najd. For the Ikhwan, the post at Busayya, a key watering hole in an important grazing area on the north-south Najd-Iraq route, became the litmus test for whether Ibn Saud would defend their rights to movement and, by extension, a broader conception of the Wahhabi-Saudi polity. In the weeks following, Ibn Saud criticized Iraq vociferously for provoking conflict by building the posts in direct violation of the terms of the neutral zone and complained about the RAF attacks, while at the same time distancing himself from the Ikhwan raids. At this point, his quandary was that he really had no interest in war on the Iraqi border but also did not want to let the British know he was not strong enough himself to control the rebellious Ikhwan groups.[41]

Throughout 1928, the Ikhwan and Ibn Saud struggled for predominance. While not outright rejecting Ibn Saud's position as rightful ruler over the Najd and Hejaz, the Ikhwan repeatedly challenged him over the nature of the Wahhabi polity and its boundaries. After a large conference in February 1928, Ibn Saud conceded, agreeing to allow the Ikhwan to lead a massive raid that month into Kuwait. In April, over twelve thousand Ikhwan tribesmen convened at Burayda to negotiate with Ibn Saud, demanding he abolish the tax on sheep, dismantle the telegraph system in the Najd, and force Iraq to take down the Busayya post. On the last point, Ibn Saud urged the Ikhwan to pause raiding for two weeks while he again negotiated with the British; if the talks failed, they could go to war.

British-convened talks in May and August in Jeddah between Ibn Saud and Gilbert Clayton to resolve the post issue broke down, but Ibn Saud still did not go to war over the Iraq frontier. Ikhwan sentiment continued to turn away from him that summer.

On November 4, 1928, Ibn Saud convened a major conference in Riyadh, again attempting to negotiate a reconciliation to resolve the tensions aggravated by the Iraqi border posts.[42] He opened by dramatically offering to abdicate, which was roundly decried amid renewed affirmations of support. But the Mutayr and Qahtan Ikhwan leadership quickly followed up with pleas that Ibn Saud lead the jihad to destroy the border posts. Ikhwan leaders queried Ibn Saud:

> You are aware that the desert belongs to us and you remember that when we protested against you for having agreed to mark a boundary in the desert. This was irregular. *Does your faith enjoin you to allow them to mark boundaries on our territory?* You told us then that the object of these boundaries was to stop quarrels and put an end to disputes, though the right of pasture in every part of the desert was still reserved to us. You further said that according to the treaty, they would abstain from the construction of posts at wells and watering places. Now we shall not rest quiet until it is ruled out that the laws of our Creed approve of the erection of these outposts, despite any mischief that may arise from them, or you solemnly declare that these outposts are no source of danger to us. Otherwise these forts will never be allowed to remain on our land. This is a matter on which we are indissolubly determined.
>
> In order that there will be no afterthought, we feel much inclined to ask you *why you did not permit us to conduct the "Jehad" (or religious campaign) with the object of upholding the supremacy of the right faith and the word of God.* We wish to recall to your mind that the sacrifices of life and property are not to be compared with the rewards which God will mete out to those who meet their end in the struggle. Anyhow, we shall comply with your instructions in this concern, but as to the presence of these outposts, there is no one who will tolerate them unless he is a mean wretch. We would fain suffer massacre and torture by you rather than provoke the wrath of God. We therefore advise you to revere his commands and avoid his interdictions. That is all we have to say and assure you that there is nothing else lurking in the depths of our hearts. (emphasis mine)[43]

These questions about territoriality, about who can demand jihad, and when and how it should be carried out constituted the crux of the authority crisis within the emergent Saudi state: Ibn Saud again begged off by asking for two months to negotiate with the British, while the Ikhwan escalated raiding into Kuwait and Iraq and against Najdi groups (including fractions of their own tribes) loyal to Ibn Saud. In response, the British deployed newly organized mobile units including armored cars and airplanes to pursue the Ikhwan tribes into the Najd. That March, Shaykh Ahmed al-Sabah of Kuwait agreed to allow the Ikhwan to use Kuwait as a base. This move profoundly redirected the Saud-Ikhwan conflict, shifting the Ikhwan's endgame toward overthrowing Ibn Saud and establishing an Ikhwan-led polity in the Najd, al-Hasa, and Hejaz.[44]

In late March, the two main Ikhwan factions, led by al-Dawish and Ibn Humayd, engaged Ibn Saud's main force at Sabila. As related at the start of this chapter, al-Dawish and Ibn Saud met in the evening of March 27, 1929, in Ibn Saud's camp to try to come to terms. According to one report, al-Dawish agreed that the Ikhwan groups would surrender but then changed his mind; according to another, al-Dawish returned to his camp to convince Ibn Humayd to accept Ibn Saud's gifts of reconciliation but that Ibn Saud made a surprise attack before he could make his case. Regardless, Ibn Saud's forces did attack at first light on March 28. With superior firepower, they routed the Ikhwan, with al-Dawish being shot in the stomach and Ibn Humayd being pursued and his forces destroyed at his base camp at al-Ghatghat.

The defeat at al-Sabila, however, did not mean the Ikhwan were done. The indefatigable al-Dawish recovered and regrouped his Mutayr forces, joined up with the Ujman tribe further east in the al-Hasa oasis close to the Persian Gulf. The Ujman, who had not participated in the Battle of Sabila, turned against Ibn Saud and joined the Ikhwan revolt after his agent tricked their leader, Didan Ibn Hithlayn, offering him hospitality then putting him in chains. In May and June, the Ujman, the Ruwalla (from the northern end of the Wadi Sirhan), and Dawish's Mutayr groups joined together in the neutral zone between the Najd and Kuwait in June 1929. Allying themselves now with King Faisal and the Shammar tribe in Iraq and with Amir Abdallah and the Ruwalla tribe in Transjordan, the Ikhwan's goal became to overthrow Ibn Saud and seize control of the Najd.

Ibn Saud, likewise, regrouped in the fall of 1929 for a final push to destroy the rebellious Ikhwan coalition. In early September, Ibn Saud convened a conference at al-Shara, a town on the road between al-Riyadh and Mecca, bringing together the loyal Ikhwan factions, the ulama, and urban representatives. The conference ratified a seven-paragraph resolution that asserted the rebellious Utayba and Mutayr tribes had to be punished, according to shari'a, and that Ibn Saud was authorized to pursue and punish them and anyone giving them aid. Having consolidated this internal support, Ibn Saud divided his forces into three groups and directed them in pincer groups to crack down on the Ikhwan. An assurance to Ibn Saud from the British that they would not allow al-Dawish or other Ikhwan leaders refuge in Iraq or Kuwait (along with a shipment to Ibn Saud of three thousand British rifles) severely hampered the Ikhwan's ability to maneuver and compete. It also cut off their strategic depth, much like the British decision to crack down on Druze crossings into northern Transjordan near the end of the Syrian Revolt or the French cutting off the Rif Republic's access into their zone in Morocco. By January, none of the major Ikhwan blocs were able to sustain any movement. On January 10, 1930, key leaders including al-Dawish, Ibn Lami, and Ibn Hithlayn surrendered to the British in Kuwait before being handed over to Ibn Saud.

With the Ikhwan-Saudi civil war finally resolved, the outstanding northern frontier issues between the Kingdom of the Najd and Hejaz and Iraq and Kuwait were also quickly settled. In January, Faisal reached out to Ibn Saud, and on February 23, 1930, the leaders met on a British carrier in the Persian Gulf to negotiate a good neighbor treaty. The Saudi-Iraqi treaty was finally signed in May 1931 in Jeddah, though it took until 1981 for both states to agree on the partition and delineation of the border through the 2,270-square-mile neutral zone specified in the 1922 Uqayr Protocol.

Tensions remained unresolved, however, with Transjordan, particularly after Amir Abdallah was peripherally involved in staging an uprising in the northern Hejaz in the spring of 1932. That April, Hamid Ibn Rifada, a Billi chief, led a group of Hejazi forces, who had trained on Amir Abdullah's agricultural estates in the Nile Delta, across the Sinai to Aqaba in Transjordan, where they were reprovisioned. In May, they crossed into Saudi territory, hoping to rally a mass movement of discontented northern Hejazi tribes but ended up with just over 1,500 men. In July 1932, the

Saudi force sent out against them roundly defeated the revolt, killing Ibn Rifada and about 370 of his men. From September 1932, the British again pushed for a treaty between Transjordan and the Kingdom of Saudi Arabia to finally resolve borderland disputes including the final delineation of the frontier (the surveys used in the 1924 agreement were found to be highly inaccurate), the status of key tribes including the Bani Atiyya and Ruwalla, and arbitration processes with regard to raiding, extradition, and indemnities. In July 1933, the two states finally signed a good neighbor agreement that settled most of their outstanding frictions.

SOUTHERN EXPANSION: THE ASIR REVOLT AND THE SAUDI-YEMENI WAR

To the south, after joining the Kingdom of the Hejaz to their growing Arabian polity in the mid-1920s, the Saudi-Wahhabi state came into direct contact with the semiautonomous province of Asir and the highland Imamate of Yemen. The Emirate of Asir, an area south of the Hejaz that stretched from the Red Sea coastlands, known as the Tihama, up over the Surat Asir mountain chain to the Najran highlands to the east, had been recognized by the British in 1915 in an effort to foment revolt against the Ottomans. In the early 1920s, the Idrissi amir in Asir then allied with Ibn Saud against the Hashemite Kingdom of the Hejaz (its northern neighbor) and Yemen (its southern). After taking over the Hejaz, Ibn Saud and the Yemen imam loosely divided Asir into respective zones of control, with Ibn Saud exercising a protectorate with a Saudi governor ruling alongside the amir and local councils.

In the early 1930s, Saudi-Yemeni rivalry in Asir drew the states into direct conflict. In November 1930, Ibn Saud and Hasan al-Idrisi renegotiated the terms of their protectorate agreement, giving the Saudis control over all of Asir and bringing them directly into contact with Imam Yahya's territory. None of this frontier, either in the coastal Tihamat Asir or the upland Najran area (the latter of which had barely been under any form of Idrissid control), was demarcated. In the Najran highlands, the Bani Yam tribe, who had never submitted to the Idrissid amir, also resisted Ibn Saud's rule, making themselves a critical swing client in this strategic, contested region. In September 1931, the Imam Yahya moved the Yemeni army into the Jabal Arw area of the Sawarat Asir range, staking a claim to broader control in the area. Struggling economically in the midst of the global depression, and concerned, as were the British, about provoking Italian intervention on behalf of the imam, the Saudis refrained from responding with force, negotiating an agreement with Imam Yahya in December that recognized his control over Jabal Arw. But the Saudis also dug in in the coastal Tihama region, developing a port at Jizan to rival the Yemeni ports further down the Red Sea coast at Hudayda and Luhiyya.

In September 1932, Ibn Saud declared the unification of his realms (the Najd, Ha`il, Shammar, Hejaz, Ahsa, and Asir) as the Kingdom of Saudi Arabia, but Asir remained an unsettled flashpoint on the peninsula. That fall, with the backing of both the Imam of Yemen and Hejazi notables in exile affiliated with the Hejazi Liberation Army (Hizb al-tahrir al-hijazi), Hasan al-Idrissi, the vassal amir in Asir, led an anti-Saudi revolt, seizing Saudi garrisons at Sahiyya, Abu Arish, and Jizan. Saudi generals, including Khalid Ibn Luway and Abd al-Aziz Ibn Musa`id, retook these positions over the winter but could not totally defeat al-Idrissi, who sought refuge with the imam in Yemen in January 1933.[45] In February, borderland tribes on both sides of the frontier revolted, with the Masariha rising up against Ibn Saud in the Tihama and the Bani Yam against Yemen in Najran, destabilizing relations between Yemen and Saudi Arabia, as both sides tried to support and quell rival proxy tribal forces. While the British and Italians supported their clients' conflicting claims to Asir, both colonial powers were wary of a direct conflict between Yemen and Saudi Arabia that could escalate into a major conflagration that might draw them in: the British wanted to maintain good relations with the imam, worried he might threaten Aden; the Italians wanted good relations with Ibn Saud, as they had long Red Sea routes from the Suez Canal linking to their colonies in Somaliland and Eritrea.

In the fall of 1933, both sides became increasingly active militarily into each other's territory, though neither side had the troop strength to prevail. The imam's focus was the Bani Yam tribe, which he pushed seventy miles north into the Najran region before being repelled in November. Saudi forces made significant gains on the Tihama coastal plain. A temporary agreement that December fell through when the Imam launched another offensive in the Najran and the Saudis responded with further attacks along the border. During the spring of 1934, the tensions between Yemen and Saudi Arabia in Asir escalated into a full-blown war. In April and May, the Saudis turned the tide, making gains across the front, first in the Najran, where they regained territory they had lost, then on the coast, where they entered the key Yemeni Red Sea port of Hudayda on April 24, 1934. The fall of Hudayda, a red line for Italy, prompted the British and Italians to both immediately anchor warships in the harbor. Despite Ibn Saud's pleas for British support for his claim to the port, they refused. The British themselves had just come to their own agreement that February with the imam, the Treaty of Sanaa, in which they recognized Yemeni independence in exchange for the imam's pledge to not attack Aden.

Ibn Saud's forces, having severely stretched their supply lines and now opposing two colonial powers, withdrew back up the coast, and the war came to a close. In early May 1934, the imam and Ibn Saud agreed to a peace agreement in the city of Taif. The imam relinquished Yemeni claims in Asir, including the Bani Yam area of Najran, and both sides mutually recognized each other's independence and sovereignty. They also agreed to a frontier line, clearly including Asir in the Kingdom of Saudi Arabia, separating the two states.

A little more than thirty years after a 1902 raid in which he reestablished Saudi control over the small Najd town of Riyadh, Ibn Saud, with affiliated tribal forces including the Ikhwan, had successfully formed an Arabian state that encompassed virtually the whole peninsula. Through the 1920s, the Sultanate of the Najd had absorbed the Kingdom of the Hejaz (unified as the Kingdom of Saudi Arabia in 1932) and pressed north and south, catalyzing military conflict on its borders with Kuwait, Iraq, Transjordan, and Yemen. The internal struggle between Ibn Saud and the Ikhwan over fluid versus fixed territorial boundaries for this emerging polity had been settled in Ibn Saud's favor by the summer of 1930, and a succession of treaties—with Iraq (1931), Transjordan (1933), and Yemen (1934)—finally began to solidify and demarcate most, but not all, of the kingdom's physical boundaries. Having gone into serious debt to finance these wars in the north and south, in 1933, Ibn Saud signed a portentous agreement with the American-owned Standard Oil company regarding exploration and exploitation of the kingdom's oil potential; the eventual influx of oil wealth would radically transform the peninsula in the next chapter of the peninsula's history, but the outlines of the Saudi polity forged through the Long Great War would hold fast up to the present.[46]

In the late 1920s and early 1930s, three more synchronic conflicts across the greater Middle East among rival political visions climaxed in the final phase of the Long Great War. In Northern Africa, to the far west, the Atlas, Jabal Saghro, and Saharan tribes in the French zone of protectorate Morocco waged a desperate jihad in a last-ditch attempt to preserve their autonomy against the onslaught of repeated summer pacification campaigns—with air power, machine gunnery, and artillery—that crushed their resistance by 1934 and established an unprecedented monopolization of force by the colonial state within the Moroccan territory. In Cyrenaica, the resilient Sanusi proto-state faced the onslaught of Italy's total colonial war in the late 1920s, including the forced relocation of most of the civilian population to brutal concentration camps, the use of devastating military technologies, and the building of a 170-mile fence along the eastern border, which eventually broke their ability to resist and sustain their autonomy. In 1934, Italy administratively unified the provinces of Tripolitania and Cyrenaica as Libya. In contrast to these examples of a colonial state eliminating internal counterimaginaries of a local political order, in Arabia and in Anatolia, this was paradoxically done by a local independent emergent state engaging in forms of internal colonialism. Kemalist Turkey mobilized a massive military campaign to crush the nascent Kurdish polity established on Mount Ararat in far Eastern Anatolia, thereafter consolidating much of the remaining territorial outlines of the post-Ottoman Republic (Alexandretta—or Hatay, in Turkish—province would be transferred from French to Turkish control in 1938), though visions of a Kurdish political order would persist.[47] In Arabia, Ibn Saud defeated the Ikhwan's rival vision of a perpetually fluid and expanding Wahhabi polity then eventually negotiated boundaries with Iraq, Transjordan, and Yemen in the early 1930s.

By the mid-1930s, the region-wide period of sustained wartime catalyzed in 1911 by French and Italian expansion into Northern Africa, which had unmade the previous political order from Morocco to Iran and through which the greater Middle East was remade into an interstate system of local and colonial polities, drew to a close. Though the region would again soon be swept up into another world war and tumultuous struggles for decolonization, none of these conflicts would fundamentally transform the political topography reimagined and forged through the Long Great War.

CONCLUSION

In the summer of 1932, a demarcation commission team including British, French, Syrian, and Transjordanian members trudged two thousand feet upward from the relative cool of the Yarmouk river valley to the brutally hot Hawran plain. Having begun down at the El Hamme railway station by the Sea of Galilee, the party was working eastward to the Jabal Tenf, surveying, then marking, the boundary between Mandate Syria and Mandate Transjordan up to a triangulated intersection point with the Iraq border. Physically, this involved mixing concrete under the summer sun and erecting cairns, spaced out along the frontier.[1]

Very roughly sketched out on a too large of a scale map in the 1916 Sykes-Picot Agreement then only partially clarified by the Franco-British Convention of December 23, 1920, this boundary had never been defined. Its final negotiation and physical demarcation was delayed for more than a decade, intentionally and nonintentionally, by both the French and British.[2] In the mid-1920s, during the Great Syrian Revolt, these borderlands had been an active front, with the French and Druze both operating extensively along and across the frontier. Eventually, the British had allowed the French to establish a *frontière de fait* south of the boundary, but the French lingered in this liminal region into the late 1920s, resettling Druze populations in villages like Semme and Umm Jimal, to shore up a buffer zone in the south.

By the early 1930s, however, the British were finally ready to figure out and settle the Syria-Transjordan border. The main reason was that they needed to also resolve the Syria-Iraq boundary—also still not defined—so they could terminate the mandate and broker the Kingdom of Iraq's entry into the League of Nations. France's territorial creep into northern Transjordan, into the precise areas the British wanted to run a railway and oil pipeline linking Iraq to the northwest Palestine port of Haifa, gave the French leverage. Regretting having given Mosul to the British a decade earlier, the French wanted as much compensatory territory as possible. Finally, after a solid month of negotiations in October 1931 in Paris, the two sides finally agreed on the border, which the League of Nations approved in January 1932.[3] Six months later, the surveying party was in the field and passed between the villages of Elemtaih and Umm al-Jimal, putting up a concrete marker; if it survived, I would have seen it driving along that boundary line in the back of the Jordanian army jeep eighty-five years later after being shot at and detained with my brother-in-law.

The next summer, in 1933, between Iraq and Syria, a similar thirteen-man commission (composed of Syrian, Iraqi, British, and French representatives) wrapped up a six-month expedition that had laboriously surveyed, negotiated (arbitrating conflicting claims about how it should pass through or around villages, salt sources, grazing lands, and most importantly, the Jabal Sinjar massif), and demarcated the border. On July 31, 1933, they installed the eighty-sixth, and final, seven-foot-high metal frontier post on the right bank of the Tigris River, just below where the Eastern Khabur joins it.[4] Somewhere along this last stretch of the border is where, eighty-one years later, the Daesh (ISIS) public relations team that I described in the preface would film the bulldozing of a border checkpoint and release it on the internet on June 29, 2014, celebrating "The End of Sykes-Picot," as they swept into the Mosul region of northern Iraq that summer.

This conclusion returns to where the book started—the Syria-Jordan border and the morphing boundaries of Iraq, Syria, Kurdistan, and the Islamic State—to underline how I hope the previous chapters have argued for a different sort of "end" to Sykes-Picot. My primary intervention has been to deeply challenge the standard genesis story of the modern Middle East: that artificial and imposed colonial borders are an original sin at the source of subsequent political conflicts in the region. By tracing out how the Long Great War unmade political worlds *and* served as the crucible in which new political worlds were imagined and put in motion, this book's alternate narrative has shown that the new map of the modern Middle East was not imposed but reshaped over time as rival colonial and local clashed violently into the 1920s and 1930s. States, identities, and spatial boundaries were transformed through war, not a peace settlement.

I focused the opening anecdote on the Syria-Transjordan border because it is here, arguably, that the Sykes-Picot standard narrative about an imposed border might be the most accurate. The British and French did eventually draw a line *somewhat* resembling the 1916 agreement that separated French Lebanon and Syria from British Palestine and Transjordan. But, it is critically important to note and account for the temporal and spatial gaps between Sykes-Picot and the actual demarcation of these borders. To start, the Sykes-Picot agreement's original designation of Palestine as an international zone became a dead letter when the British occupied it in 1917 and 1918. It then took the mandate powers until 1923 to agree on the first part of this line separating Palestine, Lebanon, and Syria, with several important adjustments in the Litani watershed, the Sea of Galilee, and the Jawlan/Golan. It then took until October 1931 for them to agree on the second part of this line between Syria and Transjordan, which was not marked off until 1932. The border between Syria and Iraq bears absolutely no resemblance to the Sykes-Picot map. France, not Britain, was originally given the entire Mosul region, but they agreed in 1920 to give Mosul to the British. As we have seen, Mosul's fate was then fiercely contested by Turkey, militarily and diplomatically, through 1926, and the actual Syria-Iraq border was not demarcated until 1933.

Thus, even in this "best case" scenario, Sykes-Picot's simplistic dehistoricization of "imposed" borders is a myth that fundamentally misrepresents how the region's political order was actually reimagined and refashioned. Borders, rather than being imposed after the fall of the Ottomans, were actually defined and demarcated—even between Syria, Palestine, Iraq, and Jordan—only after long periods of conflict, mediation, and negotiation. Across the region, from Morocco's protectorate zones to Turkey's border with northwest Iran, it took until the early 1930s for the modern Middle East's borders to start to emerge and be settled (leaving aside the ones in the Arabian Peninsula not defined until the 1970s and 1980s or in some cases up to the present).

Similarly, the standard narrative's claim about artificiality also breaks down even in the Greater Syria case. The Sykes-Picot myth primes us presuppositionally with an intuitive Edenic counterfactual in which "natural" borders could have been drawn but were transgressed. The implicit assumption is that some sort of primordial post-Ottoman ethnonational communities in fact existed and were spatially bounded, and, by extension, that the colonial and local actors had fixed ideas and preferences that were diametrically opposed. This ignores the historical record, traced throughout this book, of colonial *and* local actors repeatedly recalculating and reimagining new political futures, with adjusted social and physical boundaries, based on opportunity contexts that shifted as competing projects came into conflict and new facts on the ground were established.

From the beginning, Syria and Iraq were envisioned as separate entities by almost all the colonial and local actors (despite the ISIS theatrics on their border in 2014). For Syria, some sort of unified country was an expressed preference in 1919 for most of the population, alongside minority preferences for a Greater Lebanon or a Zionist-imagined Palestine, but, as this region was partitioned over time and as new thinkable units like Lebanon, Syria, Palestine, or Transjordan became more plausible, local populations shifted their preferences to political sovereignty and independence within these, mobilizing powerful movements and making nationalist and other types of claims over these units. In Mesopotamia the post-Ottoman process of state formation involved not partition but territorial unification. Through this consolidation period, ideas about a separate Kurdistan or Basra Republic were entertained, but colonial and local actors increasingly thought of and made claims within the imagined polity of a unified Iraq.

Thus, even in these most Sykes-Picot-esque contexts in the Mashriq, or "Arab Middle East," the longer account of the Great War presented in this book demonstrates that, like all borders around the world, the modern Middle East's political boundaries were neither artificial nor could they possibly have been "natural." Instead, they were produced as rival emerging polities came into conflict and forged the region's post-Ottoman political topography over a period of time that extended into the 1930s.

Another flaw of the standard narrative is the reification of the Mashriq story we have been discussing, using the specific Arab Middle East (that is, Lebanon, Syria, Palestine, Transjordan, and Iraq) experience to represent the history and trajectory of the whole region. If the imposition and artificiality dimensions of this narrative do not hold with the British and French mandates, they are even more farfetched in the rest of the greater Middle East. In Anatolia, the reverse happened: the emergent Kemalist Turkish Republic largely imposed boundaries on the French, Italians, Greeks, Armenians, Kurds, and even the British (in the Straits zone, though they failed in Mosul). Similarly, in Arabia, it was Ibn Saud's expansion, not colonial officials, that forced the negotiation, definition, and eventually demarcation of territorialized boundaries with Transjordan, Iraq, and Kuwait; the Trucial States on the Persian Gulf coast; and with Yemen in the 1920s and 1930s. In Iran, the Pahlavi state's consolidation, extension of state space in subduing autonomous tribal areas in Zagros and elsewhere, and struggle against British and Soviet influence also proceeded along a different trajectory than the Mashriq.

In the Maghrib, the decade-long struggles by the Rif Republic, Atlas jihads, and Sanusi polity against multiple colonial powers to preserve forms of local autonomous governance in Northern Africa also do not neatly fit in a framework of artificial and imposed boundaries that cut through what should have been "natural" units. Cyrenaica was incorporated into a unified Italian Libya (that the Sanusi leader, Idriss, eventually ruled after independence), and the Rif was subsumed in the Spanish protectorate zone. Are the boundaries of Libya artificial? Is a reunified postindependence Morocco, forcibly integrating the Rif and the Western Sahara, a natural territorial unit? Keeping the wider temporal and geographic frame of the Long Great War in place helps correct a pervasive *Mashriq* myopia, forcing us to consider the broader regional context and the spectrum of actual historical processes that shaped the modern Middle East. Across this broader canvas, there are examples of partition and unification: the one constant is that none of these were unilaterally imposed, all were worked out through extended periods of warfare.

This brings us to the Sykes-Picot narrative's third shortcoming: its diagnosis that the region's political problems stem from incorrectly drawn boundaries. My point in this book has by no means been to argue that the British and French (or Spanish, Italians, or other colonial powers) carry no historical blame. What they did wrong, however, was not how they drew borders. To reiterate: 1) Middle East borders were not imposed but produced, as they are everywhere else, over time, and, 2) a huge range of boundary configurations could conceivably have worked. As previous chapters demonstrated, political imaginaries in the region were malleable and adapted repeatedly to shifting opportunity contexts. What the European colonial powers did wrong was to repeatedly, persistently, and violently intervene, shaping the region's political institutions by buttressing authoritarian colonial state structures whose legacies continue to impact the modern Middle East. In sum, if you are going to assign blame, don't blame the borders—blame the politics and political systems colonial powers crushed or reinforced within the borders.

I will illustrate this point with the seemingly most irascible case in the region, Palestine. The British mandate sin was not drawing the borders of Palestine incorrectly. Palestine could have been larger (not splitting off Transjordan) or even smaller. At different points charted in this book, Palestinians could imagine being part of Greater Syria, even part of Egypt, and, of course, they could imagine Palestine itself as a political unit, including or without the East Bank. On the other side, different Zionist groups could also imagine multiple spatial configurations of Palestine (though there were disagreements between Revisionists and Labor about whether to give up claims to the East Bank), as the subsequent post-1948 territorial expansion and contraction of the state of Israel has proven.

What the British did wrong was to pursue an ambivalent, at times schizophrenic, ethnoreligious divide-and-rule policy in which they never midwifed representative political structures through which a Palestinian Jewish *and* Arab unified polity could emerge. Instead, they helped birth a zero-sum game of competitive Zionist and Palestinian nation-building that continues, with brutal human costs, to the present.[5] In every one of the mandate cases, the British and French actively intervened to put down nascent, local political experiments in various scales and forms of representative government (with Gouraud's violent destruction of the Damascus-based Arab constitutional monarchy being one the most glaring instances). In the place of these local emerging state structures, the British and French instead buttressed direct and indirect modes of colonial rule, intentionally and explicitly designed to inhibit solidaristic and nationalist institutions inclined toward independence that could threaten their rule.[6]

But, here it is important to not veer too far toward naively idealizing the self-determining political futures that "might have been" across the region. History rarely offers up black and white stories with clear good and bad guys; the Long Great War framework, which itself contains multiple counterfactuals to the Sykes-Picot narrative, shows us how much the making of the modern Middle East is a study in greys. For example, the Turkish Republic is the poster child of an alternate trajectory of successful self-determination, of a post-Ottoman future dictated not by the colonial imposition of artificial boundaries (apart from the contested fate of Mosul province) but by an anticolonial nationalist independence movement that forged a hugely successful polity that was viewed with admiration in the 1920s and 1930s throughout Africa, the Middle East, and Asia. The preceding chapters have shown how fraught this story in fact is, given the brutal ethnic cleansing—through genocide, war, resettlement, and assimilationist policies—enacted against Armenians, Assyrians, and Kurds during the internal colonization carried out in Turkish state-building.

The other counterfactual trajectory is the Kingdom of Saudi Arabia, another incredibly successful local state-building case that imposed its will on the post-Ottoman map. Through the 1920s and early 1930s, structures of power—in the struggles between Ibn Saud, the Ikhwan, and the ulama—were forged in ways that strongly impacted the Saudi state's development. Though beyond the scope of this book, this example of a form of "self-determination," later juiced by the influx of massive oil revenues, produced another complex and, in many ways, problematic type of post-Ottoman polity. The alternate universes in which the Rif Republic, a Sanusi state, a Kurdish entity, or an Ikhwan-led polity survived into the twenty-first century would also have likely presented equally ambivalent outcomes. In pointing out these examples, my point is not to blithely dismiss the "interrupted" democratic political futures that might have been but to emphasize that history, particularly state formation, is complicated anywhere in the world, including the greater Middle East.

If we accept the "end" of Sykes-Picot, then, what do we learn from the alternative narrative of worldmaking in the Long Great War? Overall, understanding that the making of the modern Middle East was not an event—spoken into existence by the Great Powers in Paris or San Remo—but a longer period in which processes of state, identity, and boundary formation interacted opens up wider spaces for how we think about and study the modern Middle East's history. The Long Great War, rather than cleanly marking the end or start of other periods

(Ottoman, mandate, etc.), has to be understood as its own special timeframe: a region-wide tumultuous, transitional, transformative historical moment—unparalleled in centuries before or since—that has to be studied on its own terms. There are Ottoman, Qajar, and Alawite shadows and legacies that persist through this period, as well as novel changes and new forms that emerged. Thinking about the greater Middle East—from Morocco to the Iranian Plateau—as an interconnected, complex system in which local, translocal, and international factors influenced how the post-Ottoman world was shaped also opens up important comparative questions. This framework makes us sensitive to the variation expressed across this broader regional system, recognizing an important distinction between more settled political units and the more fluid spaces in which there was dynamic competition as multiple emergent polities were imagined and competed with each other.

Similarly, analyzing the Long Great War as a distinct period deemphasizes a procrustean bed of ethnonationalism, allowing us to see the diverse array of political imaginaries that became thinkable during this period across the region—subnational, national, and supranational—and to judge them on their own terms, not based on the criteria of whether they represented "real" nationalism (secular, political, ethnolinguistic, or otherwise). With examples like the Kurds, the Palestinians, the Riffis, the Druze, and many others, we can recognize how the multiple, overlapping, perhaps contradictory, forms of local, regional, national, religious, ethnocultural, and political bonds of solidarity were activated and acted upon during this period (as they were for virtually every collective actor in this story). We do not have to succumb to the normative pressures of justifying or denying their political rights to self-determination. And, we can recognize the dynamism, not fixity, of political preferences and political futures that became imaginable and unimaginable over time. This openness to various expressions of political identity being legitimate is important for our understanding of both the past and present.

This brings us to a final question: What does the Long Great War tell us about today's greater Middle East, or, perhaps more importantly, about tomorrow? Perhaps more than anywhere else in the world, the legacies of the Great War are imminently relevant in concrete ways in the Middle East. At the beginning of the book, I emphasized that history does not repeat, but it does rhyme and echo. In the twenty-first century, successful post-Ottoman states continue to assert regional influence: Turkey is projecting neo-Ottoman aspirations in Mosul, Syria, Libya, and the Eastern Mediterranean; Iran and Israel have emerged as regional hegemons; while Saudi Arabia, and now Qatar and the United Arab Emirates, have expansionary diplomatic and military ambitions in Arabia and beyond. Russia's Middle East game has been revived with Putin's active involvement in Syria and in Libya, while the United States intervened with its largest military occupations in a generation, in Iraq and Afghanistan, and experienced a master class on the limitations of Great Power pretensions in the face of local contenders and struggles on the ground.

It is important to note that the failed state projects from a century ago also continue to shape the present. Virtually all of the cases studied in part 3—those friction points at which, because of topography and geographic juxtaposition, the most volatile, sustained, and violent clashes among emerging post-Ottoman polities persisted into the early 1930s—are echoing and rhyming a century later.[7] In the past decade, Greater Syria (the outbreak of the Syrian Civil War, the emergence of the Islamic State, the emergence of Rojava, the regional and international involvement of outside powers), the Zagros (the resumption of the Turkish-PKK civil war, the independence referendum by the Kurdish Regional Government), the Caucasus (the Nagorno-Karabakh conflict), Arabia (the Zaydi Houthi-Saudi-Emirati-Iranian conflict in the Yemen Civil War, Saudi Arabia's tensions with Qatar), Cyrenaica (the Libyan Civil War), and, finally, the Rif (the *hirak* movement) have all reemerged as the most volatile hotspots in the region. In these struggles, submerged memories and aspirations for entities like Greater Syria, and independent Kurdistan, Sanusi Barqa, or the Rif Republic, have resurfaced.

The early twenty-first century—in the wake of the 2003 U.S. invasion and destabilization of Iraq and the upheaval following the 2011 Arab uprisings, both of which helped open up the possibility for imagining a wide range of possible political futures—is witnessing a transformative transitional moment similar to that experienced a century ago. This period, of course, though greatly influenced by the Great War, will not repeat history. And, unfortunately, there is no straightforward, simple policy takeaway to be learned, other than a heavy dose of humility about international intervention and recognition of the importance and complexity of local dynamics. But, in finally forgoing the myth that the region's "Fall" is because of the original sin of imposed, artificial borders, we can see that the Middle East is neither perpetually cursed by the Great War legacy nor think that its salvation lies in either external powers or local actors simply redrawing these boundaries. The deeper issue is political. Being able to see how new worlds were created in the Middle East in the Long Great War helps us see that they can be reimagined and remade now and in the future—and therein lies hope.

NOTES

PREFACE

1. From France and Spain's inland occupation of Morocco and Italy's invasion of Ottoman Tripolitania and Cyrenaica in 1911 roughly to the end of the Saudi-Yemeni War in 1934.
2. V. M. Amadouny, "The Formation of the Transjordan-Syria Boundary, 1915–32," *Middle Eastern Studies* 31, no. 3 (1995): 533–49.
3. Closed from 2015, the Jaber-Nassib crossing was reopened by Jordan in October 2018.
4. Yoav Alon, *Making of Jordan: Tribes, Colonialism, and the Modern State* (New York: I. B. Tauris, 2007), 80.
5. *Daesh* is the word created by the Arabic acronym for the Islamic State in Iraq and Syria and is widely used, as it also sounds like "to trample down and crush" or "bigot," instead of ISIS.
6. For clips of the destruction of the border checkpoint and interviews shortly thereafter, see the *Vice* news segment with embedded reporter Medyan Dairieh, "Bulldozing the Border Between Iraq and Syria: The Islamic State," August 13, 2013, https://www.youtube.com/watch?v=TxX_THjtXOw.
7. By the summer 2015, the Peshmerga had already begun to receive support in the form of air strikes, intelligence, logistics, training, weapons, and medical aid from a global coalition including Albania, Austria, Australia, Belgium, Bulgaria, Canada, Croatia, Czech Republic, Denmark, Estonia, France, Germany, Hungary, Iran, Italy, Jordan, the Netherlands, New Zealand, Sweden, Slovakia, Turkey, the United Kingdom, and the United States. Glenn Field, "Global Support for Peshmerga Forces," *Kurdstrat*, August 7, 2015, http://kurdstrat.com/2015/07/08/global-support-for-peshmerga-forces/.
8. "Sir Archibald Mapsalot III," *The Daily Show with Jon Stewart*, Comedy Central, https://www.cc.com/video-clips/kovgs5/the-daily-show-with-jon-stewart-sir-archibald-mapsalot-iii.

9. Between Iraq and Syria, the transfer of the Mosul province from French to British control was the most significant change from the Sykes-Picot terms; in Anatolia, the Turkish war for independence kicked the French out of Cicilia; and the international administration proposed for Palestine was replaced by a British mandate. See the excellent pieces by Sara Pursley, "'Lines Drawn on an Empty Map': Iraq's Borders and the Legend of the Artificial State (Part 1 and 2)," *Jadaliyya*, June 2, 2015, http://www.jadaliyya.com/pages/index/21759/lines-drawn-on-an-empty-map_iraq's-borders-and-the, and David Patel, "Repartioning the Sykes-Picot Middle East? Debunking Three Myths," *Middle East Brief* 103 (November 2016), Brandeis University Crown Center for Middle East Studies, https://www.brandeis.edu/crown/publications/middle-east-briefs/pdfs/101-200/meb103.pdf.

INTRODUCTION

1. Despite its shortcomings and relatively recent vintage (becoming widely known as a neologism used by the American naval strategist Alfred Thayer Mahan and others from 1902), I use the shorthand term *Middle East* to reference the Braudelian-like interacting and linked system of seas, plains, mountains, and deserts stretching from Gibraltar to Hormuz. For a more nuanced discussion of the background, possibilities, and shortcomings of the concept of the Middle East, consult Michael E. Bonine, Abbas Amanat, and Michael Ezekiel Gasper, eds., *Is There a Middle East? The Evolution of a Geopolitical Concept* (Stanford, CA: Stanford University Press, 2011); and John Voll, "The Middle East in World History," in *The Oxford Handbook of World History*, ed. Jerry Bentley (New York: Oxford University Press, 2011), 437–54.
2. Arnold Talbot Wilson, *Mesopotamia, 1917–1920; a Clash of Loyalties; a Personal and Historical Record* (London: Oxford University Press, 1931), 139; Wadie Jwaideh, *The Kurdish National Movement: Its Origins and Development* (Syracuse, NY: Syracuse University Press, 2006), 173–79.
3. For an early record of the texts, see Woodrow Wilson's notes from the Paris Peace Conference published in the early 1920s in Ray Stannard Baker, *Woodrow Wilson and World Settlement: Written from His Unpublished and Personal Material* (New York: Doubleday, 1922), 4.
4. Wilson returned from Paris in the fall of 1919 to lobby for the approval of the Treaty of Versailles but was incapacitated by a stroke in late October. In March 1920, the United States Senate failed to ratify the treaty. Though the United States was an observer at the April San Remo conference and was assigned a role in western Armenia, the other Allied powers had little expectation the Americans would actively engage in the postwar Middle East.
5. In the 1915 Constantinople Agreement, Russia was promised control of Istanbul and the Bosphorus and then control of eastern Anatolia in the 1916 Sykes-Picot Agreement. To bring Italy to the side of the Allies, the British and French promised in the 1915 Treaty of London and the 1917 Agreement of Saint-Jean-de-Maurienne to recognize its interests in the Dodecanese Islands and in southern and western Anatolia.

INTRODUCTION 261

6. Treaty of Sèvres, Articles 62–64. The full English version published by the Foreign and Commonwealth Office is available at http://treaties.fco.gov.uk/docs/pdf/1920/TS0011.pdf.
7. Treaty of Sèvres, Articles 89–83.
8. The March 1912 Treaty of Fes signed by the Moroccan sultan and the French Republic recognized a French protectorate over the Alawite Empire; the French then separately recognized Spanish interests in a northern zone and in southern enclaves, including Saharan regions, that November.
9. See Robert Gerwarth, *The Vanquished: Why the First World War Failed to End* (New York: Farrar, Straus and Giroux, 2016); and Robert Gerwarth and Erez Manela, eds. *Empires at War, 1911–1923* (Oxford: Oxford University Press, 2014).
10. Peter Gatrell, "War After the War: Conflicts, 1919–1923," in *A Companion to World War 1*, ed. John Horne (London: Blackwell, 2010), 558–75. Peter Gatrell and Nick Baron apply this concept to the period after 1945; see "Violent Peacetime: Reconceptualising Displacement and Resettlement in the Soviet-East European Borderlands after the Second World War," in *Warlands*, ed. Peter Gatrell and Nick Baron (London: Palgrave MacMillan, 2009), 255–68.
11. Earlier encroachment on the de jure and de facto territories under Ottoman Empire sovereignty included Russia's steady southern expansion around the Black Sea and into the Caucasus from the late eighteenth century, international intervention in the Greek Revolt between 1820 and 1829, France's invasion of Algeria in 1830 and Tunisia in 1881, and Britain's occupation of Cyprus in 1878 and Egypt in 1882.
12. Significant military conflict took place later in the 1930s, but these instances, such as the Great Palestinian Revolt (1936–1939) or the Dersim rebellion (1937–1938), took place *within* political units that had more or less become settled.
13. Erik J. Zürcher, *The Young Turk Legacy and Nation Building: From the Ottoman Empire to Atatürk's Turkey* (New York: I. B. Tauris, 2010); Christine M. Philliou, *Turkey: A Past Against History* (Oakland: University of California Press, 2021); Cyrus Schayegh, *The Middle East and the Making of the Modern World* (Cambridge, MA: Harvard University Press, 2017); Michael Provence, *The Last Ottoman Generation and the Making of the Modern Middle East* (New York: Cambridge University Press, 2017).
14. The Great War's impact within North Africa has only just begun to be assessed in its own right; see Odile Moreau, ed., "The Maghreb: A Forgotten Front of the First World War," Special issue, *Hespéris-Tamuda* 53, no. 1 (2018).
15. See Braudel's discussion of the boundaries of the Greater Mediterranean in *The Mediterranean and the Mediterranean World in the Age of Philip II*, vol. 1 (Berkeley: University of California Press, 1995), 168–230. In contrast to Braudel's emphasis on long-term evolution, this book, perhaps paradoxically, instead presents an "event history" (*histoire événementielle*) that shows how events and processes played out rapidly across this regional system, upending and transforming political structures during this two-decade period of cataclysmic war.
16. Examples include Gerwarth and Manela, *Empires at War* and Andrew Jarboe and Richard Fogarty, eds., *Empires in World War I: Shifting Frontiers and Imperial Dynamics in a Global Conflict* (New York: I. B. Tauris. 2014). For comparative analyses, see Michael

Reynolds, *Shattering Empires: The Clash and Collapse of the Ottoman and Russian Empires, 1908–1918* (New York: Cambridge University Press, 2011); Martin Thomas, *Empires of Intelligence: Security Services and Colonial Disorder After 1914* (Berkeley: University of California Press, 2008); and James Barr, *A Line in the Sand: The Anglo-French Struggle for the Middle East, 1914–1948* (New York: Norton, 2012).

17. The reference here is to David Fromkin, *A Peace to End All Peace: Creating the Modern Middle East, 1914–1922* (New York: Holt, 1989).

18. In a recent appraisal of World War I's legacy, Eugene Rogan sums up: "The manner in which the modern boundaries were imposed by imperial fiat has destabilized the region ever since. Guided by the imperative of balancing the ambitions of rival empires, rather than in consultation with the Arab peoples concerned, the frontiers of Arab states have lacked legitimacy. A century after the Great War, Middle Eastern frontiers continue to bedevil regional stability—less on grounds of legitimacy than as a consequence of the many peoples who remain stateless (notably the Kurds and Palestinians) as a result of the wartime partition diplomacy and its consequences." Rogan, "The First World War and Its Legacy in the Middle East," in *The Oxford Handbook of Contemporary Middle Eastern and North African History*, ed. Amal Ghazal and Jens Hanssen (Oxford: Oxford University Press, 2020), 106.

19. Fromkin, *A Peace to End All Peace*, 9. The following chapters challenge almost every line in this quote.

20. Implicitly, this expresses a retrospective methodological nationalism. See the critique in Andreas Wimmer and Nina Glick Schiller, "Methodological Nationalism and Beyond: Nation-state Building, Migration, and the Social Sciences," *Global Networks* 2, no. 4 (2002): 301–34.

21. Henri Lefebvre, *The Production of Space* (Cambridge, MA: Blackwell, 1991); Neil Brenner and Stuart Elden, "Henri Lefebvre on State, Space, Territory," *International Political Sociology* 3, no. 4 (2009): 353–77; and Daniel Neep, "State-Space Beyond Territory: Wormholes, Gravitational Fields, and Entanglement," *Journal of Historical Sociology*, 30, no. 3 (2016): 466–95.

22. Since the 2003 U.S. invasion of Iraq, several pundits, fully absorbing the Fromkinian paradigm of an Anglo-French constructed modern Middle East, have mused on alternate configurations. One of the most well-known was Jeffrey Goldberg's 2008 article and accompanying map about how the United States should break up Iraq: "After Iraq," *The Atlantic*, January 1, 2008, https://www.theatlantic.com/magazine/archive/2008/01/after-iraq/306577/.

23. See Elizabeth F. Thompson, *Justice Interrupted: The Struggle for Constitutional Government in the Middle East* (Cambridge, MA: Harvard University Press, 2013) and *How the West Stole Democracy from the Arabs: The Syrian Arab Congress of 1920 and the Destruction of Its Historic Liberal-Islamic Alliance*, illustrated ed. (New York: Atlantic Monthly Press, 2020).

24. Tilly's argument about the reinforcing cycle of war-making, taxation, and state formation has, of course, generated long running debates about its merits accounting for early modern Europe itself, other important factors, and applicability beyond this context.

For a review of recent developments in these discussions, see Lars Bo Kaspersen and Jeppe Strandsbjerg, eds., *Does War Make States?: Investigations of Charles Tilly's Historical Sociology* (Cambridge: Cambridge University Press, 2017).

25. Adom Getachew, *Worldmaking After Empire: The Rise and Fall of Self-Determination* (Princeton, NJ: Princeton University Press, 2019).

26. Benedict Anderson, *Imagined Communities: Reflections on the Origin and Spread of Nationalism* (London: Verso, 1991).

27. Michelle U. Campos, *Ottoman Brothers: Muslims, Christians, and Jews in Early Twentieth-Century Palestine* (Stanford, CA: Stanford University Press, 2011); Bedross Der Matossian, *Shattered Dreams of Revolution: From Liberty to Violence in the Late Ottoman Empire* (Stanford, CA: Stanford University Press, 2014).

28. On the creation, maintenance, and evolution of this system over four centuries, see Karen Barkey, *Empire of Difference: The Ottomans in Comparative Perspective* (New York: Cambridge University Press, 2008); and Halil Inalcik, *The Ottoman Empire: 1300–1600* (London: Weidenfeld & Nicolson, 2013). On social, economic, military, and political reforms and transformation in the late Ottoman period, see Fatma Göçek, *Rise of the Bourgeoisie, Demise of Empire: Ottoman Westernization and Social Change* (New York: Oxford University Press, 1996); and Şükrü Hanioğlu, *A Brief History of the Late Ottoman Empire* (Princeton, NJ: Princeton University Press, 2008).

29. See James Scott, *The Art of Not Being Governed: An Anarchist History of Upland Southeast Asia* (New Haven, CT: Yale University Press, 2009), 6–9, on shatter zones more generally; more specifically on the Trans-Caucasus, see Reynolds, *Shattering Empires*.

30. Referring to concurrent processes in Southeast Asia, James Scott talks about the "last great enclosure movement," how modern colonial and independent states wielded new technologies to bring the ungoverned highland marches, the "Zomia" region, of the interior to heel. Scott, *The Art of Not Being Governed*, 4–9.

31. Andrew Zimmerman provides valuable insights on how historians can learn from anthropologists' move to multisited ethnography. Zimmerman, "Africa in Imperial and Transnational History: Multi-Sited Historiography and the Necessity of Theory," *Journal of African History* 54, no. 3 (November 2013): 331–40.

1. GEOSTRATEGIC QUESTIONS, COLONIAL SCRAMBLES, AND THE ROAD TO THE GREAT WAR

1. Sven Lindqvist, *A History of Bombing*, trans. Linda Haverty Rugg (London: Granta, 2012), 1–2; Ciro Paoletti, *A Military History of Italy* (Westport, CT: Praeger Security International, 2008), 134.

2. For an accessible and provocative account of Selim's world-empire-building expansion in the early sixteenth century, see Alan Mikhail, *God's Shadow: Sultan Selim, His Ottoman Empire, and the Making of the Modern World* (New York: Liveright, 2020).

3. Jamil M. Abun-Nasr, *A History of the Maghrib in the Islamic Period* (Cambridge: Cambridge University Press, 1987), 190.

4. On the legal status of late Ottoman sovereignty in Egypt, see Aimee Genell, "The End of Egypt's Occupation: Ottoman Sovereignty and the British Declaration of Protection," in *Beyond Versailles: Sovereignty, Legitimacy, and the Formation of New Polities After the Great War*, ed. Roberta Pergher and Marcus Payk (Bloomington: Indiana University Press, 2019), 77–98.
5. On the Ottoman Empire and the Eastern Question, see M. S. Anderson, *The Eastern Question, 1774-1923: A Study in International Relations* (New York: St. Martin's, 1966) and William Hale, *Turkish Foreign Policy Since 1774* (London: Routledge, 2012).
6. Though functionally autonomous, the khedival dynasty established in Egypt by Mehmet Ali technically remained under Ottoman sovereignty in international diplomacy throughout the nineteenth century. On the complex British-Ottoman negotiations over sovereignty and Egypt's legal status, see Aimee Genell, "Empire by Law: Ottoman Sovereignty and the British Occupation of Egypt, 1882–1923" (PhD diss., Columbia University, 2013).
7. Mehmet Ali's modernized Egyptian army had been previously deployed, at the behest of the Ottoman sultan, to retake Mecca and Medina in 1815 after their capture by Saudi-Wahhabi forces, and in the early 1820s, he had conducted military campaigns south into Sudan to expand his own zone of imperial control. See Khaled Fahmy, *All the Pasha's Men: Mehmed Ali, His Army, and the Making of Modern Egypt* (Cambridge: Cambridge University Press, 1997) and Afaf Lutfi Sayyid-Marsot, *Egypt in the Reign of Muhammad Ali* (New York: Cambridge University Press, 1984.)
8. On these longer population transfer flows that predate World War I, see Isa Blumi, *Ottoman Refugees, 1878–1939: Migration in a Post-Imperial World* (London: Bloomsbury Academic, 2013) and Resat Kasaba, *A Moveable Empire* (Seattle: University of Washington Press, 2009).
9. On resettlement of these refugees, see Vladimir Hamed-Troyansky, –"Imperial Refuge: Resettlment of Muslims from Russia in the Ottoman Empire, 1860–1914." (PhD diss., Stanford University, 2018).
10. Mary Lewis, *Divided Rule: Sovereignty and Empire in French Tunisia, 1881-1938* (Berkeley: University of California Press, 2013), 16–17.
11. Frederick Parsons, *The Origins of the Morocco Question, 1880-1900* (London: Duckworth, 1976); Edmund Burke III, *Prelude to Protectorate in Morocco: Pre-colonial Protest and Resistance* (Chicago: University of Chicago Press, 1976).
12. David Stevenson, "Militarization and Diplomacy in Europe Before 1914," *International Security* 22, no. 1 (1997): 131.
13. Hew Strachan, *The First World War*, vol. 1: *To Arms* (Oxford: Oxford University Press, 2001), 24–26.
14. On the idiosyncrasies of the Second Reich's colonial project, see George Steinmetz, "Empire in Three Keys: Forging the Imperial Imaginary at the 1896 Berlin Trade Exhibition," *Thesis Eleven* 139, no. 1 (April 1, 2017): 46–68.
15. On the clash of Italian and Ottoman imperial imaginaries in their incorporation of Libya into national space, see Jonathan McCollum, "Reimagining Mediterranean Spaces: Libya and the Italo-Turkish War, 1911–1912," *Diacronie. Studi Di Storia Contemporanea* 23, no. 3

(October 29, 2015). On Italy's colonial imaginary in Libya, see Claudio Segrè, *Fourth Shore: The Italian Colonization of Libya* (Chicago: University of Chicago Press, 1974).

16. Ali Minawi, *The Ottoman Scramble for Africa: Empire and Diplomacy in the Sahara and Hijaz* (Stanford, CA: Stanford University Press, 2016).

17. Ali Ahmida, *Forgotten Voices: Power and Agency in Colonial and Postcolonial Libya* (New York: Routledge, 2005), 11–18.

18. On Sanusi state formation see Edward Evans-Pritchard, *The Sanusi of Cyrenaica* (Oxford: Clarendon, 1949) and Ali Ahmida, *The Making of Modern Libya: State Formation, Colonization, and Resistance* (Albany: State University of New York Press, 2011), 73–102. Eileen Ryan details prewar Sanusi relations with the Ottomans and with European empires in *Religion as Resistance: Negotiating Authority in Italian Libya* (Oxford: Oxford University Press, 2018), 21–30.

19. Minawi, *The Ottoman Scramble for Africa*, 42.

20. Minawi, *The Ottoman Scramble for Africa*, 81–98; Abun-Nasr, *A History of the Maghrib in the Islamic Period*, 317–19.

21. Matthew H. Ellis, *Desert Borderland: The Making of Modern Egypt and Libya* (Stanford, CA: Stanford University Press, 2018).

22. Other CUP leaders were already there, as Tripolitania had long been the site to which political agitators had been banished under Abdülhamid II. Şükrü Hanioğlu, *The Young Turks in Opposition* (New York: Oxford University Press, 1995), 121.

23. On the impact of the Italo-Ottoman War on Enver and other CUP officers, see Enver Paşa, *Kendi mektuplarında Enver Paşa*, ed. M. Şükrü Hanioğlu (Beyazıt, İstanbul: Der Yayınları, 1989); McCollum, "Reimagining Mediterranean Spaces," 12; Eugene Rogan, *The Fall of the Ottomans: The Great War in the Middle East* (New York: Basic Books, 2015), 16–18; and Philip Stoddard, "The Ottoman Government and the Arabs, 1911 to 1918: A Preliminary Study of the Teskilat-i Mahsusa" (PhD diss., Princeton University, 1963).

24. On the progress of the Italo-Ottoman War, see Rachel Simon, *Libya Between Ottomanism and Nationalism: The Ottoman Involvement in Libya During the War with Italy (1911–1919)* (Berlin: K. Schwarz, 1987).

25. Renato Tittoni, *The Italo-Turkish War (1911–12)* (Kansas City, MO: Franklin Hudson, 1914).

26. Tālib Mustāq, *Awrāq Ayāmi* (Baghdad: al-Dār al-ʿArabīyah lil-Ṭibāʿah, 1989), 9–20. Also see Dina Khoury, "Ambiguities of the Modern: The Great War in the Memoirs and Poetry of the Iraqis," in *The World in World Wars: Experiences, Perceptions and Perspectives from Africa and Asia*, ed. Heike Liebau et al. (New York: Brill, 2010), 325.

2. THE MANY FRONTS OF THE OTTOMANS' GREAT WAR, 1914-1918

1. Jean Mélia, *Les Bombardements de Bône et Philippeville* (Paris: Berger-Levrault, 1927).

2. On French colonial troops in the war, see Richard Fogarty, *Race and War in France: Colonial Subjects in the French Army, 1914–1918* (Baltimore, MD: Johns Hopkins Press, 2008).

3. This book addresses *how* the Great War transformed the greater Ottoman system more than *why* the Ottomans entered the war or *why* they joined the Central Powers. Mustafa Aksakal's definitive study addresses both why questions; see *The Ottoman Road to War in 1914* (New York: Cambridge University Press, 2008).
4. Chris B. Rooney, "The International Significance of British Naval Missions to the Ottoman Empire, 1908–14," *Middle Eastern Studies* 34, no. 1 (1998): 1–29.
5. A vast literature has developed on the "home front" of the war in Europe, mostly focused on Britain and France (the role of women, propaganda, art, daily life, etc.). A few recent examples include J. A. Turner, "The Challenge to Liberalism: The Politics of the Home Fronts," in *The Oxford Illustrated History of the First World War*, New ed., ed. Hew Strachan (New York: Oxford University Press, 2014), 163–78 and Annette Becker, "The Visual Arts," in *A Companion to World War I*, ed. John Horne (London: Wiley-Blackwell, 2011), 234–47. The Ottoman home front has recently been addressed in Yigit Akin, *When the War Came Home: The Ottomans' Great War and the Devastation of an Empire* (Stanford, CA: Stanford University Press, 2018); Talha Çiçek, ed., *Syria in World War I. Politics, Economy and Society* (Routledge: London, 2016); and Leila Fawaz, *A Land of Aching Hearts: The Middle East in the Great War* (Cambridge, MA: Harvard University Press, 2014).
6. For excellent macro-treatments of the Great War in the Ottoman Middle East, see Eugene Rogan, *The Fall of the Ottomans* (London: Basic, 2015) and Ryan Gingeras, *Fall of the Sultanate: The Great War and the End of the Ottoman Empire, 1908–1922*, (Oxford: Oxford University Press, 2016).
7. Sean McMeekin, *The Berlin-Baghdad Express* (Cambridge, MA: The Belknap Press of Harvard University Press, 2012), 7–53.
8. Najwa al-Qattan, "*Safarbarlik:* Ottoman Syria and the Great War," in *From the Syrian Land to the States of Syria and Lebanon*, ed. Thomas Philipp and Christoph Schumann (Würzburg: Ergon in Kommission, 2004), 163–73; and Mehmet Beşikçi, *The Ottoman Mobilization of Manpower in the First World War* (Leiden: Brill, 2012), 86–76. Also see Melanie S. Tanielian, *The Charity of War: Famine, Humanitarian Aid, and World War I in the Middle East* (Stanford, CA: Stanford University Press, 2017).
9. In the fall of 1914, Germany fielded 4,500,000; France 3,781,000; Austria-Hungary 2,229,500; Britain 733,500; and Russia 5,000,000. See John Ellis and Michael Cox, *The World War I Databook: The Essential Facts and Figures for All the Combatants* (London: Aurum, 2001), 244.
10. Hew Strachan, *The First World War* (Oxford: Oxford University Press, 2001), 676–77.
11. Aksakal, *The Ottoman Road to War in 1914*, 177–78.
12. Going back to the Dutch Christiann Snouck Hurgronje's 1915 pamphlet and its recent critical reevaluation, see Erik Jan Zürcher, ed., *Jihad and Islam in World War I: Studies on the Ottoman Jihad on the Centenary of Snouck Hurgronje's "Holy War Made in Germany* (Leiden: Leiden University Press, 2016). On the Ottoman-German partnership, also see McMeekin, *The Berlin-Baghdad Express*.
13. The one exception was Cyrenaica, where Ottoman-German efforts to mobilize the Sanusis were successful. Hans-Ulrich Seidt, "From Palestine to the Caucasus-Oskar

Niedermayer and Germany's Middle Eastern Strategy in 1918," *German Studies Review* (2001) 24, no. 1: 1–18; Thomas Hughes, "The German Mission to Afghanistan, 1915–1916," *German Studies Review*, 25, no. 3 (2002): 447–76; and Donald McKale, *War by Revolution: Germany and Great Britain in the Middle East in the Era of World War I* (Kent, OH: Kent State University Press, 1998), 145–51.

14. From 1768 to 1914, the empire officially made six prior calls for jihad, and jihad had been used less officially numerous other times with varying valences, most recently with respect to the Italo-Ottoman War, where Turkish officers and Sanusi leaders used it to unify anti-Italian resistance. Mustafa Aksakal, "Holy War Made in Germany? Ottoman Origins of the 1914 Jihad," *War in History* 18, no. 2 (2011): 184–99.

15. James Scott, *The Art of Not Being Governed* (New Haven, CT: Yale University Press, 2009), 8–10; Michael Reynolds, *Shattering Empires: The Clash and Collapse of the Ottoman and Russian Empires, 1908–1918* (New York: Cambridge University Press, 2012), 46–81.

16. See Sabri Ateş's excellent monograph, countering the widely held notion that Chaldiran defined the border and tracing the complex local and international conflicts and tensions involved in making the boundary: *The Ottoman-Iranian Borderlands: Making a Boundary, 1843–1914* (Cambridge: Cambridge University Press, 2013).

17. Michael Eppel, "The Demise of the Kurdish Emirates: The Impact of Ottoman Reforms and International Relations on Kurdistan During the First Half of the Nineteenth Century," *Middle Eastern Studies* 44, no. 2 (2008): 237–58.

18. Janet Klein, *The Margins of Empire: Kurdish Militias in the Ottoman Tribal Zone* (Stanford, CA: Stanford University Press, 2011).

19. William Allen offers a detailed analysis of the weeks-long momentous battle in *Caucasian Battlefields: A History of the Wars on the Turco-Caucasian Border 1828–1921* (New York: Cambridge University Press, 1953), 263–85.

20. On the surge of scholarship on the Armenian genocide in the past decade, see Ronald Suny, Fatma Göçek, and Norman Naimark, *The Question of Genocide* (New York: Oxford University Press, 2011); Eric Hooglund, "New Scholarship on the Relocation of Ottoman Armenians from Eastern Anatolia in 1915–1916" (special issue), *Middle East Critique* 20, no. 3 (2011): 227–51, particularly his editor's note and M. Hakan Yavuz, "Contours of Scholarship on Turkish-Armenian Relations" in the same issue; and Fatma Müge Göçek, *Denial of Violence: Ottoman Past, Turkish Present and the Collective Violence Against Armenians, 1789–2009* (New York: Oxford University Press, 2014).

21. Hannibal Travis, " 'Native Christians Massacred': The Ottoman Genocide of the Assyrians During World War I," *Genocide Studies and Prevention* 1, no. 3 (2106): 336–38.

22. Arash Khazeni, *Tribes and Empire on the Margins of Nineteenth-Century Iran* (Seattle: University of Washington Press, 2010), chapters 4–5.

23. For an excellent treatment of Ottoman policy in Iraq, see Gökhan Çetinsaya, *The Ottoman Administration of Iraq, 1890–1908* (London: Routledge, 2006); on the Ottoman-British rivalry in the late nineteenth century Persian Gulf, see Frederick Anscombe, *The Ottoman Gulf: The Creation of Kuwait, Saudi Arabia, and Qatar* (New York: Columbia University Press, 1997).

24. Frederick Moberly, *The Campaign in Mesopotamia 1914–1918*, Vol. 1 (London: H. M. Stationery Office, 1927), 346; see also Rogan, *The Fall of the Ottomans*, 79–81.
25. One of the first tasks for the IEF at Faw was to reconnect the telegraph cables, first laid to connect the Basrah province to India in the 1860s (Anscombe, *The Ottoman Gulf*, 19–20; Rogan, *The Fall of the Ottomans*, 84).
26. See Rogan, *The Fall of the Ottomans*, 219–24, on the spring and summer campaigns up the Tigris and Euphrates.
27. Uncle to Enver Pasha, Halil Bey (later retitled Pasha) was first posted to eastern Anatolia then was redeployed in October 1915 to Baghdad province ahead of the British advance. Following the Salman Pak battle, the German field marshal over the Sixth Army, Colmar von der Goltz, put Halil Bey in charge of the force pursuing Townsend. On his recently published memoirs, see Syed Tanvir Wasti, "Halil Kut—'the Last Ottoman Pasha,'" *Middle Eastern Studies* 53, no. 5 (September 3, 2017): 820–33.
28. Edward Erickson, *Ordered to Die: A History of the Ottoman Army* (Westport, CT: Greenwood, 2001), 151.
29. Rogan, *Fall of the Ottomans*, 318–19.
30. C. R. Pennell, *Morocco Since 1830: A History* (New York: New York University Press, 2001), 181.
31. Kyle J. Anderson, "The Egyptian Labor Corps: Workers, Peasants, and the State in World War I," *International Journal of Middle East Studies* 49, no. 1 (February 2017): 5–24.
32. On Anglo-Sanusi relations and the buildup to the operations on the Egypt-Cyrenaica border, see Russell McGuirk, *The Sanusi's Little War: The Amazing Story of a Forgotten Conflict in the Western Desert, 1915–1917* (London: Arabian Publishing, 2007).
33. Ja'far al-'Askarī, William Facey, and Najdat Fatḥī Ṣafwat, *A Soldier's Story: From Ottoman Rule to Independent Iraq: The Memoirs of Jafar Pasha Al-Askari (1885–1936)* (London: Arabian Publishing, 2003). Askari's fascinating memoir details his trajectory from Libya, his participation as a commander of Faisal's army in the Arab Revolt, and his service in Iraq afterward.
34. For firsthand account of the technological and tactical innovation involved in creating these mobile units in the Western Desert, see Captain Claud Williams, *Light Car Patrols 1916–19: War and Exploration in Egypt and Libya with the Model T Ford* (London: Silphium, 2013).
35. Sayyid Ahmad supported Mustafa Kemal and was sent to negotiate with Arab tribes on the Turko-French front in the early 1920s. He departed for Damascus in 1924, then moved on to the Hejaz because the French would not let him stay. He died a decade later, in 1933, living in Medina. On Sayyid Ahmad's exile, look at Claudia Gazzini, "Jihad in Exile: Ahmad al-Sharif al-Sanusi 1918–33" (Master's thesis, Princeton University, 2004).
36. These types of societies were formed all over the Arab provinces including the Jamiat al-Basra al-Islahiya (Reformist League) in Basra and al-Nadi al-Adabi (Literary Club) in Baghdad, both founded in 1911; those in Istanbul included al-Alam al-Akhdar (The Green Banner) and al-Yadd al-Sawda (The Black Hand) in 1912 and al-Ahd (The Covenant) in 1913.

37. On the Arab Revolt, see Ali A. Allawi, *Faisal I of Iraq* (New Haven, CT: Yale University Press, 2014), chapters 5–8; for T. E. Lawrence's (self-)celebration of its success, see *The Seven Pillars of Wisdom* (Garden City, NY: Garden City Publishing, 1938)e; and Scott Anderson's deft treatment in *Lawrence in Arabia: War, Deceit, Imperial Folly and the Making of the Modern Middle East* (New York: Doubleday, 2013).
38. For military history of the Palestine campaign, see Matthew Hughes, "General Allenby and the Palestine Campaign, 1917–18," *Journal of Strategic Studies* 19, no. 4 (December 1, 1996): 59–88.

3. THE MIDDLE EAST'S SO-CALLED WILSONIAN MOMENT, 1918–1920

1. Germany with the Treaty of Versailles (June 28, 1919), Austria with the Treaty of Saint-Germain (September 10, 1919), Bulgaria with the Treaty of Neuilly (November 27, 1920), Hungary with the Treaty of Trianon (June 4, 1920), and the Ottoman Empire with the Treaty of Sèvres (August 10, 1920).
2. Woodrow Wilson, "Fourteen Points," Avalon Project, http://avalon.law.yale.edu/20th_century/wilson14.asp.
3. Margaret MacMillan, *Paris 1919: Six Months That Changed the World* (New York: Random House, 2007), 394.
4. For William Yale's longer trajectory through World War I in the Middle East, see Scott Anderson, *Lawrence in Arabia: War, Deceit, Imperial Folly and the Making of the Modern Middle East* (New York: Doubleday, 2013).
5. King-Crane Commission Digital Collection, Oberlin College (hereafter KCC). Record series 15/13/22, Box 16: King-Crane Commission (May–August 1919) Folder 3. Notes from interviews between William Yale and delegations in Jaffa, June 11, 1919. http://dcollections.oberlin.edu/cdm/ref/collection/kingcrane/id/1855.
6. Albert Lybyer, "Notes from an Interview with a Delegation in Jaffa, Met with Donald Brodie and Albert Lybyer," June 11, 1919. Record series 15/13/22, Box 16: King-Crane Commission (May–August 1919) Folder 3.Retrieved from http://dcollections.oberlin.edu/cdm/singleitem/collection/kingcrane/id/1856/rec/3.
7. Erez Manela, *The Wilsonian Moment: Self-Determination and the International Origins of Anticolonial Nationalism* (New York: Oxford University Press, 2007); Vladimir Lenin, "The Right of Nations to Self-Determination," *Prosveshcheniye*, April–June 1914, Nos. 4–6. Available at https://www.marxists.org/archive/lenin/works/1914/self-det/. In the Middle East, in part because of the more vast press distribution of President Wilson's comments (extensively discussed in journals ranging from Rashid Rida's *Al-Manar* to Nimr's *Al-Muqataam*) compared to the Communist revolutionary not yet in power, it was Wilson's rhetoric much more than Lenin's that captured the popular imagination.
8. MacMillan, *Paris 1919*; Introduction and part I of Susan Pedersen, *The Guardians: The League of Nations and the Crisis of Empire* (Oxford: Oxford University Press, 2015).

9. Chaim Weizmann, "Zionist Proposals to the Peace Conference, Feb. 3, 1919," in Meyer Weisgal, ed., *The Letters and Papers of Chaim Weizmann* (LPCW), Series A, Vol. IX (New Brunswick, NJ, 1977), 392.
10. The French brought a Moroccan to verify the translation, as they had received intelligence that Faisal was going to read the Quran and have Lawrence speak. John Mack, *A Prince of Our Disorder: The Life of T. E. Lawrence* (Cambridge, MA: Harvard University Press, 1975), 267.
11. With British urging, he had signed an agreement with Weizmann beforehand in January agreeing Palestine was not part of Syria and recognizing the Zionist presence there.
12. MacMillan, *Paris 1919*, 391.
13. See Reem Bailony, "Transnational Rebellion: The Syrian Revolt of 1925–1927" (PhD diss., University of California Los Angeles, 2015), 48–50; on the role of varying diasporic Syrian-Lebanese actors at the conference and period following, see Simon Jackson, "Diaspora Politics and Developmental Empire: The Syro-Lebanese at the League of Nations," *Arab Studies Journal* 21, no. 1 (2013): 166–90, and Stacy D. Fahrenthold, *Between the Ottomans and the Entente: The First World War in the Syrian and Lebanese Diaspora, 1908–1925* (Oxford: Oxford University Press, 2019).
14. MacMillan, *Paris 1919*, 379.
15. During the war, Sharif Pasha published a journal, *Meşrutiyet* (Constitutionalism), which was critical of the CUP leadership and their attempts to disarm Kurds. For background, see M. Atmaca, "Osmanlıcı, Konformist ve Liberal Bir Muhalif: Şerif Paşa," in Yalçın Çakmak and Tuncay Şur, eds., *Kürt Tarihi ve Siyasetinden Portreler* 1. baskı, Araştırma-İnceleme Dizisi 443 (Fatih, İstanbul: İletişim Yayınları, 2018).
16. Şerif Paşa, *Memorandum on the Claims of the Kurd People* (Paris: A. G. L'Hoir, 1919). The pamphlet was published in French and English (reprinted in the *International Journal of Kurdish Studies* (2001) 15, nos. 1–2: 131).
17. On the nineteenth-century tug of war and final 1913–1914 Anglo-Russian commission that surveyed the border, see Sabri Ateş, *Ottoman-Iranian Borderlands: Making a Boundary, 1843–1914* (Cambridge: Cambridge University Press, 2013), chapter 6.
18. On Nosratdoleh's representation of Qajar Persia at the conference and correspondence related to the Anglo-Persian Agreement of 1919, see United Nations Archives (Geneva), Private Archives (1884–1986), Firuz Nosratdoleh Papers.
19. Macmillan, *Paris 1919*, 437. On the secret 1919 Anglo-Persian agreement and domestic and international forces that prevented it from being enacted, see Homa Katouzian, "The Campaign Against the Anglo-Iranian Agreement of 1919," *British Journal of Middle Eastern Studies* 25, no. 1 (1998): 5–46.
20. Other German territories in Africa and the Pacific Islands not deemed at a stage of civilization on the cusp of self-rule were classified as a different type of mandate. On the League's definition and oversight of the various mandate classifications, see Pedersen, *The Guardians*.
21. The full text reads: "The end that Great Britain and France have had in view in pursuing in the East in the war unloosed by German ambition is the complete and definite freeing of the peoples so long oppressed by the Turks and the establishment of national

governments and administrations deriving their authority from the initiative and free choice of the indigenous populations. In order to give effect to these intentions Great Britain and France have agreed to encourage and assist the establishment of indigenous governments and administrations in Syria and Mesopotamia now freed by the Allies and in the territories whose liberation they seek and to recognize them as soon as they are effectively established. Far from wishing to impose any particular institutions on the populations of these regions, their only care is to assure by their support and efficacious assistance the normal working of the Governments and institutions which they shall have freely given themselves. To ensure impartial and equal justice for all, to facilitate the economic development of the country by promoting and encouraging local initiatives to foster the spread of education, to put an end to the divisions too long exploited by Turkish policy—such is the role that the two Allied Governments claim in the liberated territories." Middle East Centre Archives, St. Antony's College (hereafter MECA), Philby, 1/3/3/2 Draft Mandate for Mesopotamia, c. 1920.

22. On these ties and their evolution through the late Ottoman period, see Beshara Doumani, *Rediscovering Palestine: Merchants and Peasants in Jabal Nablus, 1700–1900* (Berkeley: University of California Press, 1995) and Eugene L. Rogan, *Frontiers of State in the Late Ottoman Empire: Transjordan, 1850–1921* (New York: Cambridge University Press, 1999).

23. On the devastating impact of the war on the civilian population of greater Syria, see Melanie Tanielian, *The Charity of War: Famine, Humanitarian Aid, and World War I in the Middle East* (Stanford, CA: Stanford University Press, 2017) and Elizabeth Thompson, *Colonial Citizens: Republican Rights, Paternal Privilege, and Gender in French Syria and Lebanon* (New York: Columbia University Press, 2000), chapter 1. On the spread of the influenza virus through British and Ottoman troop movements, see Kjell Lind, "The Impact of the 1918 Influenza on Greater Syria" (Master's thesis, University of London School of Oriental and African Studies, 2012).

24. Salim Tamari, *Year of the Locust* (Berkeley: University of California Press, 2011), 92.

25. For an excellent survey of the twenty-plus commissions that have been sent to assess the Palestine question since 1919, see Lori Allen, *A History of False Hope: Investigative Commissions in Palestine* (Stanford, CA: Stanford University Press, 2021).

26. James Gelvin, "The Ironic Legacy of the King-Crane Commission," in *The Middle East and the United States: A Historical and Political Reassessment*, ed. D. W. Lesch and M. L. Haas (New York: Routledge, 2007), 13–29; Ussama Makdisi, *Faith Misplaced: The Broken Promise of U.S.-Arab Relations, 1820–2001* (New York: Public Affairs, 2010), 132–46.

27. King-Crane Commission Report, submitted by Charles R. Crane and Henry Church King, August 28, 1919, 3–4, http://dcollections.oberlin.edu/digital/collection/kingcrane/id/587

28. On the internal deliberations in Damascus in 1919–1920, see Mahmoud Haddad, "Arab Religious Nationalism in the Colonial Era: Re-reading Rashid Rida's Ideas on the Caliphate," *Journal of the American Oriental Society* 117, no. 2 (1997): 253–77; Eliezer Tauber, "Rashid Rida and Faysal's Kingdom in Syria," *The Muslim World* 85, nos. 3–4 (1995): 235–45.

29. On the new forms of mass politics that emerged and flourished between 1918 and 1920, see James Gelvin, *Divided Loyalties: Nationalism and Mass Politics* (Berkeley: University of California Press, 1999), particularly the discussion on pages 150–168 on the summer of 1919.
30. Judith Yaphe, "The View from Basra: Southern Iraq's reaction to War and Occupation, 1914–25", in *The Creation of Iraq, 1914–1921*, ed. Reeva Simon and Eleanor Tejirian (New York: Columbia University Press, 2004), 19–35. See also, Eliezer Tauber, "Sayyid Talib and the Young Turks in Basrah," *Middle Eastern Studies* 25, no. 1 (1989): 3–22.
31. Rogan, *The Fall of the Ottomans*, 182–83.
32. Reidar Visser, *Basra, the Failed Gulf State: Separatism and Nationalism in Southern Iraq* (Münster: LIT Verlag, 2005).
33. Peter Sluglett, *Britain in Iraq: Contriving King and Country, 1914–1932* (New York: Columbia University Press, 2007), 21–34.
34. Wadie Jwaideh, *The Kurdish National Movement: Its Origins and Development* (Syracuse, NY: Syracuse University Press, 2006), 175–78.
35. MacMillan, *Paris 1919*, 368.
36. Nur Bilge Criss, *Istanbul Under Allied Occupation, 1918–1923* (Boston: Brill, 1999).
37. On Turko-Kurdish unity and the proceedings of the Erzurum Congress, see Bekir Baykal, *Erzurum Kongresi ile İlgili Belgeler* (Ankara: Institute of Turkish Revolution Press, 1969) and Mehmet Kırzıoğlu, *Bütünüyle Erzurum Kongresi Vol. I-II* (Ankara: Kültür Ofset, 1993).
38. Maurice Abadie, *Opérations au Levant: Les quatre sieges d'Aïnteb (1920–21)* (Paris: Charles-Lavauzelle, 1922).
39. Elizabeth Thompson traces how the Syrian-Arab Congress—encompassing both secular liberals and Islamic reformers—came together to set up an Arab, democratic, constitutional monarchy, and how this experiment was crushed by the French army months later, in *How the West Stole Democracy from the Arabs: The Syrian Arab Congress of 1920 and the Destruction of Its Historic Liberal-Islamic Alliance* (New York: Atlantic Monthly, 2020).
40. Keith Watenpaugh, *Being Modern in the Middle East: Revolution, Nationalism, Colonialism, and the Arab Middle Class* (Princeton, NJ: Princeton University Press, 2006), 160–84.
41. Philip S. Khoury, *Syria and the French Mandate: The Politics of Arab Nationalism, 1920–1945* (Princeton, NJ: Princeton University Press, 1987), 97–99.
42. Much of the Syrian nationalist leadership had already fled to Transjordan and Palestine, and then on to Cairo (Khoury, *Syria and the French Mandate*, 98).
43. Abigail Jacobson, *From Empire to Empire: Jerusalem Between Ottoman and British Rule* (Syracuse, NY: Syracuse University Press, 2011), 172–77; Benny Morris, *Righteous Victims* (New York: Knopf, 1999), 90–97.
44. Michael Provence, *The Last Ottoman Generation and the Making of the Modern Middle East* (New York: Cambridge University Press, 2017), 113, 117.
45. On buildup to the 1920 revolt, see Amal Vinogradov, "The 1920 Revolt in Iraq Reconsidered: The Role of Tribes in National Politics," *International Journal of Middle East Studies* 3, no. 2 (1972): 123–39.

46. On the British aerial bombardment in the 1920 revolt and early commitment to air governance in Iraq and Arabia, see David Omissi, *Air Power and Colonial Control: The Royal Air Force, 1919–1939* (Manchester: Manchester University Press, 1990); Priya Satia, "The Defense of Inhumanity: Air Control and the British Idea of Arabia," *American Historical Review* 111, no. 1 (February 1, 2006): 16–51; and Elmer B. Scovill, "The RAF and the Desert Frontiers of Iraq, 1919–1930," *Aerospace Historian* 22, no. 2 (1975): 84–90.
47. On the revolt, see Abbas Kadhim, *Reclaiming Iraq: The 1920 Revolution and the Founding of the Modern State* (Austin: University of Texas Press, 2012), 1.
48. The Italians had established limited relations in Asir and Yemen but did not actively intervene in Arabia until later in the 1920s.
49. Joseph Kostiner, *The Making of Saudi Arabia, 1916–1936: From Chieftancy to Monarchical State* (New York: Oxford University Press, 1993), 71–113.
50. Lisa Anderson, "The Tripoli Republic, 1918–1922," in *Social & Economic Development of Libya*, ed. E. G. H. Joffé and K. S. McLachlan (Wisbech, UK: Middle East & North African Studies, 1982), 52.
51. Lisa Anderson, "The Tripoli Republic, 1918–1922," 43–65.

4. EMERGING POLITIES IN THE EARLY 1920S

1. The account is based on the memoir of the Rif Republic's minister of foreign affairs, Muhammad Azarqan, who was taken down by Ahmad Skiraj. Previously available only in the Rabat Archives Générales, Skiraj's account was researched, contextualized, and annotated by Rachid Yachouti, in a 2010 republication, *Al-ẓal al-warīf fi muharabat al-Rif* (Rabat: Kawtar Print), 178–84; C. R. Pennell, using the original, describes the *ba'ya* in detail in *A Country with a Government and a Flag: The Rif War in Morocco, 1921–1926* (Boulder, CO: Middle East and North African Studies, 1986), 114–15.
2. Abd el-Krim's father had taken him to visit the Spanish governor on the island in 1898, and he later attended the Spanish school there for a few months in 1906. David M. Hart, *The Aith Waryaghar of the Moroccan Rif: An Ethnography and History* (Tucson: University of Arizona Press, 1976), 371–72.
3. Spain took control of Ceuta, opposite Gibraltar on the Straits, from the Portuguese in 1668, having occupied Melilla in 1497.
4. Spain's colonial interests on the northern Moroccan coast were recognized in the 1904 Anglo-French Entente Cordiale and in the 1907 Cartagena pact affirming Spain's alliance with France and Britain.
5. Sebastian Balfour, *Deadly Embrace: Morocco and the Road to the Spanish Civil War* (Oxford: Oxford University Press, 2002).
6. Harry Richards, "Room 40 and German Intrigues in Morocco: Re-assessing the Operational Impact of Diplomatic Crytpanalysis During World War I," *Intelligence and National Security* 32, no. 6 (2017): 833–48.
7. Pennell, *A Country with a Government and a Flag*, 75.

8. Germain Ayache, *Les Origines de la guerre du Rif* (Paris: Publications de la Sorbonne, 1981), 147; Pennell, *A Country with a Government and a Flag*, 91.
9. Pennell, *A Country with a Government and a Flag*, 114–16.
10. The treaty uses the term "Turkey" throughout, only referencing the Ottoman Empire in the past tense.
11. The Sèvres treaty consisted of thirteen Parts. Part I included the twenty-six articles creating the Covenant of the League of Nations. Article 22 was especially relevant for the Ottoman partition, stating, "Certain communities formerly belonging to the Turkish Empire have reached a stage of development subject to the rendering of administrative advice and assistance by a Mandatory until such time as they are able to stand alone. The wishes of these communities must be a principal consideration in the selection of the Mandatory." The twelve other parts of the treaty dealt with the Ottoman peace, setting its terms (territorial boundaries, political clauses, minority protections), administration, and economic provisions.
12. On the 1919 uprisings, see Hussein Omar's forthcoming *The Rule of Strangers: Empire, Islam and the Invention of "Politics" in Egypt, 1867—1922* (Oxford: Oxford University Press).
13. On the "semi-sovereign" status of entities like Egypt and Mount Lebanon in late-nineteenth-century Ottoman and European legal frameworks, see Aimee M. Genell, "Autonomous Provinces and the Problem of 'Semi-Sovereignty' in European International Law," *Journal of Balkan and Near Eastern Studies* 18, no. 6 (November 1, 2016): 533–49.
14. In the Treaty of Versailles, Germany relinquished all claims to the Sharifian Empire (Part IV), with articles 141–46 abrogating Germany's "right, titles, privileges" in Morocco, and German property, mining concessions, and financial interests in Morocco transferred to the Makhzen, the Moroccan state, as reparations for war damages.
15. Alf Andrew Heggoy, "Colonial Origins of the Algerian-Moroccan Border Conflict of October 1963." *African Studies Review* 13, no 1 (1970): 17–22.
16. On spatial expansion of the colonial states in Morocco, see Jonathan Wyrtzen, *Making Morocco: Colonial Intervention and the Politics* (Ithaca, NY: Cornell University Press, 2015), chapter 2.
17. David M. Hart's magisterial ethnography of the Ait Waryaghar, *The Aith Waryaghar of the Moroccan Rif*, based on fieldwork in the 1950s and 1960s, includes extensive historical coverage from the precolonial period through the rise and of the Rif government, adding granular details based on extensive interviews with participants or their descendants. C. R. Pennell's extensive study of the Rif Republic, *A Country with a Government and a Flag*, remains the most thorough and analytically rigorous treatment from the internal perspective. The following discussion here and in chapter 6 relies extensively on both publications.
18. David S. Woolman, *Rebels in the Rif: Abd El Krim and the Rif Rebellion* (Stanford, CA: Stanford University Press, 1968), 83.
19. On requests by the Khattabis for Spanish nationality in 1915, Spanish subvention for Mahammad's schooling, and tensions related to the two brothers supporting Germany and Ottoman Turkey during the Great War, see correspondence in Archivo General Militar de Madrid (hereafter AGM), Caja 1531, Capeta 2.

20. Pennell, *A Country with a Government and a Flag*, 66–68.
21. Pennell, *A Country with a Government and a Flag*, 70–75.
22. In 1839, the East India Company first secured control over the Aden port, handing over control to the Bombay Presidency. From 1917–1937, this was transferred to the Delhi-based Government of India until Aden was established as a Crown colony under the British Colonial Office. During World War I, several offices vied to manage it, including the Bombay Presidency, War Office, Foreign Office, India Office, and British High Commission in Cairo (a thank you to Lina Volin for help clarifying these successions).
23. On the synergy of reformist ideology and state-building in the first and second Saudi states in the eighteenth and nineteenth centuries, see Natana J. Delong-Bas, *Wahhabi Islam: From Revival and Reform to Global Jihad* (Oxford: Oxford University Press, 2008), chapters 1–2, and Cole Bunzel, "Manifest Enmity: The Origins, Development, and Persistence of Classical Wahhabism (1153–1351/1741–1932)" (PhD diss., Princeton University, 2018), chapters 4–5.
24. On relations among Ibn Saud, the Wahhabi ulama, and the Ikhwan, see Joseph Kostiner, *The Making of Saudi Arabia: From Chieftancy to Monarchical State* (New York: Oxford University Press, 1993), 39–42; David Dean Commins, *The Wahhabi Mission and Saudi Arabia*, (London: I. B. Tauris, 2006), chapter 3.
25. Kostiner, *The Making of Saudi Arabia*, 65.
26. James L. Gelvin, "The Social Origins of Popular Nationalism in Syria: Evidence for a New Framework," *International Journal of Middle East Studies* 26, no. 4 (1994): 651.
27. On the formation and lobbying efforts of the Syro-Palestinian Congress, see Reem Bailony, "Transnational Rebellion: The Syrian Revolt of 1925–1927" (PhD dissertation, University of California Los Angeles, 2015), 53–74.
28. The classic authoritative text on the Cairo Conference, based on exhaustive British archival records, is Aaron S. Klieman, *Foundations of British Policy in the Arab World: The Cairo Conference of 1921* (Baltimore, MD: Johns Hopkins University Press, 1970).
29. On the blending of Indian and Iraqi architectural styles in early public works construction during the British mandate, see Iain Jackson, "The Architecture of the British Mandate in Iraq: Nation-Building and State Creation," *Journal of Architecture* 21, no. 3 (April 2, 2016): 375–417.
30. Toby Dodge, *Inventing Iraq: The Failure of Nation-Building and a History Denied* (New York: Columbia University Press, 2005), 15–16.
31. Orit Bashkin, *The Other Iraq: Pluralism and Culture in Hashemite Iraq* (Stanford, CA: Stanford University Press, 2008), introduction and chapter 1.
32. James Barr traces these Anglo-French tensions over the mandates up through 1948 in *A Line in the Sand: The Anglo-French Struggle for the Middle East, 1914–1948* (New York: Norton, 2012).
33. These are exposited in Part II, "Frontiers of Turkey."
34. On the Allied occupation of Istanbul, see Nur Bilge Criss, *Istanbul Under Allied Occupation, 1918–1923* (Boston: Brill, 1999); on its longer term impact on Turkish identity, see Pınar Şenışık, "The Allied Occupation of İstanbul and the Construction of Turkish National Identity in the Early Twentieth Century," *Nationalities Papers* 46, no. 3 (May 4, 2018): 501–13.

35. Section IV stipulated that, though the Smyrna enclave remained under Turkish sovereignty (the Turkish flag was to continue to fly over the fort), Turkey transferred the exercise of sovereignty and administration to the Greek government. A local parliament was to be set up, the Greeks could station military forces there and collect customs, and after five years the parliament was to vote on whether to become incorporated into Greece.
36. The plan for Kurdistan was also to ensure the protection of "Assyro-Chaldean" and other "racial or religious minorities" in the area and look into any changes to the Turkish-Persian frontier that might be needed.
37. Nur Bilge Criss, "Occupation During and After the War (Ottoman Empire)," *International Encyclopedia of the First World War*, accessed January 4, 2021, https://encyclopedia.1914-1918-online.net/article/occupation_during_and_after_the_war_ottoman_empire.
38. Despite the British foreign secretary, Lord Curzon's aspirations to establish a permanent protectorate presence in the Caucasus, the British had neither the financial nor military reserves to do so and began to withdraw in the fall of 1919. See John Fisher, "'On the Glacis of India': Lord Curzon and British Policy in the Caucasus, 1919," *Diplomacy & Statecraft* 8, no. 2 (July 1, 1997): 50–82.
39. The report issued by the organizers ahead of the Erzurum Congress refer to "the Muslims who form one nation (*millet*), consisting of Turks and Kurds" and later references "the Muslim majority consisting of Turks and Kurds who for centuries have mixed their blood in an intimate relationship and who form the community (*ümmet*) of the Prophet" from Erik Jan Zürcher, *The Young Turk Legacy and Nation Building: From the Ottoman Empire to Atatürk's Turkey* (London: I. B. Tauris, 2010), 224.
40. David McDowall, *A Modern History of the Kurds* (London: I. B. Tauris, 2007), 186.
41. On the Koçgiri uprisings, see Robert W. Olson, *The Emergence of Kurdish Nationalism and the Sheikh Said Rebellion, 1880–1925* (Austin: University of Texas Press, 1989), 26–41; and Hülya Küçük, *The Role of the Bektashis in Turkey's National Struggle* (Leiden: Brill, 2002); *Koçgiri Halk Hareketi 1919–1921* (Ankara: Komal Publishing, 1992).
42. Matthew Ghazarian, "Obstruction as Power: Rethinking Britain's Caucasus Occupation 1918–20," *International History Review* 39, no. 4 (2017): 654–66.
43. In 1909, between twenty and thirty thousand Armenians were massacred in the midst of the counter-1908 revolution by Ottoman Muslims in the Adana province. This was catalyzed party by an accusation from Ihsan Fikri, the CUP leader in the province, that the Armenians were attempting a coup d'état to establish the Kingdom of Cilicia (hearkening back to the historic Kingdom of Armenia in the area); see Bedross Der Matossian, *Shattered Dreams of Revolution: From Liberty to Violence in the Late Ottoman Empire* (Stanford, CA: Stanford University Press, 2014), 163–70.
44. On the multivalent memory of Smyrna's burning, see Leyla Neyzi, "Remembering Smyrna/Izmir: Shared History, Shared Trauma," *History and Memory* 20, no. 2 (2008): 106–27.
45. See Laura Robson's *States of Separation: Transfer, Partition, and the Making of the Modern Middle East* (Oakland: University of California Press, 2017) on the logics of population transfer, both de facto and in 1920s' international law, with regard to Greeks, Turks, Assyrians, Armenians, and others.

5. KURDISH UPRISINGS, THE RIF WAR, AND THE GREAT SYRIAN REVOLT, 1924-1927

1. The earliest iteration of Azadî (Ciwata Azadi Kurd, or Society for Kurdish Independence) was reportedly formed in 1921 in Erzurum, by Kurdish officers in the Eighth Army Corps, perhaps in reaction to the violent crushing of the Koćgiri Revolt that summer. See Robert W. Olson, *The Emergence of Kurdish Nationalism and the Sheikh Said Rebellion, 1880-1925* (Austin: University of Texas Press, 1989), 41-51, and Martin van Bruinessen, *Agha, Shaikh, and State: The Social and Political Structures of Kurdistan* (London: Zed Books, 1992), 280-81.
2. Ugur Ümit Üngör, *The Making of Modern Turkey: Nation and State in Eastern Anatolia, 1913-50* (Oxford: Oxford University Press, 2011), 124.
3. C. R. Pennell, *A Country with a Government and a Flag: The Rif War in Morocco, 1921-1926* (Boulder, CO: Middle East and North African Studies, 1986), 185-89.
4. In the sanjak of Alexandretta, the Lausanne treaty recognized the special prerogatives the French offered the nascent Turkish Republic earlier in the 1921 Treaty of Ankara, which Turkey would continue to press until France handed it over in 1939.
5. In the 1920 Treaty of Sèvres, some variant of Armenia was used twenty-one times, while Kurds were referenced eight times. Not a single variant of either word appeared in the 1923 Treaty of Lausanne.
6. *Sacak* 139 (April 1987), quoting from the recorded speeches, instructions, and secret meeting records of the Grand National Assembly; see David McDowall, *A Modern History of the Kurds* (London: I. B. Tauris, 2007), 187.
7. McDowall, *A Modern History of the Kurds*, 130.
8. Statement made to the Grand National Assembly on April 24, 1920, quoted in *Sacak* 39 (in McDowall, *A Modern History of the Kurds*, 188).
9. For English translated version of the 1924 constitution, see Edward Mead Earle, "The New Constitution of Turkey," *Political Science Quarterly* 40, no. 1 (1925): 73-100.
10. Ironically, Gökalp himself had a Kurdish background and was a native of Diyarbakir.
11. Wadie Jwaideh, *The Kurdish National Movement: Its Origins and Development*, (Syracuse, NY: Syracuse University Press, 2006), 164-66.
12. A Kurdish area just to the northeast of the Nusabyin-Jazira axis.
13. McDowall, *A Modern History of the Kurds*, 139.
14. On Simqu's rise in the Great War and activities in the early 1920s, see Martin van Bruinessen, "A Kurdish Warlord on the Turkish-Persian Frontier in the Early 20th Century: Isma'il Agha Simko," in *Iran and the First World War: Battleground of the Great Powers*, ed. Touraj Atabaki (London: I. B. Tauris, 2006), 69-93.
15. On Reza Pahlavi's state consolidation and campaigns against Kurdish, Bakhtiyaris, and other tribal groups, see Firoozeh Kashani-Sabet, *Frontier Fictions: Shaping the Iranian Nation, 1804-1946* (Princeton, NJ: Princeton University Press, 1999), chapter 5; on Simqu, see McDowall, *A Modern History of the Kurds*, 220.
16. British intelligence estimated Oz Demir's forces numbered three hundred at the start of November, with two hundred reinforcements soon arriving, and reported that a

telegraph operating between eastern Anatolia and Rawanduz was in place (Middle East Centre Archive, St. Antony's College, Oxford [hereafter MECA], Edmonds, 1/1 Memoranda from Kirkuk 1922–1925, Edmonds to High Commissioner, Baghdad, 2 November 2, 1922).

17. MECA, Edmonds, 1/1 Memoranda from Kirkuk 1922–1925, "1 January–31 January Report."

18. MECA, Edmonds, 1/3 Kurdish Notes, "Letter from High Commissioner Dobbs to Edmonds," June 25, 1923 (No. D.O.S.O. 1098).

19. On progression of Kurdish identity and resistance to the Kemalist state-building project from the 1921 Koçgiri revolt through the 1925 Shaykh Said revolt, see Hamit Bozarslan, "Kurdish Nationalism in Turkey: From Tacit Contract to Rebellion (1919–1925)" in *The Origins of Kurdish Nationalism*, ed. Abbas Vali (Costa Mesa, CA: Mazda Publishers, 2003), 163–90.

20. Van Bruinessen, *Sheikh, Agha, and State*, 280.

21. Olson, *The Emergence of Kurdish Nationalism*, 48–51.

22. Hamit Borzarslan, " 'Being in Time': The Kurdish Movement and Quests of Universal," in *The Kurdish Question Revisited*, ed. Gareth Stansfield and Mohammed Shareef (London: Hurst, 2017), 65–67.

23. The Seventh and Eighth Corps, stationed respectively in Diyarbakir and Erzurum, were deemed unreliable due to concerns about their sympathies with the revolt.

24. Shaykh Said's body was buried anonymously by the gate and a statue of Mustafa Kemal Atatürk was symbolically erected later on the site of his hanging in an attempt to erase his memory and prevent it becoming a pilgrimage destination (Üngör, *The Making of Modern Turkey*, 132. Eighty-nine years later the newly elected Kurdish Diyarbakir municipal authorities renamed Dağkapı, one of the city's main public areas, after Sheikh Said; see Mehmet Kurt, "A Conversion to Civil Society? The Incomplete Reconfiguration of the Hizbullah Movement in Turkey," *Journal of Balkan and Near Eastern Studies* 22, no. 6 (November 1, 2020): 762–76.

25. On the mismatch between the Mosul Commission's expectations regarding taxonomies of ethnonational identification and the complicated post-Ottoman realities in Mosul, see Sarah Shield, "Mosul, the Ottoman Legacy and the League of Nations," *International Journal of Contemporary Iraqi Studies* 3, no. 2 (November 1, 2009): 217–30. For detailed notes on the itinerary, activities, and interviews conducted by the commission in March 1925 from the perspective of the British officer, Cecil John Edmonds, assigned as a representative, see MECA, Edmonds, 1/2a Mosul Commission (diary and notes) and 1/2b (statements from local delegations).

26. MECA, Edmonds, 1/4/2 Turco-Iraq Demarcation Proceedings, 1927.

27. On the massive Turkish ethnoengineering and successive phases of Kurdish deportation from southeast Anatolia from 1916 to 1934, see Üngör, *The Making of Modern Turkey*, chapter 3.

28. The "roads" and telephone network linked the main positions in the Rif and Jbala and were important both for military coordination and internal control. M'hammed (Abd el-Krim's brother) was in charge of the telephone system, assisted by boys who had been

taught how to set up the wiring by a Spanish prisoner nicknamed Antonio El Mecánico (Hart, *The Ait Waryaghar of the Moroccan Rif*, 387; Pennell, *A Country with a Government and a Flag*, 141).

29. Pennell, *A Country with a Government and Flag*, 99.
30. Abdeslam Khalafi, "La poésie de résistance au Rif: 1893–1926 (2ème partie)," 64 (August 2002), http://tawiza.byethost10.com/Tawiza64/Khalafi.htm.
31. Pennell, *A Country with a Government and Flag*, 24.
32. M. R. de Madariaga, *Abd-El-Krim El Jatabi: La Lucha Por La Independencia* (Madrid: Alianza, 2009), 67.
33. At the height of the Rif conflict, in early 1925, M'hammad bin Abd el-Krim, mentions to the *Chicago Tribune* reporter Vincent Sheean, who snuck across the front lines to interview Abd el-Krim and his brother, that he regularly reads the French and Spanish papers, which shock him with their ignorance about everything connected to the war; see Vincent Sheean, *An American Among the Riffi* (New York: The Century Xo, 1926), 233–34.
34. Abdeslam Khalafi, "La poésie de résistance au Rif: 1893–1926 (2ème partie)," 64 (August 2002), http://tawiza.byethost10.com/Tawiza64/Khalafi.htm.
35. Khalafi, "La poésie de résistance au Rif."
36. Clark Kerr to the Foreign Office, "Letter received from Abdel Kerim," December 10, 1921, FO 371/7086 W13321, The National Archives, Kew, London, United Kingdom. Cited in Carmen Baskauf, "International Dimensions of the Rif Republic: Navigating International Recognition of Anti-colonial Independence during the Interwar Period" (Unpublished thesis, Yale University, 2017).
37. "The Riff Delegation," September 6, 1922, League of Nations Archive, UN Archives Geneva, doc. 11/23217/12861.
38. "The Riff Delegation," September 6 1922, League of Nations Archive.
39. The Rif forces captured numerous Spanish soldiers in the 1921 Anwal battle. Echeverietta, a prominent Basque businessman who knew M'hammad from his time at the School of Mines in Madrid and who had previously represented the German conglomerate Mannessman in the Rif, spent four days in Ajdir (January 24–28, 1923) negotiating a ransom payment of four million pesetas (Pennell, *A Country with a Government and a Flag*, 114).
40. "The Riff Delegation," September 6, 1922, League of Nations Archive.
41. French intelligence closely tracked perceptions of the Rif War, particularly after it extended into their zone in the spring of 1925. That August, the French consul in Palestine reported Muslim and Christian support for Abd el-Krim, including a Jaffa news article hailing a "new hero of Islam who defends the independence of the national soil against two of the greatest nations in the world and invites the believers of Palestine to come to their aid," support in other papers, and fundraising in Jerusalem, Galilee, and Jaffa [Centres des Archives Diplomatiques, Nantes (CADN), SL 1051, Letter from Paul Ballereau to President of the Council, Ministry of Foreign Affairs, August 3, 1925]. For the Iraq intelligence, see CADN, SL 1051, "A.S. du Riff," Consul of France in Mesopotamia to General Sarrail, High Commissioner of the Republic, October 5, 1925. This file also contains a dispatch from Buenos Aires about the Syro-Lebanese community there organizing about the Rif War and the Syrian Revolt.

42. Service Historique de la Défense, Vincennes, France (henceforth SHD), Box 3H 102, File E3605, "Renseignements de Pologne," June 23, 1925.
43. Baskauf, "International Dimensions of the Rif Republic," 20–22.
44. See extensive studies of Spain's chemical warfare in Sebastian Balfour, *Deadly Embrace: Morocco and the Road to the Spanish Civil War* (Oxford: Oxford University Press, 2002); Sven Lindqvist, *A History of Bombing* (London: Granta, 2001).
45. John McNeill, *The Mountains of the Mediterranean World: An Environmental History* (New York: Cambridge University Press, 1992), 269.
46. Communication from Colonel Chief of Staff to General Command, Melilla (May 16, 1922). Servicio Historico Military (SHM) MICRO R469, Caja 316, Carpeta 14, Year 1922 (General Military Archives, Madrid).
47. Balfour, *Deadly Embrace*, 133–42. The Spanish military correspondence refers to the use of "ozol" and "iperita" (named after the Battle of Ypres in World War I), both of which were mustard gases.
48. See reports on Spanish daily bombing raids (TNT, incendiary, and chemical) launched from the airfield at Nador and by hydroplanes based in Melilla on villages and encampments in the eastern protectorate area in 1924 in SHM, Micro R545 C382, Carpeta 2, 1924.
49. See Spanish letters on requesting supplies (including hydrochloric acid, rubber boots, gloves, bibs, and masks) to make bombs and bimonthly shipments from Germany in SHM, Micro R545 C382, Carpeta 1, 1924.
50. Michael Clodfelter, *Warfare and Armed Conflicts: A Statistical Reference to Casualty and Other Figures, 1500–2000* (London: McFarland, 2002), 398.
51. On the final stages of the French military conquest of Amazigh (Berber) interior regions in the Atlas and Jbel Sahro ranges, see Jonathan Wyrtzen, *Making Morocco: Colonial Intervention and the Politics of Identity* (Ithaca, NY: Cornell University Press, 2015), chapters 2–3; and Moshe Gershovich, *French Military Rule in Morocco: Colonialism and Its Consequences* (Portland, OR: F. Cass, 2000). On urban anticolonialist mobilization in Morocco, see Wyrtzen, *Making Morocco*, chapter 5.
52. Michael Provence, *The Great Syrian Revolt and the Rise of Arab Nationalism* (Austin: University of Texas Press, 2009), 12–13.
53. Eugene L. Rogan, *Frontiers of the State in the Late Ottoman Empire: Transjordan, 1850–1921* (New York: Cambridge University Press, 2002), 192.
54. My discussion of the Great Syrian Revolt draws heavily on Michael Provence's fantastic study, *The Great Syrian Revolt and the Rise of Arab Nationalism*, and Daniel Neep's excellent analysis of French counterinsurgency tactics in *Occupying Syria Under the French Mandate: Insurgency, Space and State Formation* (New York: Cambridge University Press, 2012).
55. Provence, *The Great Syrian Revolt*, 51.
56. The first two high commissioners, Gouraud and Weygand, as well as many officers in the Service de renseignments, had previously served under Resident-General Lyautey in Morocco. On French colonial administrative ties in Morocco and Syria, see Martin Thomas, *Empires of Intelligence: Security Services and Colonial Disorder After 1914* (Berkeley: University of California Press, 2008) and Edmund Burke, "A Comparative View of French Native Policy in Morocco and Syria, 1912–1925," *Middle Eastern Studies* 9, no. 2 (1973): 175–86.

57. Provence, *The Great Syrian Revolt*, 53, 72.
58. Provence, *The Great Syrian Revolt*, 58.
59. Provence, *The Great Syrian Revolt*, 59.
60. Provence, *The Great Syrian Revolt*, 63–64.
61. Provence, *The Great Syrian Revolt*, 91.
62. Provence, *The Great Syrian Revolt*, 96.
63. On al-Qawuqji's fascinating trajectory from Ottoman officer, service in the French colonial military, and leadership in the Syrian Revolt then the Palestinian Great Revolt, see Laila Parsons, *The Commander: Fawzi al-Qawuqji and the Fight for Arab Independence 1914–1948* (New York: Hill and Wang, 2016). Also, on the networks of former Ottoman officers like al-Qawuqji, who played leading roles shaping the region far into the 1930s, see Michael Provence's *The Last Ottoman Generation and the Making of the Modern Middle East* (Cambridge: Cambridge University Press, 2017).
64. Fawzi al-Qawuqji, *Mudhakhirat Fawzi al-Qawuqji*. Vol. 1, 1914–1932 (Beirut: Dar al-Quds, 1975), 86–87, quoted in Eugene Rogan, *The Arabs: A History* (New York: Basic Books, 2011). 230.
65. Provence, *The Great Syrian Revolt*, 99.
66. In the early 1920s, al-Shallash had served as a liaison between Amir Abdallah in Transjordan and Ibrahim Hananu during the Aleppo resistance. He had also been sent as an emissary to the Kingdom of the Hejaz. With the outbreak of the 1925 revolt, al-Shallash returned to his home region in Deir Ez-Zor in eastern Syria to take part.
67. James L. Gelvin, *Divided Loyalties*, *Divided Loyalties* (Berkeley: University of California Press, 1998), 19–22.
68. Provence, *The Great Syrian Revolt*, 103.
69. The French bombardment decimating Damascus generated a global outcry, including among the transnational Syrian diaspora, which actively petitioned the League of Nations. Note Reem Bailony's coverage in chapter 2 of *Transnational Rebellion: The Syrian Revolt of 1925–1927* (PhD diss., University of California Los Angeles, 2015).
70. The French mandate intelligence service intercepted his letters. Provence, *The Great Syrian Revolt*, 117.
71. Provence, *The Great Syrian Revolt*, 117–18.
72. On French infrastructure and counterinsurgency urban planning in Damascus and the Ghouta, see Neep, *Occupying Syria Under the French Mandate*, chapter 6.
73. James Barr, *A Line in the Sand: The Anglo-French Struggle for the Middle East, 1914–1948* (New York: Norton, 2012), 134–35.
74. Barr, *A Line in the Sand*, 141.

6. ENDGAME STRUGGLES IN KURDISTAN, CYRENAICA, AND ARABIA, 1927–1934

1. On the conflicting Sabila accounts and dominant impression that al-Dawish and Ibn Humayd were betrayed by Ibn Saud's surprise attack, see Joseph Kostiner, *The Making*

of *Saudi Arabia, 1916–1936: From Chieftancy to Monarchical State* (New York: Oxford University Press, 1993), 135–37.

2. The neutral zones established with Iraq remained in place until the 1980s, and the boundaries with Qatar, the United Arab Emirates, and Oman were not settled until the 1970s.

3. Over 420 Kurdish "rebels" were sentenced to death that summer, though the actual number executed was likely much higher; see Ugur Üngör, *The Making of Modern Turkey: Nation and State in Eastern Anatolia, 1913–50* (Oxford: Oxford University Press, 2011), 131.

4. The British ambassador reported that the Turkish government imposed a new law in June 1927: "to transport from the Eastern Vilayets an indefinite number of Kurds or other elements. . . . The Government has already begun to apply to the Kurdish elements . . . the policy which so successfully disposed of the Armenian Minority in 1915. It is a curious trick of fate that the Kurds, who were the principal agent employed for the deportation of the Armenians, should be in danger of suffering the same fate as the Armenians only twelve years later" (David McDowall, *A Modern History of the Kurds* [London: I. B. Tauris, 2007], 199).

5. In many respects, the modern Turkish army was built to try to control Kurdistan. Between 1924 and 1989, all but one of the eighteen Turkish military engagements (including every operation after 1945 excepting the Korean War and the invasion of Cyprus), were in Kurdistan (McDowall, *A Modern History of the Kurds*, 198).

6. Mesut Yegen, "'Prospective-Turks' or 'Pseudo-Citizens': Kurds in Turkey," *Middle East Journal* 63, no. 4 (2009): 601.

7. The organizations that comprised Khoybun included Kürdistan Teali Cemiyeti (Society for the Rise of Kurdistan), Kürt Teşkilat-ı İçtimaiye Cemiyeti (The Organization of Kurdish Assembly), Kürt Millet Fırkası (Kurdish People's Party), and Kürt İstiklal Komitesi (Kurdish Independence Committee) from Egypt. Khoybun also maintained strong relations with Armenian nationalist organizations including the Dashnak Party. The first meeting of Khoybun in Bhamdoun was held in the home of Vahan Papazyan, an executive member of Dashnak originally from Van. On the origins and activity of Khoybun, see Rohat Alakom, *HoybÛn Örgütü ve Ağrı Ayaklanması* (Istanbul: Avesta, 1998).

8. On the complicated interplay of Kurds, the French mandate authorities, and the Turkish government in the production of the Turkey-Syria border from the 1925 Shaykh Said revolt through the later 1930s, see Benjamin White, *The Emergence of Minorities in the Middle East: The Politics of Community in French Mandate Syria* (Edinburgh: Edinburgh University Press, 2011), chapter 4.

9. Robert Olson, "The Kurdish Rebellions of Sheikh Said (1925), Mt. Ararat (1930), and Dersim (1937–8): Their Impact on the Development of the Turkish Air Force and on Kurdish and Turkish Nationalism," *Die Welt Des Islams* 40, no. 1 (2000): 79.

10. Senem Aslan, *Nation-Building in Turkey and Morocco: Governing Kurdish and Berber Dissent* (New York: Cambridge University Press, 2015), 56–77.

11. Kurdish original:

    Ser singa te sî girtiye
    Ala Kurd pêl didiye

Kurdan re tu Kâbe bÛye
Hêlbe Agrî Hêlbe Agrî

Hêlbe Agrî Hêlbe Agrî
Ji sawa te Tirk digirî
Te dît çawa Rom* revî
Hêlbe Agrî Hêlbe Agrî

(*Note the Kurdish use of "Rom," referencing Rome/Byzantium, for the Turks. It is similar to Tamazight referencing of "Christian" colonial enemies—France or Spain—with the same word, "irumin," in songs from this period from the Rif and Atlas Mountains). In Kadri Cemilpaşa, *Doza Kurdistan—Kürdistan Davası: Kürt Milletinin 60 Seneden Beri Esaretten Kurtuluş Savaşı Hatıratı* [The Cause of Kurdistan: The Remembrance of the last 60 Years of War of Independence of Kurdish Nation from Slavery] (Istanbul: Avesta, 2014), 123.

12. Olson, "The Kurdish Rebellions of Sheikh Said," 67–94.
13. Olson, "The Kurdish Rebellions of Shaikh Said," 85.
14. Üngör, *The Making of Modern Turkey*, 122. Also see Thongchai Winikchakul's initial influential work on the political and physical definition of Thailand, *Siam Mapped: A History of the Geo-Body of a Nation* (Honolulu: University of Hawaii Press, 1997).
15. See chapter 3, "Deportation of the Kurds, 1916–34," in Üngor, *The Making of Modern Turkey*.
16. Joost Jongerden, *The Settlement Issue in Turkey and the Kurds: An Analysis of Spatial Policies, Modernity and War* (Leiden: Brill, 2007).
17. On the Turkish press coverage of the Dersim revolt, see Taha Baran, *1937–1938 Yılları Arasında Basında Dersim* (Istanbul: İletişim, 2014).
18. Ali Abdullatif Ahmida, *The Making of Modern Libya: State Formation, Colonization, and Resistance, 1830–1932* (Albany: State University of New York Press, 1994), 95. Also, see Edward Evans-Pritchard's seminal study of the Sanusiyya, *The Sanusi of Cyrenaica* (Oxford: Clarendon, 1949).
19. Eileen Ryan details the extensive Italian-Sanusi relations and negotiations (from the precolonial era through the 1930s), including the rupture in the 1920s with the Italian shift to military conquest, in *Religion as Resistance: Negotiating Authority in Italian Libya* (New York: Oxford University Press, 2018).
20. Arielli shows the steady increase of colonial relative to metropolitan troops through the 1920s. By 1928, there were 28,558 colonial troops versus 12,672 Italian troops (the Italians included "Black Shirt" volunteers. Nir Arielli, "Colonial Soldiers in Italian Counter-Insurgency Operations in Libya, 1922–32," *British Journal for Military History* 1, no. 2 (February 5, 2015): 52.
21. Ahmida, *The Making of Modern Libya*, 74.
22. John Gooch, "Re-Conquest and Suppression: Fascist Italy's Pacification of Libya and Ethiopia, 1922–39," *Journal of Strategic Studies* 28, no. 6 (December 1, 2005): 1009–12.

23. Archivio dello Stato, Rome (hereafter ACS), Carte Graziani, Busta 7, Sc. 9, "Dieci Anni di Storia Cirenaica," R. Corpo Truppe Coloniali Della Cirenaica (December 25, 1931): 150–58. In 1931, the Italian command compiled this 238-page report on the ten-year Cyrenaica campaign following the execution of Omar al-Mokhtar.
24. ACS, Carte Badolgio, Busta 8, Letter from Graziani to Badolgio, April 5, 1930.
25. On the experience of women during the intense Italo-Sanusi conflict, including participation in battle and life interned in concentration camps, see Katrina Yeaw, "Gender, Violence and Resistance uUnder Italian Rule in Cyrenaica, 1923–1934," *Journal of North African Studies* 23, no. 5 (October 20, 2018): 791–810.
26. ACS, Carte Badolgio, Busta 8, Letter from Badolgio to De Bono and Graziani, June 20, 1930.
27. Writing to Badolgio in June, Graziani explains, "The program for the concentration camps for the subdued populations has gradually developed since the first days of my being in office. . . . We wanted to go step by step so as not to pressure the people with excessive violence and in the hope of persuading them. However, we should not delude ourselves, and we will have to resort to the concentration camps of tents along the coast to hope for more definite results that can ultimately be beneficial to the people themselves." ACS, Carte Badolgio, Busta 8, Vice-Governor Graziani to Governor Badolgio, 26 June 1930.
28. See Ali Abdullatif Ahmida, *Forgotten Voices: Power and Agency in Colonial and Postcolonial Libya* (New York: Routledge, 2005), 43–44; Ali Abdullatif Ahmida, *Genocide in Libya: Shar, a Hidden Colonial History* (New York: Routledge, 2020), chapter 3; and Nicola Labanca, "Italian Colonial Internment," in Ruth Ben-Ghiat and Mia Fuller, eds., *Italian Colonialism* (New York: Palgrave Macmillan, 2005), 27–36.
29. ACS, Carte Grazinai, Busta 7, Sc. 9, "Dieci Anni di Storia Cirenaica," 185.
30. Gooch, "Re-conquest and Suppression," 1019–20.
31. ACS, Carte Graziani, Busta 9, scatola 7, fasc. 2, Archivio Centrale dello Stato (ACS hereafter), Rome. Note from Colonel Addetto to Military Command, "Oggetto: Preventivo lavori Frontiera Orientale" (April 24, 1931).
32. For an excellent account of the centrality of the borderlands to state formation in Iraq, with excellent analysis of the Busayya post affair and of a resettlement plan for border tribes, see Carl Shook, "The Origins and Development of Iraq's National Boundaries, 1918–1932: Policing and Political Geography in the Iraq-Nejd and Iraq-Syria Borderlands" (PhD diss., University of Chicago, 2018).
33. For a recent treatment from the Kuwait perspective, see Farah al-Nakib, "The Lost 'Two-Thirds': Kuwait's Territorial Decline Between 1913 and 1922," *Journal of Arabian Studies* 2, no. 1 (June 1, 2012): 19–37.
34. Kostiner, *The Making of Saudi Arabia*, 86.
35. On the tumultuous and fluid conflicts, and rivalry between Ikhwan and Saud, in 1924–1925, see Kostiner, *The Making of Saudi Arabia*, 94–99, and David Commins, *The Wahhabi Mission and Saudi Arabia* (New York: I. B. Tauris, 2006), 80–93.
36. For an executive summary of negotiations related to Iraq, Transjordan, and the Najd from 1920 to 1928, from the perspective of the primary British adviser to Ibn Saud, Harry

St. John Bridger Philby, see Middle East Centre Archive, St. Antony's College, Oxford (hereafter MECA), Philby, 1/4/3 1928–1930 Nejd and Iraq Boundary Dispute, "Proposed Green Book on Clayton Negotiations 1928 and Nejd Rebellion."
37. Kostiner, *The Making of Saudi Arabia*, 112.
38. Kostiner, *The Making of Saudi Arabia*, 82.
39. Kostiner, *The Making of Saudi Arabia*, 113–14.
40. Kostiner, *The Making of Saudi Arabia*, 115.
41. On the centrality of the Busayya post to the Saudi-Anglo-Iraqi dispute, and its importance to Ikhwan-Saud tensions, see Daniel Silverfarb, "Great Britain, Iraq, and Saudi Arabia: The Revolt of the Ikhwan, 1927–1930," *International History Review* 4, no. 2 (1982): 222–48.
42. A full account of the proceedings of the general assembly was published the following month (December 18, 1928 issue) in *Umm al-Qura*, the official gazette of the Sultanate of the Najd and Kingdom of the Hejaz (publishing began in Mecca on December 12, 1924). See MECA, Philby, 1/4/3, 16/4 No. 8.
43. *Umm al-Qura*, December 18, 1928, MECA, Philby, 1/4/3, 16/4 No. 8, page 5.
44. Kostiner, *The Making of Saudi Arabia*, 134.
45. Kostiner, *The Making of Saudi Arabia*, 158–59.
46. Oil exploration provoked disputes starting in the mid-1930s about the neutral zone established between Saudi Arabia and Kuwait and about the Kingdom of Saudi Arabia's eastern boundaries with the British-backed emirates in Qatar and Abu Dhabi that persisted throughout the twentieth century, as did controversy over the Iraqi-Saudi neutral zone and clashes between Saudi Arabia and Oman about their border and the fate of the Buraimi oasis.
47. On the plurality of identities and local and international contestation involving the League of Nations over the fate of the Sanjak of Alexandretta in the late 1930s, see Sarah D. Shields, *Fezzes in the River: Identity Politics and European Diplomacy in the Middle East on the Eve of World War II* (Oxford: Oxford University Press, 2011).

CONCLUSION

1. The surveying party included Alec Kirkbride, Khalaf el Tel, R. Head, two Arab surveyors, six chainmen, cooks, and a tent guard on the Anglo-Jordanian side; the Franco-Syrian side included Colonel Beynet, Bahij el Khatib, a captain of the engineering corps, two infantry adjutants, a lieutenant, and twenty-five Tunisian infantrymen. For a detailed account of the summer's excursion, see Alec Kirkbride, *A Crackle of Thorns: Experiences in the Middle East* (London: J. Murray, 1956), 82–91.
2. Note that the two sides had, in the 1923 Paulet-Newcombe Agreement, been able to negotiate the borders among Palestine, Lebanon, and Syria, notably apportioning the Jawlan/Golan to French Mandate Syria and the Sea of Galilee to British Mandate Palestine.
3. For a detailed discussion of the Anglo-French negotiation of the Syria-Transjordan frontier between 1915 and 1932, see V. M. Amadouny, "The Formation of the Transjordan-Syria Boundary, 1915–32," *Middle Eastern Studies* 31, no. 3 (1995): 533–49.

4. Middle East Centre Archive (MECA), St. Antony's College, Oxford, Edmonds Box 1/2, File 4, "Rapport de la commission chargée de l'abornement de la frontière entre la Syrie et l'Iraq." Edmonds was a member of the delegation and took extensive notes (see MECA Edmonds Box 1/4/3) relevant to the Syria-Iraq and Syria-Transjordan borders.
5. See Rashid Khalidi, *The Hundred Years' War on Palestine: A History of Settler Colonialism and Resistance, 1917–2017* (New York: Metropolitan, 2020).
6. The argument in Elizabeth Thompson, *How the West Stole Democracy from the Arabs: The Syrian Arab Congress of 1920 and the Destruction of Its Historic Liberal-Islamic Alliance* (New York: Atlantic Monthly, 2020).
7. On the links between these earlier movements and present-day separatist movements, see Ariel I. Ahram's excellent *Break All the Borders: Separatism and the Reshaping of the Middle East* (Oxford: Oxford University Press, 2019).

BIBLIOGRAPHY

ARCHIVES AND LIBRARIES

ITALY

Archivio Centrale dello Stato, Rome
Ufficio Storico dell'Aeronautica Militare, Rome
Archivio Storico Diplomatico, Ministero degli Affari Esteri, Rome

FRANCE

Archives de la Ministère des Affaires étrangères, La Courneuve and Nantes
Service historique de la Défense, Chateau de Vincennes

MOROCCO

Tangier American Legation Institute for Moroccan Studies, Tangier

SPAIN

Archivo General Militar de Madrid
Biblioteca Nacional de España, Madrid

SWITZERLAND

League of Nations Archives, Geneva

UNITED KINGDOM

British Library, London
National Archives, Kew
Middle East Centre Archive, St. Antony's College, Oxford
British Empire and Commonwealth Collection, Bristol Archives, Bristol

UNITED STATES

King-Crane Commission Digital Collection, Oberlin College, Oberlin, Ohio
Library of Congress, Washington, District of Columbia
National Archives and Records Administration, College Park, Maryland
Beinecke Library, Yale University, New Haven, Connecticut

BOOKS AND ARTICLES

Abadie, Maurice. *Opérations au Levant: Les quatre sieges d'Aïnteb (1920–21)*. Paris: Charles-Lavauzelle, 1922.

Abun-Nasr, Jamil M. *A History of the Maghrib in the Islamic Period*. Cambridge: Cambridge University Press, 1987.

Ahmida, Ali. *Forgotten Voices: Power and Agency in Colonial and Postcolonial Libya*. New York: Routledge, 2005.

Ahmida, Ali. *The Making of Modern Libya: State Formation, Colonization, and Resistance*. Albany: State University of New York Press, 2011.

Ahmida, Ali. *Genocide in Libya: Shar, a Hidden Colonial History*. New York: Routledge, 2020.

Ahram, Ariel I. *Break All the Borders: Separatism and the Reshaping of the Middle East*. Oxford: Oxford University Press, 2019.

Akin, Yigit. *When the War Came Home: The Ottomans' Great War and the Devastation of an Empire*. Stanford, CA: Stanford University Press, 2018.

Aksakal, Mustafa. *The Ottoman Road to War in 1914*. New York: Cambridge University Press, 2008.

Aksakal, Mustafa. "Holy War Made in Germany? Ottoman Origins of the 1914 Jihad." *War in History* 18, no. 2 (2011): 184–99.

Alakom, Rohat. *HoybÛn Örgütü ve Ağrı Ayaklanması*. Istanbul: Avesta, 1998.

Allawi, Ali A. *Faisal I of Iraq*. New Haven, CT: Yale University Press, 2014.

Allen, Lori. *A History of False Hope: Investigative Commissions in Palestine*. Stanford, CA: Stanford University Press, 2021.

Allen, William. *Caucasian Battlefields: A History of the Wars on the Turco-Caucasian Border, 1828–1921*. New York: Cambridge University Press, 1953.

Alon, Yoav. *Making of Jordan: Tribes, Colonialism, and the Modern State*. New York: I. B. Tauris, 2007.

Amadouny, V. M. "The Formation of the Transjordan-Syria Boundary, 1915–32." *Middle Eastern Studies* 31, no. 3 (1995): 533–49.

Anderson, Benedict. *Imagined Communities: Reflections on the Origin and Spread of Nationalism*. London: Verso, 1991.

Anderson, Kyle J. "The Egyptian Labor Corps: Workers, Peasants, and the State in World War I." *International Journal of Middle East Studies* 49, no. 1 (February 2017): 5–24.

Anderson, Lisa. *The State and Social Transformation in Tunisia and Libya, 1830–1980*. Princeton, NJ: Princeton University Press, 1986.

Anderson, M. S. *The Eastern Question, 1774–1923: A Study in International Relations*. New York: St. Martin's, 1966.

Anderson, Scott. *Lawrence in Arabia: War, Deceit, Imperial Folly and the Making of the Modern Middle East*. New York: Doubleday, 2013.

Anscombe, Frederick. *The Ottoman Gulf: The Creation of Kuwait, Saudi Arabia, and Qatar*. New York: Columbia University Press, 1997.

Arielli, Nir. "Colonial Soldiers in Italian Counter-Insurgency Operations in Libya, 1922–32." *British Journal for Military History* 1, no. 2 (February 5, 2015): 47–66.

'Askarī, Ja'far al-, William Facey, and Najdat Fathī Ṣafwat. *A Soldier's Story: From Ottoman Rule to Independent Iraq: The Memoirs of Jafar Pasha Al-Askari (1885–1936)*. London: Arabian Publishing, 2003.

Aslan, Senem. *Nation-Building in Turkey and Morocco: Governing Kurdish and Berber Dissent*. New York: Cambridge University Press, 2015.

Atabaki, Touraj, ed. *Iran and the First World War: Battleground of the Great Powers*. London: I. B. Tauris, 2006.

Ateş, Sabri. *The Ottoman-Iranian Borderlands: Making a Boundary, 1843–1914*. Cambridge: Cambridge University Press, 2013.

Ayache, Germain. *Les origines de la guerre du Rif*. Paris: Publications de la Sorbonne, 1981.

Bailony, Reem. "Transnational Rebellion: The Syrian Revolt of 1925–1927." PhD diss., University of California, Los Angeles, 2015.

Baker, Ray Stannard. *Woodrow Wilson and World Settlement: Written from His Unpublished and Personal Material*. New York: Doubleday, 1922.

Balfour, Sebastian. *Deadly Embrace: Morocco and the Road to the Spanish Civil War*. Oxford: Oxford University Press, 2002.

Baran, Taha. *1937–1938 Yılları Arasında Basında Dersim*. Istanbul: İletişim, 2014.

Barkey, Karen. *Empire of Difference: The Ottomans in Comparative Perspective*. New York: Cambridge University Press, 2008.

Barr, James. *A Line in the Sand: The Anglo-French Struggle for the Middle East, 1914–1948*. New York: Norton, 2012.

Bashkin, Orit. *The Other Iraq: Pluralism and Culture in Hashemite Iraq*. Stanford, CA: Stanford University Press, 2009.

Baykal, Bekir. *Erzurum Kongresi ile İlgili Belgeler*. Ankara: Institute of Turkish Revolution Press, 1969.

Bayly, C. A., S. Beckert, M. Connelly, I. Hofmeyr, W. Kozol, and P. Seed. "AHR Conversation: On Transnational History." *American Historical Review* 111, no. 5 (2006): 1441–64.

Ben-Ghiat, Ruth. *Fascist Modernities: Italy, 1922–1945*. Berkeley, CA: University of California Press, 2001.

Ben-Ghiat, Ruth, and Mia Fuller, eds. *Italian Colonialism*. New York: Palgrave Macmillan, 2005.
Bentley, Jerry H., ed. *The Oxford Handbook of World History*. Oxford: Oxford University Press, 2011.
Beşikçi, Mehmet. *The Ottoman Mobilization of Manpower in the First World War*. Leiden: Brill, 2012.
Blumi, Isa. *Ottoman Refugees, 1878–1939: Migration in a Post-Imperial World*. London: Bloomsbury Academic, 2013.
Bonine, Michael E., Abbas Amanat, and Michael Ezekiel Gasper, eds. *Is There a Middle East? The Evolution of a Geopolitical Concept*. Stanford, CA: Stanford University Press, 2011.
Bozarslan, Hamit. "Kurdish Nationalism in Turkey: From Tacit Contract to Rebellion (1919–1925)." In *The Origins of Kurdish Nationalism*, ed. Abbas Vali, 163–90. Costa Mesa, CA: Mazda Publishers, 2003.
Braudel, Fernand. *The Mediterranean and the Mediterranean World in the Age of Philip II*. Vol. I. Berkeley: University of California Press, 1995.
Brenner, Neil, and Stuart Elden. "Henri Lefebvre on State, Space, Territory." *International Political Sociology* 3, no. 4 (2009): 353–77.
Bunzel, Cole. "Manifest Enmity: The Origins, Development, and Persistence of Classical Wahhabism (1153–1351/1741–1932)." PhD diss., Princeton University, 2018, Chapters 4–5.
Burke III, Edmund. "A Comparative View of French Native Policy in Morocco and Syria, 1912–1925." *Middle Eastern Studies* 9, no. 2 (1973): 175–86.
Burke III, Edmund. *Prelude to Protectorate in Morocco: Pre-colonial Protest and Resistance*. Chicago: University of Chicago Press, 1976.
Çakmak, Yalçın, and Tuncay Şur, eds. *Kürt Tarihi ve Siyasetinden Portreler*: Araştırma-İnceleme Dizisi 443. Fatih, İstanbul: İletişim Yayınları, 2018.
Campos, Michelle. *Ottoman Brothers: Muslims, Christians, and Jews in Early Twentieth-Century Palestine*. Stanford, CA: Stanford University Press, 2011.
Cemilpaşa, Kadri. *Doza Kurdistan—Kürdistan Davası: Kürt Milletinin 60 Seneden Beri Esaretten Kurtuluş Savaşı Hatıratı*. Istanbul: Avesta, 2014.
Çetinsaya, Gökhan. *The Ottoman Administration of Iraq, 1890–1908*. London: Routledge, 2006.
Çiçek, Talha, ed. *Syria in World War I: Politics, Economy and Society*. London: Routledge, 2016.
Clodfelter, Michael. *Warfare and Armed Conflicts: A Statistical Reference to Casualty and Other Figures, 1500–2000*. London: McFarland, 2002.
Commins, David. *The Wahhabi Mission and Saudi Arabia*. London: I. B. Tauris, 2006.
Criss, Nur Bilge. *Istanbul Under Allied Occupation, 1918–1923*. Boston: Brill, 1999.
Criss, Nur Bilge. "Occupation During and After the War (Ottoman Empire)," *International Encyclopedia of the First World War*, accessed January 4, 2021. https://encyclopedia.1914-1918-online.net/article/occupation_during_and_after_the_war_ottoman_empire.
Delong-Bas, Natana J. *Wahhabi Islam: From Revival and Reform to Global Jihad*. Oxford: Oxford University Press, 2008.
de Madariaga, Maria. *Abd-El-Krim El Jatabi: La Lucha Por La Independencia*. Madrid: Alianza, 2009.
Der Matossian, Bedross. *Shattered Dreams of Revolution: From Liberty to Violence in the Late Ottoman Empire*. Stanford, CA: Stanford University Press, 2014.

Dodge, Toby. *Inventing Iraq: The Failure of Nation-Building and a History Denied.* New York: Columbia University Press, 2005.
Doumani, Beshara. *Rediscovering Palestine: Merchants and Peasants in Jabal Nablus, 1700–1900.* Berkeley: University of California Press, 1995.
Earle, Edward Mead. "The New Constitution of Turkey." *Political Science Quarterly* 40, no. 1 (1925): 73–100.
Ellis, John, and Michael Cox. *The World War I Databook: The Essential Facts and Figures for All the Combatants.* London: Aurum, 2001.
Ellis, Matthew H. *Desert Borderland: The Making of Modern Egypt and Libya.* Stanford, CA: Stanford University Press, 2018.
Eppel, Michael. "The Demise of the Kurdish Emirates: The Impact of Ottoman Reforms and International Relations on Kurdistan During the First Half of the Nineteenth Century." *Middle Eastern Studies* 44, no. 2 (2008): 237–58.
Erickson, Edward. *Ordered to Die: A History of the Ottoman Army.* Westport, CT: Greenwood, 2001.
Evans-Pritchard, Edward. *The Sanusi of Cyrenaica.* Oxford: Clarendon, 1949.
Fahmy, Khaled. *All the Pasha's Men: Mehmed Ali, His Army, and the Making of Modern Egypt.* Cambridge: Cambridge University Press, 1997.
Fahrenthold, Stacy D. *Between the Ottomans and the Entente: The First World War in the Syrian and Lebanese Diaspora, 1908–1925.* Oxford: Oxford University Press, 2019.
Fawaz, Leila. *A Land of Aching Hearts: The Middle East in the Great War.* Cambridge, MA: Harvard University Press, 2014.
Field, Glenn. "Global Support for Peshmerga Forces," *Kurdstrat,* August 7, 2015. http://kurdstrat.com/2015/07/08/global-support-for-peshmerga-forces/.
Fisher, John. " 'On the Glacis of India': Lord Curzon and British Policy in the Caucasus, 1919." *Diplomacy & Statecraft* 8, no. 2 (July 1, 1997): 50–82.
Fogarty, Richard. *Race and War in France: Colonial Subjects in the French Army, 1914–1918.* Baltimore, MD: Johns Hopkins University Press, 2008.
Fromkin, David. *A Peace to End All Peace: Creating the Modern Middle East, 1914–1922.* New York: Holt, 1989.
Gatrell, Peter, and Nick Baron, eds. *Warlands.* London: Palgrave MacMillan, 2009.
Gazzini, Claudia. "Jihad in Exile: Ahmad al-Sharif al-Sanusi 1918–33." Master's thesis, Princeton University, 2004.
Gelvin, James L. "The Social Origins of Popular Nationalism in Syria: Evidence for a New Framework." *International Journal of Middle East Studies* 26, no. 4 (1994): 645–61.
Gelvin, James. *Divided Loyalties: Nationalism and Mass Politics.* Berkeley: University of California Press, 1999.
Gelvin, James. "The Ironic Legacy of the King-Crane Commission." In *The Middle East and the United States: A Historical and Political Reassessment,* ed. D. W. Lesch and M. L. Haas, 13–29. New York: Routledge, 2007.
Genell, Aimee. "Empire by Law: Ottoman Sovereignty and the British Occupation of Egypt, 1882–1923." PhD diss., Columbia University, 2013. https://academiccommons.columbia.edu/doi/10.7916/D8J67GH7.

Genell, Aimee M. "Autonomous Provinces and the Problem of 'Semi-Sovereignty' in European International Law." *Journal of Balkan and Near Eastern Studies* 18, no. 6 (November 1, 2016): 533–49.

Gershovich, Moshe. *French Military Rule in Morocco: Colonialism and Its Consequences*. Portland, OR: F. Cass, 2000.

Gerwarth, Robert, and Erez Manela, eds. *Empires at War: 1911–1923*. Oxford: Oxford University Press, 2014.

Gerwarth, Robert. *The Vanquished: Why the First World War Failed to End*. New York: Farrar, Straus and Giroux, 2016.

Getachew, Adom. *Worldmaking After Empire: The Rise and Fall of Self-Determination*. Princeton, NJ: Princeton University Press, 2019.

Ghazarian, Matthew. "Obstruction as Power: Rethinking Britain's Caucasus Occupation 1918–20." *International History Review* 39, no. 4 (2017): 654–66.

Gingeras, Ryan. *Fall of the Sultanate: The Great War and the End of the Ottoman Empire, 1908–1922*. Oxford: Oxford University Press, 2016.

Göçek, Fatma. *Rise of the Bourgeoisie, Demise of Empire: Ottoman Westernization and Social Change*. New York: Oxford University Press, 1996.

Göçek, Fatma Müge. *Denial of Violence: Ottoman Past, Turkish Present and the Collective Violence Against Armenians, 1789–2009*. New York: Oxford University Press, 2014.

Goldberg, Jeffrey. "After Iraq." *The Atlantic*, January 1, 2008. https://www.theatlantic.com/magazine/archive/2008/01/after-iraq/306577/.

Gooch, John. "Re-conquest and Suppression: Fascist Italy's Pacification of Libya and Ethiopia, 1922–39." *Journal of Strategic Studies* 28, no. 6 (December 1, 2005): 1005–32.

Haddad, Mahmoud. "Arab Religious Nationalism in the Colonial Era: Re-reading Rashid Rida's Ideas on the Caliphate." *Journal of the American Oriental Society* 117, no. 2 (1997): 253–77.

Hale, William. *Turkish Foreign Policy Since 1774*. London: Routledge, 2012.

Hamed-Troyansky, Vladimir. "Imperial Refuge: Resettlement of Muslims from Russia in the Ottoman Empire, 1860–1914." PhD diss., Stanford University, 2018.

Hanioğlu, Şükrü. *The Young Turks in Opposition*. New York: Oxford University Press, 1995.

Hanioğlu, Şükrü. *A Brief History of the Late Ottoman Empire*. Princeton, NJ: Princeton University Press, 2008.

Hart, David M. *The Aith Waryaghar of the Moroccan Rif: An Ethnography and History*. Tucson: University of Arizona Press, 1976.

Heggoy, Alf Andrew. "Colonial Origins of the Algerian-Moroccan Border Conflict of October 1963." *African Studies Review* 13, no. 1 (1970): 17–22.

Hooglund, Eric. "New Scholarship on the Relocation of Ottoman Armenians from Eastern Anatolia in 1915–1916" (special issue). *Middle East Critique* 20, no. 3 (2011): 227–357.

Horne, John, ed. *A Companion to World War I*. London: Wiley-Blackwell, 2010.

Hughes, Matthew. "General Allenby and the Palestine Campaign, 1917–18." *Journal of Strategic Studies* 19, no. 4 (December 1, 1996): 59–88.

Hughes, Thomas. "The German Mission to Afghanistan, 1915–1916." *German Studies Review* 25, no. 3 (2002): 447–76.

Inalcik, Halil. *The Ottoman Empire: 1300–1600*. London: Weidenfeld & Nicolson, 2013.
Jackson, Iain. "The Architecture of the British Mandate in Iraq: Nation-Building and State Creation." *Journal of Architecture* 21, no. 3 (April 2, 2016): 375–417.
Jackson, Simon. "Diaspora Politics and Developmental Empire: The Syro-Lebanese at the League of Nations," *Arab Studies Journal* 21, no. 1 (2013): 166–90.
Jacobson, Abigail. *From Empire to Empire: Jerusalem Between Ottoman and British Rule*. Syracuse, NY: Syracuse University Press, 2011.
Jarboe, Andrew and Richard Fogarty, eds. *Empires in World War I: Shifting Frontiers and Imperial Dynamics in a Global Conflict*. New York: I. B. Tauris, 2014.
Joffé, E. G. H., and K. S. McLachlan, eds. *Social & Economic Development of Libya*. Wisbech, UK: Middle East & North African Studies, 1982.
Jongerden, Joost. *The Settlement Issue in Turkey and the Kurds: An Analysis of Spatial Policies, Modernity and War*. Leiden: Brill, 2007.
Jwaideh, Wadie. *The Kurdish National Movement: Its Origins and Development*. Syracuse, NY: Syracuse University Press, 2006.
Katouzian, Homa. "The Campaign Against the Anglo-Iranian Agreement of 1919." *British Journal of Middle Eastern Studies* 25, no. 1 (1998): 5–46.
Kadhim, Abbas. *Reclaiming Iraq: The 1920 Revolution and the Founding of the Modern State*. Austin: University of Texas Press, 2012.
Kashani-Sabet, Firoozeh. *Frontier Fictions: Shaping the Iranian Nation, 1804–1946*. Princeton, NJ: Princeton University Press, 1999.
Kaspersen, Lars Bo, and Jeppe Strandsbjerg, eds. *Does War Make States?: Investigations of Charles Tilly's Historical Sociology*. Cambridge: Cambridge University Press, 2017.
Kesaba, Resat. *A Moveable Empire*. Seattle: University of Washington Press, 2009.
Khalafi, Abdeslam. "La poésie de résistance au Rif: 1893–1926 (2ème partie)," *Tawiza* 64 (August 2002). http://tawiza.byethost10.com/Tawiza64/Khalafi.htm.
Khalidi, Rashid. *The Hundred Years' War on Palestine: A History of Settler Colonialism and Resistance, 1917–2017*. New York: Metropolitan, 2020.
Khazeni, Arash. *Tribes and Empire on the Margins of Nineteenth-Century Iran*. Seattle: University of Washington Press, 2010.
Khoury, Dina. "Ambiguities of the Modern: The Great War in the Memoirs and Poetry of the Iraqi." In *The World in World Wars: Experiences, Perceptions and Perspectives from Africa and Asia*, ed. Heike Liebau et al., 325. New York: Brill, 2010. https://yale.idm.oclc.org/login?URL=http://site.ebrary.com/lib/yale/Doc?id=10476251.
Khoury, Philip S. *Syria and the French Mandate: The Politics of Arab Nationalism, 1920–1945*. Princeton, NJ: Princeton University Press, 1987.
Kirkbride, Alec. *A Crackle of Thorns: Experiences in the Middle East*. London: J. Murray, 1956.
Kırzıoğlu, Mehmet. *Bütünüyle Erzurum Kongresi Vol. I-II*. Ankara: Kültür Ofset, 1993.
Klein, Janet. *The Margins of Empire: Kurdish Militias in the Ottoman Tribal Zone*. Stanford, CA: Stanford University Press, 2011.
Klieman, Aaron S. *Foundations of British Policy in the Arab World: The Cairo Conference of 1921*. Baltimore, MD: Johns Hopkins University Press, 1970.
Koçgiri Halk Hareketi 1919–1921. Ankara: Komal Publishing, 1992.

Kostiner, Joseph. *The Making of Saudi Arabia, 1916–1936: From Chieftancy to Monarchical State.* New York: Oxford University Press, 1993.

Küçük, Hülya. *The Role of the Bektashis in Turkey's National Struggle.* Leiden: Brill, 2002.

Kurt, Mehmet. "A Conversion to Civil Society? The Incomplete Reconfiguration of the Hizbullah Movement in Turkey." *Journal of Balkan and Near Eastern Studies* 22, no. 6 (November 1, 2020): 762–76.

Lawrence, T. E. *Seven Pillars of Wisdom: A Triumph.* Garden City, NY: Garden City Publishing, 1938.

Lefebvre, Henri. *The Production of Space.* Cambridge, MA: Blackwell, 1991.

Lewis, Mary. *Divided Rule: Sovereignty and Empire in French Tunisia, 1881–1938.* Berkeley: University of California Press, 2013.

Lind, Kjell. "The Impact of the 1918 Influenza on Greater Syria." Master's thesis, University of London School of Oriental and African Studies, 2012.

Lindqvist, Sven. *A History of Bombing*, trans. Linda Haverty Rugg. London: Granta, 2012.

Mack, John. *A Prince of Our Disorder: The Life of T. E. Lawrence.* Cambridge, MA: Harvard University Press, 1975.

MacMillan, Margaret. *Paris 1919: Six Months That Changed the World.* New York: Random House, 2007.

Makdisi, Ussama. *Faith Misplaced: The Broken Promise of U.S.-Arab Relations, 1820–2001.* New York: Public Affairs, 2010.

Makdisi, Ussama. *Age of Coexistence: The Ecumenical Frame and the Making of the Modern Arab World.* Berkeley: University of California Press, 2019.

Manela, Erez. *The Wilsonian Moment: Self-Determination and the International Origins of Anticolonial Nationalism.* New York: Oxford University Press, 2007.

McCollum, Jonathan. "Reimagining Mediterranean Spaces: Libya and the Italo-Turkish War, 1911–1912," *Diacronie. Studi Di Storia Contemporanea* 23, no. 3 (October 29, 2015).

McDowall, David. *A Modern History of the Kurds.* London: I. B. Tauris, 2007.

McGuirk, Russell. *The Sanusi's Little War: The Amazing Story of a Forgotten Conflict in the Western Desert, 1915–1917.* London: Arabian Publishing, 2007.

McKale, Donald. *War by Revolution: Germany and Great Britain in the Middle East in the Era of World War I.* Kent, OH: Kent State University Press, 1998.

McMeekin, Sean. *The Berlin-Baghdad Express.* Cambridge, MA: The Belknap Press of Harvard University Press, 2012.

McNeill, John. *The Mountains of the Mediterranean World: An Environmental History.* New York: Cambridge University Press, 1992.

Mélia, Jean. *Les Bombardements de Bône et Philippeville.* Paris: Berger-Levrault, 1927.

Mikhail, Alan. *God's Shadow: Sultan Selim, His Ottoman Empire, and the Making of the Modern World.* Illustrated ed. New York: Liveright, 2020.

Minawi, Ali. *The Ottoman Scramble for Africa: Empire and Diplomacy in the Sahara and Hijaz.* Stanford, CA: Stanford University Press, 2016.

Moberly, Frederick. *The Campaign in Mesopotamia 1914–1918*, Vol. 1. London: H. M. Stationery Office, 1927.

Moreau, Odile, ed. "The Maghreb: A Forgotten Front of the First World War," Special issue, *Hespéris-Tamuda* 53, no. 1 (2018).

Morris, Benny. *Righteous Victims*. New York: Knopf, 1999.
Mustāq, Tālib. *Awrāq Ayāmi*. Baghdad: al-Dār al-ʿArabīyah lil-Ṭibāʿah, 1989.
Nakib, Farah al-. "The Lost 'Two-Thirds': Kuwait's Territorial Decline Between 1913 and 1922." *Journal of Arabian Studies* 2, no. 1 (June 1, 2012): 19–37.
Neep, Daniel. *Occupying Syria Under the French Mandate: Insurgency, Space and State Formation*. New York: Cambridge University Press, 2012.
Neep, Daniel. "State-Space Beyond Territory: Wormholes, Gravitational Fields, and Entanglement." *Journal of Historical Sociology* 30, no. 3 (2016): 466–95.
Neyzi, Leyla. "Remembering Smyrna/Izmir: Shared History, Shared Trauma." *History and Memory* 20, no. 2 (2008): 106–27.
Olson, Robert. *The Emergence of Kurdish Nationalism and the Sheikh Said Rebellion, 1880–1925*. Austin: University of Texas Press, 1989.
Olson, Robert. "The Kurdish Rebellions of Sheikh Said (1925), Mt. Ararat (1930), and Dersim (1937–8): Their Impact on the Development of the Turkish Air Force and on Kurdish and Turkish Nationalism." *Die Welt des Islams* 40, no. 1 (2000): 67–94.
Omar, Hussein. *The Rule of Strangers: Empire, Islam and the Invention of "Politics" in Egypt, 1867–1922*. Oxford: Oxford University Press, forthcoming.
Omissi, David E. *Air Power and Colonial Control: The Royal Air Force, 1919–1939*. Manchester: Manchester University Press, 1990.
Paoletti, Ciro. *A Military History of Italy*. Westport, CT: Praeger Security International, 2008.
Parsons, Frederick. *The Origins of the Morocco Question, 1880–1900*. London: Duckworth, 1976.
Parsons, Laila. *The Commander: Fawzi al-Qawuqji and the Fight for Arab Independence 1914–1948*. New York: Hill and Wang, 2016.
Paşa, Enver. *Kendi mektuplarında Enver Paşa*. Beyazıt, İstanbul: Der Yayınları, 1989.
Pasha, Shérif. *Memorandum on the Claims of the Kurd People*. Paris: A. G. L'Hoir, 1919.
Patel, David. "Repartitioning the Sykes-Picot Middle East? Debunking Three Myths." *Middle East Brief* 103 (November 2016). https://www.brandeis.edu/crown/publications/middle-east-briefs/pdfs/101-200/meb103.pdf.
Pedersen, Susan. *The Guardians: The League of Nations and the Crisis of Empire*. Oxford: Oxford University Press, 2015.
Pennell, C. R. *A Country with a Government and a Flag: The Rif War in Morocco, 1921–1926*. Boulder, CO: Middle East and North African Studies, 1986.
Pennell, C. R. *Morocco Since 1830: A History*. New York: New York University Press, 2001.
Pergher, Roberta, and Marcus Payk, eds. *Beyond Versailles: Sovereignty, Legitimacy, and the Formation of New Polities After the Great War*. Bloomington: Indiana University Press, 2019.
Philipp, Thomas, and Christoph Schumann, eds. *From the Syrian Land to the States of Syria and Lebanon*. Würzburg: Ergon in Kommission, 2004.
Philliou, Christine M. *Turkey: A Past Against History*. Oakland: University of California Press, 2021.
Provence, Michael. *The Great Syrian Revolt and the Rise of Arab Nationalism*. Austin: University of Texas Press, 2009.
Provence, Michael. *The Last Ottoman Generation and the Making of the Modern Middle East*. New York: Cambridge University Press, 2017.

Pursley, Sara. "'Lines Drawn on an Empty Map': Iraq's Borders and the Legend of the Artificial State (Part 1 and 2)." *Jadaliyya*, June 2, 2015. http://www.jadaliyya.com/pages/index/21759/lines-drawn-on-an-empty-map_iraq's-borders-and-the.

Qattan, Najwa al-. "*Safarbarlik*: Ottoman Syria and the Great War." In *From the Syrian Land to the States of Syria and Lebanon*, ed. Thomas Philipp and Christoph Schumann, 163–73. Würzburg: Ergon in Kommission, 2004.

Qawuqji, Fawzi al-. *Mudhakhirat Fawzi al-Qawuqji*. Vol. 1, 1914–1932. Beirut: Dar al-Quds, 1975.

Reynolds, Michael. *Shattering Empires: The Clash and Collapse of the Ottoman and Russian Empires, 1908–1918*. New York: Cambridge University Press, 2011.

Richards, Harry. "Room 40 and German Intrigues in Morocco: Re-assessing the Operational Impact of Diplomatic Crytpanalysis During World War I." *Intelligence and National Security* 32, no. 6 (2017): 833–48.

Robson, Laura. *States of Separation: Transfer, Partition, and the Making of the Modern Middle East*. Oakland: University of California Press, 2017.

Rogan, Eugene L. *Frontiers of State in the Late Ottoman Empire: Transjordan, 1850–1921*. New York: Cambridge University Press, 1999.

Rogan, Eugene. *The Arabs: A History*. New York: Basic Books, 2011.

Rogan, Eugene. *The Fall of the Ottomans: The Great War in the Middle East*. New York: Basic Books, 2015.

Rogan, Eugene. "The First World War and Its Legacy in the Middle East." In *The Oxford Handbook of Contemporary Middle Eastern and North African History*, ed. Amal Ghazal and Jens Hanssen, 93–108. Oxford: Oxford University Press, 2020–.

Rooney, Chris B. "The International Significance of British Naval Missions to the Ottoman Empire, 1908–14." *Middle Eastern Studies* 34, no. 1 (1998): 1–29.

Ryan, Eileen. *Religion as Resistance: Negotiating Authority in Italian Libya*. New York: Oxford University Press, 2018.

Satia, Priya. "The Defense of Inhumanity: Air Control and the British Idea of Arabia." *American Historical Review* 111, no. 1 (February 1, 2006): 16–51.

Satia, Priya. *Spies in Arabia: The Great War and the Cultural Foundations of Britain's Covert Empire in the Middle East*. Oxford: Oxford University Press, 2008.

Sayyid-Marsot, Afaf Lutfi. *Egypt in the Reign of Muhammad Ali*. New York: Cambridge University Press, 1984.

Schayegh, Cyrus. *The Middle East and the Making of the Modern World*. Cambridge, MA: Harvard University Press, 2017.

Scott, James. *The Art of Not Being Governed: An Anarchist History of Upland Southeast Asia*. New Haven, CT: Yale University Press, 2009.

Scovill, Elmer B. "The RAF and the Desert Frontiers of Iraq, 1919–1930." *Aerospace Historian* 22, no. 2 (1975): 84–90.

Segrè, Claudio G. *Fourth Shore: The Italian Colonization of Libya*. Chicago: University of Chicago Press, 1974.

Seidt, Hans-Ulrich. "From Palestine to the Caucasus-Oskar Niedermayer and Germany's Middle Eastern Strategy in 1918." *German Studies Review* 24, no. 1 (2001): 1–18.

Şenışık, Pınar. "The Allied Occupation of İstanbul and the Construction of Turkish National Identity in the Early Twentieth Century." *Nationalities Papers* 46, no. 3 (May 4, 2018): 501–13.

Sheean, Vincent. *An American Among the Riffi*. New York: The Century Xo, 1926.

Shields, Sarah D. "Mosul, the Ottoman Legacy and the League of Nations." *International Journal of Contemporary Iraqi Studies* 3, no. 2 (November 1, 2009): 217–30.

Shields, Sarah D. *Fezzes in the River: Identity Politics and European Diplomacy in the Middle East on the Eve of World War II*. Oxford: Oxford University Press, 2011.

Shook, Carl. "The Origins and Development of Iraq's National Boundaries, 1918–1932: Policing and Political Geography in the Iraq-Nejd and Iraq-Syria Borderlands." PhD diss., University of Chicago, 2018.

Silverfarb, Daniel. "Great Britain, Iraq, and Saudi Arabia: The Revolt of the Ikhwan, 1927–1930." *International History Review* 4, no. 2 (1982): 222–48.

Simon, Rachel. *Libya Between Ottomanism and Nationalism: The Ottoman Involvement in Libya During the War with Italy (1911–1919)*. Berlin: K. Schwarz, 1987.

Simon, Reeva, and Eleanor Tejirian, eds. *The Creation of Iraq, 1914–1921*. New York: Columbia University Press, 2004.

Skiraj, Ahmad. *Al-zal al-warīf fī muharabat al-Rif*. Rabat: Kawtar Print, 2010.

Sluglett, Peter. *Britain in Iraq: Contriving King and Country, 1914–1932*. New York: Columbia University Press, 2007.

Somers, Margaret. "Symposium on Historical Sociology and Rational Choice Theory 'We're No Angels': Realism, Rational Choice, and Relationality in Social Science." *American Journal of Sociology* 104, no. 3 (1998): 722–84.

Sood, Gagan. *India and the Islamic Heartlands: An Eighteenth-Century World of Circulation and Exchange*. New York: Cambridge University Press, 2016.

Stansfield, Gareth, and Mohammed Shareef, eds. *The Kurdish Question Revisited*. London: Hurst, 2017.

Steinmetz, George. "Empire in Three Keys: Forging the Imperial Imaginary at the 1896 Berlin Trade Exhibition." *Thesis Eleven* 139, no. 1 (April 1, 2017): 46–68.

Stevenson, David. "Militarization and Diplomacy in Europe Before 1914." *International Security* 22, no. 1 (1997): 125–67.

Stoddard, Philip. "The Ottoman Government and the Arabs, 1911 to 1918: A Preliminary Study of the Teskilat-i Mahsusa." Ph.D. diss., Princeton University, 1963.

Strachan, Hew. *The First World War*, Vol. I: *To Arms*. Oxford: Oxford University Press, 2001.

Strachan, Hew, ed. *The Oxford Illustrated History of the First World War*. New York: Oxford University Press, 2014.

Suny, Ronald, Fatma Göçek, and Norman Naimark, eds. *The Question of Genocide*. New York: Oxford University Press, 2011.

Tamari, Salim. *Year of the Locust*. Berkeley: University of California Press, 2011.

Tanielian, Melanie S. *The Charity of War: Famine, Humanitarian Aid, and World War I in the Middle East*. Stanford, CA: Stanford University Press, 2017.

Tauber, Eliezer. "Sayyid Talib and the Young Turks in Basrah." *Middle Eastern Studies* 25, no. 1 (1989): 3–22.

Tauber, Eliezer. "Rashid Rida and Faysal's Kingdom in Syria." *The Muslim World* 85, nos. 3–4 (1995): 235–45.

Thomas, Martin. *Empires of Intelligence: Security Services and Colonial Disorder After 1914*. Berkeley: University of California Press, 2008.

Thompson, Elizabeth. *Colonial Citizens: Republican Rights, Paternal Privilege, and Gender in French Syria and Lebanon*. New York: Columbia University Press, 2000.

Thompson, Elizabeth F. *Justice Interrupted: The Struggle for Constitutional Government in the Middle East*. Illustrated ed. Cambridge, MA: Harvard University Press, 2013.

Thompson, Elizabeth. *How the West Stole Democracy from the Arabs: The Syrian Arab Congress of 1920 and the Destruction of Its Historic Liberal-Islamic Alliance*. New York: Atlantic Monthly, 2020.

Tilly, Charles. *Coercion, Capital and European States, A.D. 990–1992*. Cambridge, MA: Blackwell, 1992.

Tittoni, Renato. *The Italo-Turkish War (1911–12)*. Kansas City, MO: Franklin Hudson, 1914.

Travis, Hannibal. "'Native Christians Massacred': The Ottoman Genocide of the Assyrians During World War I." *Genocide Studies and Prevention* 1, no. 3 (2016): 336–38.

Üngör, Ugur Ümit. *The Making of Modern Turkey: Nation and State in Eastern Anatolia, 1913–50*. Oxford: Oxford University Press, 2011.

Van Bruinessen, Martin. *Agha, Shaikh, and State: The Social and Political Structures of Kurdistan*. London: Zed Books, 1992.

Vinogradov, Amal. "The 1920 Revolt in Iraq Reconsidered: The Role of Tribes in National Politics," *International Journal of Middle East Studies* 3, no. 2 (1972): 123–39.

Wasti, Syed Tanvir. "Halil Kut—'the Last Ottoman Pasha,'" *Middle Eastern Studies* 53, no. 5 (September 3, 2017): 820–33.

Watenpaugh, Keith. *Being Modern in the Middle East: Revolution, Nationalism, Colonialism, and the Arab Middle Class*. Princeton: Princeton University Press, 2006.

Weizmann, Chaim. *The Letters and Papers of Chaim Weizmann*, Series A, Vol. IX. Weisgal, Meyer, ed. New Brunswick, NJ: Transaction, 1977.

White, Benjamin. *The Emergence of Minorities in the Middle East: The Politics of Community in French Mandate Syria*. Edinburgh: Edinburgh University Press, 2011.

White, Benjamin. "Refugees and the Definition of Syria." *Past & Present* 235 (May 2017): 143.

Williams, Captain Claud. *Light Car Patrols 1916–19: War and Exploration in Egypt and Libya with the Model T Ford*. London: Silphium, 2013.

Wilson, Arnold Talbot. *Mesopotamia, 1917–1920; a Clash of Loyalties; a Personal and Historical Record*. London: Oxford University Press, 1931.

Wimmer, Andreas, and Nina Glick Schiller. "Methodological Nationalism and Beyond: Nation-state Building, Migration and the Social Sciences." *Global Networks* 2, no. 4 (2002): 301–34.

Winichakul, Thongchai. *Siam Mapped: A History of the Geo-Body of a Nation*. Honolulu: University of Hawaii Press, 1997.

Woolman, David S. *Rebels in the Rif: Abd El Krim and the Rif Rebellion*. Stanford, CA: Stanford University Press, 1968.

Wyrtzen, Jonathan. *Making Morocco: Colonial Intervention and the Politics of Identity*. Ithaca, NY: Cornell University Press, 2015.

Visser, Reidar. *Basra, the Failed Gulf State: Separatism and Nationalism in Southern Iraq.* Münster: LIT Verlag, 2005.

Yeaw, Katrina. "Gender, Violence and Resistance Under Italian Rule in Cyrenaica, 1923–1934." *Journal of North African Studies* 23, no. 5 (October 20, 2018): 791–810.

Yegen, Mesut. "'Prospective-Turks' or 'Pseudo-Citizens': Kurds in Turkey." *Middle East Journal* 63, no. 4 (2009): 597–615.

Zimmerman, Andrew. "Africa in Imperial and Transnational History: Multi-Sited Historiography and the Necessity of Theory." *Journal of African History* 54, no. 3 (November 2013): 331–40.

Zürcher, Erik Jan. *The Young Turk Legacy and Nation Building: From the Ottoman Empire to Atatürk's Turkey.* London: I. B. Tauris, 2010.

Zürcher, Erik, ed. *Jihad and Islam in World War I: Studies on the Ottoman Jihad on the Centenary of Snouck Hurgronje's "Holy War Made in Germany."* Leiden: Leiden University Press, 2016.

INDEX

Page numbers in *italics* indicate illustrations.

Abd al-Aziz, Mawlay, 42, 43
Abd al-Hafidh, Mawlay, 43
Abdallah, Amir, 117, 156–57, *157*, 243
Abdülhamid II (Sultan), 38, 47
Abdurrahim, Shaykh, 221
Abudi Shikak Kurdish confederacy, 180
Act of Algeciras, 42
Aden Protectorate, 139, 141
administration: Anglo-Hashemite, 155; OETA, 105, 155
administrators, British colonial, 153
Aegean Islands, 137, 138
Aegean Sea, 49
aerial bombs, 31, 118, 180, 223–24, 281n69
Agadir Crisis, 10
agents, German, 74–75
agreements: Bahra Agreement, 237; good neighbor, 243, 244; Hadda Agreement, 237; Paulet-Newcombe Agreement, 285n2; secret, 14; Sykes-Picot Agreement, xiv, 4, 15, 82–83, *83*, 249
Aharonian, Avetis, 98
air power, 223–24

Ait Waryaghar tribe, 125, 135, 136, 274n17
Ajdir, Rif Republic, *191*, 193, 197
Al-Ahd (The Covenant), 108, 117
Alawites, 11, 32, 133, 134, 150
Aleppo, Syria, 87–88, 221
Alevi tribes, 223
Algeria, 33, 53, 132
Alhucemas islet, 123
Ali, Mehmet, 37, 131, 264nn6–7
Ali, Saleh al-, 27, 114, 150, 151
Allenby (General), 78, 79, 84–85, 87
alternative narratives, xiv, xvi
ambitions, 257
American Negro Labor Congress, 193
amir al-mu'iminin (commander of the faithful), 137
Amman aerodome, *157*
Ammun, Dawwud, 97–98
ammunition, 188
Anatolia, 6, 50–51, 96, 98, 107, 253; Diyarbakir, 169, 170, 185; documents on, 112; emergent polities in, 158–61, 163–64; France and, 160; Italy and, 160; political

Anatolia (*continued*)
  projects reimagining, 110–13; Russia and, 51
Anderson, Benedict, 20, 21
Andréa, Charles, 210
Anglo-French Declaration, 3, 94, 101, 110, 270n21
Anglo-Hashemite administration, 155
Anglo-Iraqi treaty, 154
Anglo-Ottoman Convention, 68, 236
Anglo-Persian Oil Company, 68
Anglo-Sanusi settlements, 120–21
Anglo-Saudi Treaty of Jeddah, 238
anniversaries, World War I, 8
Anti-Zionist demonstrations, *116*
Aqaba port, 85
Arab Army, 210
Arab East, 12, 18
Arabian Peninsula, 233–34, *234*; emergent polities in, 139–47; Great Britain and, 119–20, 140–41; political projects in, 119–22
Arab Middle East, xv, 252–53
Arab Revolt, 73, 77, 78, 79, 81, 83–84
Arab Uprisings, xii, 257
Ararat Mountain, 218, 222, 224; Kurdish fighters on, *225*; Turkey gaining, 225–26
Ararat revolt, 219–26, *222*
arbitration, 159, 233, 235
Arielli, Nir, 283n20
Armenia, 3, 4, 159, 174
Armenian genocide, 65–66, 174, 276n43
Armenian Legion, 162
armies: Arab Army, 210; British Indian Army, 71, 72; British Indian Expeditionary Force, 56; British Sinai Expeditionary Force, 84; Hejazi Liberation Army, 245; IEF, 68–69, 70–71, 268n25; Ottoman Suez Expeditionary Force, 79; Ottoman Third Army, 62, 63, 66; Russian Caucasus Army, 64; Spanish Army of Africa, 135
Armistice of Mudanya, 164, 180

Armistice of Mudros, 1, 3, 24, 67, 95, 144, 161
armistices, 38, 88, 122; formal, 10; negotiations for, 72; Ottoman-Balkan, 50
arms smuggling, 163
arrests, 65, 118, 153, 171, 184, 203, 210
artificial boundaries, xi, xv, 8, 15, 17, 250, 252–53
asabiyyet (ethnic group solidarity), 185
Asir revolt, 244–47
Askari, Jafar al-, 76, 77, 87, 268n33
assassinations, 9, 51, 52
Assyrians, 65, 174
Atatürk, Mustafa Kemal, xv
Atlas Mountains, 218
Atrash (Sultan), 151–52, 171, 199, 200, 201, 203–4, *212*
Austro-Hungarian Empire, 53
awqaf (religious foundations), 140
Az, Farid al-, 207
Azadî (Freedom) party, 170, 184–85, 277n1
Azarqan, Mohamed, 191, 192, 273n1

Badoglio, Pietro, 230, *231*
Baghdad, Iraq, 69, 70–71, 72
Baghdadi, Abu Bakr al-, xi
Bahra Agreement, 237
Bake, Hakki Mürsel, 169
Balfour Declaration, xiv, 3, 15, 86, 94, 104, 148
Balkan League, 50
Balkans, 38, 49–52
Balkan Wars, 34, 50, 51, 52
Bani Atiyya tribe, 244
Bani Yam tribe, 244, 245
Banu Zerwal tribe, 196
Barazi, Najib al-, 207
Barzanji, Mahmud, 2–3
Basic Law (Legge Fondamentale), 121
Basra province, Mesopotamia, 68–69, 70, 72, 108
Battle of Aqaqir, 77
Battle of Chaldiran, 62
Battle of Dumlupinar, 163
Battle of Gaza, 84

INDEX 303

Battle of Mosul, xi
Battle of Sakarya, 163
Battle of Tannenberg, 59
Battle of the Marne, 58
Battle of Tobruk, 48
bay'a (oath of allegiance), 123, 125, 126, 137
Bedirhan, Emin Ali, 99
Bedouin tribes, 204, 206
Bell, Gertrude, 109, 153, 154, *157*
Berenguer, Damaso, 135
Bergmann, Georgy, 61, 62
Berlin Conference, 40
betrayal, 18; British, 15; tropes, 17
Bey, Halil, 71, 268n27
bias, 9, 18
bin Ibrahim, Mahmud, 185
Bismarck, Otto von, 38
Black Sea, 33
blame, 253, 254
Bliss, Howard, 98
blockhouses, 135
Bolsheviks, 221
bombs, 208–9, 211; aerial, 31, 118, 180, 223–24, 281n69; incendiary, 194
Bono, Emilio De, 230
Book of the Independence of Syria, *114*
boundaries, xvi, 128, 254, 285n2; artificial, xi, xv, 8, 15, 17, 250, 252–53; commissions for, 159; emerging, 13; enforcing, 214–15; Ikhwan on, 241; Iraq, 250; Kingdom of Hejaz, 142; Najd region, 237; natural *versus* artificial, 17; securitized, x; spatial, 22; surveys for, 105, 249, 250, 285n1; temporary, 182; Transjordan, 158, 249–50, 251; Turkish, 173, 176; war making, 22
boundaries, political, vii, viii, 7, 8, 128, 166, 236; drawing, 9; flux of, 88
Braudel, Fernand, 13
Breslau (ship), 53, 54–55
British colonial administrators, 153
British Indian Army, 71, 72
British Indian Expeditionary Force, 56
British Raj, 141

British Sinai Expeditionary Force, 84
Brussels Line, 182, 187
budgets, 118
Busayya post, 240

Cairo Conference, 153–54, 155, 175
caliphate (*khilafa*), 176
Calthorpe, Arthur, 111
camel cavalry, 85
camps, concentration, 28, 218, 230–31, 232, 247, 284n27
Çapakçur, Syria, 221
capital, 125
capital punishment, 185
Carbillet, Gabriel, 203
casualties, 231; Hamas uprising, 207; Ottoman, 63–64; Rif War, 198
Catroux, Georges, 213
Caucasus, 261n11; de facto independence of, 99–100; emergent polities in, 158, 161–62, 276n38; fighting front, 61–67, *64*
Cavotti, Giulio, 31
Cemal (Pasha), 58, 74, 79, 81, 82, *86*, 103
Cemilpaşa, Kadri, 223
central state (*makhzan*), 136
Chanak Crisis, 164
chemical weapons, 118, 194–95, 230
chess analogy, 34, 52
Churchill, Winston, 55–56, 118, 153–54, 155, 179
civil war, x, xi; Saudi-Ikhwan Civil War, 239–44; Spanish Civil War, 198
clashes, 25, 27, 28
Clayton, Gilbert, 241
Clemenceau, Georges, 91, 148
coastline: Anatolian, 160; Northern Africa, 32
collective identities, 198
colonial administrators, 153
colonialism, 3–4, 7, 8, 17, 23, 214
colonial troops, 283n20
commander of the faithful (*amir al-mu'iminin*), 137

commissions: for boundaries, 159; Eastern Region Reform Commission, 220; Inter-Allied Commission on Mandates in Turkey, 92–94, 104–5; King-Crane Commission, 95, 98, 105–6, *105–6*, 107; Milner Commission, 132; Mosul Commission, 173, 186–87; Permanent Mandates Commission, 147; Straits Commission, 4
Committee for Union and Progress (CUP), 47, 48, 51, 58, 66, 77, 265n22
concentration camps, 28, 218, 230–31, 232, 247, 284n27
concrete, 249, 250
conferences: Berlin Conference, 40; Cairo Conference, 153–54, 155, 175; Kuwait Conference, 146, 216, 237; al-Riyadh Conference, 239. *See also* Paris Peace Conference
congress: American Negro Labor Congress, 193; Pan-Syrian Congress, 113; Sivas Congress, 112; Syrian National Congress, 1, 115, 116, 149, 272n39; Syro-Palestinian Congress, 151
Congress of Berlin, 38–39
Congress of Vienna, 35
Constantinople Protocol, 159, 260n5
control, state, 23
conventions: Anglo-Ottoman Convention, 68, 236; Uqayr Convention, 146, 216, 236, 237, 240, 243
Corradini, Enrico, 44
counterinsurgencies, Turkish, 187
courts, Rif Republic, 137
Coustillère, Eugéne, 207
Covenant of the League of Nations, 104
Cox, Percy, 119, 153, 154, 236, 237
Crane, Charles, 91, 92
Crimean War, 38
crises: Agadir Crisis, 10; Chanak Crisis, 164; July Crisis, 57; in Morocco, 40–43
Cromer (Lord), 131
CUP. *See* Committee for Union and Progress

Curzon (Lord), 100, 276n38
Cyprus, 131–32
Cyrenaica, 2, 74, 137, 139; Graziani in, 230; Italy in, 44, 45, 46, 47; Jabal Akhdar region, 227, 228, 229–30, 231, 232; Sanusi governing, 228

Daesh (ISIS), ix, 250, 259n5
Damascus: France in, 208–9, 210–11, 281n69; Jabal al-Druze and, 205–6, 208–9; Maydan quarter, 207–8; ring road, 210–11
Damascus Protocol, 81–82
Dardanelles, 80
dates, wartime, 9
da'wa (Islamic propagation), 185
Dawish, Faisal al-, 216, 217, 240, 242, 243
decrees, French, 150
defeat, of Greater Syria, 211–14
delegations, 92, 94, 97, 99, 100, 101, 206
Demir, Oz, 178, 180, 181–82, 277n16
demonstrations, Anti-Zionist, *116*
deportations, 220, 226, 282n4
Dersim revolt, 222, 226–27
Desert Song, The (play), 126, 194
desert warfare, 77
dignitaries, Muslim, 93
diplomacy, 34, 191–92, 236
diseases, 65, 79
Diyarbakir, Anatolia, 169, 170, 185
documents, on Anatolia, 112
Dome of the Rock, 86
Druze tribe, 201–5, 211, *212*, 249

Eastern Question, 33, 34–40, 56
Eastern Region Reform Commission, 220
East India Company, 68, 275n22
Egypt, 33, 46, 73–74, 75, 76–77; Khedival Egypt, 104, 264n6; Treaty of Sèvres on, 131, 132
elected council (*majlis*), 201
elections, 47, 117
elites, local, 108

Emirate of Asir, 244–47
Emirate of Diriya, 143
empires, 13, 19–20, 26. *See also* Ottoman Empire
Entente Cordiale, 41
Enver (Pasha), 55, 58, 59, 62–63, *86*
Enver, Ismail, 48
equilibrium, 19
ethnic cleansing, 255
ethnic group solidarity (*asabiyyet*), 185
ethnic identities, 2
"event history," 261n15
executions, 82, 103, 186, 208, 219, 278n24, 282n3
exile, 220–21, 268n35
expansion: jihads of, 216–17; Ottoman Empire, 32–33; pressure via European, 35–37, *36*; Rif Republic, 195–96, *196*; Saudi polity, 235–39

Faisal, Amir, 27, 105, 106, 113, 115, 149, 154
Falkenhayn, Erich von, 87
famine, 79, 103
farms, 190
fatwas, 59, 117, 118, 239
fence, 232
Fernandez Silvestre, Manuel, 135–36
festival, 117, 153
Fezzan, 45
fighters: Kurdish, 225; Sanusi, *76*; volunteer, 200
fighting fronts. *See* fronts, fighting
flags: Arab, 118; Rif Republic, 123–24
food shortages, 88
formations: nation, 16–17; worldmaking, 18–19. *See also* state formation
France, 39–40, 249–50; Anatolia and, 160; in Damascus, 208–9, 210–11, 281n69; decrees of, 150; Germany warring with, 53–54; Greater Syria and, 115, 149–52, 171–72, 199–200; Jabal al-Druze policies, 201–3; Morocco and, 41–42, 43, 133–35; political projects of, 149–52; Rif Republic and, 195–99; surrender of, 204

Franco, Francisco, 198
Franco-German tensions, 41–42
Franz Ferdinand, 9, 51, 52
free movement, 238
French Foreign Legion, 205
Fromkin, David, 15–16
"Frontiers of Turkey," Treaty of Sèvres on, 158
frontier zones, 236, 246
fronts, fighting, 56; Caucasus, 61–67, *64*; Ghouta oasis, 209–11; interdependence of, 80; Mesopotamian, 67–72, *70*; Northern African, 73–78, *75*; Ottoman home, 57–61, *60*; Ottoman Southern, 78–88, *85*
fund raising, Rif Republic, 193

Gallipoli campaign, 64
Gamelin, Maurice, 205, 212
Gardiner, C., 192
garrison villages (*hujar*), 144
Garvey, Marcus, 193
gas, mustard, 195, 280n47
general mobilization (*seferberlik*), 58, 79, 88
genocide: Armenian, 65–66, 174, 276n43; Assyrian, 65, 174
"geo-body," Turkish, 225
geographies, 26; Ottoman Empire, 12–13, 56; strategic, 236; World War I, 9, 12–14. *See also* maps
George, David Lloyd, 91, 98, 148
Germany: agents of, 74–75; France warring with, 53–54; Morocco and, 41–42, 43; Ottoman Empire and, 54–55, 57–60
Getachew, Adom, 20
Ghanim, Shukri, 97
Ghouta oasis, 208, 209–11, 212
Giolitti, Giovanni, 44–45
Goeben (ship), 53, 54–55
Gökalp, Zia, 177
gold, 210
good neighbor agreement, 243, 244
Gouraud, Henri, 115, 150, 254, 280n56
Graziani, Rodolfo, 230–31, 232, 284n27

Great Britain, 37, 38, 40, 213, 236, 249–50; Arabian Peninsula and, 119–20, 140–41; betrayal of, 15; Caucasus and, 160; Kurdish Question and, 178–82; mandates, 152–58; Mesopotamia and, 109–10, 117–19; Northern Africa and, 131–32; Ottoman Empire and, 67–72; resentment against, 117. *See also specific topics*

Greater Syria, 78, 97–98, 252; Book of the Independence of Syria, *114*; defeat of, 211–14; France and, 115, 149–52, 171–72, 199–200; Hama, 206–8; Jabal al-Druze defended by, 200–205; mandates in, 113–17, 147–52; political projects reimagining, 102–8; public opinions on, 104–5, 106–7; resources, 103; revolts in, 113–17, 171–72; Suwayda, 151; Turjman on, 103; urban centers of, 148–50. *See also specific topics*

Great Game, 37–38, 52

Great Palestinian Revolt, 214

Great Syrian Revolt, viii, x, 7, 25, 27, 199–200, 213–14; Damascus and Hama during, 205–9; Ghouta oasis front, 209–11; key terrains, *202*

Great War. *See* World War I

Greece, 111, 112, 163; Smyrna, 158, 160, 276n35; Thrace, 50

Greek Revolt, 37

grenade, 31

groups, 2, 16, 24, 150, 161; Al-Ahd, 108, 117; Azadî, 170, 184–85, 277n1; CUP, 47, 48, 51, 58, 66, 77, 265n22; Haras al-Istiqlal, 108; *harka*, 194; Khoybun, 218, 220–21, 222, 282n7

guerrilla warfare, 152, 209, 228, 232

Gulf of Sirte, 230

habitation zones, Turkish, 226

Hadda Agreement, 237

Hakkari province, Kurdistan, 182, 184

Hama, Greater Syria, 206–8

Hamas uprising, 207

Hananu, Ibrahim, 27, 114, 150–51

Haras al-Istiqlal (Guardians of Independence), 108

harka (military grouping), 194

Hart, David M., 274n17

Hasa, al- (oasis complex), 143

Hashemites, 119, 120, 142, 146, 237

hearths (*ocaks*), 223

Hejazi Liberation Army, 245

Henry, Clement, xiii

heterogeneity, 23

highland groups, 2

hirak protests, 199

Al Hoceima Bay, 123

homeland (*watan*), 176, 203–4

hope, 258

hujar (garrison villages), 144

Humayd, Ibn, 217, 242

humility, 257

Husayn, Faisal, 97, 98

Husayn, Sharif, 3, 14–15, 74, 81–83, 139–40, 142

Husayn-McMahon correspondence, xiv, 14–15, 142

Ibn Hithlayn, Didan, 242, 243

Ibn Hussein, Ali, 233

Ibn Lami, 243

Ibn Rifada, Hamid, 243–44

Ibn Saud, 28, 119– 120, 141, 142–45, 216, 233; Ikhwan at odds with, 217, 218, 234, 239, 240–41; Ikhwan fighting, 242–43; Kingdom of Hejaz and, 146, 147; Wadi Sirhan and, 237

identities: collective, 198; ethnic and religious, 2; multiple, 21–22; political, 20–21, 256; unified Muslim, 176–77

idioms, multiple, 95

Idrissi, Hasan al-, 245

Idrissi, Sayyid Muhammad al-, 77, 141, 145

IEF. *See* India Expeditionary Force

Ikhwan tribes, 144–45, 146, 216, 237; free movement of, 238; marching, *143*; I. Saud at odds with, 217, 218, 234, 239, 240–41;

INDEX 307

I. Saud fighting, 242–43; Saudi-Ikhwan Civil War, 239–44; statement, 241
imaginaries, political, 217, 254, 256
incendiary bombs, 194
indemnity, 203
Independence Guard, 117
Independence Tribunal, 219
India Expeditionary Force (IEF), 68–69, 70–71, 268n25
intelligence operations, 48
Inter-Allied Commission on Mandates in Turkey, 92–94, 104–5
interdependence, of fighting fronts, 80
interests, conflicting, 148
International Minority Movement Front, 221
invasions, 34
Iraq, 257; Anglo-Iraqi treaty, 154; Baghdad, 69, 70–71, 72; boundary, 250; British mandates in, 152–55; Kurdish Question in, 178–82; Mosul province, x, xi, xii, 109–10, 155, 251, 260n9; Saudi-Iraqi treaty, 243
Iraq Mandate, 166
irrigation, 209
ISIS, x, xi, 250, 259n5
Iskanderum (Alexandretta), Syria, 80
Islamic judge (*qadi qudat*), 125
Islamic propagation (*da'wa*), 185
Israel, 87, 117, 156, 157
Istanbul, Turkey, 54, 80, 111, 158
Italian Eritrea, 44
Italo-Ottoman War, 10, 34, 47–49, 52, 73, 137
Italo-Sanusi War, 25, 28, 218, 227–33, 229
Italy, 238, 273n48; Anatolia and, 160; Libya and, 137, 138–39; Northern Africa and, 44–46; San Remo, 3, 4, 6, 95–96, 115, 117, 148
itinerary, King-Crane Commission, *105–6*

Jabal Akhdar region, Cyrenaica, 227, 228, 229–30, 231, 232
Jabal al-Druze, Greater Syria, 214; Damascus and, 205–6, 208–9; French policies in, 201–3; Greater Syria defending, 200–205; Hama and, 206–8

Jaber-Nassib checkpoint, ix, 259n3
Jaffa, Palestine, 91, 92
Jaghbub oasis, 229
Jamal (Pasha), 201
Jerusalem, Israel, 87, 117, 156, 157
jihads, 161, 172, 175; defensive, 227; expansionary, 216–17; Ikhwan on, 241; Ottoman Empire declaring, 57, 59, 60, 71, 73, 108, 267n14; against Turkey, 183–86
Jordan, viii, ix, xii, 16, 78, 102, 200
Jordan River, 87, 105, 148, 155, 156, 158, 199
Jordan Valley, 87, 97, 103, 156
Jouvenel, Henry de, 210, 213
July Crisis, 57

Karabekir, Kâzım, 162
Kemal, Mustafa, 6, 28, 66, 112, 152, 161–62, 176–77
Khan, Khalil Badr, 179
Kharrat, Hasan al-, 208
Khedival Egypt, 104, 264n6
khilafa (caliphate), 176
Khoybun (Be Oneself), 218, 220–21, 222, 282n7
King, Henry, 91, 92
King-Crane Commission, 95, 98, 105–6, *105–6*, 107
Kingdom of Hejaz, 2, 7, 119–20, 139–40, 141; boundaries of, 142; I. Saud and, 146, 147
Kingdom of Saudi Arabia, 217, 219, 245, 246, 255, 285n46
Kitchener, Herbert, 40
KRG. *See* Kurdish Regional Government
Krim, Abd el-, 27, 123, 125, 126, 136–37, 171, 273n2; diplomatic overtures by, 191–92; global recognition of, 193–94, 279n33; officials with, *191*; resources gained by, 188; surrender of, 198
Kufra oasis, 232
Kurdish fighters, *225*
Kurdish movements, map of, *183*
Kurdish nationalists, 220
Kurdish Peshmerga, xi, xii, 259n7

Kurdish Question, 173–74; Great Britain and, 178–82; Iraq and, 178–82; Turkey and, 175–78; underlying, 187
Kurdish Regional Government (KRG), xi, 257
Kurdish uprising, 169, 170–71
Kurdistan, 155, 159, 174, 175, 215, 220–21, 276n36
Kurdistan Workers' Party (PKK), xii
Kuwait, 7, 68, 236
Kuwait Conference, 146, 216, 237

languages, 177, 183, 187, 223
Latakia region, 114, 149
Lausanne, Switzerland, 164, 165, 181
law: Legge Fondamentale, 121; martial, 79, 185, 209, 220; resettlement, 226
Lawrence, T. E., 73, 84, 85, 87, 98, 153–54; at Amman aerodome, *157*; as translator, 97, 270n10
leaders, religious, 92–93
League of Nations, 4, 93, 100–101; Covenant of, 104; S. Husayn in, 140; Mosul Commission, 173, 186–87; Rif Republic beseeching, 192
Lebanese Christian populations, 149
Lebanon, 107, 150, 155
Legge Fondamentale (Basic Law), 121
Lenin, Vladimir, 94–95, 162
letters, 81, 82
Libya, 31, 133, 137, 138–39, 227, 232–33
literature, 26
livestock, 231
loans, 59
Long Great War, vii, xvi, 10, 52; framework, 255–56; Middle East and, 8–9; three phases of, vii–viii, 11–12. *See also* World War I
loyalty, 61–62
Lyautey, Hubert, 135, 197, 280n56
Lybyer, Albert, 92, 93–94

Mahabad Republic, 227
mahkama-s (military command posts), 188–89

Mahmud (Shaykh), 110, 180–82, *181*
majlis (elected council), 201
makhzan (central state), 136
mandates, xv, 4, 18, 27, 101–2, 214, 270n20; in Greater Syria, 113–17, 147–52; Inter-Allied Commission on Mandates in Turkey, 92–94, 104–5; in Iraq, 152–55, 166; in Mesopotamia, 117–19, 147–48; in Palestine, 152, 155–58; Permanent Mandates Commission, 147
Manela, Erez, 95
manifesto, Azadî, 184–85
maps, xv, 7; of Ararat and Dersim revolts, *222*; fluidity of, 17; Great Syrian Revolt terrain, *202*; Italo-Sanusi War, *229*; Kurdish movements, *183*; Middle East 1920s political topography, *5*; Ottoman Empire expansionary pressure, *36*; Ottoman fighting front, *60*, *64*, *70*, *75*, *85*; Rif Republic expansion, *196*; of settled and emergent polities, *129*; Sykes-Picot Agreement, *83*
Marchand, Jean-Baptiste, 40
markets, weekly, 195
martial law, 79, 185, 209, 220
Masariha tribe, 245
Mauchamp, Emile, 42
Maude, Stanley, 72
Mawali tribe, 207
Maxwell, John, 74
Maydan quarter, Damascus, 207–8
McMahon, Henry, 14–15, 81, 82
Mehmed V (Sultan), 47
Melilla, Spain, 136, 190, 194
memoirs, 206
memories, 257
Mesopotamia, 6, 12; Basra province, 68–69, 70, 72, 108; fighting front, 67–72, *70*; Great Britain in, 109–10, 117–19; mandates in, 117–19, 147–48; political projects reimagining, 108–10; revolts in, 117–19, 154
Michaud, Roger, 204, 205

Middle East, 260n1; Arab Middle East, xv, 252–53; Long Great War in, 8–9; modern, vii, xvi, 250–51, 262n22; 1920s political topography, 5; worldmaking in greater, 22–26
military command posts (*mahkama-s*), 188–89
military grouping (*harka*), 194
military technologies, 24, 198, 211, 247, 263n30
Milner Commission, 132
mines, 80, 124
minority populations, 165
Misak-i Millî (National Pact), 6, 112, 173, 176, 178, 226
Mokhtar, Omar al-, xiv, 28, 78, 218, 230; Badolgio with, *231*; guerrilla warfare of, 228, 232
monastery, x
monoplane, 31
Montenegro, 49, 50
Moroccan Question, 41, 42
Morocco, xiii–xiv, 7, 11, 121–22; assaults on, 171; crises in, 40–43; emergent polities in, 133–36; France and, 41–42, 43, 133–35; Germany and, 41–42, 43; occupation of, 10; Spain and, 133–36, 273n4. *See also specific topics*
Mosul Commission, 173, 186–87
Mosul province, Iraq, x, xi, xii, 109–10, 155, 251, 260n9
Mosul Question, x, xi, xii, 173, 182, 186–87, 213
mountains, 61, 63, 134; Ararat Mountain, 218, 222, 224–26, *225*; Atlas Mountains, 218; Rif Mountains, 124; Zagros Mountains, 179–80
movement: free, 238; resistance, 112–13, 115–17, 149, 200
multiple identities, 21–22
Mushtaq, Talib, 49
Muslims, 39, 59, 140, 276n39; dignitaries, 93; solidarity of, 210; unified identity for, 176–77
Mussolini, Benito, 230

mustard gas, 195, 280n47
Mutayr tribe, 242, 243
mutiny, 184
Mutki-Bitlis road, 222
myopia, 18, 253
myths, xv, 18, 252, 257–58

Nabi-Musa festival, 117, 153
Najd-Hejaz War, First, 120, 146–47
Najd region, Arabian Peninsula, 120, 141, 142, 145–47; boundaries of, 237; state formation in, 143–44
Napoleonic Wars, 19, 35
narratives, 26–28; alternative, xiv, xvi; Sykes-Picot, 14–18, 250, 251
National Association of Colored Women's Clubs, 193
National Bloc, 213
Nationalist Association (Italy), 44
National Pact (Misak-i Millî), 6, 112, 173, 176, 178, 226
National Scientific Club, 108
nation formation, 16–17
natural boundaries, artificial *versus*, 17
Neep, Daniel, 280n54
negotiations: armistice, 72; Lausanne, 164–65, 182, 277n4; Sidi Rhuma Negotiations, *231*
networks, xii, 99, 150–51
neutrality, 58, 59, 74, 282n2, 285n46
newspapers, 104, 136, 190
Nixon, John, 69, 70
no-go zone, x
nonaggression pact, 55
Northern Africa, 12, 218, 253; coastline of, 32; emergent polities in, 133–39; fighting fronts, 73–78, *75*; geostrategic tensions in, 33–34; Great Britain in, 131–32; Italy and, 44–46; political projects in, 119–22; scramble for, 26, 34, 39, 40, 41, 44–46; settled polities in, 131–32; Spain and, 124–25. *See also specific topics*
Nosratdoleh, Firuz, 100
Nubar, Boghos, 98, 99

Nurettin (Pasha), 161
Nuri, Ihsan, 221, 222, 223

oath of allegiance (*bay'a*), 123, 125, 126, 137
Oberlin College, 91
ocaks (hearths), 223
occupations, 259n1; before *versus* during, 128; of Morocco, 10
Occupied Enemy Territory Administrations (OETA), 105, 155
October Revolution, 61, 66
OETA. *See* Occupied Enemy Territory Administrations
oil, 68, 69, 111, 157, 246–47, 285n46
Oliver, John, xiv
operations: intelligence, 48; pacification, 73, 134–35, 195, 230
opinions, on Greater Syria, 104–5, 106–7
Oppenheim, Max von, 59
Orlando, Vittorio, 91
Ottoman-Balkan armistice, 50
Ottoman Constitution, 21
Ottoman Empire, vii, viii, xiv, 1; Caucasus fighting front, 61–67, *64*; expansionary pressure on, 35–37, *36*; expansion of, 32–33; geography of, 12–13, 56; Germany and, 54–55, 57–60; Great Britain and, 67–72; home fighting front, 57–61, *60*; jihad declared by, 57, 59, 60, 71, 73, 108, 267n14; Mesopotamian fighting front, 67–72, *70*; Northern Africa and, 44–46; Northern African fighting front, 73–78, *75*; at Paris Peace Conference, 96–102; Southern fighting fronts, 78–88, *85*; unmaking of, 11, 88; variable resilience of, 34–35; World War I impacting, 56. *See also specific regions; specific topics*
Ottoman North African provinces, 1–2
Ottoman Suez Expeditionary Force, 79
Ottoman Third Army, 62, 63, 66

pacification operations, 73, 134–35, 195, 230
Pact of Darin, 238

pacts: Misak-ı Millî, 112; National Pact, 6, 173, 176, 178, 226; nonaggression, 55; Pact of Darin, 238
Pahlavi, Reza Khan, 180
Palestine, xiv, 15, 86, 103–4, 107, 254; British mandates in, 152, 155–58; Jaffa, 91, 92; resistance in, 115–17
Pan-Syrian Congress, 113
paradigms, 15–16, 17
Paris Peace Conference, 2, 3, 4, 91–92; Ottoman Empire at, 96–102; press coverage of, 104
Party of God, 206
past, present tied to, xii
Patriotic Club, 203
Paulet-Newcombe Agreement, 285n2
peace, 15, 19
Pennell, C. R., 274n17
peripheries, topographical, 23, 24
Permanent Court of International Justice, 187
Permanent Mandates Commission, 147
Persian Gulf, 69, 140, 141, 143–44, 238
Pétain, Marshal, 197
phases: Long Great War, vii–viii, 11–12; of political projects, 95–96
Picot, Georges, viii, 82
pilgrimages, 234
PKK (Kurdistan Workers' Party), xii
plateaus, 61
pledges, pro-Zionist, 155–56
poem, 189, 223, 282n11
police, 136
political communities, 26–27; unsettled, 24; war remaking, 20–22, 25
political imaginaries, 217, 254, 256
political-military networks, xii
political projects, *130*; analyzing, 126; Anatolia reimagined by, 110–13; in Arabian Peninsula, 119–22; French, 149–52; Greater Syria reimagined by, 102–10; Mesopotamia reimagined by, 108–10; in Northern Africa, 119–22; phases of, 95–96
political topography, 5, 11

polities, xi, 2, 7, 233–39, *234*
polities, emergent, 127–30, *130*, 165–66; in Anatolia, 158–61, 163–64; in Arabian Peninsula, 139–47; in Caucasus, 158, 161–62, 276n38; map of, *129*; in Morocco, 133–36; in Northern Africa, 133–39; rival, 252; Saudi, 233–35, *234*
polities, settled, 127–30, 248; map of, *129*; in Northern Africa, 131–32
populations: Greater Syria, 104; Lebanese Christian, 149; minority, 165; rural, 14, 95
present, past tied to, xii
press, 104, 118
pressure, on Ottoman Empire, 35–37, *36*
Principles of Turkism, The (Gökalp), 177
prisoners, 188, 193
projects. *See* political projects
promises, 94
protectorate zones, 52, 251
protocols: Constantinople Protocol, 159, 260n5; Damascus Protocol, 81–82
proto-states, 160
Provence, Michael, 280n54
public opinions, on Greater Syria, 104–5, 106–7
punishment, capital, 185

qadi qudat (Islamic judge), 125
Qajars, 32
Qarawayn University, 190
Qawuqji, Fawzi al-, 206–7

Rabban Hermizd monastery, x
Rahman, Abd al-, 179
raids, 240, 241
railways, 57, 84, 87, 124, 157, 204, 212
Rashidi tribe, 144
Rauf, Hussein, 110–11
Rayyis, Mohamed al-, 206
recognition, of Krim, 193–94, 279n33
reconnaissance, 197
Reform Society, 108
refugees, 39, 162, 163

religious foundations (*awqaf*), 140
religious identities, 2
religious leaders, 92–93
religious lodges (*zuwayya*), 227–28
reparations, 96
resentment, 117
resettlement law, 226
resilience, of Ottoman Empire, 34–35
resistance movements, 112–13, 115–17, 149, 200
resolution, of Mosul Question, 186–87
resources: Greater Syria, 103; Krim gaining, 188
revolts, 128, 153, 261n12; Arab Revolt, 73, 77, 78, 79, 81, 83–84; Ararat, 219–26, 222; Asir, 244–47; Dersim, 222, 226–27; in Greater Syria, 113–17, 171–72; Great Palestinian Revolt, 214; Greek Revolt, 37; in Mesopotamia, 117–19, 154. *See also* Great Syrian Revolt; uprisings
Rif Mountains, 124
Rif Republic, xiii, xiv, 7, 122, 123–24, 125–26, 214; emergent polity of, 135–39; expansion of, 195–96, *196*; fall of, 188, 194–99; fund raising for, 193; global reach of, 189–94, 279n41; rise of, 188–94; spatial configuration of, 195; statements from, 192; travel permits, 189; uprisings, 171
Rif War, xiii, 25, 172, 190, 195–99, 279n41
Rikabi, Ali Rida Basha al-, 205
ring road, Damascus, 210–11
rivalries, personal, 210
Riyadh Conference, al-, 239
Rogan, Eugene, 262n18
Roosevelt, Theodore, 42
Royal Air Force, British, 118, 182
rural populations, 14, 95
Russia, 33–34, 37, 38, 39; Anatolia and, 51; Caucasus and, 162, 261n11
Russian Caucasus Army, 64
Russian Revolution, 66
Russo-Ottoman War, 38, 39, 62
Russo-Turkish War, 19, 33

Ruwalla tribe, 145, 237, 242, 244
Ryan, Eileen, 283n19

Sabah, Ahmed al-, 242
Said, Nuri al-, 87, 169, 170–71, 183–85, 187; execution, 186, 219, 278n24; Kurdish movement of, *183*
salvation, 258
Samuel, Herbert, 153, 156, *157*
Sanders, Otto Liman von, 57–58, 87
San Remo, Italy, 3, 4, 6, 95–96, 115, 117, 148
Sanusi, Idris al-, 121, 228
Sanusi, Muhammad bin Ali al-, 45
Sanusi tribe, 45–46, 48, 74–78; emergent polity of, 138, 139; Italo-Sanusi War, 25, 28, 218, 227–33, 229; religious lodges, 227–28; troops, 76
Sanusiyya (Sufi order), 74
Sarıkamış, 63, 65, 67
Sarrail, Maurice, 171, 202–3, 208
Saud, Ali, 147
Saudi Arabia, 235
Saudi-Ikhwan Civil War, 239–44
Saudi-Iraqi treaty, 243
Saudi polity, 233–39, *234*
Saudi-Yemeni War, 11, 235, 244–47
School of Mines, 190
Scott, James, 263n30
scramble, for Northern Africa, 26, 34, 39, 40, 41, 44–46
sea, 35, 41; linkage of, 140; war at, 49
secret agreements, 14
secret societies, 81–82, 108, 268n36
secularizations, 170, 183
securitized boundaries, x
security, 149
seferberlik (general mobilization), 58, 79, 88
self-determination, 92, 93, 94–95, 109, 122, 156, 255
Selim, Memduh, 221
Selim I (Sultan), 32
Serbia, 53
Şerif, Mehmet, 98–99

Seven Years' War, 19
Sha'alan, Nuri al-, 145, 237
Shafaq, Ali. *See* Demir, Oz
Shallash, Ramadan al-, 207, 210, 281n66
Sharif, Sayyid Ahmed al-, 73, 74, 75, 77, 121, 228; exile of, 268n35; Sanusi with, 76
Sharifian Empire, 44
"shatter zones," 23, 62, 126, 161, 173–74
Shikak, Simqu, 180
ships, 53, 54–55
shortages, food, 88
Siba'i, Mazhar al-, 206
Sidi Rhuma Negotiations, *231*
Sivas Congress, 112
skirmishes, 116
smuggling, arms, 163
Smyrna, Greece, 158, 160, 276n35
snow, 63
social engineering, of Turkey, 220, 223
Society for the Advancement of Kurdistan, 99
soil, fertile, 200
soldiers, ix
solidarities, 21, 185, 210, 227, 256
songs, 189, 190–91, 282n11
Souchon, Wilhelm, 54, 55, 59
Spain, 43, 121, 122, 123, 273n3; Morocco and, 133–36, 273n4; Northern Africa and, 124–25; Rif Republic and, 189, 192, 194, 197–99, 279n39
Spanish Army of Africa, 135
Spanish Civil War, 198
spatial boundaries, 22
Special Organization, 48
Standard Oil, 246
state control, 23
state formation, 25, 27, 28, 126–27, 252; boundaries and, 22; as complicated, 255; failed, 257; Najd region, 143–44; war and, 19–20
Stoltzenberg, Hugo, 194–95
Straits Commission, 4
Straits of Gibraltar, 124
Straits zone, 96, 158, 160, 164

Sudan, 131–32
Suez Canal, 57, 73, 79
supplies, 75–76, 77, 132, 200, 222, 229
surprise attacks, 85
surrender: French, 204; of Krim, 198
surveys, boundary, 105, 249, 250, 285n1
suspicions, 213
Suwayda, Greater Syria, 151
Switzerland, 164, 165, 181
Sykes, Mark, viii, 82
Sykes-Picot Agreement, xiv, 4, 15, 82–83, *83*, 249
Sykes-Picot narrative, 14–18, 250, 251
Syria, viii, ix, 84, 93; Aleppo, 87–88, 221; Çapakçur, 221; Iskenderum, 80. *See also* Greater Syria
Syrian National Congress, 1, 115, 116, 149, 272n39
Syrian Question, 91, 151
Syro-Palestinian Congress, 151

tactics, delaying, 59
Talaat (Pasha), 64–65
Talu, Ibrahim Haski, 221–22
Tamari, Salim, 103
Tangier, 133
taxes, 136, 137, 210, 227, 236, 239
technologies: military, 24, 198, 211, 247, 263n30; state-controlled, 239
telephone system, 189, 278n28
Telgrama de Rif (newspaper), 136, 190
tensions: Franco-German, 41–42; geostrategic, 33–34; in Northern Africa, 33–34; political, 1
Thompson, Elizabeth, 272n39
Thrace, Greece, 50
Tigris River, 70, 169
Tilly, Charles, 19, 262n24
topographies, 5, 11, 23, 24, 197
Townshend, Charles, 70–71
trade routes, 35, 41
Transcaucasia, 66–67, 111
Transcaucasian Democratic Federative Republic, 161

Transjordan, 156, 157–58, 213, 236, 249–50, 251
translators, 97, 270n10
travel permits, Rif Republic, 189
treaties, 4, 49, 181, 269n1; Anglo-Iraqi, 154; Anglo-Saudi Treaty of Jeddah, 238; multiple, 91; postwar, 16; Saudi-Iraqi, 243; severe, 96
Treaty of Algeciras, 133
Treaty of Ankara, 162–63, 173, 179, 277n4
Treaty of Bardo, 132
Treaty of Brest-Litovsk, 66
Treaty of Darin, 144
Treaty of Fes, 43, 261n8
Treaty of Kars, 162, 173
Treaty of Lausanne, xiv–xv, 6, 137, 172; negotiations, 164–65, 182, 277n4; scholarship on, 10
Treaty of Moscow, 162
Treaty of Muhammara, 146, 216
Treaty of Sanaa, 246
Treaty of San Stefano, 38
Treaty of Sèvres, xiv, 4, 6, 127–30, 274nn10–11; on Egypt, 131, 132; on "Frontiers of Turkey," 158, 276n35; word usage in, 277n5
Treaty of Versailles, 100, 101, 127, 260n4, 274n14
Treay of Akramah, 138
trenches, 54
Tribal Criminal and Civil Disputes Regulation, 109
tribes, 235–36; Ait Waryaghar, 125, 135, 136, 274n17; Alevi, 223; Bani Atiyya, 244; Bani Yam, 244, 245; Banu Zerwal, 196; Bedouin, 204, 206; Druze, 201–5, 211, *212*, 249; Masariha, 245; Mawali, 207; Mutayr, 242, 243; Rashidi, 144; Ruwalla, 145, 237, 242, 244; Ujman, 242; Utayba, 243. *See also* Ikhwan tribe; Sanusi tribe
Tripoli, 44, 45, 49
Tripolitania, 31, 44, 45, 46, 47, 137, 138
Tripolitanian Republic, 2, 7, 121, 138
tropes, betrayal, 17
Tunisia, 33, 39–40, 44, 132

Turjman, Ihsan Hasan al-, 103
Turkey, 161–65, 169, 170–71, 174; Ararat Mountain seized by, 225–26; Ararat revolts in, 219–26, 222; boundaries of, 173, 176; Dersim revolts in, 222, 226–27; "geo-body" for, 225; habitation zones of, 226; Istanbul, 54, 80, 111, 158; jihads against, 183–86; Kurdish Question in, 175–78; social engineering of, 220, 223
Turkish Air Force, 224
Turkish National Assembly, 170
Turkism, 177, 223
typhus, 65

Ujman tribe, 242
ultimatums, 115
Umm al-Jimal ruins, ix
unity, 176–77
University of Texas, Austin, xiii
upheaval, vii
uprisings, viii, ix, 6, 199; Arab Uprisings, xii, 257; Hamas, 207; Kurdish, 169, 170–71; mass, 184; Rif Republic, 171; staging, 179
Uqayr Convention, 146, 216, 236, 237, 240, 243
urban centers, Greater Syria, 148–50
Utayba tribe, 243

Varnier, Maurice, 133
Venizelos, Eleftherios, 111
Volpi, Giuseppe, 138
volunteer fighters, 200

Wadi Sirhan region, 236, 237
Wahhab, Abd al-, 143
war, viii, xvi, 165, 247–48; boundaries made by, 22; desert warfare, 77; guerrilla warfare, 152, 209, 228, 232; political communities remade by, 20–22, 24; at sea, 49; states made and unmade by, 19–20; worldmaking and, 18–19. *See also specific topics; specific wars*
War for Independence, 169, 177–78, 183
watan (homeland), 176, 203–4
water, 84
weaknesses, Ottoman Empire, 35
weapons, 118, 188, 194–95, 230, 247. *See also specific weapons*
Weizmann, Chaim, 97, 270n10
Wilhelm II (Kaiser), 41–42, 57
Wilson, Arnold, 2–3, 109, 117, 153, 154
Wilson, Woodrow, 3, 91–92, 95, 97, 98, 101, 260n4
Wilsonian Moment, 95, 113, 122
winter, 62, 63, 65
worldmaking, 255; greater Middle East, 22–26; war and, 18–19
World War I, xiv, 8; eastern theater, 1; geographical scope, 9, 12–14; Ottoman Empire impacted by, 56; prelude to, 47–49; re-periodizing, 9–12; Rogan on, 262n18. *See also specific topics*

Yahya (Imam), 141, 244–45, 246
Yale, William, 92
Young Turks, 47, 48, 99

Zaghlul, Saad, 7, 132, 153
Zagros Mountains, 179–80
Zionism, 155–56, 254
Zionist Organization, 97
zone: frontier, 236, 246; no-go, x; protectorate, 52, 251; "shatter zones," 23, 62, 126, 161, 173–74; Straits, 96; Turkish habitation, 226
zuwayya (religious lodges), 227–28